Sponsored by the National Academy of Education

Issues in Education Research

Issues in Education Research

Problems and Possibilities

Ellen Condliffe Lagemann
Lee S. Shulman

Jossey-Bass Publishers
San Francisco

Jossey-Bass books and products are available through most bookstores. To contact Jossey-Bass directly, call (888) 378-2537, fax to (800) 605-2665, or visit our website at www.josseybass.com.
Substantial discounts on bulk quantities of Jossey-Bass books are available to corporations, professional associations, and other organizations. For details and discount information, contact the special sales department at Jossey-Bass.

 Manufactured in the United States of America on Lyons Falls Turin Book. This paper is acid-free and 100 percent totally chlorine-free.

Chapter Seven epigraph from Spindler, G. D. (ed.), *Education and Anthropology.* Copyright © 1955 by Stanford University Press. Used with permission of the publishers.
Chapter Seven excerpts from Bloch, M. "The Uses of Schooling and Literacy in a Zafimaniry Village." In Street, Brian V. (ed.), *Cross-Cultural Approaches to Literacy.* Cambridge, England: Cambridge University Press, 1993. Reprinted with the permission of Cambridge University Press.
Chapter Twelve excerpts from Gloria Ladson-Billings. *The Dreamkeepers.* San Francisco: Jossey-Bass, 1994. Used by permission of Jossey-Bass, Inc., Publishers.
Chapter Twelve excerpts from "For colored girls who have considered suicide when the academy's not enough: Reflections of an African American Woman Scholar" by Gloria Ladson-Billings. Reprinted by permission of the publisher from Neumann, A., & Peterson, P. L. (eds.), *Learning from Our Lives: Women, Research, and Autobiography in Education* (New York Teachers College Press. © 1997 by Teachers College, Columbia University. All rights reserved.), pp. 52–70.

Library of Congress Cataloging-in-Publication Data

Issues in education research : problems and possibilities / edited by Ellen Condliffe Lagemann and Lee S. Shulman for the National Academy of Education, Commission on the Improvement of Education Research.
p. cm.
Includes bibliographical references and index.
ISBN 0-7879-4810-1
1. Education—Research—United States Congresses. 2. Educational change—United States Congresses. I. Lagemann, Ellen Condliffe. II. Shulman, Lee S. III. National Academy of Education. Commission on the Improvement of Education Research.
LB1028.25.U6I77 1999
370'.7'2073—dc21   99-11010

FIRST EDITION
HC printing   10 9 8 7 6 5 4 3 2 1

CONTENTS

INTRODUCTION

THE IMPROVEMENT OF EDUCATION RESEARCH: A COMPLEX, CONTINUING QUEST

Ellen Condliffe Lagemann
Lee S. Shulman

What is "good" education research? What is "less good" or even "bad" education research? Should there be universal standards in this very broad and diverse domain of scholarly inquiry? If so, who should create them? By what means? And if standards should and could be formulated and agreed on, how should they be disseminated and enforced, and by whom? Not surprisingly, these questions provoked heated debate when they were raised at a meeting of the National Academy of Education (NAE) in the fall of 1991. The result, almost a decade later, is this collection, commissioned and reviewed by an NAE study group, the Commission on the Improvement of Education Research (CIER).[1] NAE formed the commission in 1992 to review the current state of education research and to make recommendations for improvement. This book, *Issues in Education Research: Problems and Possibilities*, represents the first half of our assignment. A companion publication, intended to deal with the second half, will be available in the near future. Together they address what has always been, and will remain, central to the academy's purpose: improving education through the improvement of education research.

The questions that led to this book were provoked by three matters of concern to the academy—concerns that are no less significant for the health of the field today than they were ten years ago. The first was how to safeguard the

---

[1]Members of the commission are Charles L. Bidwell, Ann L. Brown, Jerome S. Bruner, Allan Collins, Ellen Condliffe Lagemann [cochair], and Lee S. Shulman [cochair].

quality of the research being carried out. As a society of scholars and education leaders dedicated to the promotion of scholarship that can improve practice, policy, and public understanding of education in all its forms, NAE has frequently reviewed and commented on the state of education research. This was done thirty years ago in a volume that Lee J. Cronbach and Patrick Suppes edited, *Research for Tomorrow's Schools: Disciplined Inquiry for Education* (Cronbach and Suppes, 1969). And with many studies in between, it was done most recently in a report of an NAE study group on funding priorities for education research, entitled *Research and the Renewal of Education,* led by Michael W. Kirst and Diane Ravitch and administered by Thomas James, Jr. (NAE, 1991). The second report called attention to some of the domains of practice and policy that have been significantly changed as a result of research carried out over the past ten or fifteen years. Among other things, it observed that progress in research-based knowledge was now jeopardized by serious declines in public and private support for research in education. While primarily calling for increased funding, the report recommended that efforts be made to ensure the continued high quality of education research (NAE 1991, p. 42).

A second concern had to do with the state of American education. Following publication of *A Nation at Risk* in 1983, school reform became a top priority for policymakers nationwide. Beginning with a somewhat monolithic push for "excellence in education," which usually meant a more streamlined curriculum, more homework, and higher achievement as measured by standardized tests, reform efforts diversified during the 1990s. Some groups emphasized systemic reform, others school-based innovations built around general principles. In some instances improved pedagogy was seen as essential, in others enriched curricula, and in still others more "professional" teachers. If ever there was a time when evaluation and longitudinal studies of school change were needed, it is now. Historically school reform in the United States has been intermittent and cyclical. Too often eras of high expectations and significant change have ended in disillusionment. To prevent that occurring at the end of the twentieth century and to help ensure that this cycle of reform would be sustained, research seemed essential—"real" research, that is, to be distinguished from reports based merely on opinion, ideology, or personal experience.

Finally there was recognition that the field was undergoing significant change. Studies in education are always defined by some combination of five attributes: purposes, problems, settings, investigators, and methods. Studies in education vary in the ways in which different scholars frame different problems to be investigated in different settings, relying on a variety of methods that are intended to advance different particular purposes. Some studies are theoretical, some practical. Some are conducted by social scientists, others by mathematicians, and still others by teachers or administrators. Education research is sometimes undertaken in a university laboratory, sometimes in a school classroom, and sometimes in a library or archive. The methods used can be experimental, anthropological, or philosophical. The purposes of the research can involve school improvement, theoretical advance, or both.

Important changes have been occurring, and are continuing to occur, in all the attributes of educational study. The problems, topics, or issues deemed most important to pursue have shifted recently. For a long time many of the core problems or topics for education research were defined by the fundamental psychological processes of learning, such as memory, transfer, and problem solving. The research problems were expected to be general—How does learning occur?—rather than focused on the subjects of the school curriculum—How do students' prior conceptions of conservation affect their learning of physics? Even those who opted to study basic general processes looked almost exclusively at the nature of learning, not considering teaching as a proper topic of investigation. Today that has changed. Now scholars are more inclined to analyze particular interactions and general phenomena interpreted within a particular context. What the anthropologist Clifford Geertz (1973) called "thick description" is now evident in education research as well as in many of the social sciences. General questions that artificially separate teaching from learning, and teaching and learning from the school subjects around which they take place, have given way to more narrow-gauged, nuanced, and multifaceted inquiries.

Education research has also changed in the settings in which the research is conducted. For many years the settings for education research tended to be psychological laboratories that could be carefully controlled or classrooms that had been made over to resemble laboratories as closely as possible. Other studies were conducted with carefully designed questionnaires, inventories, or interviews susceptible to the same strategies for achieving control that operate in laboratory settings. Education researchers often argued that if the setting for an investigation were not a laboratory but rather the buzzing, booming confusion of a real classroom, it would be impossible to generalize from its characteristics to those of classrooms in general. As part of a shift to more particular and even microlevel studies of the complex phenomena involved in education, the settings for education research have also changed. Scholars today are much less likely to restrict their work to laboratories or to rely entirely on methods that could offer the controlled reliability of a laboratory. Now they are increasingly inclined to study, and even participate in, actual schools and classrooms.

The shift in the focus of research to education settings has been accompanied by changes in the training and background of different researchers—an equally important force in defining investigations in education and in reorienting the field. Education has always been studied by scholars from a wide range of disciplines with a wide range of scholarly affiliations. If psychologists predominated among the first generation of researchers in education, they could usually count historians, philosophers, and sociologists among their colleagues. Increasingly scholars trained in disciplines were joined by ones trained in education itself, if not in educational measurement, then in some other special field of education, like curriculum, school administration, counseling, and the like. Today the universe of discipline-trained and often discipline-based scholars has increased to include, among others, anthropologists, linguists, and economists, and the educationist camp has been increased by the addition of more and more practitioners, especially principals and teachers. The changing backgrounds of those who do education research encouraged the trend toward more field-based research and, in some instances, has encouraged collaborations between and among researchers of different primary affiliation and perspective and opened up new sets of problems for inquiry.

Of course, as the disciplinary backgrounds and professional affiliations of researchers have changed along with the settings and problems for education research, so have the methods used. For many decades the methods of psychology predominated in education research. Early in the twentieth century, they largely (but not entirely) eclipsed older methods, notably those associated with history and philosophy. Recently, however, psychological methods have been increasingly supplemented by the ethnographic methods of anthropology, the discourse procedures of linguistics and sociolinguistics, and the "think-aloud" and other forms of protocol analysis of cognitive science. If those methods derive from the changing backgrounds of scholars involved in education research, the move away from laboratory research has also fostered the use of more field-appropriate techniques for observation, reflection, and sense making. The keeping of journals in written or video formats, the writing of autobiographies, and the presentation of research in other narrative forms is now more and more commonplace. In addition new developments in related social and behavioral sciences, especially statistics, have also been used by education researchers.

Last but far from least important, education research has always been undertaken for a myriad of different purposes, and those different and changing purposes continue to stimulate change. Some research is intended to discover or invent new theoretical understandings of particular educational processes or phenomena. Some is intended to develop new methods, techniques, or strategies for solving specific problems. Some educational inquiries are designed to gather more complete data about particular schools, students, neighborhoods, or content areas. Others are undertaken to apply previously acquired understandings in the amelioration or improvement of current educational conditions, whether of practice or policy. Still others begin from a wish to connect or integrate previously distinct areas of theory, practice, or policy. In some cases research is pursued to improve particular forms of practice or inform specific policies. In others the research seeks to test or extend a theoretical formulation in a related discipline such as psychology or sociolinguistics. Sometimes research is undertaken to evaluate or understand the impact of practice in a particular school or classroom. Other times it is directed at the formulation of generalizations or principles. And often research is undertaken in the interest of a particular ideology or value system to which the investigators are committed. Whatever the purposes are, they have a driving influence on the research that results.

COMBINING THE BEST OF NEW AND OLD STYLES OF RESEARCH

By and large the changes evident in education research are positive and in need of encouragement. That said, there is an inescapable yin and yang to change: positive changes or beneficial reforms seem always to be associated with at least some unintended, less positive consequences. It is interesting, for example, to contemplate an extraordinarily perceptive summation of the changes already occurring in education research by Philip Jackson of the University of Chicago in a 1990 American Educational Research Association (AERA) presidential address. As Jackson explained, there has been a "decline of interest on the part of many of us in what used to be looked upon as our main business, which was the discovery of rules and principles of teaching and of running schools that would prove to be universal or nearly so in application and invariant or nearly so over time. That dream of finding out once and for all how teaching works or how schools ought to be administered no longer animates nearly as many of us as it once did" (Jackson, 1990, p. 7). While one can applaud the retreat from research befitting the long-held belief in what historian David Tyack (1974) so aptly termed the "one best system" approach to schooling, one must also ponder the downside to the more local, small-scale, case-focused styles of research that have become more popular recently. Will we lose all bases for generalization? Does that matter? If so, how might the benefits of a local orientation be preserved without giving up entirely on the search for universals—or, more likely, near universals?

If that possibility warrants thought, so does a problem that has emerged as a result of a trend toward more anthropological, field-based, narrative styles of research. When well done, studies in this mode can yield valuable, richly nuanced analyses of all sorts of educational phenomena and contexts. But the operative phrase is "when well done," and many studies have not been well conceived and have not been carried out by people with appropriate training in what is often called (imprecisely) "ethnography." At a time when one could almost say that the new slogan in education research is "everyone his or her own ethnographer," thought needs to be given to finding ways to support the development of observational studies without losing all the discipline and rigor of formal ethnographies. More generally the question is, Can the best of new developments be combined with what is worth preserving from older styles, orientations, and perspectives?

THE WORK OF THIS BOOK

NAE empaneled the Commission on the Improvement of Education Research to survey and evaluate changes in education research so that work of high quality might continue to foster improvements in educational policy and practice. Here, then, is a set of commissioned essays that presents the current ferment in this field. The essays differ strikingly in position and point of view. Two of those included in the book's first part, for example, contemplate the historic situation of education research and reach very different conclusions. Theodore R. Mitchell and Analee Haro believe that there are inherent, inescapable tensions in education scholarship that will always make it a somewhat troubled enterprise. David K. Cohen and Carol A. Barnes, by contrast, are much more optimistic. Arguing that one can identify quite a few instances of influential education research, Cohen and Barnes believe that scholarship in education has become more powerful of late and that it has had considerable effect on both public perceptions and discourse and policymaking.

Another important issue illuminated by the different positions represented in this book has to do with the role of disciplines and even disciplined thinking. Some authors—notably Elisabeth S. Clemens and Kathleen Hall—believe changes in the disciplines drive changes in education research. Clemens implies this and suggests the importance of social studies of science and organizational analysis for education research. Hall also implies the importance of the disciplines, in her case with an analysis of the thought of European scholars such as Pierre Bourdieu.

Other contributors are essentially unconcerned with the disciplines, focusing entirely on the relevance of research to practice. Speaking from long experience as a school leader, Deborah Meier takes this position and pleads for new, less quantitative and mechanistic approaches to educational assessment. Still others believe that seeking relevance too directly has been harmful to education research. Shirley Brice Heath makes this point, for example, and argues passionately the importance of centering the education of education researchers in the social disciplines.

Many chapters deal with questions concerning the education of education researchers. This is the central concern of Anna Neumann, Aaron M. Pallas, and Penelope L. Peterson, who maintain that the insights into practice that researchers in training who have been teachers bring to their studies need to be more fully respected and embraced. It is also the central concern of Alan H. Schoenfeld, who insists that in the education of education researchers "there is no canon, there are no core methods, this is not a time of normal science, and there are myriad models of mentoring." Despite that, Schoenfeld suggests that there are ways to ensure that students learn to recognize the strengths and weaknesses of different perspectives and methods and become skillful in deploying them. Concerned that education research accurately report the experience of minority members, Vanessa Siddle Walker argues that graduate training should be reformed to help researchers become more sensitive to questions of culture—the culture a researcher brings to research, as well as the culture of those under investigation—and to the articulation of a researcher's commitment to improve the lives of those under study.

Relationships between theory and practice are always important in discussions of education research, and such relationships are addressed in many of the chapters. Drawing from their experience as teachers studying what is involved in trying to teach well, Deborah Loewenberg Ball and Magdalene Lampert describe some of what they have learned. The importance of grounding conversations about teaching in a common context—for example, the case of a student's learning about even and odd numbers—is one of the insights they explore as they detail the wide range of questions they have grappled with while trying to find productive ways to represent practice. Another chapter that is centrally concerned with relationships between theory and practice is the one written by James G. Greeno and a group of his colleagues at the Institute for Research on Learning. They describe how and why their collaboration to help design and develop a mathematics curriculum was successful. Although claims about the benefits to be had from researchers, teachers, and curriculum developers working together to create environments in which children can learn effectively are common, cooperation is more difficult than many appreciate. Greeno and his colleagues show that, while also providing a case study of the ways in which barriers can be surmounted.

In addition to the issues that run through several chapters and sometimes provoke considerable divergence between and among the various authors, there are many others raised by a single author. Thus, Roy D. Pea reviews new possibilities for improved communication using the World Wide Web, and Jerome Bruner closes the book with a plea to understand education research as a "cultural science."

Without our mentioning every chapter, the point may be clear. *Issues in Education Research: Problems and Possibilities* is intended as an introduction to the tensions, dilemmas, issues, and promise that currently characterize education research. The book sets out to flag some issues about which scholars have major disagreements and others that are just beginning to arise as scholars contemplate the significance for research of changes that have occurred in practice and policy as well as in research over the past ten to twenty years. The book does not cover and map every issue important to education research and its improvement. It does not deal with questions related to research funding or to the quality of educational publishing; it treads lightly over matters related to the continuing professional development of scholars in education and over matters concerning the dissemination of research. And having begun in a debate about standards for research, it tends to skirt that question. Its purpose instead is to demonstrate that education research is in a state of flux and to invite wide consideration of what that means for the training of education researchers and the sponsorship and conduct of education research.

In the course of its deliberations, the Commission on the Improvement of Education Research concluded that one way to improve education research is to attempt to stimulate discussion and debate. A scholarly field as broad, diverse, and important as education will thrive when questions of purpose, significance, validity, and usefulness are widely, publicly, and carefully debated. Such debate should encourage self-consciousness and experimentation among established scholars and a sense of excitement and open possibility among younger scholars. It should help frame the matters of quality and standards with which we are ultimately concerned.

Those matters cannot be easily resolved because there are difficult, perhaps impossible, trade-offs essential to them. For example, peer review is a widely used device that can be helpful in verifying the importance and reliability of a research report before it is published. But peer review can also stand in the way of bringing out high-quality, original work that is not entirely governed by existing scholarly styles and conventions. Without peer review, one runs the risk of publishing flawed material that experts in the subject would quickly recognize as problematic. But relying on peer review may limit creativity and the dissemination of new, critical ideas. Clearly, existing mechanisms for judging competence and reliability are flawed and imperfect, and yet a field of research without widely respected criteria for distinguishing the sound from the spurious will not be able to contribute worthwhile advice to those in search of expertise and will be held in low public repute. What, then, is one to do?

We do not believe that it is a retreat from the problem to suggest that what we need is to talk about finding ways to ensure quality in education research. Rather, we believe that discussions at faculty and professional meetings, conversations among staff and trustees of public and private funding agencies, and public debate in journals and on the Web can create the conditions out of which shared conceptions of "good," "less good," and even "bad" research can emerge. Such discussion and debate may not be a sufficient approach to improving education, but it is surely a necessary one. If this book encourages it, its goal will have been met.

References

Cronbach, L. J., and Suppes, P. (eds.). *Research for Tomorrow's Schools: Disciplined Inquiry for Education.* New York: Macmillan, 1969.

Geertz, C. *The Interpretation of Cultures.* New York: Basic Books, 1973.

Jackson, P. W. "The Functions of Educational Research." *Educational Research,* 1990, *19,* 3–9.

A Nation at Risk: The Imperative for Educational Reform. Washington, D.C.: U.S. Department of Education, 1983.

National Academy of Education. *Research and the Renewal of Education.* New York: National Academy of Education, 1991.

Tyack, D. B. *The One Best System: A History of American Urban Education.* Cambridge, Mass.: Harvard University Press, 1974.

ACKNOWLEDGMENTS

The work of the National Academy of Education's Commission on the Improvement of Education Research has been generously supported by both the Carnegie Corporation of New York and The Spencer Foundation. We are grateful to Karin Egan, our program officer at Carnegie Corporation, and to John Barcroft, former vice president, and John Williams, current vice president, of The Spencer Foundation, for their patient and steadfast belief in this project.

Avery Russell, director of publications at Carnegie Corporation, worked with us as a freelance editor in revising and finishing this book. Her keen eye for logic, her insistence on clarity, and her apt sense of just the right word have improved the chapters immeasurably. It is not an exaggeration to say that the book might not have been completed without her help, for which we will always be grateful.

E. C. L.
L. S. S.

THE EDITORS

Ellen Condliffe Lagemann is professor of history and education, chair of the Department of Humanities and the Social Sciences, and director of the Center for the Study of American Culture and Education at New York University. She is president of the National Academy of Education.

Lee S. Shulman is president of the Carnegie Foundation for the Advancement of Teaching. He was the first Charles E. Ducommun Professor of Education at Stanford University, where he retains an affiliation. He is a past president of the National Academy of Education.

THE CONTRIBUTORS

Deborah Loewenberg Ball is a professor of education at the University of Michigan. She studies teaching and teacher learning in the context of teacher education and policy.

Carol A. Barnes is a senior research associate in the School of Education at the University of Michigan.

Charles E. Bidwell is the William Claude Reavis Professor of Sociology and Education at the University of Chicago. His primary research interest is the effect of the social organization of schools on students' life chances.

Jerome Bruner is a professor at New York University, where he currently works on the relation of law and psychology.

Elisabeth S. Clemens is associate professor of sociology at the University of Arizona and author of *The People's Lobby: Organizational Innovation and the Rise of Interest Group Politics in the U.S., 1890–1925.*

David K. Cohen is the John Dewey Collegiate Professor in the School of Education at the University of Michigan.

Karen A. Cole is a research scientist at the Institute for Research on Learning. She is an educational psychologist specializing in assessment equity, teacher professional development, and mathematics education.

Allan Collins is a professor of education and social policy at Northwestern University and research professor of education at Boston College.

Randi A. Engle is a doctoral student at Stanford University who specializes in multimodal explanations and conceptual learning during conversation.

Shelley Goldman is a senior research scientist at the Institute for Research on Learning and a consulting professor at Stanford University. She is an anthropologist of education who specializes in designing and researching classroom learning environments.

James G. Greeno is a research fellow at the Institute for Research on Learning and a professor of education at Stanford University. He is a cognitive scientist who specializes in studies of conceptual learning, reasoning, and understanding.

Kathleen Hall is an assistant professor in the Graduate School of Education at the University of Pennsylvania. She is an anthropologist whose research focuses primarily on issues related to education, immigration, and race relations in the United States and Great Britain.

Analee Haro is a doctoral student in the Graduate School of Education and Information Studies at the University of California, Los Angeles.

Shirley Brice Heath is professor of English and Linguistics at Stanford University and senior scholar at the Carnegie Foundation for the Advancement of Teaching.

Jennifer Knudsen is a researcher at the Institute for Research on Learning and a doctoral student at Stanford University. She is a mathematics educator who is currently directing mathematics education projects and researching change in reforming teachers' practices.

Magdalene Lampert is a professor of education at the University of Michigan. She studies teaching and teacher development and has interests in the potential of new technologies in these fields.

Beatrice Lauman is a doctoral student at Stanford University. She is a philosopher of education, specializing in mathematics education.

Charlotte Linde is a senior research scientist at the Institute for Research on Learning and consulting professor at Stanford University. She is a linguist specializing in studies of the use of narrative and other semiotic resources for institutional and individual remembering.

Ray McDermott is a research affiliate at the Institute for Research on Learning and a professor of education at Stanford University. He is an anthropologist who specializes in cultural analysis of education.

Deborah W. Meier is principal of the Mission Hill School in the Boston public school system. She is the founder of New York City's Central Park East schools and the author of *The Power of Their Ideas*.

Theodore R. Mitchell is a historian of education, particularly interested in issues of citizenship and the state. He is currently on leave from UCLA at the J. Paul Getty Trust.

Anna Neumann, associate professor of education at Michigan State University, conducts research on learning and intellectual identity development across the course of scholarly lives.

Aaron M. Pallas is a professor of education and affiliate professor of sociology at Michigan State University. He studies the intersection of school organization, educational stratification, and the life course.

Roy D. Pea is director of the Center for Technology in Learning at SRI International in Menlo Park, California, and consulting professor in the School of Education at Stanford University.

Penelope L. Peterson studies learning in multiple contexts. Her recent books include *Restructuring in the Classroom: Teaching, Learning, and School Organization* (with Richard Elmore and Sarah McCarthey) and *Learning from Our Lives: Women, Research, and Autobiography in Education* (with Anna Neumann).

Alan H. Schoenfeld is Elizabeth and Edward Conner Professor of Education at the University of California at Berkeley and president of the American Educational Research Association.

Vanessa Siddle Walker is an associate professor in the Division of Educational Studies at Emory University. She specializes in historical models of African American schooling.

Issues in Education Research

PART ONE

EDUCATION RESEARCH AS A PROBLEM IN THE HISTORY AND SOCIOLOGY OF EDUCATION

CHAPTER ONE

An Auspicious Moment
for Education Research?

Ellen Condliffe Lagemann

Interest in research on education is on the rise in the United States. The causes for this are multiple and the possible outcomes unclear. As the chapters in Part One suggest, education research has frequently influenced public discussion and public policy, although often in subtle and complicated ways (Suppes, 1978; Atkins and Jackson, 1992, p. 2). At the same time, it has to be acknowledged that studies of education tend to "get no respect." Indeed few other areas of serious scholarship have ever been more scorned and demeaned. Education research has been accused of ignoring important questions while reinforcing practices that stand in the way of fundamental reform. It has never been a professionally dominated field of study and as a discipline has been internally fragmented. Recently Carl Kaestle (1993) noted, in a report of interviews with thirty-three education researchers and federal agency officials, that education research has had "an awful reputation." A prime reason for this, he said, has been the persistent belief that research rarely leads to improvements in practice. Although there are abundant examples of current and past research-based innovations in classrooms, these have often been short-lived, or their precise research lineage has not been known to the teachers involved. Instances of effective linkages between research and practice have therefore gone unnoticed.

Despite the possibility that education research may have had more influence on practice than its "awful reputation" suggests, there is no denying that the field has faced and is facing difficult and multifaceted problems. The question is, Can things be improved? Will it be possible to increase the applied value of education research, to strengthen its relevance to problems of public policy, to magnify its capacity to contribute to our most fundamental understandings of human behavior, while also raising its dangerously insufficient funding base? Even if no one can provide definitive answers to these questions, it is possible to draw some conclusions about the preconditions for needed changes—conclusions that are rooted in historical precedent.

NEW DEVELOPMENTS IN EDUCATION RESEARCH

The rising interest in education research stems from several sources, making it an optimum time to assess the requirements for bringing more coherence to the field. The primary source is perhaps the 1983 publication of *A Nation at Risk,* which castigated America's "mediocre performance" in education and called on the nation's leaders and citizens to support reforms. The alarm this report sounded caused many individuals and groups that had not paid much attention to K–12 schooling previously to become involved in school reform, setting in motion quite different efforts to strengthen school curricula and increase the academic achievement of all children. Some of these efforts have focused on raising standards nationally or within a district or particular school; others have sought to change the culture of schools; still others have involved carefully planned interventions that can be uniformly adopted by otherwise different schools. Which of these reform strategies work, and under what conditions? Jonathan Crane (1998), director of the National Center for Research on Social Programs in Chicago, argued in a recent review of a number of evaluation studies that unless these questions are answered, there will be no way to know which programs are worth replicating on a large scale and which programs should be discontinued. His contention is that funding for reform initiatives should be linked to funding for evaluation research—a call voiced with increasing frequency among public and private funders, school board members, educators, and researchers themselves.

In addition to the spur from school reform, interest in education research has increased as a result of new developments in academe. A long-standing problem in education scholarship has been the division between theory and practice. Of late, recognition of this issue, combined with new basic knowledge about human development and behavior, has prompted changes in the ways that increasing numbers of scholars who study education conduct their work. Rather than generating theory at a distance from practice settings, more researchers are now working in classrooms. More are also working in multidisciplinary teams and regarding teachers as partners in their research.

This concern with developing effective strategies for clinical research has encouraged some researchers to become teachers and some teachers to become researchers in order to study classroom practice from the inside, rather than limit their work to the laboratory or library. Using videotapes and journals, teacher–researchers are attempting to make their experience working in classrooms generally available for discussion and analysis.

The search for effective strategies for clinical research has also fostered the emergence of a variety of research communities that cross disciplinary and institutional lines in order to put researchers who begin with different perspectives into newly collaborative relationships with each other and with school personnel. More often than not, the studies undertaken by such groups blur long-established lines separating research and development from evaluation, the result being a continuing process of inquiry-based school improvement rather than a more controlled and limited experiment or intervention.

A notable example of classroom-based research is the work in San Francisco Bay Area urban classrooms that Ann Brown has led for almost a decade. As she is the first to admit, Brown was once a traditional psychologist who sometimes tested children in cages to avoid test corruption through social and verbal interaction with them (Brown, 1994). As she began to move out of the laboratory to observe children in classrooms, she became interested in the problems they had learning to understand lengthy texts. With Annemarie Palincsar, she developed a strategy to help with this, called "reciprocal teaching" because it involved taking turns at summarizing, asking questions, and otherwise interpreting and teaching about a text.

Interest in studying and developing this intervention led Brown and her collaborators to develop what is now called "communities of learners." Expressly intended to use the resources of actual public school classrooms, these experimental settings have enabled Brown, working with teachers in their classrooms, to identify, describe, analyze, and assess a variety of methods to foster learning. All the methods Brown has identified fit with the project's "first principles"—for example, the belief that learning is social in nature, that metacognition (or learning about learning) is essential to education, and that individual differences should be acknowledged and built on. In addition, while constantly being refined in practice, these first principles are being elaborated into a new theory of learning that is derived not only from psychology and in-school experimentation and learning, but also from "pertinent branches of linguistics, sociology, and anthropology, and by studies of out of school learning . . . apprenticeship and on-the-job training . . . and studies of communities of professional scientists" (Brown and Campione, 1994).

Efforts such as Brown's to address long-standing divisions between theory and practice have been matched by significantly more attention to problems of generalization in education. This has heightened scholarly interest in distilling meaning from the often conflicting findings of disparate surveys and experimental studies. One result has been the further development of methods for aggregate analysis, notably the method commonly known as meta-analysis or research synthesis. These methods may help to clarify once murky areas of controversy about the significance of different resources, practices, and modes of organization in schools. Matters of generalization are mirrored by new efforts to study the particular, in the form of case histories, biographies, and institutional portraits, and then to ponder what such "local" descriptions can reveal about educational phenomena in general.

Myriad efforts are also under way to understand better what knowledge is in education and how, when, and in which forms knowledge can be deployed to improve teaching and enhance student learning. Such studies have called attention to the role of reflection in the education of educators and to the importance of subject-related pedagogical knowledge. They have also prompted analysis of the social situations that give meaning to knowledge and of the mediating circumstances that enable teachers to "use" the knowledge they gain through programs of professional development. Thinking about the meaning of knowledge in education has focused attention on teaching for understanding rather than simply for purposes of recall or mental training.

Another development on the academic side that may lessen the sometimes great divide between theory and practice in education concerns the growth of so-called qualitative research over the past ten to fifteen years. Until relatively recently most education research has tended to rely on quantitative measures, often derived from psychological constructs about teaching, learning, and human behavior. Qualitative research moves away from that template and encompasses everything from formal ethnographic studies to informal case histories and autobiographies. By some definitions, it includes everything that is not quantitative! As Elliot Eisner and Alan Peshkin (1990) explained in introducing the published proceedings of a conference they convened at Stanford University in June 1988, qualitative research is still quite controversial. Indeed there are four quite different views. Some scholars believe that qualitative research is a valuable complement to quantitative studies; others see it as "a soft and less trustworthy version of the real stuff" that is only "good for exploratory work"; still others see it as a sign of the maturing of education scholarship, more traditional quantitative methods being, to these scholars, the ones that are "suspect"; and still others believe that there really is not much difference in the merits of quantitative and qualitative research, both needing to meet high standards of value and validity (Eisner and Peshkin, 1990, p. 11).

Despite mixed opinion, qualitative research has great potential for capturing the complex layers of meaning that always coexist in any classroom or in any educational experience. Certainly accounts by researchers who are also K–12 teachers, notably Deborah Loewenberg Ball and Magdalene Lampert (see Chapter Sixteen), suggest that to be the case. In "How Do Teachers Manage to Teach? Perspectives on Problems in Practice," for example, Lampert (1985) presented the multiple, often conflicting demands of living in a classroom with children and working hard to teach. Her account of fifth-grade boys and girls sitting on opposite sides of the room, which raises a host of questions about where the teacher should stand, instantly resonates with anyone who has been in such a situation. At the same time, she carefully conveys important research insights about the constant dilemmas and ambiguities that teachers face.

All of these developments augur well for the future of education research. At the same time, much work remains to be done if the field is to thrive and continue making a contribution to basic knowledge, educational improvement, and public policy. Most important, ways will have to be found to ensure the high quality of the research undertaken, to improve its credibility, and to secure a steadier and more adequate flow of funds. The President's Panel on Education Technology (1997) recently noted that funding for education research relative to overall education expenditure is minuscule. The panel pointed out that in 1995 "the United States spent about $70 billion in prescription and nonprescription medications, and invested about 23 percent of this amount on drug development and testing. By way of contrast, our nation spent about $300 billion on public K–12 education in 1995, but invested less than 0.1 percent of that amount to determine what educational techniques actually work, and to find ways to improve them" (p. 96). Surely a cogent case can be made for greater public and private expenditure to enhance the understanding and nature of our education system.

Accomplishing all these goals for education research will, in my view, depend on self-conscious efforts to build a strong research community with a shared set of goals and standards for education scholarship. If history is any guide, it is the absence of such a distinct knowledge community that has left the field open to periodic criticism for its lack of rigor, relevance, and validity. Because of this, education scholarship has been vulnerable to all sorts of problems and shifts in direction over its entire hundred-year history, never developing widely shared traditions for criticizing, authenticating, and accumulating knowledge and prey to fragmentation and conflicting purposes.

PROBLEMS OF COMMUNITY EXAMINED

For the field to succeed in building a strong research community, certain historical attributes that have limited both the real, and even more the perceived, value of education study will have to be acknowledged, addressed, and then overcome. The first of these is the contested nature of education research, which has deep-seated roots (Lagemann, 1997). The second is the pluralistic character of the enterprise, and the third is its public character.

Contested Nature of Education Research

Ever since the late nineteenth century, when education was first established as a university subject in the United States, the very idea that education could be a field of research has been repeatedly called into question. When Paul Hanus arrived at Harvard University in 1890 to become its first full-time education faculty member, he discovered that most of his new colleagues thought the very idea of "educational science" was bogus. The philosopher George Herbert Palmer is said to have quipped about Professor Hanus that "he bore the onus of his subject" (quoted in Kucklick, 1977). Hanus's friend and colleague at Stanford University, Ellwood Patterson Cubberly, endured similar disdain, leading one of his peers to confess later that among many Stanford faculty members, "'Education' was hardly considered to be up to the dignity of [either] a 'Science' or an Art'" (Sears and Henderson, 1957, p. 57). Sentiments like these persist to this day.

If education scholarship is contested in the sense that the very possibility of research and expertise in education is suspect, it is also contested in a second sense. Among those engaged in studying education, there have been, and continue to be, constant charges and countercharges concerning the merits of different methods, findings, and problem statements. At least among education researchers, the dance is well known. Quantitative types challenge qualitative types, and the reverse; disciplined-based scholars question the rigor of studies undertaken by education-based scholars, and education-based scholars query the relevance of studies done by their discipline-based colleagues. Teacher–researchers, in turn, are inclined to ignore the theories spun by university types, and university types are equally inclined to be dismissive of the very notion of teacher research. Leaving aside differences derived from differing roles and professional identities, more often than not studies of the same problem reach fundamentally different conclusions. As one interviewee told Kaestle (1993), "For every study in education research, there are an equal number of opposing studies" (p. 29). Charges and countercharges among people engaged in education research reduce the credibility of the enterprise and make it difficult to find common ground.

Needless to say, too, the close association between education research and teaching has tended to limit its credibility. Since the mid-nineteenth century, teaching has been viewed as "women's work." As such, it was presumed to be more affective than intellectual. Understood as an extension of what were presumed to be a woman's natural propensities to nurture and inspire virtue, teaching was viewed through a gendered lens that precluded defining it as a vocation requiring the skilled use and application of specialized knowledge. In a variety of ways, this association further undermined claims to respect for education research as a rigorous form of scholarship.

Education Research as a Pluralistic Enterprise

In addition to being a contested domain of scholarship, education has encompassed a massive array of subject matters—from management to pedagogy to measurement to curriculum theory to community studies—and has been expected to illuminate and perhaps foster more effective practices among a wide range of different participants, from kindergarten teachers, junior high school foreign language instructors, senior high school math teachers, and school principals to Washington policymakers. To scan the program for an annual meeting of the American Educational Research Association (AERA) is immediately to encounter education research's pluralistic character. Usually more than one hundred (thin) pages long and written in tiny print, the program includes sessions on everything from school finance reform to methods for encouraging self-esteem among seventh-grade students in coeducational math classes to innovations in achievement testing to the philosophy of Paolo Freire. As its twelve sections and innumerable special interest groups testify, AERA is a very large and constantly expanding umbrella for its almost twenty-four thousand members. Although it serves many very useful purposes, it cannot be accurately described as a community of researchers—an association of colleagues and peers.

Moreover, as a pluralistic enterprise, education scholarship has been assessed according to the metrics of value employed in a large number of very disparate professions and subprofessional groups as well as a wide range of disciplines. Historians of education, psychometricians, linguists, reading specialists, sociologists skilled in survey research, and organization theorists may all engage in education research, but few among them would think about problems of method and significance in the same way.

In sum, while contributing in its own right to the growing complexity of the field, the pluralistic nature of education research has fueled debates about the pros and cons of different ways to study education.

Public Character of Education Research

Education research is inevitably a more public enterprise than is research in many other fields, bearing as it does on a domain of public life and public policy that has been—and should be—of interest to ordinary citizens. After all, pretty much everyone has been to school. As Kaestle (1993) discovered in his interviews, "Everybody's been in fourth grade, so everybody knows what good teaching is. You can't make your own ICBM or cure cancer, but you know how history is taught and you know how kids should be disciplined" (p. 27).

The methods and language of education research, moreover, have usually been neither so abstract nor so arcane as to be beyond the understanding of the nonexpert, attracting frequent lay consideration and comment. Recall Walter Lippmann's (1922a–1922e) famed challenge to the supposed "research findings" generated by World War I mental testers like Lewis Terman and the more recent public challenges in California to new standards for mathematics instruction. Because these emphasized developing mathematics understanding more than drill and practice in computation, they encouraged instruction that was very different from what most parents had experienced. This caused alarm.

Whatever one makes of this example, the point is that critics on the right and the left, some well informed and some not, have felt competent and entitled to read, interpret, comment on, and even evaluate "educational science." This is much less likely to happen in more esoteric fields such as medicine, physics, and economics. For better or worse, the apparent accessibility of education research to public understanding reduces the authority or "expertness" associated with it.

Far more important than this, however, is the linkage of education research to public policy development. Education has always been the favored form of social intervention in the United States, making the findings of education studies of more than passing interest to a relatively wide lay audience and opening the field to public scrutiny. Beginning in the seventeenth century, education has been counted on to fulfill most of our vital social goals. The Puritans passed the famous Deluder Satan Act, mandating schooling to help ensure piety and virtue. Horace Mann's generation in the mid-nineteenth century expected public schools to develop moral character, foster economic progress and social equality, and ensure political unity. Their descendants in the twentieth century have looked to the schools to overcome poverty and racial prejudice and more recently, to prevent pregnancy, AIDS, and car accidents and nurture a multiplying variety of literacies—civic, scientific, artistic, and the like. Schools, in short, have been asked to carry forward this society's most important public business, and research on schooling has tended to reflect the different shifts, divisions, and conflicts over education's purposes.

BUILDING A DISTINCT RESEARCH "COMMUNITY"

The contested, pluralistic, and public character of education research has meant that, in a very real sense, it has been inaccurate to think of it either as a field in itself or as an identifiable congeries of fields. Even to call it a domain of scholarship might exaggerate the degree to which one could identify lasting agreements among one or several groups concerning what education is and should do and how the ensuing activities should be systematically investigated. Although many people have engaged in activities that could be described as education research, there has not been a clearly discernible research community associated with education.

Without a distinct research community, education scholarship has never developed widely shared traditions fostered through common patterns of professional socialization as have other areas of scholarship. Historically and today, there has not been a common route to becoming an education researcher. Trained in virtually all the faculties of the university, not only schools of education but also schools of arts and science, public policy, law, and social work, scholars of education find jobs in all the faculties of the university. Neither as graduate students nor subsequently as full-fledged scholars are they exposed to common conceptions of what education is or to common conversations concerning the ethical responsibilities of education research. With differences in training thus having magnified differences in primary professional affiliation, scholars of education have had few, if any, reasons to develop a sense of mutual professional recognition, which is, after all, a crucial part of professional socialization.

In other fields, community-wide standards for research that have been established through professional training have frequently been reinforced and maintained by professional publications and associations. Once again, in education that has not been the case. From the first years of the twentieth century, journals devoted to education research have multiplied in number, focus, audience, and the criteria used to determine which research deserves publication. In consequence, professional research journals in education have done little to create norms around which a community might coalesce.

And what of professional associations? Early in the twentieth century, the National Society of College Teachers of Education (NSCTE) aspired to become an umbrella organization for all university-based scholars of education. Trying to distinguish its members from teachers, including normal school teachers who might claim to be engaged in research, the NSCTE was not able to generate a lasting sense of community among its briefly united members. The differences that divided them proved stronger than their common identification as professors of education, the result being a steady proliferation of less broad, more specialized associations, each with its own purposes and membership requirements. Even within the American Educational Research Association, there is little sense of community and few common standards to distinguish good from bad research, or significant from trivial.

Lacking a strong research community and the common standards of scholarship that can grow from that, education research has been more powerfully directed by seemingly removed events and shifts in national mood and priority than by questions derived from previous research. That is because goals for education have usually been derived from general national goals, and the apparent validity of education research has usually depended on the degree to which research has been perceived as useful in the immediate pursuit of those goals.

In the 1950s, for example, anticommunism and the cold war fueled new demands for "excellence" in education, which usually meant the highest possible levels of achievement for the academically most able. These new aspirations stimulated new research and development activities, which generally took the form of "course improvement" projects that were intended to anchor the various school subjects in the structures of the relevant disciplines. Developing the "new math," the Physical Science Study Committee (PSSC) version of physics, and other new curricula also involved new teams of discipline-based scholars in education. In the process, the education-based scholars who had previously dominated efforts to study and reform school curricula were displaced.

What is more, their earlier efforts to develop practical curricula were discontinued. Although today it is easy to criticize some of their efforts, especially the ones known as "life-adjustment" courses, which sometimes deteriorated into little more than discussion of boy–girl relationships and information about manners, dress, and speech, pre–World War II curriculum study was directed toward finding ways to strengthen the holding power of secondary schools. The goal was to prevent a wide range of noncollege-bound students from (what we now call) dropping out. When national goals shifted, that purpose, which was later embraced by such groups as the William T. Grant Foundation's Commission on Work, Family, and Citizenship (1988), was moved aside.

As these examples show, education research, no less than education policy, has had a pendulum-like history. Without a research community to generate shared standards of significance and validity, it has been difficult to create a consensus concerning central questions for investigation, sustain the pursuit of those questions over reasonably long periods of time, and develop the social structures necessary to translate research findings into actual improvements in practice. In consequence, methods and findings have multiplied without in any way being sifted, aggregated, and transformed to generate further research. The situation has been analogous to scores of separate firecrackers popping, with all the attendant noise and smoke but none of the dazzlingly clear illumination that can be associated with a well-calibrated fireworks show.

GOALS AND STANDARDS FOR EDUCATION RESEARCH

What, then, is to be done? Building a knowledge community in education will require, first and most important, self-conscious efforts to agree on goals and standards for education research. Goals and standards for research represent a crucial part of the intellectual infrastructure of any knowledge community, but there has been little lasting consensus about what these should be among scholars of education. In the past, in fact, it has been the absence of widely agreed-on goals and standards that has allowed shifts in direction to undermine promising lines of investigation.

To build the necessary intellectual infrastructure, there will have to be unprecedented collaboration among a wide variety of institutions and associations, public and private. Neither major education research associations like AERA, the National Academy of Education, the American Educational Studies Association, and the National Society for the Study of Education nor more specialized groups like the John Dewey Society, the National Conference of Professors of Educational Administration, the National Association for Research in Science Teaching, or the Society for the Study of Curriculum History represents the full universe of scholars who study education. Even so, it is possible to imagine that groups like these could be convinced to come together to discuss strategies for community building. Whether those strategies would entail a differentiation of roles and responsibilities among them or a congress-like effort to work together to assess research needs, review and evaluate current knowledge, and link knowledge to practice as well as to continuing research, the self-interest of all such groups should inspire a willingness to explore common problems, especially public skepticism and associated declines in funding, and the new potential for more powerful research that is implicit in new research methods, styles, and collaborations. If the result of conversations among groups were consensus concerning at least some goals and some standards, that might help to overcome competition and fragmentation.

Public and private funding agencies would also need to be involved in this effort. More often than not, new directions in research have depended on the willingness of a private foundation or a government agency to back a particular researcher or a particular approach to research. In consequence, funding agencies have exercised a great deal of control over which problems and research methods have and have not been developed. Widely diversified in their priorities in education and their approaches to philanthropy, funding agencies have perhaps unwittingly fostered the contested, pluralistic, and public character of education research and, in so doing, have helped preclude the possible emergence of a distinct research community. Obviously such agencies need to be free to support innovations, and obviously too they must be able to operate with significant institutional autonomy and discretion. But public and private agencies that are interested in education and in tested, research-based improvements in education have a stake in developing a more unified community than has heretofore existed among scholars of education. Hence, they need to take part in discussions among education associations concerning strategies for collaboration.

Last but hardly least, university deans, especially deans of schools of education, must be brought into the conversation about goals and standards for education research and, through them, faculty members. The reason for casting the net widely is that the training of education scholars is not the sole responsibility of the schools of education but a function that is distributed across the university. Goals and standards for education research also need to be articulated with changes in the humanities, psychology, and the social sciences, with new conceptions of law and public policy and with new approaches to public administration. Unless agreements on direction are reviewed, tested, refined, and constantly developed by multiple circles and new generations of scholars, they will quickly become inert codes of conduct rather than vital blueprints for action.

Fortunately, there appears to be growing support for the kind of community-building conversations sketched above. In fact, in June 1998, the National Education Research Policy and Priorities Board and the Office of Educational Research and Development of the U.S. Department of Education convened a two-day meeting to discuss national directions in education research planning. Attended by representatives from federal agencies, professional associations, foundations, and schools of education, the meeting testified to widespread concern with improving education research through better and more widely collaborative agenda setting and longer-term and more cumulative directions for research.

To build a true knowledge community in education, however, two more elements, which are often overlooked, will be necessary. The first is to bring teachers into the conversation about the purposes and uses of education research. Old paradigms for education research assumed that knowledge about teaching and learning would be generated by (usually male) scholars working in university laboratories and libraries and would then be transmitted to (mostly female) K–12 teachers, who would translate the findings of research into daily classroom practice. We know now that if research is to have a positive effect on teaching and learning, then teachers must be full partners in education. As Ann Brown once said in commenting on the ways that teachers often change the ideas she develops through research, "I'm totally dependent on a gifted teacher" (quoted in Kaestle, 1993, p. 26).

If her remark is any indication that teachers should be involved in discussions of research agenda and research standards, then it will be important to ponder how this can be done effectively. Many teachers are not at all interested in research. In most cases, neither their training nor their job descriptions mandate that they stay abreast of research literature—or that they change their approach to teaching based on research findings. To accomplish either would require different and time-consuming new learning, which is rarely rewarded in one's school or by school districts. Clearly, therefore, if a true knowledge community in education is to include teachers, efforts will have to be made to bridge current divisions between teacher education and the education of scholars in education and to change the incentive structures that currently make it somewhat irrational for teachers voluntarily to read about and engage in research.

The second element crucial to the formation of a knowledge community in education is much greater attention to educating the public about education in all of its complexities. To take hold, internal efforts to build community must be supported from the outside. Education researchers need to communicate more effectively with all the constituencies that influence education: members of school boards, elected bodies, and the press; governing authorities in higher education; and laypeople generally. They also need to engage their colleagues throughout the academy and its knowledge-generating affiliates—think tanks, consulting companies, and the like—in conversation about research in education. Unless all this is conceived as part of community building, then the old "awful reputation" of education research will persist.

Members of the lay public and scholars outside education know little about the particular challenges of studying education. Their basic familiarity with public education leads them easily to believe that there is not much to study. Lacking an understanding of the intellectual and practical difficulties of the field, they are inclined to dismiss research evidence, preferring to rely on tradition or their own experiential knowledge when asked to make a decision about some educational matter. Since most educational matters are decided by nonexperts, that is a problem that scholars of education overlook at their peril. To do so is to undermine the possible gains to be made from efforts to negotiate a broad general consensus concerning goals and standards for research.

The challenges facing scholars of education interested in improving prospects for research are immense. They are grounded in education's history and are compounded by phenomena that have nothing directly to do with education research—everything from the rise of postmodernism, which has tended to erode the authority of all knowledge, to a continuing retreat from earlier, more generous conceptions of public responsibility, which has tended to undermine belief in everything associated with public education, including school boards, "ed schools," and even teachers. Needless to say, too, if one is mindful of the history of education scholarship, one must acknowledge that in the past there have been repeated efforts to improve education research and that few of those have succeeded in creating a consensus about goals and standards. That notwithstanding, the cautionary insight available from history should not preclude renewed, perhaps more historically informed, efforts to change the status quo. Indeed, to do less than learn from the past in order to secure better prospects for newly promising research in education would be to abandon a hundred-year quest that, however flawed, has yielded significant gains in knowledge and in education policy and practice. Clearly the necessity is to recognize both the problems and the promise of the present moment and to find ways to act in support of ever more cumulative, insightful, humane, and useful research in the future.

References

Atkinson, R. C., and Jackson, G. B. (eds.). *Research and Education Reform: Roles for the Office of Educational Research and Improvement.* Washington, D.C.: National Academy Press, 1992.

Brown, A. L. "The Advancement of Learning." *Educational Researcher*, 1994, *23*, 5.

Brown, A. L., and Campione, J. C. "Guided Discovery in a Community of Learners." In K. McGilly (ed.), *Classroom Lessons: Integrating Cognitive Theory and Classroom Practice.* Cambridge, Mass.: MIT Press, 1994.

Commission on Work, Family, and Citizenship. *The Forgotten Half: Pathways to Success for America's Youth and Young Families.* New York: William T. Grant Foundation, 1988.

Crane, J. (ed.). *Social Programs That Work.* New York: Russell Sage Foundation, 1998.

Eisner, E., and Peshkin, A. (eds.). *Qualitative Inquiry in Education: The Continuing Debate.* New York: Teachers College Press, 1990.

Kaestle, C. "The Awful Reputation of Educational Research." *Educational Researcher*, 1993, *22*(1), 23–31.

Kucklick, B. *The Rise of American Philosophy: Cambridge, Massachusetts, 1860–1930.* New Haven, Conn.: Yale University Press, 1977.

Lagemann, E. C. "Contested Terrain: A History of Education Research in the United States, 1890–1990." *Educational Researcher*, 1997, *26*, 5–17.

Lampert, M. "How Do Teachers Manage to Teach? Perspectives on Problems in Practice." *Harvard Education Review*, 1985, *55*, 178–194.

Lippmann, W. "The Mental Age of Americans." *New Republic*, 1922a, *32*, 213–215.

Lippmann, W. "The Mystery of the 'A' Men." *New Republic*, 1922b, *32*, 246–248.

Lippmann, W. "The Reliability of Intelligence Tests." *New Republic*, 1922c, *32*, 275–277.

Lippmann, W. "Tests of Hereditary Intelligence." *New Republic*, 1922d, *32*, 328–330.

Lippmann, W. "A Future for the Tests." *New Republic*, 1922e, *33*, 9–10.

National Commission on Excellence in Education. *A Nation at Risk: The Imperative for Educational Reform.* Washington, D.C.: U.S. Department of Education, 1983.

Panel on Education Technology. President's Committee of Advisors on Science and Technology. *Report to the President on the Use of Technology to Strengthen K–12 Education in the United States.* Washington, D.C.: U.S. Government Printing Office, March 1997.

Sears, J. B., and Henderson, A. D. *Cubberly of Stanford and His Contribution to American Education.* Stanford, Calif.: Stanford University Press, 1957.

Suppes, P. (ed.). *Impact of Research on Education: Some Case Studies.* Washington, D.C.: National Academy Press, 1978.

CHAPTER TWO

Research and the Purposes of Education

David K. Cohen
Carol A. Barnes

Education research is a field of inquiry in which most work is applied and whose results, in the United States, are regularly the object of public interest and political passion. One possible reason for the interest and passion is the subject, which includes matters of considerable public importance: the effects of teaching, the nature of learning, the costs and benefits of schooling, and the schools' role in reducing poverty, increasing productivity, and improving economic competitiveness. Yet interest and passion seem to vary among nations, for the results of similar inquiries are more placidly received in corporate and consensual societies, where there is less argument and more deference to authority. Citizens in such nations appear tacitly to delegate most decisions about the ends and means of schooling to specialists in professions, ministries, and schools. Another reason is history, or habit: Americans have disagreed about schooling ever since we have had schools; educational argument seems to be a national pastime. Seventeenth-century Calvinists vehemently argued about how to instruct the young, and the habit has persisted despite or perhaps because of increasing religious and cultural pluralism.

Still another reason for interest in research on schools is that our political system was carefully arranged to open it to popular access and to restrain government

This chapter was written for the National Academy of Education's Commission for the Improvement of Educational Research, cochaired by Ellen Condliffe Lagemann and Lee S. Shulman. Thanks to Ellen Lagemann, who had several helpful suggestions concerning revision.

influence in education and other domestic matters. It is difficult to imagine a political system better suited to engendering arguments about schools, of which Americans seem so fond, or to open schools to the influence of those arguments. All manner of information about schools is used in and generated by the ensuing disputes, research included. Ours is a nation of part-time populists, who regularly dispute, subvert, and overturn the decisions of government officials and professionals in education. The past fifteen years of school reform, and argument about it, are the latest in a nearly unbroken era of reform and controversy since World War II. The growing movement for charter schools and choice is only the most recent evidence of efforts to restrict professional and government influence in schooling. Research has been widely used in both, and both developments have generated a good deal of research.

RESEARCH AND THE SCHOOLS' PURPOSES

If it is not news that American arguments about schools have been a steady accompaniment to research on them, it may be a bit more surprising to find that political dispute and systematic inquiry often have been handmaidens. Many researchers consider politics a distraction from the more dispassionate methods of social science, but in the United States at least, they often seem to be allied. One case in point arose in the 1840s, near the very beginning of the common school crusade, when allies of Horace Mann struggled with conservative school administrators for control of the Boston schools. Mann's colleagues campaigned for a more humane and progressive pedagogy, more equal schooling for African Americans and the poor, and a more rational school administration. Several of these Boston liberals won election to the Grammar School Committee and then tried to launch what may have been the first organized education research program in U.S. history. They composed a new and intellectually demanding citywide examination to assess the more progressive academic goals they thought schools should pursue. Members of the committee descended on the schools, where they administered the exam to all students, interviewed the grammar school masters, and observed lessons. They analyzed the data and composed a school-by-school report in which they depicted students' performance in most schools as dismally weak. The central problem in students' performance was their lack of deep knowledge and a parallel inability to reason about the questions they had been asked. Committee members portrayed the grammar masters and their antiquated, mindless, fact-and-memorization pedagogy and passion for discipline and control as the villains of the piece. Mann's allies proposed a new curriculum and pedagogy that would be more intellectually ambitious and engaging for students. They also argued that a more rational school system would employ research, including regular assessment of students' performance by a new central school agency, to monitor schools and inform corrective action (Cohen and Barnes, 1995; Mann, 1868, 1951; Parsons, Howe, and Neal, 1845; Messerli, 1972; Katz, 1971).

Education research in the United States thus seems to have been born in a major political battle over whether public education should become more humane, equal, and rational or God-fearing, authoritarian, and traditional. Disputes over schools' purposes were central to all the arguments, and research on how schools achieved their purposes was a central element in the reformers' program and arguments about it.

Disputes about schools' purposes, and related entanglements with research, became even more common six decades later in the progressive era. Educators, reformers, and public officials struggled to adjust public education to their various pictures of how a more urban, populous, diverse, and industrial society would work. Many researchers saw the schools' purposes as a matter of helping industrial capitalism work better and aligned themselves with business-oriented reformers. E. L. Thorndike, George Strayer, and others envisioned America as a developing social meritocracy of ability and achievement married to a developing economy of efficiency. They sought to create schools that would help to align the society with the economy by educating young members of one for suitable positions in the other. In a small 1911 volume, *Individuality*, Thorndike wrote, "Specialization of schools is needed not only to fit pupils for special professions, arts, trades, and the like, but also to fit the schools to original differences in the pupils" (Jonçich, 1962, p. 125). Applied research, in the form of school surveys, student testing, and curriculum evaluation, was central to their program. Thorndike cautioned education reformers not to "expect too much of education." Rather, "like good men of science they should measure and know, and like good engineers" allow a factor of safety (p. 133).

These researchers believed that more efficient and meritocratic schools would better serve America, both by using modern management to improve systems' performance and by matching students' studies with their social destinies. Many educators also seemed to bet that such work would offer them a way to improve their academic positions, to do more consequential public service, and thus to improve their social situation. Schools would be guided by research on them and their students and, thus informed by science, would better serve the developing industrial order. Thorndike, Strayer, and others worked in an era in which the professionalization and institutionalization of social research had begun in earnest, developments from which they benefited and to which they contributed.

John Dewey, Lucy Sprague Mitchell, George Counts, and others of a more radical persuasion worked the same issues but from a very different perspective. They wanted a more equal and cooperative America, and they wanted schools to combat the evils of industrial capitalism and help build a more humane society. They opposed testing, curriculum tracking, and the influence of business on schooling. But research was not central to their program, for they relied more on argument than on inquiry and evidence. George Counts (1922,

1929) took a few opportunities to collect evidence on the operation and effects of the existing schools. The Eight-Year Study was a major effort to assess the effects of progressive schooling. But this work aside, empirical research did not figure prominently in the progressives' rhetoric of criticism or reconstruction.

Institution building was more prominent, but that was limited as well. With the brief exception of the Dewey School and a few longer-running progressive private schools, they did not try to invent examples of the schools for which they argued. Bank Street, Wheelock, Pacific Oaks, and Lesley colleges recruited and educated professionals for service in either mainstream or alternative schools, but they were a few drops in a huge and growing bucket of conventional practice. There is no evidence that progressives tried to turn these colleges into a broader national strategy to change schools by changing the people who worked in them.

Opportunities to link ideas about the schools' purposes, professional service, and research thus were more rare in this dissenting tradition than in the line of work that Strayer and Thorndike pioneered. For better or worse, professional service for the left-wing progressives came to be dissent accompanied by tiny islands of progressive practice, rather than efforts to inquire systematically into the problems of the public schools or the operation of alternatives. Dewey wrote extensively about education, and he offered thoughtful arguments for more equality and more challenging instruction in public schools. But his educational writings defined no agenda for further inquiry. Although his writing about the schools was salient to issues of great interest and importance, he rarely suggested lines of further inquiry, experimentation, and research. Even his Laboratory School, which he did bill as an experiment, did not seem to be systematically documented, with the exception of the Mayhew and Edwards (1966) volume many years later. Neither he nor any of his associates published any evidence on the school's effects for students.

As a result, left-wing progressives on the problems of the dominant school regime, the creation of educational alternatives on a large scale, and research on their effects never gained a foothold in either university research or the public domain. Dewey's ideas never became a regular part of the research and graduate education mainstream, which is one reason for their modest effect in public education. Dewey's very different conception of the purposes and practices of schooling remained outside the central organizations and research agendas of public education. Graduate research and education in education were instead largely defined by Thorndike's views, his agenda for inquiry, and his graduate students.

Research and public affairs became more entangled after World War II, as social research grew along with the phenomenal expansion of higher education, and school criticism and reform became a regular feature of public life. The era opened with a sustained chorus of university-led complaint about the purposes and methods that professional educators had embraced in life adjustment education and their mind-numbing effects in the schools. That attack on the schools' purposes was soon followed by the U.S. Supreme Court's decision in *Brown v. Board of Education of Topeka* (1954), which announced that the entire Jim Crow educational regime in the South was illegitimate and henceforth illegal (see *Brown v. Board of Education of Topeka,* 1951; and also *McLaurin v. Oklahoma State Regents for Higher Education,* 1950; and *Sweat v. Painter,* 1950). If ever there was a significant change in the purposes of American schooling, it was that move from state-sponsored racism.

Academic researchers played a central role in both developments. Scientists and humanists were the chief critics of public education in the postwar decade; Arthur Bestor, James B. Conant, and Admiral Hyman Rickover were among the leading figures, and the professors took a central role in the invention of new and intellectually much more demanding purposes for public schools. Their agent for this effort was curriculum, but the purpose was to shift the aims and content of schooling radically, at least for the more able students. Social scientists also played a central role in *Brown*: they brought evidence and argument to bear for the plaintiff's claims and, as the desegregation cases grew, played an increasingly important role in efforts to define, create, and criticize a racially neutral school system (see, for example, the effects of segregation, Appendix to appellants' briefs in *Brown,* 1952).

By the late 1960s social science had become the chief means for investigating the effects not only of desegregation but of Great Society school improvement programs, social policy more broadly, and the schools themselves, especially their effects on academic performance and achievement later in life. That development brought research closer to the center of political arguments about the purposes and effects of educational and social policy and about the fairness of American society, where it remains. One reason for that development was that research revealed, with growing force and clarity, how much education counted for occupational and economic performance later in life. If schooling counted for the things about which most Americans cared deeply, then research on schooling was no frill. Another reason for the growing importance of research was that just as Americans became more sensible of their growing entanglement with economies overseas (courtesy of competition with the Japanese over cars in the 1970s and 1980s) social researchers began to report how poorly American schoolchildren stacked up against their European and Asian peers. The message was that American students did poorly in a world perspective, but the medium was sociology, economics, and psychology. Social scientists reported on the differences among national school systems, explained the sources of the differences, and offered advice about what might be done (Stevenson and Stigler, 1992).

If the links between politics and research on schools' purposes have often been close, they have not been simple. In some cases research that bore on the schools' purposes was closely and deliberately tied to political arguments. That certainly was the case with Mann's allies, much of the work of Strayer and

Thorndike, some of George Counts's work, and many more recent studies of issues related to school segregation and other public policy matters. But in some other cases, research has had a more inadvertent bearing on public affairs. One increasingly common case in point is when conventional disciplinary work, like research on human capital formation, becomes salient to public affairs because social or political developments highlight issues of social investment.

Political concerns and research are directly linked in both of these cases, but as research has grown in volume and autonomy, more and more of it has been done within the academy. Although it bears on matters of public concern, it is increasingly carried out and communicated in specialized scientific channels. The growth of the academy thus has increased the difficulty of members' communication with the society that supports them. Research and public affairs have become a species of parallel play; concerns and arguments within research roughly mirror those in the larger society, without contact between the two.

THE EFFECTS OF SCHOOLING

One of the chief ways that researchers have contributed to the conversation about schools' purposes has been to issue dismal reports on how schools affect learning—or fail to affect it. Horace Mann's allies stirred up a hornet's nest of local controversy with their report that most grammar schools failed to educate most students. Joseph Meyer Rice did something of the same sort nationally at the end of the nineteenth century with his studies of how students in city schools across the country performed on the tests that he devised and administered. Some might say that Mann's colleagues and Rice were not professional researchers, but these men did have some specialized knowledge, saw it as crucial to school improvement, and tried to invent more.

There were many more inquiries into the effects of schooling topics during the nineteenth and twentieth centuries (see Cohen and Neufeld, 1981). But what contemporary researchers would recognize as systematic inquiry into the effects of schooling began only after World War II, as survey research, mathematical modeling of social processes, and computerized information processing enabled large-scale data collection and analysis in which the attributes of many schools, students, and educational resources could be related. James Coleman's 1966 *Equality of Educational Opportunity Survey* (EEOS) usually is seen as the first major effort of a scientific sort.

Although Coleman did not set out to create a dispute, his work nevertheless had some of the same effects—stirring up controversy by poking it with a stick of evidence—as had the work of Mann's colleagues and Rice earlier. His study became central to political arguments that raged well past the report's publication. The study was sponsored by the U.S. Office of Education (USOE), pursuant to an obscure subsection of Title IV of the 1964 Civil Rights Act. With the leadership of Alexander Mood, an educational statistician then serving as assistant commissioner for educational statistics in USOE, Coleman and his colleagues had undertaken the congressionally required national survey of schools and students to report on patterns of inequality. But with Mood's agreement they also collected evidence that would enable them to analyze the relations along students' family backgrounds, schools' educational resources, and students' achievement.

Much to everyone's astonishment, the analysis revealed less inequality in access to resources than had been expected. Differences among schools in the allocation of such resources as libraries, teachers' experience and education, per-pupil expenditures, science labs, and other facilities were much more weakly related to students' race and class than had been expected. A larger surprise was that differences among schools in those same educational resources were weakly related to differences among schools in student performance. Differences among schools' libraries, their teachers' experience and education, their per pupil expenditures, science labs, and other facilities had little or no effect on differences in students' achievement. Although teachers' verbal ability was related to their students' performance, the most powerful predictors of students' performance were their parents' educational and social backgrounds, in comparison to whose effects school resources were trivial. Schools' social and economic composition was also related to students' performance: disadvantaged students who attended school with more advantaged students did better than those similarly situated who attended school with others who were disadvantaged

Coleman's report was startling and corrosive, for the results were starkly opposed to long-established professional opinion and public belief about schools. His report raised fundamental questions about public policy, including the wisdom of investment of more dollars in schooling (Mosteller and Moynihan, 1972; Moynihan, 1968). Despite the astonishment, the results had not come out of scientific left field. Many small studies in earlier decades had shown that the school resources conventionally thought important were weakly and inconsistently related to student performance. A large and quite compelling study—Project Talent—had been undertaken nearly a decade earlier with no public fanfare and produced similar results. Project Talent was a longitudinal study of students and secondary schools that enabled researchers to weigh the effects of school resources on students' achievement near the end of high school, given knowledge of students' achievement at the beginning of high school. The analyses were published in blandly inconspicuous scientific reports that offered even more convincing evidence about the weak differential effects of educational resources on student achievement.

The EEOS confirmed this large, and largely unknown, study, but because it was a government report and because the civil rights movement and other policy changes had increased interest in liberal social policies, Coleman's study became a central element in political dispute about education. Although it had been intended chiefly to report on the extent of inequality in the schools, it helped to usher in a period of much more vivid public controversy about the schools' effects on learning and the implications for educational policy.

Coleman's report on the effects of schools' social composition encouraged political liberals, but everything else about the report discouraged them. That effect was fed by a small eruption of disappointing evaluations of Project Head Start, Title I of the 1965 Elementary and Secondary Education Act (ESEA), and other Great Society school improvement programs. The evaluations were undertaken or sponsored by social scientists who went to Washington, D.C., in the New Frontier and Great Society eras. They hoped to improve the effectiveness of government programs by improving knowledge of their effects. Although they were more technocratic than political in their intentions, the evaluation reports followed on the heels of the Coleman study, during the slow collapse of President Lyndon B. Johnson's ambitions for domestic reform and the growth of the conservative movement in American politics. The combination created something of a crisis in education and education research, for accumulating evidence seemed to suggest that conventional educational resources and ameliorative interventions were weakly effective at best (McLaughlin, 1975). These reports were coupled with persistent evidence that what counted most for students' performance was their families' social and economic status, their race, and their own incoming school achievement. That led many to conclude that researchers were claiming that schools "made no difference," an idea that was reinforced in 1972 by the publication of *Inequality* by Christopher Jencks and several colleagues (1972).

No one had claimed, or could have claimed, that schools made no difference. For one thing, no researcher had compared the performance of American students to that of their peers in another nation that was in every respect similar, save that there were no publicly provided schools. For another, there was the evident fact that students learned a great deal in school; algebra and French do not spring spontaneously to the minds of American adolescents. Coleman's, Jencks', and other studies showed only that when schooling was nearly universally provided and when the allocation of educational resources among them was relatively equal, differences among schools in those resources did not seem to be strongly related to differences among schools in students' performances. Although there were great differences in average achievement across schools, and especially troubling achievement differences between schools that enrolled the children of affluent and poor parents, differences in the educational resources that most people thought significant, like money spent or the education of teachers, were at best weakly related to student performance differences.

But even on a cautious interpretation of the research, it seemed to suggest that allocating more money to schools that enrolled many more poor children would be unlikely to improve achievement, a conclusion that was powerfully reinforced by the disappointing evaluations of programs like Title I of the 1965 ESEA, which entailed just such compensatory resource allocation. Conservatives used the evidence to call for cutbacks in Title I and other liberal programs. That troubled liberals, but the evidence was even more troubling because it appeared to suggest that schools did not serve, in Horace Mann's often-quoted phrase, as "the balance wheel of the social machinery." Rather than reducing the educational effects of America's larger social and economic inequalities, schools appeared to transmit and perhaps harden them. (On this point, see the varying views of Bowles and Gintis, 1976; Jencks and others, 1972.)

In reaching that conclusion, commentators forgot that no one had done research on that nonexistent-comparison America that was in all respects similar to the one Coleman and others investigated, save that public schools did not exist and schooling could only be purchased in the market. Had such miraculous research been done, investigators could have estimated both the effects that having a public school system had on the inequalities in knowledge and skill with which students entered school and on the economic and occupational consequences of schooling. This point was lost in the arguments, even though a moment's thought would have revealed that in societies in which schooling could only be purchased in the market, differences between affluent and poor students in access and achievement would be much greater than in societies in which nearly everyone attended school.

One reason that these developments were so startling was that the research challenged the American faith in the power of exposure to school. Since the eighteenth century we had thought that social environments were a powerful influence on the development of mind and that better environments could cure all manner of mental and moral problems. It was thought that schools, asylums, prisons, libraries, and other formal institutions could undo the damage done by irresponsible families, slum neighborhoods, papist doctrine, family poverty, and other social evils (Rothman, 1971; Katz, 1971; Cohen, 1985; Ravitch, 1974; Kaestle, 1983). But research and evaluation seemed to challenge that faith directly. In addition, they questioned the commonplace educational resources—teachers' education, books, science labs, money spent on schools, and the like—that educators had long told Americans would make better schools better. These were the indicators that parents and teachers used to make judgments about the quality of education—and the resources for which Americans regularly paid state and local taxes.

It seemed incredible that everyone should have been so completely incorrect, especially when educational opportunity played such a central part in American ideas about equality and social policy. On some accounts, equal educational opportunity was the American substitute for social policy in employment, welfare, and family support (Katznelson and Weir, 1988; also Wier, Orloff, and

Skocpol, 1988), so if schools did offer equal opportunity, then little else need be done. But if educational opportunity was as unequal as the research seemed to suggest, something was very wrong with the idea that America offered equal opportunities for accomplishment and with the view that schools were the central agent of equality.

However incredible, the subversive findings turned out to be influential, and in surprisingly different ways. Some conservative commentators embraced the results and used them to support their skepticism about Great Society programs and liberal social policy. President Nixon and his advisers—who were no friends of social research, regarding researchers as a generally hostile group of liberals —later used the results as part of the justification for proposals to turn Title I of the 1965 ESEA into a revenue-sharing scheme. They argued that state and local officials would know better what to do with the money than remote federal bureaucrats.

Less predictably, President Nixon accepted the plan of Daniel Patrick Moynihan, at that time the president's chief adviser for domestic affairs, to improve research and proposed to create the National Institute of Education (NIE) to do more research on the issues that Coleman and others had raised. The idea made friends on both sides of the congressional aisle, and became law. For the first time in U.S. history, a federal agency sought to improve education by investigating how schools worked. Studies that had seemed to create a crisis in liberal social policy and the reputation of education research somehow also helped to set a more focused and prominent mission for education research and to promise a rosy future for research funding.

The NIE did not have a happy life, and its funding soon looked less rosy. But the subversive research that contributed to its invention also helped to stimulate a contrary line of inquiry, much of it funded by the NIE. Beginning in the early 1970s, research on schools, teaching, and learning began to prosper. Many researchers moved from a focus on schools to teachers, in an effort to figure out whether some teachers were unusually effective and why. David Berliner, Jere Brophy, William Cooley, Tom Good, and Gaea Leinhardt were among the leading figures in this line of work, and Brophy summarized the evidence in the mid-1980s. There were unusually effective teachers, as judged by the magnitude of students' gains on standardized tests, and their practice seemed very different from that of their less effective peers. More effective teachers seemed to plan lessons carefully, select appropriate materials, make their goals clear to students, maintain a brisk pace in lessons, check students' work regularly, and teach material again when students seemed to have trouble learning (Brophy and Good, 1986). They also spent much more time on instructional tasks (Cooley and Leinhardt, 1985; Berliner, 1979). Such teachers had coherent strategies for instruction and deployed lessons, books, and other resources in ways consistent with the strategies. They believed that their students could learn and that they had a large responsibility to help. They had definite objectives and orga-nized instruction to achieve them. Although typically quite traditional and didactic, these teachers' lessons were well thought out, well organized, and well paced. Typically the teachers used conventional tests and texts but as part of a well-crafted strategy to improve children's learning.

Many other teachers did not have coherent strategies for instruction and deployed resources in a scattered and inconsistent way. They had vague objec-tives, and their lessons were not well thought out or well organized. Classroom work typically was badly paced, and teachers either did not regularly check to see how students were doing or, if they did check, did not make many midcourse corrections to accommodate students' responses. John Goodlad (1984) reported that more than half of elementary students told the members of his research team that they "did not know what they were supposed to do in class." Teachers of this sort did not exert themselves to make educationally fruitful connections with students; many acted as though they believed that their responsibility was only to "present the material" and let students get it if they could. When such teachers worked with children from disadvantaged circumstances, they often acted as though students could handle only watered-down instruction.

Other researchers did similar work at the school level, probing connections between schools' collective characteristics and student performance. Ronald Edmonds began by trying to figure out whether some schools produced unusu-ally large achievement gains, and when he found some, he tried to identify what distinguished them from run-of-the-mill schools. Edmonds and others reported that faculty members in unusually effective schools shared a vision of the pur-poses of instruction, agreed that their school's purpose was to promote students' learning, and believed that they were responsible for helping students to learn. Teachers had a strong commitment to students' academic success, and their principals' leadership helped to create and sustain these beliefs and practices (Edmonds, 1979, 1984).

Critics soon pointed out crucial methodological problems with this line of work, including interannual variation in effectiveness (Rowan, Guthrie, Lee, and Guthrie, 1986) and problems in reasoning from schools with unusually high per-formance to more ordinary schools (Purkey and Smith, 1983). The method-ological problems might have kept researchers away if they had closely followed their methods textbooks, but they pursued Edmonds's insight anyway, embroi-dering and deepening it (Purkey and Smith, 1985). Despite the problems, his work offered an appealing way to depict the differences between strong and weak schools.

This line of inquiry gained credibility as evidence accumulated. A group of researchers collaborated on the most comprehensive study (Bryk, Lee, and Hol-land, 1993), changing this tradition of work as they capitalized on it. They found that more effective high schools were more likely to have teachers who shared a commitment to their students and believed that they had an obligation to help students achieve academic success. Faculty members in these schools were collegial, had extensive contact with students in and out of class, and had high morale. Students were likely to study the same curriculum, for there was little curriculum tracking. Anthony Bryk and his colleagues portrayed effective high schools as communities in which students and teachers took responsibility for each other academically and socially. Although students in such schools had higher achievement, what is especially noteworthy is that achievement differences between advantaged and disadvantaged students decreased over the high school years. That reversed the pattern in typical secondary schools, which were much more fragmented and anomic. Teachers, staff members, and students in these weaker schools shared no common vision of instructional purposes and made no common commitment to students' success, and there was no common curriculum. There was instead low morale, with little collegiality or contact among teachers and students outside class, and achievement differences between advantaged and disadvantaged students increased over the high school years.

This sketch of recent research on the effects of teaching and schooling reveals some surprising features of research on schools' purposes. One is that seemingly dismal reports on the schools' achievement of their purposes had constructive as well as some worrying consequences, because one element in research decisions is a dialectic among researchers. Research that seemed so negative in the context and afterglow of the Great Society stimulated researchers to ask questions they might never have asked had the troublesome work never been done. Another is that opponents of research sometimes advance it when inquiry about the purposes and effects of schooling suits their purposes. Richard Nixon's electoral victory reminded educators and researchers that support for schools and ameliorative social programs might not continue forever on faith. More evidence that social programs were ineffective could encourage changes in the politics and economics of education that would damage research and schools. The conservative turn in U.S. politics, which seemed an enemy of investment in schooling, offered researchers incentives to investigate schools' effectiveness, a development that was repeated in the 1980s and continues today.

Thus the previous two decades saw both unparalleled dispute about schools' purposes and effects and a remarkable flowering of research on those matters. One reason for the flowering was that research came to seem more useful across the political spectrum. Liberals found it increasingly useful because, for the first time, research on the purposes of schooling raised fundamental questions about the schools' effects and effectiveness, and public discussion of the research alerted them to the importance of such knowledge. Political conservatives increasingly found education research to be a handy tool as cross-national studies reported dismal comparisons between U.S. and other nations' schools, and national surveys revealed similar patterns. Because these findings reinforced conservative critiques, they supported expensive national and cross-national studies in the 1980s that they might earlier have brushed off as politically irrelevant or a frill. But as conservative proposals for charter schools have been adopted, conservatives have found it useful or necessary to support or submit to the same sorts of research and evaluation that they earlier urged on public schools and liberal programs (Berman and others, 1998; Manno and others, 1997; Witte, 1994; Greene and others, 1996; Greene and Peterson, 1996).

EFFECTS OF RESEARCH ON THE EFFECTS OF SCHOOLING

Research on the schools' purposes and effects has had larger impacts as well. One is that research on schooling plays a larger role in public discourse about education now than it did thirty years ago. It figures more prominently in executive branch discussions of schooling and in congressional deliberations. It is used increasingly to justify and attack programs, and it has a more prominent role in foundation reports and the actions of state governments. In these ways and others, research has helped to change the ways that Americans think about schools and how they act on them.

These changes did not occur because particular studies shaped particular decisions, for social research typically is not influential in that way. The changes are instead associated with the growing role of social research as a language for advocating, explaining, and justifying ideas and decisions. This influence of research might be regarded as linguistic: research shapes the ideas, claims, and evidence that are in good currency in political discourse by shaping the vocabulary and syntax of thought and speech. Research on the purposes of schooling has helped to alter Americans' ideas about those purposes and the schools' part in achieving them.

One key example of such influence is the increasing focus on results in public and professional discussion of schooling. Before the 1960s public debate about schools was focused much more on the allocation of resources, the availability of access, and the content of curriculum. There was little systematic attention to results, even though they were tacitly assumed to be implied in resources allocated and curriculum used.

The initial and absolutely fundamental contribution of Coleman, Jencks, and other researchers was to raise deep questions about that assumed connection; by the late 1960s resources no longer could be assumed to ensure student performance. That was a fundamental rupture in inherited ideas about schooling, and it occurred as the result of efforts to model schooling processes mathematically, in input-output terms. One might say that the formal models only made explicit what educators and citizens always had assumed—that students in better schools did better because their schools were better. But the process of trying to fit an input-output model to data on school resources and student performance enabled Project Talent researchers and Coleman explicitly to test an assumption that never had been held up for inspection on any scale. The result dramatically called attention to the lack of those direct connections between resources and results that nearly everyone, including the researchers, had expected to find.

The rupture had several effects. One was to help to bring school outputs out into the open as the chief focus for both schools and research. Many critics and commentators responded to the research and evaluations by arguing that if conventional resources did not produce the desired school outcomes, something else should be done. The late 1960s and early 1970s thus saw the first eruption of efforts to focus schools explicitly on results, in proposals for performance contracting, outcome accountability, and program evaluation. None had the desired effects, but all were part of an increased effort to reorient schooling to results.

In fact, the continuing failure to find tight connections between resources and results created potent incentives, in and around the research enterprise, to figure out what was wrong, in order to explain why the connection was weak and to figure out how it might be strengthened. The apparent ineffectiveness of schools and programs created opportunities for skeptics, conservatives, and advocates of efficiency to call for scientific evaluation determining whether schools and interventions improved students' achievement. That rhetorical stance and the ensuing evaluations helped to keep the focus on results. The broken connection also put liberals, service providers, and program advocates on the defensive, increasing the incentives for them to invest in research and acquiesce in the novel idea that intervention programs, which had once seemed self-evidently desirable, should be evaluated to see if they improved results (McLaughlin, 1975).

One consequence was progressive public and political attention to what had been termed "accountability." In the 1970s state governments began to collect and publish data on student performance, often school by school—an idea that would have been treated as unthinkable just a decade before. The motives for these initiatives were mixed, but one was to encourage schools to pay more attention to student outcomes by making the information public and allowing citizens and educators to compare and draw their own conclusions. The concern with accountability has grown since then. Most states now have well-established accountability systems, and a few state and local agencies have quite sophisticated means of collecting and publishing data on schools' performance. These are premised on the sense that schools should be responsible for students' performance and the belief that schools should be penalized if they fail to produce results. Recent state school reforms in Texas and Kentucky are perhaps the clearest expression of those ideas.

Another stimulus for the attention to results was research on the role of schooling in status attainment and economic performance. Decades of research had shown that, on average, students who stayed in school longer got better jobs and earned more money. Some recent work suggests similar payoffs to student achievement (Jencks and Phillips, 1999). Researchers also reported evidence that the occupational and economic importance of schooling has increased, probably because many jobs require more knowledge and skill than formerly. This work grew more sophisticated and convincing as it used longitudinal rather than cross-sectional data and offered evidence pointing to the causal links among school attainment, income, and occupational status.

These developments added resonance to the sense that results were the appropriate way to think about schools; they also drew public attention to results. Reports of schools' performance are by now a regular feature in newspapers, magazines, and other media. Newspapers publish annual state assessments; critics argue about the meaning of the reports, and they lock horns about the appropriateness of particular assessment instruments. Concern about the schools' production of results never has been higher, and arguments about results have never been more intense. The movement for standards-based reform is only the most recent and significant manifestation of results-oriented thinking about schools, for a central idea in the movement is that schools should be responsible for achieving explicit outcomes, based on clear academic standards (Resnick and Resnick, 1989). This movement has helped to intensify attention to results as reformers and researchers try to conceptualize and design assessments that will more faithfully represent standards for school performance and offer students more opportunities to display their thinking. One mark of the change is that among the many arguments about standards-based reform, there has been little dissent from the idea that school improvement should focus on school outcomes.

Social research thus has increasingly shaped the language used to understand and discuss social and educational problems. It has especially focused attention on students' academic performance, as that is measured in formal assessments. And these changes in public discourse have been accompanied by others, also drawn from the vocabulary and syntax of social science. Input-output models of social processes, a key feature of the new language arising from modern economics and sociology, have helped to frame the focus on results by picturing schools as agents of production. The idea of schools as learning "factories" is at least as old as Thorndike and Bobbitt, but only in the past three decades has there been an analytic apparatus that social scientists can use to model schooling processes formally in input-output terms and thus help reorganize political and public debate around such models.

To argue that research has had a linguistic influence is not to imply that this is a matter of mere talk. Language often shapes behavior by influencing how we read and define situations, what problems we see, how we define solutions, and what action we believe is possible. Franklin D. Roosevelt's language had a significant effect on American politics and social policy, in part because he spoke about the Great Depression in ways that recognized privation and legitimized ameliorative action. Hitler's language had a powerful effect on German behavior in the 1930s and 1940s, in part because he used it effectively to mobilize national pride, prejudice, and a sense of collective identity and to legitimize violence against Jews, dissenters, gypsies, and homosexuals. President Clinton's success in using language to portray congressional Republicans as dangerous enemies of education and health care in 1995 and 1996 assisted his legislative efforts at the time, his subsequent campaign for reelection, and the 1998 congressional elections. The language of the Supreme Court's decision in *Brown v. Board of Education of Topeka* had an enormous effect on Americans' behavior in part because it accepted that black Americans had been right all along about the injustice of Jim Crow, that white America had been wrong, and that remedies were in order. The Court thus legitimized black expression, which had long been politically buried, and led to a range of actions from lunch counter sit-ins to voter registration.

Changes in the language of social research seem to have had similar consequences. For instance, when Title I of the ESEA was initially passed in 1965, the legislative focus was on channeling more educational resources to the schools that disadvantaged students attended. Advocates may have assumed that students' achievement would improve, but there was only the most modest attention to results (McLaughlin, 1975). When Title I was reauthorized in 1994, however, the legislation focused heavily on results: it now calls for states to set explicit standards for student performance, for Title I no longer aims to channel resources to schools but to improve student performance. The legislation also proposes to hold schools and districts responsible for performance. States are required to hold local schools and districts "accountable" for student performance, offer assistance to schools failing to improve that performance, and close schools or reassign staff if they do not succeed. That is a remarkable shift, in both the nation's single most important federal public school program and the very idea of government responsibility in school improvement. With Title I and Goals 2000, the Clinton administration declared that student outcomes were the purpose of school improvement and that government was responsible for those results. Although the administration's position capped developments over several decades, it was a momentous change.

The change was not isolated. The past decade has seen an unprecedented migration of researchers into school improvement efforts, all seeking to improve student achievement. Robert Slavin, an education researcher at Johns Hopkins University, used a program of research to define, test, and develop Success for All, an elementary school intervention designed to improve achievement for disadvantaged students. Henry Levin, an economist of education at Stanford University's Graduate School of Education, developed the Accelerated Schools

Program, with roughly the same purpose. James P. Comer, a Yale University psychiatrist, developed an intervention program for young children that seeks to improve education for disadvantaged students by improving family–school connections and social service coordination. Bryk, an education researcher at the University of Chicago, has taken a central role in the Chicago school reforms, including the development of an intervention program to improve literacy performance in low-income schools. E. D. Hirsch, a professor of English at the University of Virginia, has developed an intervention program designed to improve performance by focusing on traditional conceptions of academic subjects.

The entry of these and other researchers into school improvement is unprecedented, in both the researchers' focus on results and their effort to work in practice. They have begun to redefine the role of research in schooling by redefining the researcher's role. Of course, some academics previously tried to improve schools by doing research on learning and teaching, developing curricula, and writing texts, but few worked directly as school improvement. Dewey and Thorndike wrote texts and devised tests. The researcher-intervenors discussed here assumed that changing schooling will require more than such isolated academic instruments as tests, texts, or a laboratory school. If our view of the influence of social science is roughly correct, then the increased focus on results (due in part to changes in the language of research itself) has enabled research to become a more direct agent of school improvement and the researcher to become a more direct agent of change.

For an account of this sort to be convincing, however, it also must explain why Americans might have been receptive to the language of research. The supply of research alone could hardly be the cause of more influence, since research journals are not required reading for citizens and officials. A more plausible explanation lies in the increased importance of expertise in many enterprises and occupations and the expanding number of channels for the use of expert knowledge. For instance, nonprofit foundations were staffed in the 1950s by well-educated amateurs who had little specialized professional preparation. Now these agencies hire specialists with advanced degrees who were educated as researchers and speak that language. Foundations increasingly use research in their deliberations, in various task forces, and in reports that they hope will influence public opinion.

The growth of analytic agencies in and around government was a similar development. There were only a few state and federal agencies of this sort in the 1950s and even fewer nongovernment think tanks. Both sorts of offices have multiplied since the mid-1960s and are staffed by a new class of knowledge professionals who have specialized professional degrees in various social sciences. They conduct and manage research and other advice based on research to consumers in and out of government. The existence of these agencies and the presence of social science–trained professionals have encouraged a larger role for

research in conversations within executive and legislative agencies and in relations between such agencies and other groups.

The demand for social research thus can be traced at least in part to a larger
population of specialized analytic agencies and professionals whose work concerns social problem solving. More agencies now define their mission as social
problem solving through analysis, and more people are paid to speak and write
about social problems and public policy. These professionals have learned to
speak the language of social science and use it to frame problems and possible
solutions. They read research and consult researchers because they have learned
that is where authoritative knowledge is found. And they work in agencies
whose mission and survival depend on the use of research. Both the agencies
and their staffs have been supported partly by university social science departments and policy analysis programs that specialize in educating professionals
to work in just such agencies. Postgraduate education of that sort was entirely
unavailable in the 1950s, but the programs have prospered since then, sending
thousands of students to work in analytic offices, government, private agencies,
foundations, and community agencies.

SCIENTIFIC PROGRESS?

Thus far we have told a tale of increasingly sophisticated understanding of and
agreement on how schools work. Beginning from research that seemed to under-
cut schools' claims to effectiveness, knowledge about teaching and schooling
has produced consistent evidence of educational effectiveness. One distinctive
thread in the new work has been the broadened definition of educational
resources to include teachers' goals and strategic actions, their professional commitments and knowledge, the knowledge that they have and the skills that they
deploy, and how these enable them to guide students' use of materials and facilities. Researchers have also included in educational resources various collective
attributes of schools and classrooms, such as leadership, shared goals, and collegiality.

These shifts mark a continuing movement in scholarly interest away from
conventional conceptions of educational resources—such as teachers' qualifications and school facilities—toward particular instructional practices and organizational arrangements and the knowledge, skill, and culture that these entail.
Educational inquiry also increasingly defines resources in terms of their salience
to outcomes, rather than assuming that connection. None of this denies the significance of instructional materials, facilities, and teachers' formal qualifications; it implies, rather, that their salience depends on how teachers deploy
them. Materials, facilities, teachers' formal qualifications, and the like are only

potential resources in this view. Whether they become actual depends on what teachers make of them, and that depends on teachers' knowledge, skills, and professional commitments, as well as on the organizations in which they work.

This new picture of educational resources is not simple. The differences that researchers discern in schools' and teachers' effectiveness are subtle and relatively difficult to manipulate because the resources are complex and because manipulating professional action, knowledge, and norms is a more complex undertaking than increasing salaries, building better schools, and revising standards for hiring. The new ideas about resources are less easy for policymakers or members of the public to grasp than money, bricks, and mortar, nor do they lead easily to clear policy initiatives. Worse, knowledge about schooling has become more subtle at the same time that public life in the United States has become more simplistic; as research complicates our view of schooling processes, American politics has grown more addicted to partisan and ideological sound-bite sloganeering.

That contrast is particularly important because the recent research seems to imply more professional and less political influence on schools. If key educational resources center on professional action, norms, and knowledge, then inventing a more accomplished professionalism will be one key to school improvement. Such professionalism can be supported and encouraged by public agencies, but it can be done only by the professionals in question. One of the most prominent policy innovations of our era has been the National Board for Professional Teaching Standards (NBPTS). This private professional group has devised standards and examinations for school teachers in an effort to raise standards for teaching and place governance of the standards and examinations in the hands of professionals rather than government.

American politics does not offer many openings for such work. Policy initiatives come and go in a brief and unstable issue–attention cycle, in which state and federal policy goals, programs, and issues change regularly. There is little time for careful analysis and policy formation or for learning from experience with previous initiatives. The politics of education reveals increasingly deep division about the purposes of schooling. Although the recent research seems to imply more deference to professionals, politicians seem inclined toward more ideologically inspired intervention, and there are sharper partisan differences over education policy. The NBPTS has thus far secured significant state and federal support, but its growing success has been attacked.

Research cannot solve these problems, for they are political and professional in origin. But researchers could make a more subtle contribution to solving them if they produced more substantial results and presented them with more convincing authority. Attention to and support for research in economics or health care has not visibly suffered from the recent increases in ideological warfare and partisan conflict, and it is just at this juncture that the frailty of social science progress in education becomes apparent. Our earlier account stressed the important work that has been done since the early 1970s, but it did not mention equally important work that has not been done. For instance, studies of effective schools seem simply to have stopped after producing suggestive results. No one devised and tested interventions based on the research, nor did anyone then organize field trials of the surviving designs. Similarly, research on effective teaching did not progress very far from studies of the unusually effective teachers. Brophy organized research and experiments that tested some of the ideas derived from his field studies, but the logical next steps for this entire program of inquiry, like larger experiments with well-defined treatments, were not tried (Mosteller, 1972). The same could be said of work that William Cooley and Gaea Leinhardt and other researchers began. Sponsors and researchers instead moved on to new topics, leaving suggestive but incomplete work behind. The research opened up important new lines of inquiry, but because the studies were typically small and used varied methods, it is unclear how far anyone can generalize from them. These limitations also mean that there are no general estimates of the magnitude of effects on students' achievement relative to other influences. In addition old issues have resurfaced as several researchers claim to have shown that traditional resources do influence student performance, as do, according to evidence from an experiment, sharp reductions in class size (Hedges, Laine, and Greenwald, 1994; Mosteller, 1995; Mosteller, Light, and Sachs, 1996). The researcher-initiated interventions sketched a few pages earlier, however, are reported to have produced little of the expected effects on student achievement (Millsap et al., 1997).

Researchers have improved understanding in the sense that they have opened up new vistas, raised more fundamental problems, and offered suggestive evidence. But they have not produced convincing theoretical formulations, consistent and compelling findings for the new ideas, or convincing support for courses of action (see, for example, Cohen and Weiss, 1977, on school desegregation). Moreover, although researchers agree on many matters, they have not yet reached scientific consensus. Some critical issues, like the cumulative effects of teaching on students' performance, have gained little attention, and some old issues remain undecided.

How this bit of history turns out will depend partly on developments in the next decade or two. If researchers organize to encourage more cumulation of knowledge on the issues discussed here, more convincing advice based on solid evidence might be possible. But that would require researchers to create stronger social guidance for topic choice in investigations of schooling and stronger canons about acceptable research methods that would encourage more comparability in studies. It would also require incentives for cumulative research programs and support for research, development, and assessment of interventions, including experiments of several sorts.

Such things are technically possible, but they would be quite difficult to arrange. One reason is that they would be very costly, requiring many times the amount of money now invested in education research and development. There have been precious few sustained efforts to link research and improvement, let alone to link them in ways that are well conceived, carefully managed, adequately supported, and closely tied to sound evaluative research. One reason has been the pitifully weak support for educational research and development, much bemoaned among researchers. But a more fundamental reason is that the education research and development field is so diverse and diffuse, and intellectually so weakly governed, that education researchers never have come together to devise a rational agenda and seek support for it.

Another reason that more cumulative research would be difficult to arrange is that it would require more consensus about methods of inquiry in education research than now exist. Creating consensus would cut across many competing grains in the field. Cumulation of knowledge is a serious problem in large areas of social research, partly because the enterprise cannot depend on replicated studies to winnow out weak hypotheses. Historical change and context variation change relationships and threaten validity in social studies of nearly any sort. Few competing hypotheses are entirely invalid, so many competing explanations coexist. The relative absence of such threats in the physical and biological sciences means that there are real individual incentives for investigators to replicate others' studies and real intellectual payoff in such work. But in social science these incentives are reduced by historical and situational variation, the partial validity of many hypotheses, and the ensuing incentives for researchers to make reputations by focusing on one of several hypotheses, thus dispersing knowledge. Scientists can achieve more cumulation only by the sort of self-conscious priority setting and guidance of research decision making that we sketch here.

Even if some greater consensus were achieved, success in such an enterprise also would require persistent good judgment in the collective guidance of education research—something that would be difficult to arrange even for a few years, let alone over the longer term. It is much easier to rely on a combination of very general guidance and individual incentives in the marketplace of ideas. That works in sciences in which knowledge structures are strong, but in social studies of schooling it has had the perverse effect of encouraging a species of small-scale buccaneering individualism that reduces collective understanding and knowledge cumulation. One could argue that the rather fragmented character of research fits with the divided and episodic nature of politics and public discourse about schooling in the United States. Politics and public discourse may support fragmentation within research and decrease the possibilities for cumulation by offering researchers incentives to contribute in fragmented and episodic rather than cumulative ways. The irrationalities that some researchers have discerned in the relationship of public discourse, politics, and research may be as much an artifact of the culture of American politics as evidence of inherent incompatibility.

CONCLUSION

This account of research on the purposes of schooling offers a somewhat surprising view of the relationship of research on schools' purposes, politics, and policy. The past three decades have been a period of growing political and ideological conflict about schools, yet also of broadened interest in and attention to education research and in improving research. The improvements are encouraging, but researchers have not capitalized on that work with efforts either to deepen and confirm findings or to make more rational decisions about research programs. We see hopeful signs, including growing attention to differential effectiveness among teachers and schools and more sophistication in the investigation of such matters. There also has been the beginning of a tradition of research-based, knowledge-generating clinical intervention in schooling. That sort of endeavor has been missing from the education research enterprise for nearly the entire century of its existence, crippling its capacity to change the social allocation of resources to schools, observe the consequences for students and educators, and inform practice and policy. The lack of systematic intervention that is linked to careful research also has contributed to the scattered and frequently inconclusive character of research and the inability to decide what had been solidly learned from a very important tradition of deliberate inquiry. If some elements of a more fruitful approach have appeared, our consideration of them should help to reveal how much remains to be done.

References

Berliner, D. C. "Tempus Educare." In P. L. Peterson and H. J. Walber (eds.), *Research on Teaching* (pp. 120–136). Berkeley, Calif.: McCutchan, 1979.

Berman, P., and others. *A National Study of Charter Schools: Second-Year Report.* Washington, D.C.: U.S. Department of Education, Office of Educational Research and Improvement and National Institute on Student Achievement, Curriculum, and Assessment, 1998.

Bowles, S., and Gintis, H. *Schooling in Capitalist America: Educational Reform and the Contradictions of Economic Life.* New York: Basic Books, 1976.

Brophy, J., and Good, T. L. "Teacher Behavior and Student Achievement." In M. C. Wittrock (ed.), *1986 Handbook of Research on Teaching* (pp. 328–375). New York: Macmillan, 1986.

Bryk, A. S., Lee, V. E., and Holland, P. B. *Catholic Schools and the Common Good.* Cambridge, Mass.: Harvard University Press, 1993.

Cohen, D. K. "Origin." In A. G. Power, E. Farrar, and D. K. Cohen (eds.), *The Shopping Mall High School: Winners and Losers in the Educational Marketplace* (pp. 233–306). Boston: Houghton Mifflin, 1985.

Cohen, D. K., and Barnes, C. A. *High Standards, All Children, and Learning: Notes Toward the History of an Idea.* Prepared for Carnegie Corporation of New York, Task Force on Learning in the Primary Grades, February 1995.

Cohen, D. K., and Neufeld, B. "The Failure of High Schools and the Progress of Education." *Daedalus*, 1981, *110*, 62–89.

Cohen, D. K., and Weiss, J. A. "Social Science and Social Policy: Schools and Race." *Educational Forum*, May 1977, 393–413.

Cooley, W., and Leinhardt, G. (1985). "The Instructional Dimensions Study." *Education Evaluation and Policy Analysis, 2*(1980): 7–25.

Counts, G. *The Selective Character of American Secondary Education.* Chicago: University of Chicago Press, 1922.

Counts, G. *The Senior High School Curriculum.* Chicago: University of Chicago Press, 1929.

Edmonds, R. R. "Effective Schools for the Urban Poor." *Educational Leadership,* 1979, *37*, 15–27.

Edmonds, R. R. "School Effects and Teacher Effects." *Social Policy,* 1984, *15*, 37–39.

Equality of Educational Opportunity. *Harvard Educational Review,* 1968, 38.

Goodlad, J. *A Place Called School.* New York: McGraw-Hill, 1984.

Greene, J. P., and Peterson, P. E. "Methodological Issues in Evaluation Research: The Milwaukee School Choice Plan." Occasional Paper 96–4, No. ED402682. Cambridge, Mass.: Harvard University, 1996.

Greene, J. P., and others. "The Effectiveness of School Choice in Milwaukee." Occasional Paper 96–4, No. ED402682. Cambridge, Mass.: Harvard University, 1996.

Hedges, L. V., Laine, R. D., and Greenwald, R. "Does Money Matter? A Meta-Analysis of Studies of the Effects of Differential School Inputs on Student Outcomes." *Educational Researcher,* April 3, 1994, pp. 5–14.

Jencks, C., and Phillips, M. "Aptitude or Achievement: Why Do Test Scores Predict Educational Attainment and Earnings?" In S. Mayer and P. Peterson (eds.), *Learning and Earning: How Schools Matter.* Washington, D.C.: Brookings Institution, 1999.

Jencks, C., and others. *Inequality: A Reassessment of the Effect of Family and Schooling in America.* New York: Basic Books, 1972.

Jonçich, G. M. *Psychology and the Science of Education: Selected Writings of Edward L. Thorndike.* New York: Teachers College Press, 1962.

Kaestle, C. F. *Pillars of the Republic: Common Schools and American Society 1780–1860.* New York: Hill & Wang, 1983.

Katz, M. B. (ed.). *School Reform: Past and Present.* Boston: Little, Brown, 1971.

Katznelson, I., and Weir, M. *Schooling for All.* New York: Basic Books, 1988.

Leinhardt, G. "Instructional Time. A Winged Chariot?" In C. W. Fisher and D. C. Berliner (eds.), *Perspectives on Instructional Time* (pp. 263–282). New York: Longman, 1985.

McLaughlin, M. *Evaluation and Reform: The Case of ESEA, Title I.* Cambridge, Mass.: Ballinger, 1975.

Mann, H. "Horace Mann on the Value of Written Examinations in the Schools, 1845. *Common School Journal* (Massachusetts), Oct. 1." In E. W. Knight and C. L. Hall (eds.), *Readings in American Educational History* (pp. 493–499). New York: Appleton-Century-Crofts, 1951. (Originally published 1845.)

Mann, H. "Annual Reports of the Secretary of the Board of Education. Report for 1843." In *Annual Reports on Education* (pp. 230–417). Boston: Walker, Fuller, 1868. (Originally published 1865.)

Manno, B. V., Finn, C. E., Bierlein, J. L. A., and Vanourek, G. "How Are Charter Schools Different? Lessons and Implications." Charter Schools in Action Project: Final Report. Hudson Institute's Educational Excellence Network, 1997.

Mayhew, K., and Edwards, A. *The Dewey School.* New York: Atherton Press, 1966.

Messerli, J. *Horace Mann: A Biography.* New York: Knopf, 1972.

Millsap, M., Herman, R., and Stringfield, S. *Strategies for Educating Disadvantaged Children.* Washington, D.C.: U.S. Department of Education, 1997.

Mosteller, F. "The Tennessee Study of Class Size in the Early School Grades." *Future of Children,* 1995, *5*(2), 113–127.

Mosteller, F., Light, R., and Sachs, J. A. "Sustained Inquiry in Education: Lessons from Skill Grouping and Class Size." *Harvard Educational Review,* 1996, *66*, 797–842.

Mosteller, F., and Moynihan, D. P. (eds.). *On Equality of Educational Opportunity.* New York: Random House, 1972.

Moynihan, D. P. "Sources of Resistance in the Coleman Report." *Harvard Educational Review,* 1968, *38*, 23–36.

Newmann, F. M., and Wehlage, G. G. *Successful School Restructuring: A Report to the Public and Educators.* U.S. Department of Education, Office of Educational Research and Improvement. No. R11Q00005-95. Madison: Center on Organization and Restructuring of Schools, University of Wisconsin–Madison, 1995.

Parsons, T., Howe, S. G., and Neal, R. H. *Reports of the Annual Visiting Committees of the Public Schools of the City of Boston.* City Document No. 26. Boston: J. H. Eastburn, City Printer, 1845.

Purkey, S. C., and Smith, M. S. "Effective Schools: A Review." *Elementary School Journal,* 1983, *83*(4), 427–452.

Purkey, S. C., and Smith, M. S. "School Reform: The District Policy Implications of the Effective Schools Literature." *Elementary School Journal,* 1985, *85*(3), 353–389.

Ravitch, D. *The Great School Wars: New York City, 1805–1973: A History of the Public Schools.* New York: Basic Books, 1974.

Resnick, L. B., and Resnick, D. P. "Assessing the Thinking Curriculum: New Tools for Educational Reform." In B. R. Gifford and M. C. O'Connor (eds.), *Future Assessments: Changing Views of Aptitude, Achievement, and Instruction.* Norwell, Mass.: Kluwer, 1989.

Rothman, D. *The Discovery of the Asylum: Social Order and Disorder in the New Republic.* Boston: Little, Brown, 1971.

Rowan, B., Guthrie, L., Lee, G., and Guthrie, G. P. *The Design and Implementation of Chapter 1 Instructional Services: A Study of 24 Schools.* Contract No. 400–85–1015. Washington, D.C.: U. S. Department of Education, Office of Educational Research and Improvement, Far West Laboratory for Educational Research and Development, 1986.

Stevenson, H., and Stigler, J. *The Learning Gap: Why Our Schools Are Failing and What We Can Learn from Japanese and Chinese Education.* New York: Summit Books, 1992.

Wier, M., Orloff, A. S., and Skocpol, T. (eds.). *The Politics of Social Policy in the United States.* Princeton, N.J.: Princeton University Press, 1988.

Witte, J. F. *Milwaukee Parental Choice Program: Fourth-Year Report.* No. ED385891. Madison: Robert M. LaFollette Institute of Public Affairs, University of Wisconsin, 1994.

CHAPTER THREE

Poles Apart

Reconciling the Dichotomies in Education Research

Theodore R. Mitchell
Analee Haro

ducation," quipped a colleague recently, "is the Rodney Dangerfield of the social sciences: it never gets any respect." This seems particularly pertinent today. On the one hand, those of us who are responsible for the financial h"ealth of the research enterprise watch as foundations and corporations transfer their support for education research to programs that provide funds directly to schools. In the process, we become acutely aware that the search for viable investments in ideas about education has come less and less to focus on research. Even within the most highly regarded universities, institutional reviews of education departments raise issues about the legitimacy and quality of education research. The elimination of the University of Chicago's education department, home to John Dewey, Charles Judd, and others in the pantheon, speaks volumes about the current crisis in education research. What is one to make of all of this?

One might take an optimistic view, drawing the inference that education research or, more broadly, disciplined inquiry in education (see Cronbach and Suppes, 1969, pp. 14–19), has succeeded in building a body of knowledge sufficient to address the problems of teaching and learning and that what is left is a mop-up job of implementing what we know. This is what many of the leading lights thought about physics in 1800, and it probably, in one variation or another, explains some of the current disregard for scholarly research in education. A more likely explanation for the loss of support lies less in education research's successes than in its perceived failures.

The history of complaint about education research is as long as the history of the enterprise (see Cronbach and Suppes, 1969, chaps. 2, 3). This fact is itself a puzzle. What is it about education research that has made it such a durable target?

Our hypothesis is that the "science of education" over the past 150 years has been characterized by fundamental and unresolved tensions between three fundamental polarities: those between applied and basic research, those between a Newtonian and pragmatist view of education science, and those between inquiry into educational purposes and educational processes. At any one time, the strength of these opposing forces determines the shape of scholarly work within it. The precise balance between the forces changes, but always in ways limited by the force at the opposite pole. The result has been a history of temporary equilibria that determine the focus, scope, and social aims of education research. These equilibria are and have been inherently unstable, being as much about what the research does not accomplish as about what it does. In this way, education inquiry is always under fire from contending interests.

THE TENSION BETWEEN BASIC AND APPLIED INQUIRY

There has been a fundamental tension between basic research in education and its associated disciplines, on the one hand, and applied research, on the other. This tension was captured well by the National Academy of Education's (NAE) Committee on Educational Research in 1969. That group characterized the opposing poles as "inquiry for conclusion" and "inquiry for decision." Disciplined inquiry aimed at conclusions refers to research work that is generated and guided by scholars who are seeking to understand some phenomenon. That understanding may be incremental, or it may be frame-breaking. In either case the conclusions drawn are intended to build up the stock of knowledge regarding basic processes in, say, teaching and learning. The latter domain of inquiry, aimed at decisions, concerns questions initiated by either scholars themselves or interested practitioners and policymakers and that are designed to guide action. Whether constructed as "basic" and "applied" or "inquiry for conclusions" and "inquiry for decisions," the demands for one or the other have been unrelenting and too often seen as mutually exclusive.

Demands for basic or conclusion-driven inquiry have come mainly from inside the academy and are shaped by the deepest social norms of the scholarly tradition. As Dewey (1929) defined it, inquiry in education should parallel that of other "sciences." By that he meant specifically that "discovery and organization of material go on cumulatively, and that one inquirer can repeat the researches of another, confirm or discredit them, and add still more to the capital stock of knowledge" (p. 9). For scholars outside faculties of education, who nonetheless focus on issues in or germane to education, established disciplinary paradigms provide a structure for the development of this kind of "scientific" practice. Scholars in education have struggled for status among core disciplines in the arts and sciences by seeking to create such a scientific approach, in part through the creation of scholarly associations, refereed journals, and a national academy to signify and disseminate exemplary contributions. As efforts to generate a body of significant science, these have yielded less than extraordinary results. NAE's Committee on Educational Research concluded in 1969 that "not more than one-tenth of the doctoral dissertations in education and not more than one-tenth of the work published in the less well-edited journals, even today, are respectable works of serious inquiry" (Cronbach and Suppes, 1969, p. 226).

Although progress has been made, education research has not yet thrown off the stigma of this assessment. Efforts to generate legitimacy within the academy have met with only partial success (see Cremin, Shannon, and Townsend, 1954; Powell, 1980; Russell, 1937; Sears and Henderson, 1957). At Stanford University, for example, it was not until the middle of the twentieth century that education faculty members were allowed to serve on the university committee on academic appointments and promotions (Sears and Henderson, 1957). At the University of California, Los Angeles (UCLA), Ph.D. committees in education must still include one or more faculty members from outside education to ensure a kind of rigor not expected among education faculty alone.

In part, this perception of a lack of scientific or scholarly rigor derives from the perceived special attentiveness of education faculty to the demands for applied or decision-focused inquiry (Cronbach and Suppes, 1969; see also Bright and Gideonse, 1967; Sieber and Lazarfeld, 1966). Coincidentally, this demand— the pull to practice—comes from outside the tight social world of the academy —from practitioners and policymakers. To these individuals, who are called on to manage and improve the nation's educational institutions, the value of disciplined inquiry in education has always been proportional to its direct applicability to problems and issues of the day. Henry Barnard, in his role as first commissioner of the U.S. Bureau of Education, fell into disfavor among the patrons of the bureau during the late 1860s, in part because of his insistence on supporting broad philosophical inquiry rather than jumping headlong into policy debates over the education of former slaves. His catholic taste and scholarly sensibility—traits that had suited him well as editor of the *Journal of Education* —were anathema to politicians and decision makers, whose interest in answers overwhelmed Barnard's own interest in questions (MacMullen, 1991). The attitude of decision makers toward education research has always been one of impatience at the scholarly process. Conversely scholars are disdainful of the appetite for untested truths among those who labor day to day in schools.

Ironically but predictably, attempts to resolve the tension between basic and applied inquiry have resulted in bodies of work that, in attempting to accommodate both demands, satisfy neither. One such failed approach has been the attempt to raise to the level of science work that is aimed primarily at influencing practice. One of the most significant areas of university-based education inquiry during the first decades of the twentieth century, for example, focused on the discovery and development of efficient modes of educational administration. Critical to the "methodology" of such endeavor was the school survey, a vehicle by which faculty members and their graduate students, usually for a substantial fee, would gather data in schools about the structure of the curriculum, the classification of students, and the qualifications of the staff and then apply a predetermined template of reforms based on the professor's prior understanding (see Callahan, 1964; Tyack, 1974; Tyack and Hansot, 1990). Today we would call these consulting arrangements, but at the time they were regarded as state-of-the-art research in educational administration. To examine any one of these surveys is to be struck by their attention to detail, their mechanical nature, and their voluminous size. More striking, though, is the often ambiguous connection between the information gathered and the recommendations that followed.

The survey of New York City schools in 1911–1912 under the guidance of Paul Hanus, Harvard University's first full-time education faculty member, ran twelve volumes, cost more than $100,000, and contained strong recommendations regarding the expansion of school programs and administrative staff (Hanus, 1913). The report also urged that control of the schools be removed from the hands of the municipal government and placed in the hands of professional managers. Angered at these recommendations, the survey's sponsor commissioned an alternative survey that recommended greater economies, a reduction of staff, and *tighter* control by municipal government over school affairs. Ernest Carroll Moore, then at Yale University and shortly to join Hanus at Harvard before moving west to found UCLA, pointed out that the contending reports agreed "pretty completely as to the essential facts" but diverged "radically as to the meaning of these facts." Many in the New York schools, beginning with the Superintendent, William Maxwell, condemned the entire survey as a fiasco, accusing Hanus and his colleagues of "arrogance" and of suffering a "preconceived and doctrinaire point of view." Associate superintendent Andrew Edson called the recommendations "more visionary than practical," derived not from evidence but from the researchers' "inner consciousness" (quoted in Powell, 1980, p. 95).

The New York experience was a bruising one all around. For practitioners and policymakers, the "science" of education inquiry proved to be hopelessly ambiguous. For researchers, including Hanus and Moore, this assessment drove them to armor their conclusions with even more facts. Spurred on by this need, Hanus, Moore, and their colleagues at Teachers College, Columbia, at Stanford, and at the University of Chicago developed full-fledged research programs in educational administration that became factories for the generation of descriptive data.

Assessing the state of research in the field of educational administration in 1927, Walter Monroe observed that "many educators, including most superintendents and principals, appear to think of education research as consisting of the activities of collecting, organizing, and disseminating information about schools. According to this point of view, the researcher is primarily a combination of high-grade accountant and publicity agent" (Monroe and others, 1927, pp. 325–326). Far from being discounted, this kind of descriptive work became the substance of doctoral training in education during the 1920s and 1930s. The reaction inside the academy was predictable. In Harvard style, George Herbert Palmer, professor of philosophy, simply dismissed Hanus and his ilk. "Professor Hanus," Palmer sneered, "bore the onus of his subject" (quoted in Lagemann, 1996, p. 7). As David Tyack and Elisabeth Hansot have shown in *Managers of Virtue* (1988), this period of congruence between education inquiry and educational practice was also a period of great skepticism among the academic faculty regarding the place of education research in universities. Equally skeptical were practitioners who were not satisfied by the discoveries being made in the universities.

If the strategy of turning practical inquiry into science failed to satisfy the demands of either practitioners or scientists, a second strategy of developing a science that influenced practice fared equally badly. The earliest significant experiment along these lines was John Dewey's Laboratory School at the University of Chicago. There, beginning in 1896, Dewey attempted to place an organization of structured inquiry, not descriptive but experimental, at the precise intersection between science and practice. Dewey's main aim was to use experimental practice as a way of driving forward the conclusion-based science of education. "It is not," he stated, somewhat vexed at those who saw the school as a production facility for new pedagogies, "the primary function of a laboratory to devise ways and means that can be put to practical use, so it is not the primary purpose of the school to devise methods with reference to their direct application in the graded school system." Instead, Dewey argued that "it is the function of some schools to create new standards and ideals and thus to lead to a gradual change in conditions" (Dewey, 1896, pp. 417–418).

Like the education surveys, the Laboratory School also failed to satisfy demands for either relevance or research. Professional educators carped on two fronts: first, that the school did not attend to practical implementation of its pedagogies and, second, that even when it did, the school itself was not "typical" enough to inform practice. At the other pole, university faculties criticized, and continue to criticize, such efforts for not employing rigorous enough scientific techniques. This crossfire suggests that for Dewey and for many of those who have followed, the middle ground between the two poles of applied and basic inquiry is more like a no-man's land (Dewey, 1943; Cronbach and Suppes, 1969, pp. 49–52).

Ultimately the professional and lay community that surrounded the Laboratory School had its own way with the inquiry practiced there. The insatiable demand for practical applications combined with the "human desire to prove that the scientific mode of attack is really of value," brought "pressure to convert scientific conclusions into rules and standards of classroom practice," thereby short-circuiting much of the experimentation at the school (Dewey, 1929, p. 18). The popularity of the work done at the school at once provided ample testimony to its success as a model and ultimately sowed the seeds of the school's decline, as the rapid cycle of discovery and innovation lent the perception of faddishness to proposed advances (for a solid analysis, see Cronbach and Suppes, 1969, pp. 50–51).

Dewey's ultimate fate in this regard is indicative of still a third mode by which the tension between inquiry for conclusion and inquiry for decision has been reduced: through the widespread appropriation by decision makers and policymakers of research findings that are aimed at, and best suited to, building up the stock of basic knowledge. California today is in the middle of a renewed battle over reading instruction between whole language teaching and phonics. Advocates of each position cite evidence from learning theory, cognitive science, and countless studies of classroom performance in defense of their conclusions. Study is used to contradict study, and battle lines have been drawn, often at the extremes of the debate.

In the normal course of scholarly debate in the experimental sciences, extreme positions are gradually modified (think of pharmaceutical research) as more applied research develops a clearer sense of the marginal benefits of one or another "treatment." Moreover, "clinical" research often develops treatments that bring competing strands of research together into play as elements of a unified strategy. In education we are too often deprived of this mediating force of rigorous clinical trials. Experiments are designed, by their nature, to reduce complexity. As Dewey (1929) put it, "There is no science without abstraction, and abstraction means fundamentally that certain occurrences are removed from the dimension of familiar practical experience into that of reflective or theoretical inquiry" (p. 17). Thus abstracted, understandings derived from "reflective or theoretical inquiry" do not fit easily back into the realm of "familiar practical experience," at least not without mediation. Experimental results are thus inherently unsuited as solutions to the messy, complex problems of schools. What has been needed, and little provided, is a set of intermediate institutions whose purpose it is to take research findings and create from them "clinical" approaches and clinical tests. Instead what happens too often, as in California today, is that unripe research has been applied, and in its most strident form, to the development of policy without the benefit of scholarly friction. As an added problem, the very stridency of the advocacy has developed a rather strict ideological signification to opposing positions, further polarizing what might have been an interesting scientific debate. Speaking of his own experience in the Laboratory School as well as of the school survey movement, Dewey observed in 1929 that "there is a tendency to convert the results of statistical inquiries and laboratory experiments into directions and rules for the conduct of school administration and instruction. Results," he went on to say, "tend to be directly grabbed . . . and put into operation." The problem with this path, although appealing to all of us who have sought and seek to apply the best research thinking to the problems of schools, is that "there is not the leisure for that slow and gradual independent growth of theories that is a necessary condition of the formation of a true science" (pp. 17–18).

Like Dewey and the Laboratory School, today's scholars are often pulled to create policy determinations and curriculum recommendations from basic research findings before those findings have been subjected to scholarly scrutiny within a clinical environment. The advocacy and "promotion" that result from this premature transformation of conclusion-focused inquiry into decision-focused inquiry, while answering the call from the field for relevant work, does a disservice to both the field and the community of education researchers. For professionals this process produces partial and relatively simplistic solutions to real and complex problems; for researchers, it produces scorn and derision (Cronbach and Suppes, 1969, pp. 51, 68, 233).

Altogether, the basic tension between basic and applied research has been one of the most vexing problems facing education researchers inside and outside faculties of education. The pressure from sources internal to the academy to emphasize basic research and from outside to produce useful research findings has misshaped the research enterprise, leading to general frustration. Ironically the 1990s have seen breakthroughs in "conclusion-focused" inquiry, in areas as disparate as cognitive science and classroom sociology (*Review of Education Research,* 1990–1995). To turn these breakthroughs into meaningful policies and programs, however, will require the renewal of authentic clinical research in education, with its own identity and norms. But in order for this to happen, two other historical tensions in education research must be resolved as well.

NEWTONIAN AND PRAGMATIST
SOURCES OF A SCIENCE OF EDUCATION

The tension between basic and applied inquiry is not simply a struggle over the social value of one or another type of inquiry, nor is it exclusively a tension between the needs of scholars and practitioners; it is also reflective of a more fundamental unresolved tension between two views of education as a science and, indeed, of science itself. Like the earlier tension, this one too owes much to a distinction between those who produce inquiry and those who consume or seek to consume it. At one pole are Newtonian notions that seek universal "laws" in education that have universal applicability. While largely discredited among active investigators across disciplines, the idea of universal laws continues to dominate the lay view of science and continues to shape the use, if not the production, of disciplined inquiry in education, drawing "false universals" from studies with much more limited ambitions and aims. At the other pole are the inheritors of the pragmatist tradition, for whom context plays a determining role in understanding educational phenomena. Here the internal dynamics of the research community threaten to make context the only text and to pull inquiry into an abyss of particularism.

Early education research, rising as it did in the nineteenth century, contributed to the idea that there were universal truths to be found, if only the right method could be discovered and employed. Like other of the fledgling social sciences, education research embraced the Newtonian view of cause and effect at just the time the natural sciences began to eschew deterministic, mechanistic understandings of the universe (Haskell, 1977). Thus, education "scientists" sought to push their field along the well-worn path of the so-called hard sciences, earning legitimacy through association with accepted, but aging, paradigms. The earliest education research, like early research in most other fields, focused on basic description, observation, and speculation. Henry Barnard's *Journal of Education* was devoted to such description. An analysis of the table of contents of Barnard's journal from its beginning in 1855 until 1865 shows that approximately 60 percent of the entries dealt with descriptions of educational practice in a variety of states and nations and 25 percent with practical suggestions to teachers; 15 percent represented disciplined inquiry in the form of philosophical or psychological essays. The last, often translations of important historical documents, represented a significant effort to create for educators a kind of dialogue that combined the scholarly with the practical (*Journal of Education*, 1855–1865).

Taxonomy followed description, as early American scholars of education sought to classify different educational practices and structures. Comparative studies were important elements of this taxonomic exercise. The early reports of the U.S. Bureau of Education are chock-full of comparative studies of education in Europe. Simultaneously the same bureau began to collect and disseminate raw data from the schools and districts across the country. While the bureau passed from Barnard's hands first to John Eaton, then to N. H. R. Dawson, and finally to philosopher-schoolmaster William Torrey Harris, it maintained and even enhanced its role as a repository of broad educational thinking, anchored by the increasing weight of descriptive statistical studies (Leidecker,

1946, chap. 24). Also during this period, states and major cities opened their own research bureaus to pursue the collection of data at a local level. Until the turn of the twentieth century, these data were allowed to speak for themselves, with little or no accompanying analysis or interpretation and less connection to policy. In terms of its "scientific" identity, education inquiry in the United States was already tending heavily toward the empirical, but other elements of that identity remained less clear.

Developments during the last decade of the nineteenth century changed that as the psychology of William James, John Dewey, Edward Thorndike, and G. Stanley Hall gave education research its basic persona, if not its basic personality. As psychology emerged as a discipline, it quickly became the queen of what Dewey called later the "sources" of the science of education. Of the four, Hall and Thorndike were far more susceptible to Newtonian images of the discipline they were working to build. Hall's "child study" and his claims for the universal findings of developmental psychology fit him well for the Clark University faculty, whose strength had been in engineering and the natural sciences. Thorndike's experimentalism pushed forward the "scientism" of both psychology and education. This approach suited both for stardom among education professionals and the lay public, eager for the kind of answers educational psychology was ready to provide (Clifford, 1968). James was the most detached of the four, working hard to maintain a philosophical approach to the development of psychology, including, importantly, insisting on a moral component to the developing discipline. Yet James as well was convinced of the ultimate "science of the mind," from which could be derived general and universal truths (James, 1899).

Ironically, it was James's protégé, Josiah Royce, who leveled one of the first challenges to the Newtonian view. An idealist philosopher whose tendencies led to long and tortured discussions of pure forms, Royce was nonetheless struck by the complexity of the educational process and the impossibility of discovering a "universally valid" set of rules about education. In education, he argued, "it is the detail that will concern you more than the type." In considering the student, there are those things "that science abstracts from and ignores" that one "most needs to know." History, social condition, the interdependent identities of teacher and student: "all these things will properly interfere with" the development and application of education as a science. "This being the case," Royce argued, "there is, indeed, no `science of education,' whose formulas will not need at the right moment to be forgotten" (Royce, 1891, pp. 22–23). But Royce could only describe the problem. It was Dewey who most clearly articulated the pragmatist dependence on context as a method of investigation and discovery. For Dewey it was critical to distinguish between theories that were universal in a general way and the universal application of those theories. Speaking of the principle of "universal application" in his *Sources of the Science of Education* (1929), he made the point clearly, using the same language as Royce had: "No conclusion of scientific research can be converted into an immediate rule of educational art." This cannot be so because "there is no educational practice whatever which is not highly complex; that is to say, which does not contain many other conditions and factors than are included in the scientific finding" (p. 19).

Thus context, the source of complexity, did not rule out in Dewey's mind the development of a "science" of education, but it did give that science particular characteristics. Foremost among these, for both Dewey and Royce, was the idea that the possibility of a scientific domain of education inquiry was paired with an impossibility of the universal scientific application of that inquiry. For both, and indeed for others, this was more than the simple problem of inappropriate "use" of the science; it was a characteristic of both the general scientific enterprise and the particular enterprise of inquiry in education. Precisely by reducing "complexity" through experimental (and later statistical) means, universalistic theory building makes education research unsuitable for direct application.

Unfortunately this subtle observation was lost on many who sought to turn inquiry in education into a prescriptive exercise and a mechanical form of science more suited, in Royce's words, to the "seventeenth and eighteenth centuries" than to the twentieth (Royce, 1891, pp. 16–17). Indeed, as leading education researchers became more sophisticated in understanding the limits of their disciplines, other researchers and practitioners moved in the opposite direction, "grasping," in Dewey's phrase, research results and turning them into rules and policies. The pull toward a Newtonian approach to education inquiry continued to distort the shape of research and ideas about the nature of the science of education.

If, on the one hand, research that aims at universally applicable theory is defeated by the recognition of multiple contexts, then research that aims at modest, context-sensitive conclusions is defeated by demands that it be more universal. This is true of both experimental research, in which context is controlled, and contextualized research of the sort that is done within school settings. For good and responsible reasons, scholars in education in the past twenty years have undertaken more particularistic studies that seek to carve out limited areas of inquiry within which interaction between variables can be understood. Not only experimental studies but also detailed ethnographies of classrooms and schools have rejected the universal claims of Newtonian science and have asserted an epistemology of incremental understanding, whereby knowledge is created not with the aim of developing one single explanatory model, but of creating situated understanding of multiple educational environments.

This trajectory toward narrowly focused studies has had multiple effects. First, it has annoyed consumers of research, who still crave universalistic answers. Second, it has served to narrow the domains of expertise within which scholars operate and to restrict the domain of conversation over the research products and their knowledge claims. Third, it has produced a great deal of scholarly work whose value is less than the sum of its parts because context sensitivity becomes not only an antidote to false universality but a barrier to generalizations of all kinds, theoretical or practical, basic or applied.

Ironically, therefore, in an attempt to create better and more responsible science, the retreat from universals has created and supported an enterprise that is frustratingly obscure and infuriatingly elusive to those outside the academy. To those inside the academy, the shift to narrower studies that are better rooted in context has done much to increase the status of individual research projects; however, the same resistance to generalization inhibits the development of theory and reinforces the most basic concerns about education as a field.

THE TENSION BETWEEN EDUCATIONAL PURPOSE AND PROCESS

Questions about the nature and significance of education research play out in a third, less visible but no less important, kind of tension: that between inquiry into educational purposes and inquiry into educational processes. In a 1927 survey, Carter Alexander defined education research as the effort "to discover, in the light of the purposes of education commonly acknowledged, the most efficient procedures in the organization, supervision, finance, and evaluation of the program of educational service" (p. 1). There could be few clearer explications of the "process" science of education as it is commonly viewed. By identifying research as the set of projects that takes place within the boundaries of "the purposes of education commonly acknowledged," Alexander disqualifies that research from playing a part in the definition of those educational purposes. For much of its history, education inquiry adhered to the boundary Alexander and his colleagues drew. From school surveys to testing, much of education research of whatever stripe has worked within and been unconscious of the broader questions of purpose (see Travers, 1983). An analysis of the 130 topics for which papers were published in the National Society for the Study of Education (NSSE) yearbook from 1902 to 1974, for example, shows that fewer than 10 percent dealt explicitly with educational aims or purposes. There are several reasons for this.

First, isolated by their professional colleagues in universities, many education researchers made common cause with professionals in the nation's emerging school districts (Lagemann, 1996, pp. 9–10). The needs of practice, to which this research attended, were by their nature process needs. Second, these lines of inquiry became institutionalized as the students of the early school surveyors, for example, became the next generation of faculty members in schools of education (Tyack and Hansot, 1988, pp. 129–152). Third, through a process by which members of the education faculty established their legitimacy through relevance to the needs of practitioners, broader questions were left to scholars in the core letters and sciences departments, exacerbating a division between inquiry about purpose and inquiry about process that persists today. Thus, in the sociology of Jane Addams and the economics of Richard Ely, one finds more fundamental inquiry regarding the purposes of education than one does in contemporaneous writings by George Drayton Strayer and Ellwood Patterson Cubberly. Of course, in these disciplinary domains, education was only one of several foci, and so questions of purpose, thus segregated, became diluted by the demands of the broader disciplines in which these scholars worked (Cronbach and Suppes, 1969).

The effects of the segregation of faculties of education from faculties in the core disciplines, coupled with internal dynamics among both groups, contributed to the segregation of inquiry about aims from inquiry about process. In the 1950s scholars and politicians began to rebel against this separation. At the level of the classroom, university faculty members in the disciplines crossed over into questions of process as they began to be openly critical of the curriculum in the schools, arguing that it was both inadequate in terms of rigor and antiquated in terms of content. Arthur Bestor (1983), a historian at the University of Illinois, captured the mood of these critics by arguing that "we have permitted the content of public school instruction to be determined by a narrow group of specialists in pedagogy, well-intentioned men and women, no doubt, but utterly devoid of the qualification necessary for the task" (p. 50). What followed, as Ellen Condliffe Lagemann (1996) has demonstrated, was a reassertion of influence, indeed a reassertion of control by disciplinary faculty in the establishment of curricular goals and the creation of curricular materials designed to achieve those goals. As Lagemann found, by 1975, the National Science Foundation alone had spent more than $130 million on course improvement projects and another $565 million on new curricula and teacher training. As this last number suggests, disciplinary scholars extended their efforts well beyond defining curricular goals, working to improve the level of disciplinary understanding among teachers and, failing that, to create curricular materials that were "teacher proof."

The movement to reconnect the discipline-based faculty with the schools and with education inquiry had a salutary effect on the content level of curricular materials and resulted in increased attention within the university to issues of precollegiate education. The negative effects of this reassertion of influence by the discipline-based scholars were twofold. First, it sustained a rhetoric that continued to divide ends and means but defined them differently. In this new language, the ends of education consisted nearly exclusively of the mastery of content, and content was captured as the domain of the subject area specialists. Means came to be defined as soft-edged ideas about children and pedagogy and the mechanical operations of school organization. Second, by first exacer-bating the distinction between ends and means, demeaning inquiry about process, and associating process-focused inquiry with faculties of education, the movement deepened the active tension between scholars in the disciplines and faculties of education regarding the proper boundaries of the work of each.

But the movement acted in the opposite direction as well. At the same time that *Sputnik* brought the nation's scientists into a conversation about educa-tional processes, the growth of the civil rights movement raised new questions about the broader social goals of education. For some, the stark evidence that schools did not open doors to opportunity for large segments of the citizenry stood in sharp contrast to the public's understanding of the purposes of schools. For other people, reformist notions that schools should become tools for social mobility and not tools for ordering relationships between groups struck an equally discordant, if opposing, note. For still others, the idea that schools could become avenues of access to the opportunity structure seemed like a fine, if unlikely, possibility. What were schools for? What did they achieve? These were not new questions, but they were also not the primary questions asked by schol-ars of education, whether inside or outside faculties of education.

There were, of course, important exceptions, which only proved the rule. The social reconstructionists who clustered around Dewey and George Counts at Columbia University and Teachers College in the 1920s and 1930s took these questions as their primary focus and developed not only an important discourse about the aims of education in a democracy but also a significant model of col-laboration between the faculty in the disciplines and the faculty in education. For the social reconstructionists, the aims of education were not simply impor-tant to education; they mattered to society as a whole. As Dewey (1929) put it even before his Columbia years, "What a society is, it is, by and large, as a prod-uct of education" (p. 75). By turning the society–education equation around—seeing society as an expression of its education rather than the reverse—Dewey and his colleagues established the importance of a scholarship devoted to edu-cational purposes. It is not surprising, then, that the pull to address educational purposes during the 1960s and 1970s created a Dewey revival and a revival of inquiry into the ends of education.

Beginning with President Lyndon B. Johnson's launch of the Great Society, during which he told an accepting Congress that "the answer to all our national problems comes down to a single word . . . education," much inquiry in edu-cation has focused on aims, in two ways. The boom in evaluation research and in inquiry regarding the effects of education programs in general has attempted to answer the question of purposes analytically: What have we achieved? In the more humanistic disciplines of philosophy and history, scholars have asked these questions through a close reading of the practices and processes, as well as of the outcomes, of educational practice. Implicit in much of this work is a contrast between the stated goals of education in America and its results. Low rates of literacy among school leavers, some of them graduates, provide a lively contrast, for example, to our national commitment, made explicit by Thomas Jefferson, to a literate citizenry. A less-developed literature, mainly by philosophers, attempts to use the dissonance between what we do and what we say to initiate a broad discussion about the future purposes of education in American society. These efforts, courageous as they are, are often discounted by school professionals for their lack of an explicit plan from moving from here to there, illustrating once again the ways in which the bifurcation between purposes and process creates tension within the education research community and between that community and the professional and lay consumers of that inquiry.

This is not to say that the renewed focus on educational purposes has been without effect. The increased understanding of the achieved ends of schooling, as opposed to the *ascribed* ends, has given the public a sense of urgency about improving schooling. The more developed analytic capacity to evaluate programs has helped funders better understand the impact of their work. But, as Lagemann argues, these very advances have had the paradoxical effect of calling the bulk of education research into question by demonstrating the ineffectiveness of many programs and reforms.

ANTINOMIES AND AUTHORITY

The three major tensions outlined above have too often been dealt with in dichotomous fashion. Within the profession there are divisions between those who do basic research *or* who do applied research, between those who believe in universal claims for their work *or* who have a more contextualized view of science, and between those who pursue inquiry about educational purposes *or* who pursue inquiry about educational process. As implied in the analysis above, the magnetic force around each of these poles is created by the distinct and independent orbits of the social world of the academy and the social world of the profession. Despite efforts of many individual researchers and practitioners, the isolation of research and practice has remained strong and had detrimental effects. On the one hand, education practitioners have become more and more isolated from research findings that, even though not immediately applicable to practice, can and should help reframe professional thinking about practice. On the other hand, academic researchers, disconnected from the field, are asking questions that are less and less pertinent to education and, we would argue, less fertile in general as a result.

In this context, what suffers most is the authority of the education researcher. Drawn in multiple directions by the antinomies inherent in the history of education inquiry, they have been unable to stake out their own unique territory and establish agreements about such basics as what constitutes good research and what constitutes valid theory building.

Those who today are withdrawing their support from education research are voting not to support the current perceived equilibrium in education inquiry, in which research is becoming at one and the same time more basic—that is, disconnected from practice and more context sensitive—so much so as to be inconclusive; *and* more and more directed to educational purposes rather than educational means. Those inside the academy who act or think of acting to eliminate education programs do so either from their perception that the equilibrium is overbalanced in the opposite ways—that education research is too applied, too connected to practice, and too directed to educational means—or that, accepting the practitioners' view, education inquiry has lost its connection to practice and should be practiced in social science departments. What is important is not the question of whether any of these perceptions is accurate, but rather of how these equilibria are achieved and how they can be managed, not simply endured.

ARGUMENT FOR A COMMON GROUND

At this point, one might well argue for a more balanced approach to education inquiry, in which the communities of researchers and practitioners came to focus more on the commonalities in their work than upon its differences. For Royce this common ground was defined by a partnership between art and science, where research provided a general set of propositions that then become raw material for teachers whose artful adaptation of these general principles transformed dry science into live education. For Royce, "there is, indeed no 'science of education' whose formulas will not need at the right moment to be forgotten." But Royce was also clear that knowing the science is a precondition to forgetting it. It makes a great difference, he stated flatly, whether "you do possess the science that you can be wise enough at the right moment to forget" (Royce, 1891, p. 23). This partnership, in which science and art play distinct but mutually supportive roles, is perhaps the dominant way in which professionals and researchers have attempted to establish a common ground. Most teacher training programs are based on some variant of this notion, and the development of clinical faculty lines in schools of education attempt, among other things, to provide novices with exemplars of how one takes science and turns it into art.

Other attempts to create common ground seek to establish inquiry itself as a common enterprise that joins academics and professionals. Dewey called on education professionals to promote "scientifically developed attitudes"—on teachers, in particular, to engage as "investigators" in the activities of their own classrooms. For Dewey, the science as well as good practice depended on "direct participation of those directly involved in research" (Dewey, 1929, pp. 30, 47–48). Teacher-researcher models of the 1970s and "reflective practitioner" ideals of the 1980s attempted to settle the common ground between academic research and practice. Today even more substantive "inquiry" models seek to base discussions of practice *and* of research on collaborative work between faculty members in higher education and those in schools (Oakes and others, 1994).

A third attempt to reach common ground seeks common purpose among scholars inside and outside organized faculties of education. Dewey railed against the separation of education research from the disciplines that give it strength and vigor. To him, this "segregation of [education] research . . . tends to render it futile." Thus isolated, much education research tends "to exaggerate minor points . . . and to grasp at some special scientific technique as if its use were a magical guarantee of a scientific product" (Dewey, 1929, p. 50). Here too much common ground has been established. Collaboration between discipline-based scholars, education faculty members, and practitioners has infused the development of national curriculum frameworks with uncommon energy and wisdom. In California so-called subject matter projects join education researchers and practitioners with scholars in the disciplines to develop curriculum guidelines in basic areas and to provide training and professional development for teachers. These have been important efforts, and there are many more like them across the country. More to the point, they have begun to yield real fruit, if only in terms of recreating a debate about education that extends well beyond the walls of schools of education. Nothing demonstrates the new robustness of this debate as powerfully as did the recent battle over National History Standards. Whatever its sources, for our purposes what is most telling is the purposefulness with which the issue was taken up by practitioners, education faculty, and professional historians. Critically, the battle lines were *not* the traditional fault lines between research and practice or between education faculty and history. Rather, the battle was fought along ideological, political, and even intellectual divisions, leading one to imagine that the common ground between research and practice and between discipline-based inquiry and education might be habitable after all (McMillen, 1995)

THE ROAD AHEAD

The question that faces all of us who are interested in a robust future for both education inquiry and educational practice is whether these tensions and traps are indeed inherent or whether we can move toward a more stable and generative set of relationships between researchers of all stripes, professionals, and members of the public. This is indeed the question that lies at the center of this book, and there are clearly no easy answers. Perhaps the historical record can yield some insights.

The Need for Mediating Institutions

First, the tension between basic and applied research has over time implied a prior understanding that research "results" will be applied to educational practice and that the natural flow is from the laboratory to the classroom. Thus educational "science" has been a source of answers for those engaged in practice. Too seldom have we turned the question around, looking, as Dewey suggested, to "educational *practices* [to] provide the data, the subject-matter, which form the *problems* of inquiry." For Dewey and for many of us looking to move beyond the tension between applied and basic research, it is important to imagine that "concrete educational experience is the primary source of all inquiry and reflection" (Dewey, 1929, pp. 33, 56). Recent scholarship has been heartening in this regard, and holds much promise to integrate research and practice in powerful ways (*Review of Education Research,* 1990–1995).

Second, the criticism is often made that not enough education research makes it into the classroom. We believe that the history shows a different problem: that *too much* unmediated research finds its way into classrooms, producing a frustrating oscillation between this week's findings and last week's. Teachers with whom we work complain that their professional development is highly colored by in-service training programs that move from fad to fad, driven by researchers and those who would apply research to practice. Overall, education is lacking the mediating structures available in other spheres that institutionalize dialogue about research and practice. Clinical trials and the approval process for drugs and devices, clinical training of practitioners in which researchers participate, and the overall culture of interaction between clinicians and researchers in academic medical centers create institutionalized environments, for example, in medicine, that act as mediating forces. Although not perfect by any means, the presence of these institutionalized forms helps create a buffer of professional consideration between the creation of new knowledge and its consumption in the medical enterprise. In the other direction, the existence of these institutionalized forms of mediation establishes a norm whereby research is conducted in an environment connected to practice. In education, research bureaus and laboratory schools—earlier forms of mediation—have fallen into disuse. In Los Angeles and elsewhere, however, efforts to create stable partnerships between universities and schools—rich partnerships that extend beyond the training of new professionals to encompass inquiry and research—may create just this kind of mediating environment.

Third, the expectations of parents and the broader public are misfocused. Here too the lack of mediating institutions helps perpetuate the tensions and traps that have plagued the research community. Public expectations, as well as the expectations of some professionals, remain rooted, as we have seen, in a deterministic view of the educational process. There is great hunger for *the* answer and little patience for *an* answer to complex problems, such as those facing urban children. As with the problem of unfiltered research, this hunger leads to the rapid appropriation of solutions that may or may not have a relationship to the issues at hand. (This is the classic example of the garbage can model of decision making raised to the level of social decision making.) Indeed, the most significant recent attempts to reconcile all of these persistent tensions have been the remarkable and unprecedented efforts of university scholars, in and out of education, to serve as human bridges between the poles that have tended to pull at the enterprise of education research. Ted Sizer, James Comer, Robert Slavin, and Henry Levin have all made the transit of research into practice, and of purposes into practices, their personal task. The enterprises they have built are distinct but share the common feature of having established local areas of common ground among practitioners, researchers, and, perhaps most important, communities. The critical theme of their work is that common ground can only be established locally, through active and personal engagement. This view, and the apparent successes of much of their work, has begun to frame the way we think about school reform and the way we think about education research.

A Call for More Public Discourse

The efforts of such scholars to put research knowledge into practice have been extraordinarily powerful, engaging teachers, researchers, and parents in discussions of educational aims and means and developing a sense of common purpose around the task of educating children. Yet as powerful as they have been at the local level, these efforts, be they Accelerated Schools or Coalition of Essential Schools, suffer from their own success (Goldberg, 1996; Levin, 1988). In addition, they have become formulas for success rather than tools for continued improvement, and in this they represent the durability of the most intransigent tension: that between deterministic views of educational science and more pragmatic, inquiry-based views. This is a problem mainly of consumption —of a national appetite for solutions to the frustrating and complex problems facing education. It is a hunger that includes voters, parents, some school professionals, university presidents, and, increasingly, funders of education inquiry. The result has been to ascribe to these and other projects more answers than questions and to repeat the problems that so beset Dewey and the Laboratory School in the early years of the century. Moreover, as foundations place money in "program-only" enterprises, such as the Annenberg Challenge Grants Program, they amplify the institutional effect of this appetite, increasing the magnetism of deterministic and sometimes reductionist approaches to education inquiry.

Already we are seeing predictable results, as the public looks too soon for implicitly promised "results" from these research-based enterprises (Stecklow, 1994). The consequences of this trend have been, once again, to call into question the efficacy of education inquiry. At the other extreme, parents and the public are skittish about change, research driven or not. Voters in particular entertain every proposal for change with a skeptical eye, wondering why we need to change a system that is recognizable and familiar. What both of these trends suggest to us is the lack of public discourse about education of the kind that informs the public about business and economics, for example. The business press, although certainly given to faddishness in its most popular forms, is a bruising forum that does create a fairly robust dialogue about both the environment in which business operates and the internal challenges facing industries, companies, and the economy as a whole. In this sense the business press serves a mediating function between the research community and the public that the education press is only beginning to create. The *New York Times* has long had an education page that serves this function; other papers across the country, notably the *Los Angeles Times* and the *Sacramento Bee*, have begun similar efforts.

Finally, and most fundamental, education inquiry needs to find its own internal compass and its own internal gravity. The ability of the polarities that we have discussed to pull research in differing directions is a testament to both their power and the lack of internal gravity within the field. In establishing the foundations for our own inquiry, we could do no better than to remember Dewey's remark that "until educators get the independence and courage to insist that educational aims are to be formed as well as executed within the educative process, they will not come to consciousness of their own function." Without that sense of duty to define education and then build it, he warned, "others will then have no great respect for educators" (Dewey, 1929, p. 74). With that, our inquiry, our questions, our methods, and our findings take on real meaning and real significance. We can do no less for the profession or for society.

References

Alexander, C. *Educational Research: Suggestions and Sources of Data with Specific Reference to Administration.* New York: Teachers College Press, 1927.

Bestor, A. *Educational Wastelands.* (2nd ed.) Urbana: University of Illinois Press, 1983.

Bright, R. L., and Gideonse, H. D. *Education Research and Its Relation to Policy.* Washington, D.C.: U.S. Department of Health, Education and Welfare, 1967.

Brim, O. B. *Knowledge into Action: Improving the Nation's Use of the Social Sciences.* Washington, D.C.: National Science Foundation, 1969.

Callahan, R. *Education and the Cult of Efficiency.* Chicago: Phoenix, 1964.

Clifford, G. J. *Edward Thorndike: The Sane Positivist.* Middletown, Conn.: Wesleyan University Press, 1968.

Cremin, L., Shannon, D., and Townsend, M. A. *History of Teachers College, Columbia University.* New York: Columbia University Press, 1954.

Cronbach, L. J., and Suppes, P. (eds.). *Research for Tomorrow's Schools: Disciplined Inquiry for Education.* New York: Macmillan, 1969.

Dewey, J. "The University School." *University Record,* 1896, *1,* 417–418.

Dewey, J. *The Sources of a Science of Education.* New York: Horace Liveright, 1929.

Dewey, J. *Schools and Society.* Chicago: University of Chicago Press, 1943.

Goldberg, M. F. "Here for the Long Haul: An Interview with Theodore Sizer." *Phi Delta Kappan,* 1996, *77,* 685–687.

Hanus, Paul H. *School Efficiency: A Constructive Study Applied to New York City; Being a Summary and Interpretation of the Report on the Educational Aspects of the School Inquiry.* New York: World Book Company, 1913.

Haskell, T. *Authority and the Social Sciences.* Urbana: University of Illinois Press, 1977.

James, W. *Talks to Teachers on Psychology: And to Students on Some of Life's Ideals.* New York: Holt, 1899.

Lagemann, E. C. *Contested Terrain: A History of Education Research in the United States, 1890–1990.* Chicago: Spencer Foundation, 1996.

Leidecker, K. *Yankee Teacher: The Life of William Torrey Harris.* New York: Philosophical Library, 1946.

Levin, H. M. *Accelerated Schools for At-Risk Students.* New Brunswick, N.J.: Center for Policy Research in Education, 1988.

McMillen, L. "Revised History Standards Appear to Satisfy Critics of Earlier Version." *Chronicle of Higher Education,* April 12, 1995, p. A16.

MacMullen, E. *In the Cause of Education.* New Haven, Conn.: Yale University Press, 1991.

Monroe, W., and others. *Ten Years of Educational Research: Suggestions and Sources of Data with Specific References to Administration.* New York: Teachers College Press, 1927.

Oakes, J., and others. "Center X: A Concept Paper." Working paper, UCLA Graduate School of Education and Information Studies, 1994.

Powell, A. *The Uncertain Profession: Harvard and the Search for Educational Authority.* Cambridge, Mass.: Harvard University Press, 1980.

Review of Education Research, 1990–1995. Washington, D.C.: American Educational Research Association, 1990–1995.

Royce, J. "Is There a Science of Education?" *Educational Review,* 1891, *1,* pp. 16–17.

Russell, J. *Founding Teachers College: Reminiscences of the Dean Emeritus.* New York: Teachers College Press, 1937.

Sears, J., and Henderson, A. *Cubberly of Stanford and His Contribution to American Education.* Stanford, Calif.: Stanford University Press, 1957.

Sieber, S., and Lazarfeld, P. *The Organization of Educational Research in the United States.* New York: Bureau of Applied Social Research, 1966.

Stecklow, S.T. "Critical Thought; Acclaimed Reforms of U.S. Education Are Popular But Unproved; Ted Sizer's Methods Stress Reasoning over Rote; Gains Aren't Measurable; Ambiguity and Faculty Spats." *Wall Street Journal,* December 18, 1994, p. A1.

Travers, R. M. W. *How Research Has Changed American Schools: A History from 1840 to the Present.* Kalamazoo, Mich.: Mythos Press, 1983.

Tyack, D. B. *The One Best System: A History of American Urban Education.* Cambridge, Mass.: Harvard University Press, 1974.

Tyack, D.B. and Hansot, E. *Learning Together: A History of Coeducation in the United States.* New Haven: Yale University Press, 1990.

Tyack, D.B., and Hansot, E. *Managers of Urban America: Public School Leadership in America 1820–1980.* New York: Basic Books, 1982.

CHAPTER FOUR

Needed

Thoughtful Research for Thoughtful Schools

Deborah W. Meier

*Out walking one night I came upon a man circling under a lamppost. I asked
him, "What did you lose?" "My watch," he said. "Are you sure you lost it here?"
"Actually," he admitted, "I lost it over there [he gestured into the dark], but the
only light I can find is over here, so that's where I decided to look."*

There has been too much research on schools built around the stuff that
is easiest to look at—standardized, quantitative data that meet a particular set of psychometric criteria. What we need, however, is to understand what is off there in the dark. Keeping our eyes narrowly focused around
the lamppost has helped us avoid asking aloud: "So what—and what for?"

We know that the so-called hard stuff—test scores, attendance data, dropout
statistics—is not "hard" at all; it is soft and sloppy and highly accessible to our
not-disinterested manipulations. Yet whenever I ask my colleagues why they
continue to trust judgments based on such flimsy evidence, they chorus back:
"It's the only stuff we have. Anyway," they add more softly, "our own voices
and accounts are not considered credible."

But it may also be that reliance on existing forms of quantitative data serves
a purpose that we dare not name.

Our curious dependency on a certain kind of "hard," or what Ted Chittenden, author and cognitive psychologist at the Educational Testing Service, calls
"indirect," data can be partly explained by the all-too-human desire for simplicity and exactitude. The "direct" data—actual live children engaged in the
thing itself, rather than subsamples of presumably related activities—require
arguable interpretations and thus can produce complicated and ambiguous
results. George Madaus, holder of the Boisi Chair of Education and Public Policy
at Boston College, made the same point in his testimony to the Education Committee, Massachusetts House of Representatives (July 15, 1998). In criticizing a

new teacher test, he noted that it "flies in the face of a fundamental measurement principle . . . . A direct measure of whatever skill or ability you are interested in is . . . preferable to any paper-and-pencil test. Further, even when a paper-and-pencil test is used, it should be validated against a direct indicator of the skill or ability."

The public, we are told, will never buy that. Even at New York City's Central Park East and now Boston's Mission Hill schools, which I have been associated with for so many years, we have accepted this prejudice and used numbers (as well as narrative and anecdotal data) to report certain forms of direct observation.

It seems to comfort folks. And the education research community has helped to create the public's willingness to settle for it. Rather than being an antidote to such oversimplification, experts and academics have fostered the dependency. If these well-informed persons use test scores almost exclusively to verify their judgments and treat such data as though they were the *real thing*, is it any wonder that the lay public believes that the true "ends" of education are best summarized by reference to quantitative measures of aptitude and achievement? In fact, it seems a scholarly quibble (or hopelessly romantic) to suggest that the ends of education do not neatly correspond to test scores.

But suppose the emperor wears no clothes. Suppose virtually all the data that schools and school systems are accustomed to use rest not only on outmoded ends but, worse, on a huge but useful deception. This chapter considers that possibility and suggests other, more valid approaches to the assessment of children's academic performance.

I got a call one night from a wise friend who had played a critical role in the formation of a new elementary school designed exclusively for at-risk youngsters. "We're starting our fourth year, and I'm ready to call it quits," she said resignedly. "Our kids can't read." Given her past glowing accounts of this school, I was floored. "Didn't you notice this before?" I asked.

"No," she replied, "because third grade is the first year they get tested, so it has just shown up."

"But," I persisted, "you trust the people you hired to run the school. You spend a lot of time there too. How come they never noticed that the kids couldn't read?"

"We all somehow deceived ourselves, I guess," she concluded.

I proposed that we visit the school together and find out for ourselves if the students could read. We would rely only on the direct data: we would listen to a sample of students actually reading.

And we did just that. We randomly picked nearly one-fifth of the students in first through fourth grades and read with them. We did not find a single nonreader. Most of the children read aloud from "grade-level" books they had never seen, and "with expression." They made reasonable efforts to pronounce unknown words and carried on good discussions about the text. And they also knew a lot about books, authors, words, and language, although they were probably not yet as proficient as their more advantaged peers.

A week later, still stunned by these results, my friend said to me, "Debby, could we have been wrong?"

Well, maybe our sample was skewed, I suggested. No, she insisted, she had checked on that. Still, somehow . . .

We both laughed.

What she had on her hands was a political, not a reading, problem. The school's future funding required better scores. She needed techniques that would raise their scores while not interfering with the reading performances that we had witnessed. The challenge was to figure out a way to make sure the children's current low scores did not undermine their self-esteem and their continued impressive progress as readers.

It should not have surprised me when a year later my friend called to tell me that we had been right. The proof: "Our new test scores just came out, and they confirm our judgment." But even she needed this additional "evidence," although she knew that what had changed was not the children's ability to read but their ability to demonstrate it on this particular test. Test scores still seemed more "real."

WHAT STANDARDIZED TESTS MEASURE

If my personal account is not aberrant and my friend is not an oddball, then there clearly is a problem. This nation is spending inordinate amounts of energy trying to produce not better and more enthusiastic readers, but better test takers. No independent evidence exists that the two are the same thing or are produced by the same methods. The gradual replacement in schools of all other forms of judgment by this one particular mode of assessment, despite decades of attack, cannot be merely a misunderstanding or a shortcut born of economy—although both are essential to the deception. If the existing model were viewed as not merely harmless but dangerous, a more expensive solution might be found. After all, beloved medical cures have been discarded, though not easily, once they have been acknowledged to be bad for our health.

Yet a twenty-year effort to replace the traditional standardized test with more authentic forms of assessment—exhibitions, portfolios, oral defenses, performances, and the like—has foundered not merely on the grounds of expense but on the seemingly irreconcilable conflict between what is authentic and what psychometrics will allow. The conventional view is that only psychometrics can speak with objective certainty and that all tests must meet their criteria. As we will see, this view has made direct assessment appear almost impossible.

The Role of Rank Ordering

The stubborn fact may be that the particular rank order that psychometrically reliable testing alone seems to produce remains both politically and educationally useful. Our society tolerates such testing not because it is scientific, but because many people want a rank order—that is, some form of normal, or bell, curve. It seems to confirm a commonsense observation that since most of those in positions of power and influence score well, something important is being tested. Furthermore, there are just enough exceptions—surprises—to make those with social and political power feel that such tests cannot be entirely self-serving.

But above all, perhaps traditional testing allows researchers, educators, and policymakers to do things that otherwise would be very hard to do. This relatively cheap instrument makes it possible to diagnose and compare with elaborate tables and charts children, schools, and systems with fairly predictable results (Meier, 1974). By conforming to a set of "industry" rules, the test makers claim the right to promise the public that the score of a test taker would not change much if the person took a similarly constructed test, or took the same one on a different day, and, furthermore, that the results can predict this test taker's success at similar kinds of tests taken at some time in the future.

Although the quality and quantity of the procedures that must be met are certainly greater for psychometrically well-designed tests than for other forms of judgment, the mystique of their infallibility far outstrips what the actual design can support. There is clear evidence, for example, that the results across different, equally "valid" commercial tests do not match each other, even though the rules of psychometrics would make this seem impossible. Furthermore, measurement error is far too great for the high-stakes decisions it is used for. Worse still, when children are read the questions aloud, removing any need to know how to read, one would suppose that their scores would go up substantially. The tests may not even be measuring the skill in question. But for many low scorers, this makes little or no difference. The test is often not measuring "knowing how to read," but rather the children's difficulty comprehending certain kinds of subject matter and vocabulary and their different interpretations based on different experiences. The "distracters" (wrong answers) are, in fact, intended to serve that latter purpose: to pick up on common misinterpretations that children might reasonably make. Thus the irony. Machine-scored multiple-choice tests can be 100 percent reliable even though they may be measuring something different from what was advertised.

Impact of Coaching to the Test

In the "olden days"—when I went to school and when I began teaching—it was the tests that schools and teachers designed themselves that were considered the centerpiece of teaching and learning and that formed the basis of in-school authority. When external, norm-referenced tests were administered, schools and teachers were strictly prohibited from preparing students for them, except at the beginning of the actual test session and then only by repeating the explicit script the test maker prepared for this purpose. Students were told there was no way to prepare—except with a good night's sleep. On testing day, teachers instructed students not to guess what the right answer was, even when, in fact, wild guessing could substantially improve one's score and there was no penalty for wrong answers. As I recall, we teachers believed that the scoring machines could detect guesses, just as it is now claimed the tests can detect cheating (too many erasures, perhaps, or when the erasures always result in a change from wrong to right answers). These alien tests, like the equally secret world of IQ testing, belonged to a different domain—the domain of "science." Even the scores were kept secret from the general public (although parents were informed about their own children's scores).

When I began teaching I obeyed all these instructions, albeit with increasing reluctance, because I was told that only thus could the playing field be made level for all children. During the 1960s, however, test scores became public. Newspapers began to report scores, comparing schools and systems to each other. The race was on. Eventually parents, teachers, schools, and school systems began to realize they could improve students' scores with better and longer preparation. Leading the way were for-profit organizations (such as Kaplan and Princeton Review) that tapped into the anxieties of more powerful parents over the emerging influence of the Scholastic Aptitude Test (SAT) in deciding who got into which prestigious college. As public pressure on schools to account for results grew—even for traditionally low-scoring students—the users of the regular standardized K–12 tests stopped obeying the publisher's prohibitions, at first covertly and eventually by systemwide decree. By the 1970s, what is now benignly called curriculum alignment began to occur. Schools went into the business of designing what and how they taught in order to match the tests. For example, teaching the right answers to the items *likely* to be found on a reading test became the way to teach reading. Correlation became causation without missing a beat.

In the mid-1960s when I arrived in New York City, most city schools showed that the vast majority of students were scoring below the fiftieth percentile in reading and math on the MAT (Metropolitan Achievement Test). The city press had just begun its relentless annual public ranking of schools based on this test. The schools responded in due course so that within a half-dozen years the number above grade level rose dramatically. At the same time, no one claimed that public school children in New York City had made a breakthrough in reading, and no high school reported that it was getting better-prepared students. Districts unabashedly offered special programs aimed specifically at students performing just below "grade level." (Interestingly, the scores nearly always plummeted when students made the transition to middle or junior high school.

The absence of a homeroom teacher accountable for both teaching and testing reading may be one reason for this otherwise inexplicable drop.)

Given the nature of the instrument, however, teaching to the test can only temporarily improve the odds, since only rank order counts, not one's absolute score. For example, if Mary gets seventy-two answers right on a fifth-grade test, she falls into the sixty-third percentile, which is her reported score. (Other forms of reporting data may be included, the most common being "grade level," the least common being stanines, which is a more accurate portrayal of the meaning of scores on the bell curve.) The reported score presumes that this is where Mary would stand if the entire population of fifth graders had taken the test. But by this logic it follows that improved scores based on improved preparation eventually requires the test maker to renorm the test, by changing either the score sheet or the actual test.

Even with renorming threatening the future, no school or school system could afford to ignore the temporary advantage of test-specific preparation in a society that judged its schools by their students' test scores. Superintendents, after all, rarely lasted long enough in one position to worry about renorming. In contrast to older assumptions, it was now implicitly acknowledged that a student taking two different tests, each of which claimed to test reading, might not get the same score on both. And, in fact, it became general knowledge within the field that certain tests were "harder" than others for certain populations. Furthermore, it turns out that it makes a difference if one coaches to a *particular* test. Coaching "in general" is far less useful than coaching to a particular test. Finally, it makes a difference when a test was last normed. The reason that testing programs are sometimes switched by school systems is worth examining. It often coincides with a new school or school administration that has a short-term stake in demonstrating that students are not doing as well as the public may have thought and that the new team thus faces enormous difficulties based on past poor leadership. This is especially the case where new administrators honestly face what they know are inflated test scores based on past overpreparation for a particular testing program.

Efforts to raise scores at all costs would at least be harmless if the tests themselves were a good way both to teach and measure reading. But the nature of both the tests and the coaching misleads us and misdirects teaching. The trouble is that the low scores misled educators into spending more time and resources teaching the basic skills of reading and in coaching for the tests and less time on rich subject matter (history or science) or good literature. Concern for test scores led New York City in the 1970s to eliminate elementary school libraries and replace them with high-tech "reading labs." Time is finite, so we spent our time on what literally counted.

Reading is often only a small part of the children's problem. When a few researchers many years ago asked children why they selected a particular answer, their responses suggested that something quite different was going on. That "something" may be closer to the mysterious quality that IQ tests also tap, which my ancestors, among others, appeared to lack three generations ago when they first came to America in droves. Jews and southern Europeans scored near the bottom on early IQ tests at the turn of the century and quite a few years into the twentieth, while northern Europeans scored near the top. Asians scored very low too, despite the current view of their talents. But years of immersion and success in American life erased those disparities.

What these researchers discovered is the same thing that I learned in the late 1960s when I tried to find out why my bookworm son scored so poorly in his third-grade reading test in New York City—a discovery that was confirmed in my interviews with children in Central Harlem, which I later wrote about (Meier, 1974). Even if they could read the original item aloud accurately, summarize it orally, and interpret it sensibly (as we had asked the children to do in my friend's school), they might not get the right answer on the test. Poor children and minority children in particular gave what appeared at first glance to be irritatingly "wrong" answers. What the test missed is what can be learned only by questioning the students. Although the children were reading quite well, in the usual sense of that word, they were interpreting the text differently, or were baffled by particular references, vocabulary, and subject matter assumptions. These factors affect some subgroups of children far more than others and can have a substantial impact on a child's test scores on any given test day.

In short, test scores are not merely weak indicators of higher-order skills, or affective and aesthetic strengths, but even of what we ordinarily think of as just plain "reading comprehension" skills. The kinds of items that would pick up gross errors in literal reading—the straightforward "know-how" questions—are intentionally few since a test that rests on such gross distinctions would not produce a normal curve. Thus the vast majority of what schools successfully teach and children successfully learn is intentionally left off such exams.

It was this form of testing—designed much like IQ tests—toward which the original prohibition against coaching was directed. The test makers needed items that would allow them to predict ahead of time how many children would get each answer right and wrong; they needed items they expected to stand the test of time (for at least a decade or more). The tests would work only if one had reason to believe this claim. The accuracy of the test makers' predictions depended on items that schools were unlikely or unable to teach directly, but which differentiated children from each other. That is precisely what enabled these tests to be so useful: to predict future performance. Even to try to coach children on items intended to serve such a purpose would contaminate the scoring system itself and make all scores unreliable predictors of the future. This explains why the SAT was originally not called an achievement test but an "aptitude" test. Coaching therefore undermines precisely what the test makers have so carefully designed. (Consider my amazement when, teaching in Project Head Start in 1965–1966, I was told that our goal was to raise IQ scores and that we should therefore focus our curriculum on teaching the specific kind of knowledge that was used on IQ tests. It went against everything I understood at this point in my life about the meaning of IQ.)

The Fallacy Revealed

What is puzzling is how it was ever imagined that such an instrument could measure the *nation's* progress at creating a better-educated citizenry. What psychometrics was offering was a promise of "no change" over time—just a picture of who belonged where along the immutable bell curve. Americans were, to their credit, unwilling to admit that a child's socioeconomic status was already a better and cheaper predictor of a child's and school's place on the normal curve. In the society of the past, where school success was only one among many ways to succeed, the issue of exactly what was being measured could be bypassed without too much fuss. No one seemed wildly distressed by the secrecy surrounding testing until the 1960s. It took the increasing importance placed on school success and the 1960s thrust toward social and racial egalitarianism to force the issue into the open. Even so, few dared to claim what virtually all educators and the larger public had come to realize: that schooling was powerless to eliminate the advantage—the edge—that comes with being advantaged (never mind uglier racist or ethnic assumptions about where groups would stand on the normal curve). Indeed, as the producers of *Sesame Street* discovered in their early assessments of the program's impact, the already advantaged are more, not less, likely to take advantage of the best and newest learning schemes. Even fewer people were willing to acknowledge that leveling the playing field would require far more radical and targeted reforms than those being proposed (and not just changes in schools), beginning with abandonment of a form of measurement that promised no change. If a way were discovered to get all children to read better, faster, and earlier, nothing would appear to have changed as long as children were measured by these kinds of tests. Such a breakthrough would produce a difference only if the frontrunners were refused access to these same new and better learning schemes. That is hardly likely to happen, nor should it.

When Coaching Is an Abuse and When It Is Not

If the public *wants* tests that produce a reliable and predictable rank order, then it has them, and people should stop abusing and misusing them with coaching.

Coaching to change scores, even if it often succeeds in this respect, far less often improves reading and can even endanger good reading. For one thing, it masks the real problems that low scorers are having, which more often lie beyond "reading programs" and the whole-phonics-versus-whole-language debate. On the surface a test can be about the skill being tested, but the connection between that skill and what students are having difficulty with can be very different.

Of course, coaching for tests is not always an abuse, depending on the test and its purpose; it can even be quite appropriate for certain kinds of tests. Coaching is standard for a driver's test, because that test is not designed so that coaching will destroy its scoring system. There is no mandate, for example, that scores must follow a particular curve. A road test simply and literally measures driving competence: the more people who pass, the merrier. The preparation is in keeping with the nature of the task. In contrast, preparing for an eye test (by prior access to an eye chart) would not serve us well. The purpose of this test is strictly diagnostic, and coaching would cover over a problem that needs uncovering. Its purpose is not to determine how well Americans are "seeing" absolutely and comparatively; rather, it is to help each particular child see better. Wouldn't it be nice if reading tests did the same? At least occasionally?

In standardized school tests, however, science has given us tests that produce a reliable, predictable rank order that does not change over time and that matches predicted future success at schooling—as long as the test is not abused.

What the Public Has Bought

Coaching on standardized tests is an abuse if the users—the audience—think they are getting something else. What the public thinks it has bought is a combination diagnostic instrument that can inform teaching and learning, a measure of whether an individual child can read and what percentage of all children can do so. They think that what the test makers are offering them is more or less like a driver's test, separating those who can from those who cannot. Especially where their own child is concerned, they want the chance to check the results, to get as close as they can to what went "wrong." But since the questions and answers on the actual test must remain secret—unlike our driver's test—it is impossible, without cheating, to "show" parents, teachers, or the child himself or herself what the mistake was, meaning the nature of the ignorance in question. Yes, of course, parents and laypersons would also like a single unambiguous and simple number that stands in for all this complexity. But they want it only if it is possible. Simple information is what they got, not honest information.

Although it is easy to point to parents, lay citizens, and politicians as the culprits in their wholesale dependence on traditional tests, there is more to it than this. In a world where expertise is honored (how else can one survive?), the blame lies at least partly with the educational statisticians, researchers, and psychometricians who lent their names, reputations, and work to accrediting such data, even in their much-abused and misused forms. If these test data were good enough for these experts and all their task forces, is it so surprising that Mom and Dad and the average school board member would take them seriously?

It was the professionals, above all disinterested ones like researchers and scholars, who offered the general public psychometrics nearly a century ago as the answer to all its desires: short, sweet, cheap, simple to rank, seemingly precise and certain, and with results that confirmed society's expectations. These professionals bear some responsibility for what the public now thinks it can have—for example, that the test score gap between high and low scores on standardized tests can be closed. Just as good doctors do not pretend to certainty, even on matters of life and death, educators should not have done so either.

Any test has its own parameters, its own rules, requiring one to ask particular and different questions. Out-of-classroom educational experts and researchers were and still are needed to act as guardians of the information pool on which wise decisions have to be made in a democratic society. Instead the experts have helped contaminate that pool. By both their actions and inactions, members of the profession have not only encouraged the growth of such tests, but have allowed standardized norm-referenced tests to serve a myriad of conflicting purposes that no single test, even a good one, can possibly fulfill. A test that was intended to serve individual parents, classroom teachers, the school district, politicians, and the lay public does not, it turns out, do well by any of them. Parents and teachers have mainly needed diagnostic information: How well are the students getting what it is they are being taught? In what different ways do different students learn best? That is not of much interest to politicians or the broader lay public. And none of these tests is designed well for sorting people on the basis of the particular skills they need to succeed in their institution, trade, or occupation, be it as a police officer, an undergraduate at Harvard, a student at medical school, or a member of a drivers' club. No single test can sort for all these high-stakes purposes, each of which rests on a different set of dispositions, habits, and skills.

In addition, the degree of measurement error in standardized tests is considerable; it is certainly too large to serve us well where the stakes are high and when decisions will be made that determine the future course of a young person's life. The younger the children are, the greater the measurement error is, yet we are seeing more and more testing of very young children. Colleges and employers may find they have institutional needs for arbitrary cut-offs that cannot be justified by statistical evidence, but educational practitioners do not have to use cut-offs for their own teaching and learning purposes—for decisions they make between kindergarten and twelfth grade. A 3.3 score and a 3.9 score are statistically the same. Yet in many localities a child with a 3.3 gets automatically held over, while a child with a 3.9 is patted on the back.

Test data, by the way, are not the only form of "hard data" that have misled the public about the performance of schools. New York City for years counted graduation rates by calculating the percentage of twelfth graders who graduated. This meant that in places like the Bronx, where little more than a third of the students ever made it to the twelfth grade, the press would on occasion release Board of Education data claiming 90 to 97 percent graduation rates! Who knows how "dropouts" are figured? Some cities do not call students dropouts who leave after reaching the age of eighteen; others do not if the students leave before they reach high school. Many schools and school systems disguise dropouts by checking off that the students are moving to another state or country—Puerto Rico, Mexico—if at all possible without regard to whether they are likely to be continuing their schooling. I leave aside the many ways that principals can, if enough is at stake, play with attendance data. New York City once upped its citywide attendance records by simply counting noses at a different time of day. Imagine my surprise to discover that in California and Massachusetts, daily attendance data include as "present" students who are not in attendance if they have a note from home. National comparisons of "incidents" and suspension rates are based on wildly different criteria and frequently depend on particular local consequences; more incidences reported may lead to more security guards or more accusations of racism and bad management.

What the community of educators can and should be faulted for is having let this kind of stuff appear to be hard data just because some data are better than none.

TOWARD A NEW PARADIGM

Some of these faults—like how to count dropouts and attendance—could be fixed, although this would require the cooperation of a better-educated press. But the student testing model now used for charting progress is unfixable. Painfully needed is a new paradigm to replace norm-referenced testing. The one we are using is part and parcel of the historical fact that schools have been as much as anything else about sorting children. The capacity of scores to predict the future was built around the assumption that schools could not and should not have an impact on rank order. Now that we claim to want something different from our schools, the technology we invented for a different age is grossly unfit to do the job.

Our society is accustomed to tests that serve as scientifically neutral stand-ins for decisions that many other societies make solely on the basis of wealth or social status and others delegate to people they trust. Democratic ideals and a healthy antiaristocratic bias were in part responsible for bringing into existence the granddaddy of all modern psychometrics, the American IQ test. But as Stephen Jay Gould has so dramatically demonstrated in his *The Mismeasure of Man* (1981), IQ tests came with their own baggage of biases. All of our most reputable standardized tests, no matter what they purport to measure, have been modeled on the IQ test. There are more sophisticated ways to get the samples, score the tests, and report the results; there are even some new gimmicks. But there have been no breakthroughs in the basic technology of "scientific" testing in nearly a hundred years, and none is to come.

Rather than the technology, it is the idea on which the technology rests—the idea that there is a way around the fallibility of well-educated judgment—that is at fault. Standardized norm-referenced tests stand in stark contrast to what a democratic school system should be all about—what Thomas Jefferson called schools that educate our "discretion." They ignore the aspect that democratic society ultimately rests on: an educated citizenry trained to exercise judgment, with all its fallibility, uncertainty, and messiness, a messiness kept in check by a combination of healthy skepticism and public debate, not a pretense to certainty built around a network of secrecy.

At a time in history when it is claimed that our society must educate all its children well and that all children must be trained to use their intellects in sophisticated ways—a proposition contrary to the concept of normative tests—the continued popularity of this outmoded form of testing among those who know better needs addressing, and in a hurry. Some of the technology of psychometrics can be constructively used for testing small, random, uncoached samples of students in order to make comparisons as well as track changes over time. Such use, without high-stakes consequences, would not require norming; nor would measurement error matter. Studies could be made of the reasoning behind the ways that different groups of students respond to the same questions in order to learn something from such responses, not just mark them wrong. This kind of research could assist us in teaching, rather than labeling, children.

But beyond the more constructive use of such tests, there need to be different approaches to assessing students and their schools—approaches that speak directly to parents, teachers, and communities, helping them to understand their children better and track their progress over time. We have reached the point where the traditional testing system threatens all schools, particularly those that serve the most vulnerable.

As long as the man and woman on the street and powerful policymakers believe they can answer profound questions of student capacity, teacher efficacy, different forms of pedagogy, and even the impact of family structure (to mention just a few) by analyzing in myriad statistically sophisticated ways the latest available test data, we are in trouble. Instead of recognizing this, however, we are in the midst of a new and more far-reaching effort to use such data for even more grandiose purposes.

Currently policymakers are demanding nationwide improvement in test scores (or else); many are pushing for the creation of one uniform set of interconnected nationally norm-referenced tests to replace all the other forms of confusing human judgments. They think that such an airtight system of testing will finally bring coherence to an overly decentralized education system, put pressure on localities and lazy practitioners, ensure that all children are measured fairly (and frequently), and make it hard for anyone to rely on their ill- or well-intentioned biases. In the process each child, family, and teacher will finally have the truth about where they stand in the grand scheme of things and what they have to do about it—of course, raise their score. We have finally squared the circle.

Such proposals can only help the exodus from public schooling altogether by those with the means to flee. Centralized school systems with their sure-fire consequences may be okay for other people's children, but they are unlikely to appeal to users with choices.

Building the New Paradigm

Of course, there *are* alternatives and lots of good folks who care and believe in them. The problem is not that there are no better ways. It is actually not so hard to build assessments that "merely" help us see where students stand in a continuum or assortment of skills. In fact, they were invented decades ago, have been used for ages by school people, and are still around. Standardized criterion-referenced testing, which came into vogue in the 1970s, was intended to do something of the sort. Unfortunately, criterion-referenced tests could not resist psychometrics, and in the name of reliability they ended up as simply longer traditional tests with more subscores.

By the mid-1970s, some reformers went a step further. They rested their alternative ideas on other familiar forms of assessment, most of which divided learners into only two categories: pass–fail. They looked at how Ph.D. candidates are judged, how architects are certified, and at older forms of public exhibition—from the Boy Scouts, to 4-H, to bar mitzvahs. They noted that driver's tests matter a lot, but no one gets ranked. Oddly enough, pass-fail is all that counts in the bar exam, although preparation for the bar is much joked about by those who have passed the exam for its irrelevance to lawyering. Red Cross lifesaving tests are pass-fail. My own children had to be able to swim halfway across the lake before they could take the canoe out on their own. They could do it with speed and form, or they could comfortably float and dog paddle. There were some uncertains that required retesting, where my husband and I disagreed on how "comfortably" my son was dog paddling.

There are circumstances, school reformers of the 1980s noted, when "coaching" for tests makes sense. Ted Sizer, chairman of the Coalition for Essential Schools, and Grant Wiggins, a much-published author and expert on secondary school assessment, argued more than a dozen years ago for schools built around exit exhibitions of competence. They saw good coaching as precisely the task of good teaching. There was nothing wrong with aligning ends and means. Good teaching always has this in mind.

An important national movement in the 1980s was built to try to wean us away from the old paradigms to new ones built on authentic forms of performance. There were, and are, differences of opinion between the proponents of these new paradigms on many issues, but all have agreed that their work stands in stark contrast to the older psychometric model. Their work fundamentally rests on the concept that it is possible and desirable to review actual novice performances relying on the judgment of one's peers or would-be peers (the experts). Many proponents of such forms of assessment would even argue that becoming adept both at exhibiting one's competence in this fashion or at being able to make judgments about such exhibitions is at the heart of their definition of a good education.

Advocates of traditional "scientific" testing might suggest that these systems of making judgments are too "political" and sloppy for making important life decisions. But if the central purpose of schooling in a democratic society is to train fallible human judgment, it makes sense to assess schools in ways that do honor to this essential purpose also.

Maybe the obvious alternatives are avoided for precisely this reason, because they require us to describe what is good enough and then stand behind it, rather than rely on nameless others to set our standards. In the 1980s and early 1990s Vermont pioneered a statewide assessment system that was built around collections of student work. The exciting thing about this short-lived portfolio approach was that it required all the state's teachers to look at the work youngsters produced in the classrooms of their colleagues and make judgments about it. It required, in other words, that teachers in the state take responsibility for their opinions. Such approaches to assessment hold us all accountable in deeper ways. They provoke us to wonder whether most of us are "good enough" and, if not, whether it matters. They stimulate debate about the purpose of public schooling, a debate that would be both hard work and inevitably contentious and might not lead to consensus.

So we pretend that it is all pretty simple. After all, doesn't everyone want a school that "works"? Is that really so hard to define? Isn't that where most children get high scores? Aren't the scores indicators of doing well at school, and if they are not, can't school be reformed so there is better alignment? Soon enough, scores define purpose. In the absence of better answers, why not?

When asked why one must go to high school, most young people will answer, "To get a diploma so I can go to college." Why go to college? "So I can get a better-paying job." Rare is the student who says of either high school or college, "So I can *learn something* of intellectual or social value to me." The value of the certificate lies not, therefore, in what one has learned but in its scarcity. Its value can be raised by making it harder to pass—by devising either a tougher test or a tougher scoring system. High-prestige schools have higher cut-offs (pass–fail dividing line), low-prestige schools low ones. No one ever has to remember or agree on what it is we value so highly that we require all our children to devote nearly two involuntary decades to mastering it. The test is a hurdle, not an accomplishment.

"All Children Can Learn"

A new idea has been unleashed: all children can learn things of intellectual importance. It is still an amazing claim, and in the world of tomorrow perhaps a critical one. It is surely the most exciting national challenge our country faces. But it will be a cruel hoax if we do not alter the way we measure all our children.

Tackling purposes can change this potential hoax into a realizable dream. That is why it has been at the center of the best reform ideas. It was the central point of Ted Sizer's much-acclaimed *Horace's Compromise* (1985), Neil Postman's *The Ends of Education* (1996), John Goodlad's *A Place Called School* (1984), and many other books that have encouraged a healthy, though not widespread, debate about the essential purposes of schools. From 1975 to 1995 governors, think tanks, national task forces, and disciplinary leaders all began to echo at least some of the rhetoric of these writers. Among the many initiatives in the early 1990s was a widely acclaimed national effort to spearhead systemwide reform launched by President Bush and U.S. Undersecretary of Education David Kearns (former chief executive officer of Xerox Corporation). Called the New American School Development Corporation (NASDC), it invited reformers throughout the country to compete for the prestigious designation as a NASDC model. There were remarkable similarities among most of the models proposed, as well as among the final five selected for full funding.

Whether launched by professed liberals or conservatives, phrases like *higher-order thinking* or *critical thinking, problem solving, teamwork, learning for understanding,* and *performance-based assessment,* along with *decency, character, compassion,* and *awareness of the ideals and feelings of others* (the diversity stuff) were increasingly "in." People who disagreed on many fronts joined forces in praising the National Council of Teachers of Mathematics (NCTM) frameworks, instruction in reading that rested on the use of good literature, and a science education curriculum that rested less on rote memory and more on learning to experiment and reason scientifically. No one, except what was seen as the extreme "Christian right," blinked for a while. The dissension came over pedagogical details: the balance between memory and discovery, the role of group versus individualized teaching, more phonics or less, and what constitutes evidence of success.

During this same period, cities and states as well as a variety of interesting national reform networks initiated changes in the way students were being educated and schools organized. Unlike overhauling a factory, changing schools had to take place amid the arduous daily tasks confronting schools and teachers. We could close a factory for retooling but not a school. School change also bumped up against ordinary people's ideas of what made sense, their own memories of past experiences at school, their fears about novelties and experiments being practiced on their children. And, finally, school change had to respond to the sixty-four-thousand-dollar question: "How do you know this new way is better?" All of these factors had to be answered before changes were even launched, much less fully established. It is a problematic task at best. But it did not help when we agreed, however begrudgingly, to answer the last question—"Does it work?"—with instruments that came out of a different history to serve a different purpose.

To the latter question the experts and school practitioners who were seeking serious change had some alternate, if hard-to-sell, answers. Public exhibitions, performance assessments, portfolios, school quality reviews by external experts, and longitudinal data based on real-life success were suggested. They were well accepted in many other fields of work, and with enough effort from the highest authorities and sufficient time, the public might have bought them as good ways to assess their schools. A rash of states and publishers began to play with how to do this on a large scale, while on a smaller scale individual schools and teachers began to try out their own forms of defining and exhibiting achievement. California tried on a large scale to build a new assessment system that was standardized in some traditional ways but deviated radically in others. Vermont went even further and introduced statewide portfolio assessment. Kentucky tried a statewide system of authentic testing. New York State launched a task force to develop a new approach to statewide regents' testing that would combine some form of standardized tests and some locally devised alternative assessments, along with schoolwide peer review that borrowed from British practice. Even the testing of teachers launched by the National Board for Professional Teaching Standards opted for portfolios, video observations, interviews, performance reviews, and written essays rather than standardized multiple-choice testing, and it refused to consider scoring by the bell curve, despite the enormously increased cost and time involved. Highly reputable folks in the various academic associations agreed to develop similarly sophisticated forms of student assessment in each discipline.

All claimed to be in agreement that the old tests—whatever their virtues—could not tackle the lofty new missions. What was needed, if the nation were serious about wanting the best for all children and their teachers, were new but rigorous ways to assess student and system progress toward meeting these goals.

The new formats exposed the enormous weak underbelly of America's schools —how little of what we taught was exhibitable. In schools in which students were rarely writing and rarely talking (at least about schoolwork), what was there to exhibit? The reformers viewed this as one of the positives—that such new forms of assessment might drive schools into rethinking their practices. Children tested on performance would have to be taught how to perform.

This in turn led to an interesting nascent debate about what kind of ultimate performances students were to be prepared for. Who were the audiences? The connection between tests and performances on real-life tasks by people outside of school settings became more relevant. The scores of traditional tests, in their grand abstractedness, masked such connections and left fuzzy the relevance of in-school training to out-of-school purposes.

Subverting the Idea

In the midst of this very fragile and healthy debate about purposes, and while the lay public remained largely ignorant of what the fuss was all about, the test makers and their allies noticed a flaw: these new forms of assessment, which depended on the educated judgments of thousands of practitioners, including sometimes even parents and lay citizens, did not mesh with the world of psychometrics, and any attempt to make them do so would be inordinately expensive, not least because they would require the retraining of teachers and test givers. As constituted, they lacked a scientific base. In fact, the more authentically the trait assessed was, the more it involved the people closest to the children—sometimes even the children themselves—the less it met such a requirement. In "real life" these judges were too much like other jurors—like movie critics and publishers, often disagreeing, and sometimes in substantial ways. In short, the new forms of assessment were more expensive, they were harder to explain to the public, and they lacked what the old tests had: instant familiarity. The policymakers responded to these arguments by demanding that the nascent experiments conform to more standardized formats: less choice of topics, clearer guidelines for essays or scientific experiments, more standardized questions (that were also less authentic). They agreed that "better" rubrics with less wiggle room should be designed and that scorers needed to be trained to produce more consistency—to act more like the machines they were replacing.

In addition, as the late 1990s rolled around, attention began to focus on whether the cut-offs were tough enough. By this time, "tough" had become synonymous with cracking down on precisely those closest to the students—their permissive or misguided or ignorant families and teachers. The steam behind the idea of building a new paradigm was gone. The old tests emerged stronger than ever. (An odd test that has all the faults of both paradigms was also born of this new mood. Like the traditional tests, it is entirely paper-and-pencil, are very long, and claim to be able to arrive at highly precise numerical scores with indisputable cut-offs. They are based, however, not on years of careful reliability or validity studies, but on the judgments of appointed and centralized panels. I speak here, for example, of the new Massachusetts student and teacher tests that seem to be leading a new trend in testing, which needs attention from the research community for its equally serious potential for abuse and misuse.

It is hardly surprising, then, that the sentence "All children can learn" has finally been filled in by the ludicrous "All children can learn to pass any sound psychometrically designed test with equally high scores." Lake Wobegon has gone national; and, if not, someone is just not working hard or smart enough.

The fragile reform consensus began to fall apart. Literature-based instruction, nontracked classrooms, interdisciplinary instruction, and even the seemingly unassailable NCTM standards are increasingly under bellicose attack for failing to produce improved test scores. The attack comes not only from places like the conservative American Enterprise Institute but also from the mainstream American Federation of Teachers. Nervous supporters of these past reforms are responding by watering down the boldness of their ideas. Overnight, school people are being given new messages in direct conflict with the ones they were scolded for not embracing last year (probably most breathe a sigh of relief). Restructuring buildings, not changing the way teachers and children work together, is now "in." And cynical teachers know that this too shall pass.

As long as tests are designed to produce a set rank order, children and schools can at best change places with each other. If the demand is for "tougher" standards, schools can raise the cut-off point so that fewer pass. But meanwhile the dumbing down involved in the organization of schooling around getting the "right" answers on such tests will continue to be ignored. Over time a new consensus may develop that concludes that it is the mantra about "all children" that is passé, not the tests. The "realists," with an eye on the political desirability of cutting expenditures, will be able to claim that the bell curve is destiny.

RETHINKING THE GOALS

What could change this gloomy prognosis? If we wanted all our friends and neighbors, nay even our enemies and potential rivals, to be "equally" well educated, and if we believed that there might be more than one "politically correct" definition of *well educated*, maybe we would be willing to give up on our current dependence on psychometrics and all that goes with it. Maybe then we would turn to some of the not-so-complex alternatives that already exist: both old-fashioned school assessments like exhibitions and the myriad assessments used in other fields of endeavor. Maybe we would recognize that the heart of any good assessment system is that it fosters the kind of healthy intellectual debate that democracy depends on. In this context, psychometrics might have a contribution to make, but it would not dictate the terms of the debate. In such a context, school restructuring would not be an end in itself but simply a tool for creating the kind of lively exercise of judgment needed to raise children well. Big schools versus small ones; interdisciplinary versus disciplinary; teamwork versus solitary work: all would be debated in relationship to the purposes of education, not their impact on test scores.

But unless the emperor is exposed, why should the public invest in an expensive and more complex alternative? If one seeks to adopt the novel and the exciting idea that all children could and should receive an education as demanding and as powerful as the one largely reserved for a small elite, this will not be easy to realize. It is a fragile, still untested, and hardly well-funded idea, and it will remain unattainable by statistical fiat if current assessment practices are not rethought, if the "stuff" out there away from the streetlight does not become the center of our attention—the stuff that will get us talking, even arguing, about what it really is we want our children to become. What we need is a frank and occasionally raucous debate about the habits of heart and mind that we hold ourselves publicly accountable for nurturing in the next generation of our fellow citizens, within a spirit of compromise and tolerance for more than one answer.

The research community will need to become part of this debate. The argument I make in this chapter is that researchers have been using existing "hard data" as the base data of much of their research on educational practices and student performance—this despite the fact that such data are at best corrupt and at worst built around a false paradigm, false at least with respect to the purposes for which it has been used. Not only does this make much of their research questionable, but it has played a major role in making the test scores respectable.

At a time when the overuse of testing is drowning out good practice and when testing is actually cutting off debate about purposes, researchers could provide a powerful voice of sanity. Good conversation about the connections among purposes, practices, and assessment will not lead to simple answers—and it will be hard to conduct. But it might lead to a better-educated citizenry, on which better schooling ultimately rests.

References

Goodlad, J. I. *A Place Called School: Prospects for the Future.* New York: McGraw-Hill, 1984.

Gould, S. J. *The Mismeasure of Man.* New York: Norton, 1981.

Madaus, G. Testimony to the Education Committee, House of Representatives, State of Massachusetts, July 15, 1988.

Meier, D. W. *Reading Failure and the Tests.* New York: Workshop Center, School of Education, City College of New York, 1974.

Meier, D. W. "Why Reading Tests Don't Test Reading." *Dissent,* Fall 1981, pp. 457–466.

Postman, N. *The Ends of Education: Redefining the Value of School.* New York: Knopf, 1995.

Sizer, T. *Horace's Compromise.* Boston: Houghton Mifflin, 1985.

Wiggins, G. *Assessing Student Performance.* San Francisco: Jossey-Bass, 1993.

PART TWO

CHANGING CONFIGURATIONS IN EDUCATION AND SOCIAL RESEARCH

CHAPTER FIVE

Sociology and the Study of Education

Continuity, Discontinuity, and the Individualist Turn

Charles E. Bidwell

The example of the interdependence of theoretical and methodological movements in social science and in social science research on education that I present in this chapter illustrates how social science research on education is subject to, and responsive to, the same field of intellectual and institutional forces as is social science generally. I focus on a paradigm shift in sociology that has had transformative effects on sociological scholarship. This shift was fully evident by the 1960s, and its consequences have been particularly visible in sociological research on education. I draw on sociology and on relationships between sociology and education research for my example because this discipline is the one I know best.

The paradigm shift was marked at its inception by a sudden, sharp rise in emphasis on explaining social phenomena in individualist terms. There was a concomitant decline of emphasis on the analysis of structural relationships in societies and on their major institutions and organizational forms. This change of intellectual focus I call the *individualist turn*.

Empirical sociologists turned away from comparative research and reliance on the field observation of socially structured situations, replacing these methods with extensive use of surveys of large populations of individuals. The responses of these individuals to questionnaires and other instruments designed to measure their individual states of mind, individual states of being, and individual patterns of behavior became the objects of analysis.

The individualist turn was most pronounced in the study of social stratification and social mobility, where research has come to center on variation in individuals' occupational attainment and on the distribution of life chances among persons. This research is commonly known as *status attainment research*. The study of education, which had been of keen interest to a number of the sociological founding fathers, gained a new legitimacy and importance in the sociological enterprise because, within the status attainment frame, education itself could be thought of as an individual attainment and as a resource that people could use in the labor market.

Despite the individualist turn, there were some notable continuities in sociology that link the work of earlier scholars with those who followed in a more strictly institutional or cultural tradition. In addition, from the 1950s onward, much else has been afoot in sociology, including the appearance of hermeneutic and critical analysis. Nevertheless, until quite recently these developments remained on the margins of the mainstream of sociology, and it is the mainstream that I want to examine. Now there is much ferment, in both theory and method, in sociology and cognate disciplines, so that provocative new pathways for social science and education research are opening. The two chapters that follow explore two of these pathways in some detail, one deriving from a new methodological and political self-consciousness in social anthropology, the other from investigations of local and public or cosmopolitan knowledge.

THE SOCIOLOGICAL HERITAGE IN THE STUDY OF EDUCATION

By midcentury sociologists interested in education could choose among five principal theoretical traditions, each with a distinctive substantive focus:

- Education in the class and status group relations of types of societies
- Education as a cultural expression and medium of social control
- Schools in the social fabric of communities
- Organizational structures and processes of schools
- Education and social mobility in major historical societies

These five sociological traditions have a fundamental element in common. The phenomena that each seeks to explain are components of social organization or culture that pertain to whole societies or to major parts of societies. The principal things to be explained also are social organizational or cultural.

Education in Class and Status Relations: Max Weber

The first of these traditions comes primarily from Max Weber's comparative studies of historical societies. In large part his was an effort to classify societal forms and uncover the processes underlying variation of these forms in time and space. Although Weber did not write systematically about education, at various points in *Economy and Society* (1968) he dealt with one or the other of two major educational topics: the relationships between types of education and types of status group relations and the consequences of change in the nature of these relations for the structure and curricula of universities.

Weber explained how the access of status groups to university education and how the political capacity of these status groups to influence policies, govern access, and influence offerings differ from one historical society and era to another. He drew out this analysis most fully with respect to the European societies of his day and, in them, the emergence of a university curriculum devoted to specialized programs to prepare for the professions and bureaucratic offices.

Weber argued that the growing scope and supremacy of rational modes of thought and bureaucratic organization rendered the liberal arts largely irrelevant to the status, occupational, and political interests of a rising commercial and professional bourgeoisie. He concluded that the university curriculum and provisions governing access to the universities would necessarily become endemic issues of political contention in the liberal-democratic European states.

Education as a Cultural and Social Expression: Emile Durkheim

Emile Durkheim's writings on education form a distinctive strand in his body of work. This corpus includes *The Evolution of Pedagogy* (1977), an analysis of the rise and development of university education in France. Durkheim treats the evolution of the French university from its medieval origins in part as an expression of the idea of universal knowledge. But it also is a matter of evolving organizational forms (for example, autonomy and progressive differentiation into faculties and subject matters), which could be explained as outcomes of an interplay of demographic and ecological forces. These forces provided favorable conditions for the interest-driven action of corporate groups, including at various times groups of teachers, church officials, students, and organs of the newly forming state.

Durkheim's work also includes *Moral Education* (1961). These lectures were given at the Sorbonne in 1902–1903 when the secularizing Third Republic was entering its fourth decade. Here, Durkheim proposes education as a secular basis for values and habits of conduct, and thus for social order. Socialization in school would supplant socialization in the church and family. Durkheim considers how the capacity of schools to socialize students for citizenship in the secular nation-state is provided by classroom social structure, the consequent daily round of life in the classroom, and a curriculum dominated by rational knowledge. This analysis is grounded on a prior analysis of the structural and moral character of the rising national state—in particular, the weakening of such primordial bonds as those of kinship and local community, the flattening of social differences in the face of a common national citizenship, and, as in

Weber, the decline of traditional beliefs and the rise of science, skepticism, and rationality.

In the blossoming national age of rationalism and declining tradition, Durkheim concluded, socialization in the bosom of the family is a parochial socialization for difference and individual uniqueness rather than citizenship, so that the more appropriate preparation for citizenship is to be found in the school, which treats children as members of a shared social category (the students in a given school class) and can expose them to a cosmopolitan culture of science and reflective thought. Here, no less than in his sociological history of French education, the approach and the conceptual apparatus are social structural and cultural.

Education, Community, and Social Control: The Chicago School

The founders of the Chicago school of sociology, including Albion Small, W. I. Thomas, Robert Park, and Ernest Burgess, had a considerable interest in education as one of the institutional foundations of social control. This view is elaborated most fully in the essays on social control in Park and Burgess's *Introduction to the Science of Sociology* (1921). Park and Burgess gave social control a capacious definition: any process through which a social group can consider and affect the ends and means of its collective activity.

For the Chicago sociologists, the primary issue was to identify processes that promote the integration of various levels of social formation, from very large societies to small communities. Accommodation and assimilation provide the structural and cultural foundation of social control. Education becomes a central "device" of social control (Park and Burgess, 1921, p. 339) by virtue of its efficiency in maintaining the cultural basis of social interchange: the community of language, belief, and sentiment that undergirds capacity for the collective guidance of collective activity. It is individual persons, of course, who are educated, and the mediation of social processes through the behavior of individuals is implicit throughout. Still, the focus is on the collective outcome rather than its substrate in what people do individually.

The Social Organization of Schools: Willard Waller

The analysis of the social organization of the school received its first definitive statement by Willard Waller in *The Sociology of Teaching* (1932), which at its core is a structural analysis of the American high school. Waller provides an explanation of key structural attributes of these schools. He begins with the work that schools do, in particular the dilemmas that confront teachers and students as they go about their work. For teachers, these dilemmas arise from the nature of teaching: how to balance intimacy and social distance in a context in which the teacher must be both supportive and judgmental. For students, the dilemmas arise from subordination to the authority of parents and community,

and derivatively to that of teachers and principals, who require them to be educated. Students try to find paths of least effort through their class work. In a
way reminiscent of workers on many a shop floor, they band together to deflect
or resist teachers' standards of performance.

Waller does not limit himself to the classroom. He discusses how social control in the school itself may be achieved, especially through athletics and other
collective representations that permit students to identify with the school and
form positive bonds with others in the school.

Undergirding the whole of Waller's structural analysis of the high school is
a penetrating discussion of limits placed on high schools by local constituents.
These limits derive from the subordination of school officials to local elites, who
in effect become political agents in the matter of education, insisting on preserving the school as "a museum of virtue," in which young people are safe-
guarded from the moral compromises of adult life and exposed to the rudiments
of an ennobling (if not practically useful) high culture.

Waller gives much attention to the ways in which these structures and
events, in combination with systems of popular and professional beliefs about
the nature of school knowledge, divorce the school from the natural world of
childhood (Cohen, 1989). He is concerned with the consequences of this dis-
tancing not only for the experiences of individual students and teachers, but
also for social control in the school and for the school's coherence as an organization. Thus, Waller presents the first rounded account of the nature of
schools as organizations to be encountered in either the sociological or the educational literature.

Education and Social Mobility: Pitirim Sorokin

I have left Pitirim Sorokin on social mobility to the last because the topic of
social mobility is substantively central to the individualist turn in sociology and
the sociology of education. Sorokin (1927) asserts that all societies must con-
tain "channels of vertical mobility, which are as necessary as channels for blood
circulation in the body" (p. 180). *Social Mobility* (1927) is Sorokin's attempt to
show how historical societies differ in the primary institutional channels
through which talent of various kinds—mental, physical, and moral—circulates
upward and downward. Sorokin presents a series of propositions about the relative prominence of one or another of these mobility channels—social institutions like commerce, the church, the military, the schools—within which
individuals are prepared, tested, and allocated to stratified social positions
according to technical proficiency and moral fitness.

The conditions affecting the primacy of one or another of these institutional
channels include historical circumstance (such as periods of war during which
the military is a prime mobility channel or religious enthusiasm in which
expanding denominations and sects provide substantial mobility opportunities).

They also include economic characteristics that affect the relative importance of economic organizations and professions.

Sorokin views education as a significant mobility channel in most periods and historical societies, its effect on the incidence and rates of vertical mobility depending primarily on the degree to which a society's schools are under the control of an elite (an aristocracy or owners of capital, for example) that limits the access of persons of lower social standing.

Although social mobility at root is a movement of persons, Sorokin is not interested in explaining variation in the life chances of these individuals. Instead he is interested in the rates of movement of persons in and out of the various strata in a society, especially the degree to which elite strata remain closed and therefore self-reproducing. He examines the consequences of these rates for a society's health, especially the degree to which blockages in a society's mobility regime prevent a refreshment of talent or moral probity among its economic, political, or religious leadership.

In his stress on the efficient allocation of talent and moral fitness to social positions, Sorokin forecasts the soon-to-appear functionalist analysis of social stratification and its consequences for social integration and productivity. The functionalist analysis, however, led much of sociology, and sociological studies of education with it, in a very different direction than the institutional approach that Sorokin and the greater number of earlier European and American sociologists took for granted as the foundations of their scholarship.

THE INDIVIDUALIST TURN AND
THE STUDY OF STATUS ATTAINMENT

World War II disturbed the course of sociological scholarship worldwide, but by the 1950s in the United States the individualist turn had gained dominant theoretical and methodological force. This development was no less true of sociological work on education than of sociology in general. Institutionally centered work moved from the center to the periphery of the discipline. Part and parcel of this movement, the rise of the status attainment paradigm was accompanied by a prodigious proliferation of research on the distribution of individuals' occupational and educational life chances in the American population. The contrast with Sorokin on social mobility is clear and sharp.

Status attainment research is an effort to uncover the mechanisms at work in individuals' lives that explain their social mobility. The principal achievements studied are occupational (job prestige, income, and so on). The portion of the life course under analysis usually is bounded by schooling and occupational maturity (often the job held at age forty-five). In status attainment models, the predictors of attainment, like attainment itself, are attributes of individuals, such as their total years of schooling, their early occupational aspirations, or parental occupational prestige or educational attainment.

Peter Blau and Otis Dudley Duncan, in *The American Occupational Structure* (1967), made the definitive statement of the status attainment paradigm. They applied it to a major set of survey data about the social origins, education, and occupational histories of a national sample of American males who had entered full-time employment in different periods of American social and economic change.

Their basic theoretical model is simple. The respondent's occupational prestige at age forty-five is predicted by the prestige in 1962 (the date of the survey) of his first full-time job, the number of years of education he had attained, and the occupational prestige of his father's job, along with the number of years of education that his father and mother had completed. This model is arranged in such a way that the attributes of the respondent's parents can affect his occupational attainment (the first job and the job in 1962) both directly and through the respondent's educational attainment. The respondent's year of school, in turn, can affect his 1962 occupational prestige both directly and through the prestige of his first job.

For present purposes, this model has two noteworthy characteristics. First, it makes no explicit assumptions about the correspondence of occupational prestige ranks with such social strata as classes or status groups. Indeed an accompanying, highly influential methodological contribution of Duncan was the development of a reliable scale that assigns prestige scores to a large array of jobs. The scale is based on survey responses of national samples of U.S. adults (Duncan, 1961). It has proved to be replicable over time and across economically developed national societies.

Whereas a formulation like Sorokin's conceives of vertical mobility as movement between discrete social strata, here vertical mobility is presented as attainment along the continuum of prestige scores, whether the mobility occurs between generations (that is, the difference between father's occupational prestige and son's occupational prestige) or within an individual life (that is, the difference between the prestige of a first job and a later job).

Second, the model does not represent the mechanisms through which these various effects may take place. For example, if parental occupational prestige has a direct effect on the occupational prestige of the son's first job, net of any effect of son's educational attainment, this effect presumably measures some sort of occupational inheritance, but of what kind? Is it an advantage conferred by family wealth, connections, the influence of upbringing within a particular set of values or expectations, or something else?

In other words, the social organization of occupational mobility and the interplay of social structural and normative forces in mobility processes remain essentially implicit. Blau and Duncan draw a variety of inferences about such matters from their data. To this end, they make excellent use of comparisons between the attainment patterns of birth cohorts, but explicit theoretical attention remains on the individual. Society becomes a context in which institutional forms are not clearly seen, given the assumption that social status is continuous. This context remains in the background, while individuals' movement toward occupational maturity is in the foreground analytically. This implicitness of social and cultural mechanisms is no less true of Blau and Duncan's treatment of education, which appears only as years of school completed.

An influential attempt to model the processes involved in educational attainment itself was made by William H. Sewell and his colleagues at the University of Wisconsin (Sewell, Haller, and Portes, 1969), as part of a longitudinal study of the status attainment of a birth cohort of non-farm Wisconsin males. In the Wisconsin model, the individual's ultimate occupational attainment (again measured by prestige) is influenced most immediately by educational attainment, and both kinds of attainment are presented as functions of prior aspirations. These aspirations, in turn, are affected by significant others' influence, arising in face-to-face encounters that allow the other either to serve as a model for the individual or to communicate expectations for behavior.

No more than the Blau-Duncan model does the Wisconsin model incorporate the social organizational or cultural matrix of the events that it represents. In the Wisconsin model, influence on educational attainment during the school years is expected to come from three principal sets of others: parents, teachers, and peer friends. Yet neither family structure, nor school organization, nor the friendship circle appears in the Wisconsin model. Sewell and his collaborators, like Blau and Duncan, trace the sources of educational and occupational attainment ultimately to family social status. But because family social status is measured by continuous indicators, their model, like Blau and Duncan's, does not directly address variation in life chances associated with class or status group differences in family resources, values and beliefs, or opportunities for education.

Following quickly on the appearance of *The American Occupational Structure* and early papers from Sewell's project, the literature on educational attainment expanded rapidly, keeping pace with the growth of the entire status attainment literature. The work on educational attainment includes a series of major studies that provides a fuller specification of the student's environment of significant others and their influence (among others, Alexander and Eckland, 1973; Kerckhoff, 1974; Rehberg and Rosenthal, 1978; Williams, 1972). These studies remained mute about the social structural and cultural systems within which the processes of educational attainment presumably take place.

In sum, by the mid-1970s, research on status attainment had largely supplanted all other research on social mobility and social stratification in the United States, taking a dominant place in the core sociology journals (in particular, the *American Sociological Review*, the official general research journal of the American Sociological Association). Very few sociologists now were giving sustained empirical attention to issues of class or status groups, although a growing number of sociologists, primarily on the theoretical side of the discipline, were reviving Marxian ideas about class relations in society in a challenge to the reigning attainment paradigm. (See, for example, Wright, 1979.)

The symbiosis of sociological and educational inquiry during this period can be seen clearly in *Equality of Educational Opportunity* (Coleman and others, 1966). This early venture into large-scale policy research on education opened the sociological study of education to the status attainment paradigm, now focused directly on the processes affecting individual students' academic achievement. Responding to the growing political force of the civil rights movement, the Congress had commissioned a study of national scope. Harold Howe, U.S. Commissioner of Education, specified the charge of the study as an examination of "the lack of availability of educational opportunity for individuals by reason of race, color, religion, or national origin, in all levels of public education" (Coleman and others, 1966, p. iii).

James Coleman became the director of this study and, with the sociologist-collaborators whom he assembled, addressed four questions:

1. How much racial and ethnic segregation can be observed in the public schools?

2. How equally are educational opportunities distributed among the students in these schools?

3. Grade by grade, how much do students vary in academic achievement?

4. To what extent are differences in achievement associated with differences between schools in quality of education?

The study was based on survey data collected from a large sample of public elementary and high schools and of students in those schools. Educational opportunity and quality of education were measured by the amounts of resources available in the schools, such as per pupil expenditures, number of library books per pupil, and school-level averages of teachers' verbal ability. The validity of these measures and the appropriateness of the methods of data analysis (the estimation of student-level ordinary least squares regression models) were the subject of heated debate for some time after publication of the study. (See Mosteller and Moynihan, 1972.)

Few questions were raised about the individualist paradigm within which the study was framed. I want to stress that Coleman and his collaborators used essentially simple models that fall within the general status attainment rubric. Note that the phenomenon to be explained was the academic attainment of individual students. Among students comparably placed in the school grades, this individual achievement was to be accounted for by such attributes of the student as race and parental education and by the measures of school resources. Note that the latter measures, no less than the former, were treated in the analysis as if they could be attached to each student individually. Thus, the study in effect became a study of an individual student's access to resources that he or she might use in the pursuit of academic success, or that the teacher might use to help the student toward higher grades or higher test scores.

With the analysis framed in this way, Coleman and his colleagues found that personal attributes of these students were far and away more powerful predictors of achievement than attributes of their schools. Although in the descriptive results, modest between-school differences of attainment were seen, these differences essentially disappeared in the multivariate analysis. They were reduced to differences of student background. Coleman and his colleagues did compare results for regions of the country and found differences between the South and other regions, but these comparisons focused on the values of the attainment parameters as they occurred in various parts of the country—an ecology of educational status attainment, if you will.

Given the spirit of the times and the political climate of the mid-1960s, it is no surprise that this study gained the keen attention of policymakers, many of whom had counted on education as a tool to use in combating unequal educational opportunity, and the no-less-keen attention of social scientists who were themselves attuned to issues of opportunity and equality in the United States. Two streams of research followed on the heels of what came to be known as the Coleman report: studies in the tradition of the Wisconsin model concerned with the social psychology of academic aspiration and attainment and studies attempting to find properties of schools that would make them effective environments for students' attainment. (For a trenchant discussion of these literatures, see Dreeben, 1994.) In each case, the focus now was on the attaining individual student and the way resources for attainment were distributed among schools and therefore, presumably, between individual students.

These two streams have converged in work on ability grouping in the lower grades and tracking in the secondary schools, reviewed in an extended critical essay by Oakes, Gamoran, and Page (1992). This research has remained essentially social psychological, concerned with the ways in which ability groups and tracks provide a context for the achievement of individual students. It has yet to address ways in which curricular strata in schools, thought of as part of their social organization, affect a school's capacity to operate. We have learned a good deal from this research about the distribution of individual life chances, but not a great deal about how schools work and, therefore, how their workings affect the creation of educational opportunities.

SOURCES OF DISCONTINUITY

How are we to account for the triumphal march of the status attainment paradigm through sociological studies of mobility and stratification and sociological studies of the school? I think that converging forces in the intellectual, methodological, and social organization of American social science very nearly overly determined the outcome. As a result of these forces, the post–World War II years in the United States presented social science with a vastly different research environment from what had been in place in the 1920s, 1930s, and 1940s. To my mind, five sets of forces are of particular importance.

First, before 1950, sociological research was concentrated in a very few universities, mainly in the Midwest. By 1950 centers of active research in sociology had diffused substantially, to both coasts and a growing number of midwestern universities as well. In particular, with the rise of Harvard sociology and Parsonian functionalism in the 1950s, along with generative work in new survey analysis at Columbia, the sociology department at the University of Chicago lost its singularly preeminent position in the discipline.

At the same time, research funding (measured in constant dollars) was much more modest in the earlier decades than later, and it was concentrated on the few active research centers. A close tie between the department of sociology at Chicago and a handful of private foundations that supported social science was at the core of this relationship. These donors gave their support with few strings attached. (On these matters, see Bulmer, 1984.)

This environment favored small-scale research, centered in the library or in fieldwork in a few theoretically interesting settings, with reliance on the comparative method for purposes of generalization. It also was an environment that did not encourage significant challenges to reigning theoretical and conceptual paradigms.

Second, to a degree as a spillover effect of the compelling concept of science as an endless frontier, the postwar period saw the federal government (through the National Science Foundation and the National Institute of Mental Health, in particular) and a new breed of policy-oriented foundations (such as the Ford Foundation) come to the fore to support social science. Sociology was one of the key recipients of this support. Where the earlier generation of benefactors had taken a relatively disinterested view of the directions to be followed by the social scientists they supported, the new wave of funders had clear policy objectives and targeted their support accordingly. Issues of equity, especially the distribution of educational and economic opportunity, were central items on this agenda. Great numbers of sociologists happily subscribed. These changes in the social science landscape in themselves opened a broad and smooth entryway into the study of individuals' life chances in school and in the labor market.

Third, the 1950s were marked by mutually supportive technological and methodological developments in social science that turned attention to the individual level of analysis and explanation. The years following World War II saw the appearance of high-speed calculation and ancillary hardware (like the IBM counter sorter) that allowed even independent scholars to reduce large amounts of data to manageable units quickly and efficiently and then to proceed with their quantitative analysis.

This development provided one of the prime bases for the equally rapid development of survey research as a key method in social science. In addition, this was the time when the first generation of survey research organizations grew dramatically: the Bureau of Applied Social Research at Columbia University, the National Opinion Research Center at the University of Chicago, and the Institute for Social Research at the University of Michigan. Growth of the survey research enterprise was stimulated by the equally rapid growth of public opinion polling (the Gallup and Roper organizations, most notably).

The measurement of public opinion had received a substantial methodological boost during World War II from governmental concern for assessing the effectiveness of propaganda. This effort resulted in the development of precise methods for asking questions and assessing the reliability of the answers received, in interviews and through the use of questionnaires. Employment of these techniques in market research created a substantial demand for the services of survey research organizations. Subsequent use of these techniques to measure all sorts of social phenomena, including phenomena previously the province of comparative social structural and cultural analysis, was natural.

The development and expanding topical scope of survey research were furthered also by the appearance of methods of multivariate quantitative analysis, especially ordinary least squares (OLS) estimation. In its logic, OLS does not differ from earlier methods devised to analyze survey data that are based on the cross-tabulation of the frequency distributions of two or more categorical variables. (See Lazarsfeld, 1955; Stouffer and others, 1949; Rosenberg, 1968.) Nevertheless, OLS for many purposes is far superior because it can be used with continuous variables and with many predictor variables simultaneously.

OLS permits the researcher to work with a large body of data like the questionnaire responses of a sizable sample of research subjects. One can evaluate such models as the status attainment model, estimating effects of each predictor on an outcome (like the effect of paternal occupational prestige on son's occupational prestige), net of the effects of all other variables in the model (like the effect of son's educational level on son's occupational prestige). Simply from the technological and methodological standpoints, it was no accident that virtually all status attainment research and research on educational attainment and school effects have employed survey data, analyzed with OLS and its successors.

OLS imposes a notable limitation on the user. It can be used appropriately with data from only one level of aggregation. Thus, for example, if it is to be used in the analysis of data about individuals' attitudes or behavior, the data cannot also include measures of their social or cultural situations, unless these measures are treated as if they indicated attributes of the individual respondent. Thus, Coleman and his colleagues treated measures of school attributes as if they were attributes of the individual students in these schools.

In this way, the movement toward survey research, undergirded by the tools of multivariate analysis, provided a powerful impulse toward individual-centered social science. In the process, mechanisms involved in relationships between social attributes of social and cultural environments and the attitudes and behavior of the individuals surveyed could be inferred but not directly measured. Attention to these mechanisms, to say nothing of relationships and mechanisms at the level of society and culture themselves, inevitably moved toward the background and out of the field of vision of many sociological researchers, including those interested in education.

Fourth, we must take into account a powerful drive among midcentury social scientists to be, and to be recognized as, legitimate, generalizing scientists. Sociologists from Durkheim and Weber forward have engaged in sociological research as a generalizing enterprise and, concomitantly, as a rejection of historicist analysis of singular, particular cases (whether singular societies or singular types of formal organizations, for example). The comparative method was a step away from historicist analysis, and survey analysis was a seemingly larger one. It permitted generalization from data gathered about large populations of persons, potentially disparate in their demographic attributes and social situations. Thus, although in principle OLS analysis can be applied to any level of aggregation, including relationships between structural and cultural attributes of collectivities, the tendency toward applications at the individual level was reinforced.

At the same time, partly as an effort to gain legitimacy in the realm of the sciences and partly as a result of more autonomous epistemological developments, it became a dictum for most empirical social scientists to explain any relationship between social or cultural aggregates in terms of constitutive individual-level processes. Thus, a relationship between the specialization of work in an organization and the organization's administrative form might be explained by failures of individual specialist workers to communicate with one another that stimulated administrative intervention. Just as particle physics has sought to explain properties of matter, so the analysis of individual action intervening between aggregate social states would explain the nature of those states and their patterns of change.

Sociologists have become increasingly preoccupied with the "micro–macro problem," that is, with identifying the processes through which social forms emerge from individual and dyadic actions and the mechanisms through which social forms constrain what people think and do (Blau, 1964; Coleman, 1990). As long as OLS held methodological sway, the micro-macro problem could not be attacked directly with empirical evidence, and sociological attention remained fixed on the micro-level of analysis, thereby reinforcing the individualist turn.

Fifth, consider the profound effect of sociological functionalism. Functionalism entered American sociology from British anthropology. The anthropological functionalists (Rivers, 1913; Malinowski, 1926, 1939; Radcliffe-Brown, 1935) were influenced by physiological conceptions of the biological organism as a system in which each process contributes to the whole organism's welfare. They sought to explain elements of social structure and culture "by their function, by the part which they play within the integral system" (Malinowski, 1926, pp. 132–133). It was the intention of the leading functional theorists in sociology, Talcott Parsons (1951; Parsons and Bales, 1952) and his student Robert Merton (1949), to refine and use this general approach to explain properties of social structure and to explicate the operation of social processes.

Like the Chicago sociologists, Parsons had a special interest in processes of social control, which he defined as the problem of social integration. In particular, Parsons was interested in how the parts of a structurally and normatively differentiated society could be coherent and orderly and how such a society could change adaptively without losing its essential form. This definition of social control is similar to that used by Park and Burgess. Nevertheless, as Parsons elaborated it in *The Social System* (1951), the analysis of social control had much to do with the problem of deviance, that is, the departure of individuals' behavior from the normative expectations governing their roles in society.

Deviance might be conceptualized at the level of a whole collectivity, as a rate similar epistemologically to the mobility rates that Sorokin studied. Parsons, however, focused on the genesis of the individual acts that would comprise such a rate. His analysis is twofold. He depicts social structural mechanisms that would weaken an individual's tendency to deviate, such as the isolation of already-deviant persons from others in the society in prisons or enclosed worlds of criminality. He gives equal attention to the psychodynamic processes that affect an individual's willingness and ability to follow role expectations as a consequence of the strength and durability of that person's "internalization" of these role norms and the institutionalized values on which Parsons assumed they were based.

In this formulation, compliance is subject to rewards and punishments, and the rewards and punishments that are central in Parsons's theory arise in face-to-face relationships—relationships between the person in question and other individual actors to whom that person is related, such as parents, employers, colleagues, and friends. Thus, although Parsons probed deeply into the micro-macro problem, for him the fundamental social processes are micro-social. Their consequences for social integration in fact are attributed primarily not to societal or other larger-scale collective events, but to events within the individual personality, in a context of immediate, local social experience. During the 1950s, Parsons's functionalist theory of the social system and its controlling processes became the dominant theoretical approach in sociology, and its dominance gave its own strong impetus to the individualist turn.

CONTINUITIES IN SOCIOLOGY AND THE SOCIOLOGY OF EDUCATION

Despite the pervasiveness of the individualist turn and the concomitant dominance of the status attainment paradigm, certain sociologists and fields of sociological research continued in the institutionalist, comparative tradition. A selective review of these continuities will be instructive.

Formal Organizations and the Organization of Schools

In the sociological study of formal organizations, the comparative approach has remained strong, although now involving comparisons between different types of organizations rather than different societies. The objective of this work is to explain variation in organizations' structural form. In the 1960s, Charles Perrow (1970), Joan Woodward (1967), and James Thompson (1967) developed sociotechnical theory, while others, again including Thompson (1967) and, as well, Paul Lawrence and Jay Lorsch (1967) and Jeffrey Pfeffer and Gerald Salancik (1978), developed resource dependence and contingency theories.

The proponents of the sociotechnical approach traced variation in organizational form to variation in production technology (for example, relating the steepness of a hierarchy of offices to the degree to which steps in production are interdependent). The proponents of resource dependence and contingency theory have found sources of variation in organizational structure in properties of organizations' environments (for instance, the proposition that the more powerful units in an organization are those that deal with the turbulent, unpredictable sectors of its environment).

These theories do not fit the case of schools very well, and the theoretical puzzle that they present has had a generative effect on further organizational analysis. For James March and his collaborators (see especially March and Olsen, 1976) and Karl Weick (1976), the puzzle was the peculiar fact that school systems have a substantial administrative apparatus without evidently strong administrative involvement in the oversight of instruction and despite generally placid, predictable environments.

To resolve this puzzle, Weick proposed that some organizations, like schools, can display "loose coupling," especially between the organization's productive activities and its administrative cadre. Stimulated by this proposition, the next generation of organizational theorists has argued that organizational form is responsive less to instrumental problems of administration or control than to the power of ideas, systems of meaning, and normative structures (both professional and popular) to shape understandings of what a proper organization of a given kind (a school, a hospital, a government agency, a company) looks like and how it operates. These understandings, they continue, constrain the structures and processes of the organizations themselves. (See Meyer and Rowan, 1978; DiMaggio and Powell, 1983.)

Cross-National Comparisons of Educational Systems

Cross-national comparisons and the analysis of historical societies have continued variously in research on the rise and expansion of national educational systems and studies of the implication of education in national economic and political development.

In 1962 Martin Trow published a widely cited paper on relationships between education and social stratification in which the approach is very much like that of Sorokin. That is, the expansion of education in contemporary societies is seen as a response to expansion and contraction in the labor market, mediated by the testing and allocating processes that occur in schools. Some ten years later Randall Collins (1975) presented a subtle, stratification-based analysis in which, following Weber, he treated access to education and forms of education in the present day as matters of intense status group competition and conflict.

To date, the analysis of educational expansion as an outcome of class or status group conflict has been less influential than demand-based explanations (for example, Craig, 1981; Garnier and Hage, 1991; and Walters, 1984). Demand-based theory, however, has been challenged by scholars who move beyond narrower class or status conflict formulations into accounts that consider political processes involving multiple corporate actors and correspondingly multiple bases of interest formation.

This theoretical development owes much to the work of the English sociologist Margaret Archer (1984). Archer presented a systematic theory to explain variation in the emerging form of educational systems that incorporates many of the elements of Durkheim's focus on the interaction of group interests in the rise of the French universities. She applied this theory to comparative national cases.

The 1960s saw the appearance of a substantial sociological enterprise involving research into relationships between educational provision and the economic and political emergence and stabilization of developing nations (among others, Anderson, 1963; Foster, 1965; McGinn, 1980). This work was part of a larger movement involving studies of societal "modernization" that has strong Weberian roots. (See Inkeles and Smith, 1974; Lipset, 1979.)

John Meyer and various collaborators (Meyer and Hannan, 1979; Meyer, Kamens, and Benavot, 1992; Meyer, Ramirez, and Soysal, 1992) have undertaken a systematic program that has roots in both of these lines of inquiry, investigating the sources of an apparent convergence of structures and curricula in the national educational systems of the post–World War II world. This research draws heavily on propositions about the global diffusion of understandings of the nation-state, of citizenship, and of the role of education in state building to explain observed organizational and curricular convergence among national educational systems.

The older institutional and comparative tradition, then, is far from dead, but the continuity has been far from stultifying. It seems fair to say that the areas of continuity are also areas of theoretical ferment. The continuities are dynamic, with outcomes for our sociological understanding of education that are not yet clear. By now status attainment research has become both conceptually and methodologically routine, and it is from the livelier sociological fields like those I have described that research advances are likely to come.

That there are continuing strands of institutional and comparative studies of education can be attributed in part to the efforts of tough-minded, independent scholars. But it is notable that the substantive areas in which their work has advanced are, by virtue of the social and political organization of sociology, domains that have enjoyed substantial intellectual and programmatic independence of the field of forces that have acted on the status attainment enterprise.

Both the study of organizations and the study of national development have strong bearing on fields of social practice, in the United States and elsewhere. These connections have in each case created potent networks of supporting constituencies in the academy, governments, business, and the world of international agencies. This connectedness has opened sources of research funding and policy support that have stood considerably apart from the policy issues that have motivated support for status attainment research. Thus, my examples of discontinuity and continuity in sociology and in the sociology of education teach the same lesson: that social science and social science research in education are part of a single community of intellectual and professional fate.

References

Alexander, K. L., and Eckland, B. *Effects of Education on the Social Mobility of High School Sophomores Fifteen Years Later (1955–1970)*. Chapel Hill: Institute for Research in Social Science, University of North Carolina, 1973.

Anderson, C. A. "The Effect of the Educational System on Technological Change and Modernization." In Bert F. Hoselitz and Wilbert H. Moore (eds.), *Industrialization and Society* (pp. 259–276). London: Mouton, 1963.

Archer, M. S. *Social Origins of Educational Systems*. Thousand Oaks, Calif.: Sage, 1984.

Blau, P. M. *Exchange and Power in Social Life*. New York: Wiley, 1964.

Blau, P. M., and Duncan, O. D. *The American Occupational Structure*. New York: Wiley, 1967.

Bulmer, M. *The Chicago School of Sociology: Institutions, Diversity, and the Rise of Sociological Research*. Chicago: University of Chicago Press, 1984.

Cohen, D. K. "Willard Waller: On Hating School and Loving Education." In D. J. Willower and W. L. Boyd (eds.), *Willard Waller on Education and Schools* (pp. 79–107). Berkeley, Calif.: McCutchan, 1989.

Coleman, J. S. *Foundations of Social Theory.* Cambridge, Mass.: Belknap Press of Harvard University Press, 1990.

Coleman, J. S., and others. *Equality of Educational Opportunity.* Washington, D.C.: U.S. Government Printing Office, 1966.

Collins, R. *Conflict Sociology.* New York: Academic Press, 1975.

Craig, J. E. "The Expansion of Education." *Review of Research in Education,* 1981, *9,* 151–213.

DiMaggio, P. J., and Powell, W. W. "The Iron Cage Revisited: Institutional Isomorphism and Collective Rationality in Organizational Fields." *American Sociological Review,* 1983, *48,* 147–160.

Dreeben, R. "The Sociology of Education: Its Development in the United States." In Aaron M. Pallas (ed.), *Research in Sociology of Education and Socialization* (Vol. 16, pp. 7–52). Greenwich, Conn.: JAI Press, 1994.

Duncan, O. D. "A Socioeconomic Index for All Occupations." In Albert J. Reiss, Jr. (ed.), *Occupations and Social Status* (pp. 109–131). New York: Free Press, 1961.

Durkheim, E. *The Evolution of Educational Thought.* London: Routledge and Kegan Paul, 1977.

Durkheim, E. *Moral Education.* New York: Free Press, 1961.

Foster, P. W. *Education and Social Change in Ghana.* Chicago: University of Chicago Press, 1965.

Garnier, M., and Hage, J. "Class, Gender, and School Expansion in France." *Sociology of Education,* 1991, *64,* 229–250.

Inkeles, A., and Smith, D. H. *Becoming Modern.* Cambridge, Mass.: Harvard University Press, 1974.

Kerckhoff, A. *Ambition and Attainment.* Washington, D.C.: American Sociological Association, 1974.

Lawrence, P. R., and Lorsch, J. W. *Organization and Environment: Managing Differentiation and Integration.* Cambridge, Mass.: Division of Research, Graduate School of Business, Harvard University, 1967.

Lazarsfeld, P. F. "Interpretation of Statistical Relations as a Research Operation." In Paul F. Lazarsfeld and Morris Rosenberg (eds.), *The Language of Social Research.* New York: Free Press, 1955.

Lipset, S. M. *The First New Nation: The United States in Historical and Comparative Perspective.* New York: Norton, 1979.

McGinn, N. *Education and Development in Korea.* Cambridge, Mass.: Harvard University Press, 1980.

Malinowski, B. "Anthropology." In *Encyclopedia Britannica*. First Supplementary Volume (pp. 132–133). New York: Encyclopedia Britannica, 1926.

Malinowski, B. "The Group and the Individual in Functional Analysis." *American Journal of Sociology*, 1939, *44*, 938–964.

March, J., and Olsen, J. *Ambiguity and Choice in Organizations*. Bergen, Norway: Universitetsforlaget, 1976.

Merton, R. K. "Manifest and Latent Functions." In *Social Theory and Social Structure* (pp. 21–81). New York: Free Press, 1949.

Meyer, J. W., and Hannan, M. (eds.). *National Development and the World System: Educational, Economic, and Political Change*. Chicago: University of Chicago Press, 1979.

Meyer, J. W., Kamens, D., and Benavot, A. *School Knowledge for the Masses*. Bristol, Pa.: Falmer, 1992.

Meyer, J. W., Ramirez, F. O., and Soysal, Y. N. "World Expansion of Mass Education, 1870–1980." *Sociology of Education*, 1992, *65*, 128–149.

Meyer, J. W., and Rowan, B. "The Structure of Educational Organizations." In M. W. Meyer (ed.), *Environments and Organizations* (pp. 78–109). San Francisco: Jossey-Bass, 1978.

Mosteller, F., and Moynihan, D. P. (eds.) *On Equality of Educational Opportunity*. New York: Random House, 1972.

Oakes, J., Gamoran, A., and Page, R. (1992). "Curriculum Differentiation: Opportunities, Outcomes, and Meanings." In P. W. Jackson (ed.), *Handbook of Research on Curriculum* (pp. 570–608). New York: Macmillan, 1992.

Parks, R. E., and Burgens, E. W., (eds.). *Introduction to the Science of Sociology*. Chicago: University of Chicago Press, 1921.

Parsons, T. *The Social System*. Glencoe, Ill.: Free Press, 1951.

Parsons, T., and Bales, R. F. (eds.). *Toward a General Theory of Action*. Cambridge, Mass.: Harvard University Press, 1952.

Perrow, C. *Organizational Analysis: A Sociological View*. Belmont, Calif.: Wadsworth, 1970.

Pfeffer, J., and Salancik, G. R. *The External Control of Organizations: A Resource Dependence Perspective*. New York: HarperCollins, 1978.

Radcliffe-Brown, A. R. "On the Concept of Function in Social Science." *American Anthropologist*, 1935, *37*, 395–396.

Rehberg, R. A., and Rosenthal, E. R. (1978). *Class and Merit in the American High School*. New York: Longman, 1978.

Rivers, W. H. R. "Survival in Sociology." *Sociological Review*, 1913, *6*, 293–305.

Rosenberg, M. *The Logic of Survey Analysis*. New York: Basic Books, 1968.

Sewell, W. H., Haller, A. O., and Portes, A. "The Educational and Early Occupational Attainment Process." *American Sociological Review,* 1969, *34,* 82–92.

Sorokin, P. *Social Mobility.* New York: Harper, 1927.

Stouffer, S. A., and others. *The American Soldier: Adjustment During Army Life.* Princeton, N.J.: Princeton University Press, 1949.

Thompson, J. D. *Organizations in Action: Social Science Bases of Administrative Theory.* New York: McGraw-Hill, 1967.

Trow, M. A. "The Democratization of Higher Education in America." *European Journal of Sociology,* 1962, *3,* 231–262.

Waller, W. *The Sociology of Teaching.* New York: Wiley, 1932.

Walters, P. B. "Occupational and Labor Market Effects on Secondary and Post-Secondary Expansion in the United States, 1922–1979." *American Sociological Review,* 1984, *49,* 659–671.

Weber, M. *Economy and Society.* New York: Bedminster Press, 1968.

Weick, K. "Educational Organizations as Loosely Coupled Systems." *Administrative Science Quarterly,* 1976, *21,* 1–19.

Williams, T. "Educational Aspirations: Longitudinal Evidence on Their Development in Canadian Youth." *Sociology of Education,* 1972, *45,* 107–133.

Woodward, J. *Industrial Organization: Theory and Practice.* London: Oxford University Press, 1967.

Wright, E. O. *Class Structure and Income Determination.* New York: Academic Press, 1979.

CHAPTER SIX

From Society to School and Back Again

Questions About Learning in and for a World of
Complex Organizations

Elisabeth S. Clemens

D oes education prepare students for futures as good citizens, competent workers, and innovative researchers or entrepreneurs? A conviction that the correct answer is yes has long influenced both the political will to invest in education and many of the questions scholars asked about the relation of schooling and society. Of late, however, doubts have multiplied. Policy debates stumble over evidence that there is no straightforward relationship between educational spending and educational outcomes. Parents voice concern over the extent to which what students do learn in school helps them later in life. Although investment in education still appears to be a critical source of economic growth, there is little consensus over the mechanisms that link schooling and life beyond school. Like the barrier between the bloodstream and the brain, some fundamental disconnection seems to exist between formal education and the challenges presented by the larger world.

This disquiet echoes among scholars. The confidence of sociologists in addressing the relation between school and society has been shaken by empirical findings and theoretical claims. Repeatedly studies have failed to find the robust associations between educational resources and outcomes that common sense would have predicted. Theorists have argued that this weak connection between inputs and outputs is a central feature of the education system. Informed by their study of "institutionalized organizations" like schools, John Meyer and Brian Rowan (1977) asserted that the success of these organizations "depends on factors other than efficient coordination and control of productive activities. Independent of their productive efficiency, organizations that exist in highly elaborated institutional environments and succeed in becoming isomorphic with these environments gain the legitimacy and resources needed to survive" (p. 352).

Schools present one face to external audiences and quite another to their primary constituency: their students. The practical activity of schools, most importantly in the classroom, appears decoupled from the state agencies established to evaluate whether schools are performing well. Such decoupling raises further questions about the consequences of what it is that students do learn. If classrooms are effectively insulated from educational policy, how can we understand —and enhance—the capacity of education to produce effective workers and citizens?

More certainty and optimism can be found by approaching these questions from a different direction: How do knowledge, skills, or social ties produced in one setting carry over to other settings? Asked in this way, the question of how schooling relates to the rest of social life can be addressed by using recent theoretical advances in two areas of interdisciplinary scholarship: the social studies of science and organizational analysis. Scholars in these areas have paid extensive attention to the advantages of combining ethnographic, textual, and institutional analyses with more traditional sociological methodologies, such as survey or experimental research.

The potential benefits of applying insights from both areas to education research are suggested by three organizing questions: How do individuals extend what they learn in one setting, or in relation to one problem, to other settings or problems? What are the ties that link students, teachers, and administrators to opportunities in other social realms? How are schools or other educational organizations articulated with other social institutions?

These questions are posed within the context of a moment of economic transformation that invites reflection on the relation of schooling to the world of work. To the extent that American schools have prepared students for the workforce, they have been criticized for instilling obedience to hierarchy, adherence to routine, and deference to authority (Bowles and Gintis, 1976). Yet what was once a virtue in the eyes of economic elites may now be a vice insofar as recent economic developments often require greater technical literacy, flexibility, and ability to work within teams performing complex activities. For the sake of simplicity, this new economy may be characterized by an increasingly prominent knowledge-based sector (finance, research, professional services), a declining manufacturing sector, and a growing personal services sector in which direct interaction with clients rather than the manipulation of symbols is the central activity (Reich, 1991).

Against this highly stylized backdrop, one can then ask what sort of learning or capacity to learn is required to succeed in a "learning organization." Rather than assuming that education *should* prepare students for work or that it *does* so prepare them, this chapter explores the question, "What if"? Given a certain trajectory of economic development, *what if* schools really attempted to prepare students to succeed in that economic world? What questions would education researchers want to ask in order to ascertain how such a task should be approached and how well it is accomplished?

APPROACHES TO LEARNING ACROSS DOMAINS

Current research in the sociology of science and organizational analysis poses relational questions about learning: To what extent do individual organizations or laboratories present distinctive settings for a process of learning that is fundamentally situated (Lave and Wenger, 1991)? What is it that individuals, specifically students, acquire in one setting that is then applied to another?

In both the social studies of science and organizational analysis, the answers begin from an assumption of bounded rationality. Rather than simply learning more—whether specific information or generalized analytic skills—people acquire scripts and recipes (Powell and DiMaggio, 1991), exemplars (Kuhn, 1977), or "packages of theory and technology" (Fujimura, 1988) that are more or less applicable to other problems or settings. This orienting assumption is consistent with results from cognitive psychology that demonstrate differences in the task behavior between novices and experts (Scribner, 1984) and show how the organization of what people already know influences how they will acquire new knowledge (Kuhn, Garcia-Mila, Zohar, and Anderson, 1995). The assumption also opens the study of knowledge acquisition to the use of qualitative methods across a variety of settings for learning and the application of whatever is learned. Building on an appreciation that learning is fundamentally situated, these arguments raise important questions about how what is learned is organized and then applied to new situations.

Situated Learning

This concern for how knowledge is applied across domains is at odds with much recent ethnographic work in science studies. The latter line of research emphasizes the decidedly local character of scientific or expert knowledge: "All scientific work is situated—done in particular spaces, times, and locations, with particular material practices. Nothing is predetermined. Moreover, the material practices are differently constructed by the various participants in specific situations," write Adele Clark and Joan Fujimura (1992, p. 5). Moving away from images of scientific knowledge as an objective and widely accessible body of shared theories and facts, contemporary sociologists of science are as likely to distinguish among tacit, or local, forms of knowledge and public knowledge (Knorr-Cetina, 1981), often linking the former more closely to core processes of scientific discovery and innovation.

In this respect, the sociology of science echoes studies of the profoundly situated character of learning in both formal schooling institutions and everyday settings (Lave and Wenger, 1991). In an important study of scientific diffusion, for example, H. M. Collins (1982) emphasizes the role of interpersonal contacts and site visits for acquiring the tacit knowledge and craft skills needed to build a particular type of laser successfully: "The major point is that the transmission of skills is not done through the medium of the written word" (p. 54). Although scientific publications played a role in alerting research groups to what had been accomplished in other institutions, the "public" knowledge of the disciplines is portrayed as peripheral to the process of diffusing the innovation. For Collins, this finding has profound methodological implications. Whereas "paradigm groups" have been defined by shared adherence to a set of articulated scientific principles, theories, or research findings, Collins argues that

> an important difference between members of different paradigm groups (as I am using the idea) lies in the contents of their tacit understandings of the things that they may legitimately do with a symbol or a word or a piece of apparatus. Because the process of learning, or building up tacit understandings, is not like learning items of information, but is more like learning a language, or a skill, it must be investigated differently. To ask respondents directly for the sources of their tacit knowledge, or to assume that sociograms based on responses to questions about articulated knowledge necessarily picture the diffusion or development of tacit knowledge, is to confuse concept formation with information exchange [1982, p. 46].

If learning and innovation are essentially local, those who study broader social processes of learning and the cumulation of knowledge (or devise policies for education) must surely despair. Close ethnographic study of knowledge acquisition and transmission may tell us something about how the craft sense necessary to build a particular laser in a particular set of British laboratories was acquired, but a more transposable or multipurpose theory of knowledge acquisition appears, at least aesthetically, at odds with this vision of the profoundly situated or local character of scientific learning. The puzzle may be stated as a paradox: learning is fundamentally situated, yet most actors do not encounter novel settings or problems as utter dopes. What actors already know about settings and practices must, in some way, be at least partially transposable, if not necessarily generalizable.

Fortunately the ethnographic turn within the sociology of science has provided a corrective to its own profoundly situated understanding of expert knowledge. One of the founding pieces of this literature emphasized the inscription of knowledge for subsequent use in the laboratory, for transmission to others in the research group, or for more general diffusion to audiences of both specialists and generalists. From this perspective, the laboratory appears "as a system of literary inscription, an outcome of which is the occasional conviction of others that something is a fact" (Latour and Woolgar, 1986, p. 105; Latour, 1987, chap. 1).

This line of investigation draws attention away from the overwhelmingly local character of tacit knowledge to the processes by which what was once tacit is made public. These processes involve not only conventions of public discourse but also the invocation of more generally shared scripts—frameworks or narratives within which formerly local or tacit knowledge is imbued with connections to the more articulated terrain of public knowledge. While it may indeed be impossible to reproduce tacit understandings from such public knowledge (Collins, 1982, p. 54), it is equally difficult to acquire tacit knowledge without some shared public knowledge. Consequently a better understanding of the frameworks employed to link local to public knowledge is critical for understanding how education qualifies one to join that company of educated men and women.

The Importance of Narratives

In its emphasis on the frameworks that organize knowledge, the sociology of science intersects with prominent criticism directed at current pedagogical practice: the lack of attention paid to the importance of narratives in structuring learning at all levels through university education. In cognitive terms, such narratives serve as scaffolds for isolated discoveries or situation-specific learning. They "highlight what is canonical and expected in our way of looking at them, so that we could more easily discern what is 'fishy' and off-base and what, therefore, needs to be explicated" (Bruner, 1996, p. 125). In addition to identifying anomalies, narratives are tools for constructing parallels across different domains; at a motivational level, they help to answer the question of what purpose is served by this learning (Postman, 1995). Finally, narratives may serve as tools for discerning "what kind of situation this is" and thus for shaping the appropriation of prior learning to new settings.

These insights have provoked passionate calls for renewed concern with the provision of narratives in the process of education, but they also raise empirical questions for education research. Given that most students do manage to link events or facts into narratives, what sorts of narratives do they employ? Although my colleagues in history describe a subset of history majors who care only to learn lists of facts, many, if not most, students are not of this species. Consequently it is important to ask what narratives or frameworks they have found to order their knowledge. It is possible, after all, that the most widely available frameworks may distort or transform findings and events in systematic ways.

As Bruno Latour argues in his brilliant *The Pasteurization of France* (1988), by retelling a familiar tale of scientific genius in the style of Tolstoy's *War and Peace*, we can see beyond the typical hagiography of history or science with its emphasis on the "great man" or "genius." As with fiction, the scientific literature provides "stories that define for us who are the main actors, what happens to them, what trials they undergo"—to reassess "what one man can do," whether it is Napoleon, Kutuzov, or Pasteur (Latour, 1988, pp. 9, 13). For example, in a poll published in the *Washington Post* (Morin, 1996), respondents with the least accurate knowledge about current economic conditions—the rate of unemployment, inflation, corporate profits—were also the most likely to identify the president as having significant control over economic outcomes. To the extent that the "great man" narrative obscures the complex roles of Congress, corporations, financial markets, and other factors, this framework for organizing information produces impotent political diagnoses.

With respect to narratives, therefore, one may pose questions of equity in addition to those of excellence or adequacy. Are there categories of specific facts and findings that are consistently difficult to incorporate in the most available narratives? Are there patterned absences in the repertoires used by children to link specific discourse? Heilbrun argues that the limited available narratives for women's lives have made it difficult for them to write about those lives and, for many women, to figure out what to do after the dominant sequence of courtship, marriage, and childbearing has been played out or when it has not been completed. By extension, the distribution of narratives for interpreting and structuring action in the world may well shape the divergent experiences of members of a society.

Models for generating such a historical demography of narratives or scaffolds may be found in a rapidly growing line of work that extends across the study of organizations, social movements, and political history. Best exemplified by the work of Charles Tilly on repertoires of contention, this approach begins by asserting that individuals have mastered a repertoire or tool kit of modular forms of action or scripts or schema of interpretation. For the study of collective action, this assertion leads to procedures for coding contentious actions as they are reported in newspapers or other documents and tracking the shifting composition of repertoires over time and between nations (Tilly, 1995). For a study of discourse, one might track vocabularies, themes, characters, or plots in a variety of interviews or textual materials (Dobbin, 1994; Lamont, 1992). For an ethnographic study of the workplace, the changing distribution of interaction scripts across settings and over time provides an appropriate research strategy (Barley, 1986).

The mapping of such organizing frameworks or narratives also illuminates the interplay of learning within school and other social experiences. Extracurricular cultural capital matters not only because the children of more prosperous families tend to have more of it, but also because students from different backgrounds often possess different overarching narratives or frameworks that help them to order what is worth learning and why (Willis, 1977). The consequences of such organizing frameworks are not limited to formal education.

Transposing Learning

The literature on narratives highlights the processes by which fragments of learning are linked to frameworks within a single domain. But narratives alone do not provide an adequate answer to the question, What is it that individuals, specifically students, acquire in one setting in order to use it on another? Vivian Paley (1984), for example, noted how *Star Wars* provided a template for understanding hierarchy: "The children think a great deal about leaders and followers. They are increasingly aware of the social order that exists beyond their control. This is particularly true of the boys, whose tendency to play in large groups makes the establishment of leaders essential. The huge *Star Wars* cast enables everyone to be someone's boss. In the playground after lunch, Jonathan announces that he is Sandman. 'I'm the boss of the Jawas!' he says, although no one present is identified as the Jawas" (p. 23). Borrowed from popular culture, this vivid imagery of social hierarchy could be used—albeit imperfectly—to think about friendships among students.

Here again, ethnographic research in the sociology of science provides a useful starting point. Whether one begins from a belief in the profoundly local character of knowledge or from an assertion that shared paradigms (or research programs) define meaningful communities within science, the existence of scientific conversations that transcend locales or cross-disciplinary boundaries is theoretically problematic (Clemens, 1986). Consequently there has been growing interest in the character of boundary objects that facilitate collaboration or the transmission of knowledge across groups that differ in either tacit knowledge or disciplinary commitments. In her work on cancer research, Fujimura (1988) has argued that a "scientific bandwagon" was facilitated by the development of a "'standardized' package of oncogene theory and recombinant DNA technologies": "A package of theory and technology is a clearly defined set of conventions for action that helps reduce reliance on discretion and trial-and-error procedures" (p. 261; on the "transparency" of technologies, see Lave and Wenger, 1991, pp. 102–103). In contrast to the emphasis on situatedness in recent theories of learning (Lave and Wenger, 1991; Rogoff and Lave, 1984), a wide variety of theoretical perspectives in sociology and organizational analysis emphasize that schema are "transposable" (Sewell, 1992), that much innovation is rooted in analogical thinking, and that the real action in social life stems precisely from such operations.

This argument retains the emphasis on the embedded character of knowledge that characterizes many laboratory ethnographies, but treats the boundaries between locales as problematic, not absolute. Fujimura's interest in how "black-boxed" packages (to use Latour's terminology) help to stabilize the relations among or articulation between locales of scientific activity speaks directly to the question of how what is learned in one locale has consequences for what is known or done in another. Framed in these terms, research directed to the question of whether students can "learn to learn" through the mastery of general formulas or techniques would address the specific types of boundary objects that are observed in use in other settings or later in time. Narratives or familiar plot lines may serve as such boundary objects.

Beyond the construction of objects or packages that are designed to bridge either locales of inquiry or domains of knowledge, work in both the sociology of science and organizational analysis repeatedly identifies a second general mechanism for linking domains: analogy or metaphor. By making assessments that this situation or problem resembles another to which an appropriate response is already known, actors extrapolate prior learning to new challenges. In revisiting the concept of paradigm, for example, Thomas Kuhn (1977) argued that this highly influential (but ambiguous) term should be replaced by the concept of a disciplinary matrix, to include a scientific community's "preferred analogies" and "exemplars," which are "concrete problem solutions, accepted by the group as, in a quite usual sense, paradigmatic" (pp. 297–298). Thus a second project of cultural mapping would seek to identify the population of models for analogizing, either as found in instructional materials or as employed in use by students as they seek to make sense of new topics or problems.

Thick descriptions of the process by which children and adults analogize from one domain to another would also speak to the debate over the extent to which learning in a changing society with high rates of information flow should stress general formulas (or "tools for learning") or deeper understandings of specific domains of knowledge that might serve as the basis for the construction of powerful analogies. Here again methodologies developed to map changing repertoires of action or discourse could be easily appropriated.

This image of learning inverts—at least momentarily—the relationship between information and interpretation evident when E. D. Hirsch (1996) asserts that "cognitive research shows that there is an unavoidable interdependence between relational and factual knowledge, and that teaching a broad range of factual knowledge is essential to effective thinking both within domains and among domains" (p. 157). A more profoundly analogical model of learning would suggest that it is not so much the broad range of facts that matters as deep knowledge of a sufficient number of topics, allowing a student to construct the rich analogies that lead to innovative solutions.

THE ROLE OF LEARNING IN LEARNING ORGANIZATIONS

By emphasizing the extent to which learning must bridge domains or institutions, the preceding discussion has assumed a particular kind of social world—one constituted of multiple, often fragmented settings for social action. Within such a world, some settings may be more intimately linked than others to learning processes. Prominent in commentaries on the modern economy, for example, are claims that an increasingly important set of organizations can be characterized as "learning organizations" (Corcoran, 1993; Rheem, 1995). While quite susceptible to enthusiasm, this literature does provide a tool for describing certain systems of social organization within which analogical learning is particularly important and, by extension, for thinking about the patterns of social relationships in which learning is facilitated.

This shift in the level of analysis reveals a second set of potentially fruitful synergies between education research and recent developments in sociology. Turning from the individuals who learn skills to the networks that exist among those who have stakes in the organization of schooling, education researchers have demonstrated the importance of the ties among schools, families, and other community actors for the quality of educational outcomes (Bryk, Lee, and Holland, 1993; Coleman, Hoffer, and Kilgore, 1982). Yet here too there is room for much mutually advantageous exchange among research areas. Sociologists of science, notably Latour, have elaborated the ways in which knowledge is a medium for "enrolling allies" from other arenas—a practical skill useful to school administrators and students alike. Organizational sociologists have refined the analysis of ties, moving from analyses of resource dependency to the multiplex character of ties and the varying consequences of networks for getting jobs or other benefits (Granovetter, 1973). Pedagogical innovations, such as the increasing use of group work at all levels of the curriculum, speak to the generative capacity to form new ties that is often associated with discussions of social capital. At the level of both individual networks and the organization of schools or districts, these developments underscore the utility of analyzing the structure of learning situations.

The question of how to organize to promote learning has taken on new salience with recent economic developments. For some years now the pages of the popular business press have been heralding the dawn of a new sort of economy, one in which the economic health of the United States will be secured by its ability to reorganize industries (or promote new industries) to enhance flexibility, innovation, and learning. As former U.S. Secretary of Labor Robert Reich (1991) has argued, "The real economic challenge facing the United States in the years ahead—the same as that facing every other nation—is to increase the potential value of what its citizens can add to the global economy, by enhancing their skills and capacities and by improving their means of linking those skills and capacities to the world market" (p. 8). Two questions remain, however: What skills? and, How are these linkages to be formed? One place to begin addressing these issues is the growing literature on those organizations that are held out as exemplars of the economy to come: learning organizations.

Before linking studies of new economic forms to questions of educational practice, one must begin by confronting a level of analysis problem: in the former literature, organizations rather than individuals do the learning. On first inspection, therefore, the catchphrase *organizational learning* promises more than it delivers to those concerned for education. Read with an eye to questions of schooling, the literature on organizational learning has surprisingly little to say about processes of cognition. Instead these studies frequently attribute the capacity to learn to the structure of relations among individuals within an organization or among organizations within a field or industry. Expansive and heterogeneous networks may increase organizational learning (Powell, Koput, and Smith-Doerr, 1996, p. 118; Stinchcombe, 1990), whereas an organization's experience with managing the complex coordination of activities among departments may produce competency traps in which mastery of a less-than-optimal procedure discourages the learning of new methods (Levitt and March, 1988, pp. 322–323). Implicitly these arguments incorporate elements of a transmission model of learning; how well an organization learns appears as a function of the extent and variety of new information to which it is exposed.

To the extent that such arguments do address "what people know," the implications for formal education are more explicit. Organizational learning is described as "routine-based, history-dependent, and target-oriented" (Levitt and March, 1988, p. 319)—in other words, field-specific rather than generalized. On first inspection, this context-dependent quality of learning would seem to overwhelm anything that could be carried by an individual from school to work. Like ethnographic research in the sociology of science, the locality of learning appears to foreclose any possibility of using knowledge across multiple settings. Precisely because learning is portrayed as *consistently* path dependent, however, a more general claim can be advanced:

A complete learning cycle is one in which individual cognitions and preferences affect individual actions, which affect organizational choices, which affect environmental responses, which affect individual cognitions and preferences. . . . Although the ambiguities of history compromise the linkages, organizations continue to "learn" as though the cycle were complete. As a result, a theory of organizational learning has to comprehend both the ways in which ambiguity affects the cycle and the dynamics of learning under such conditions [March, 1988, p. 13].

The ability to detect these paths of bounded organizational learning would be a valuable skill to teach children. Fortunately, exemplar-based strategies of education organized around a particular style of narrative offer promising possibilities. A prescription for just such an approach has been offered by Neil Postman. Following William James's claim that "you can give humanistic value to almost anything by teaching it historically," Postman argues that the teaching of subjects as narratives of questions, solutions, errors, and innovations can provide a compelling framework within which to integrate fragments of learning (1995, p. 113; Toulmin, 1972, pp. 145–260). Juxtaposed against research into organizational learning, this proposal also has the apparent advantage of providing students with exemplars for the type of critical reflection on organizational choice required for a more conscious strategy of learning in complex environments.

This learning may also require familiarity with certain kinds of social interaction, an insight suggested by Jean Lave and Etienne Wenger's (1991) work on "legitimate peripheral participation." As their discussions of midwifery in the Yucatán and meat cutting in modern supermarkets make explicit, what and how such actors learn depends greatly on the ways in which social interaction is structured to facilitate learning, particularly through exchanges between relative experts and novices across various tasks within a work setting. In a valuable addition to this point, Yrjö Engeström's (1993) study in Finnish medical clinics illustrates how the organization of work activities shapes the extent to which individual practitioners are able to build on what the organization already knows about patients (through its technology of data collection and storage) in the course of clinical interactions. Such recent research on learning highlights how the intersection of the organization of tasks with the organization of knowledge constructs distinctive opportunities for learning within various settings.

These insights from the literatures on organizational, and organized, learning frame a series of questions for those who would transform formal education to suit the needs of the economy that is to come. First, how can students be prepared repeatedly to relearn their jobs or to acquire new ones? Second, how can students be prepared for the type of cognitive work valued in these new forms of economic enterprise? Third, how can students be aided in acquiring the expansive, heterogeneous networks that are associated with both learning organizations and individual economic success?

Much of the answers to the first and second of these questions may lie in studies such as those discussed in the preceding section. A clearer understanding of how people make use of existing knowledge (whether as mastery of fact or as tools for learning) to address problems in a new domain or setting will have practical implications for strategies of coping with an increasingly flexible economy and the shift from single to serial careers (Reich, 1991, p. 178). The third question, however, points to another issue rarely addressed in research literatures oriented to the study of individual cognition or economic attainment: insofar as networks matter for everything from job mobility to social support, to what extent do different schooling arrangements provide students with different forms or degrees of connectedness?

The dependence of social networks on educational experiences is popularly recognized as one of the core benefits of an elite university education. If it is not what you know but whom you know that matters, then the returns to education will reflect the degree to which universities nurture both social ties and the skills to make more ties in the future. At the level of primary and secondary schooling, research has focused overwhelmingly on the relation of families to schools. But it is possible to ask to what extent different arrangements—for example, neighborhood schools versus magnet schools—have consequences for the density, extensiveness, and durability of students' social networks, which sociologists have demonstrated are crucial resources for finding jobs and facilitating mobility (Granovetter, 1973).

With respect to the generation of network ties, some critics have argued that many schools are institutionally isolated: they "are not only characterized by self-contained classrooms, they are self-contained organizations with few links to the outside world" (Doyle, 1990, p. 131). One of the factors credited with the success of Catholic schools has been the embeddedness of activities in interactions between school and community as well as between students and adults, including teachers, parents, and alumni (Bryk, Lee, and Holland, 1993, chaps. 5, 11). On this score, current efforts to include community service as a regular component of secondary education are worthy of considerable attention. The institutionalization of voluntarism may well increase the extent of students' connections to the community, but the formalization of these programs may alter the character of those ties for students who would have volunteered in any case.

Sociological studies of networks also suggest that what someone knows has consequences for what social ties she or he will form. Juxtaposing Pierre Bourdieu's (1984) theories of cultural capital with current sociological work on the structure of social networks, Paul DiMaggio (1987) asks why surveys of attendance at cultural or recreational events reveal little of the isomorphism of economic class and class culture that "reflection" models of culture would lead us to expect. Instead, he argues, "the well-educated and persons of high occupational prestige do and like more of almost everything. . . . Being a successful member of the middle class requires some mastery of prestigious status cultures; but it is abetted by an easy familiarity with cultures of occupation, of region, and of ethnicity as well" (1987, pp. 444, 445). Although debates over the role of cultural indoctrination in education have emphasized the opposition of national culture to distinctive group traditions, research on social networks suggests that a case can be made for instrumental multiculturalism. Building on studies of bilingualism and of families formed across divisions of race or religion, this question might lead to a clearer understanding of how students (and adults) learn to "culture-switch" when moving across domains or constructing expansive, heterogeneous social networks.

DiMaggio's concern for the mapping of cultural capital onto social strata, however, provides an important caveat to the premise that the "learning" that happens at managerial (and elite technical) levels within complex organizations provides an appropriate exemplar for rethinking the organization of education. This claim of appropriateness must be questioned in a society where many, perhaps most, students will go on to work in service or manufacturing jobs that require few of the capacities for learning, criticism, and innovation that figure so prominently in the celebratory discussions of the postindustrial economy (Martin, 1989). Critics of the "elevated standards" approach to school reform have argued that by taking the college-bound, middle-class student as the norm, these reforms will erode the capacity of schools to retain, and with luck to aid, students who have no intention or expectation or desire to pursue this educational path.

Yet if we focus not on academic requirements but on the skills to develop powerful analogies, to criticize received learning, and to construct networks that link social groups, these are precisely the sorts of skills that have been used by political challengers throughout American history (Clemens, 1997). How the political and economic consequences of trying to learn from learning organizations would be assessed by all those concerned with educational reform is, of course, quite another question.

TOWARD AN ANALYSIS OF INSTITUTIONAL ARTICULATION

Understanding the organization of what students learn and the ties that link schools to other social activities lays the foundation for an analysis of institutional articulation. Studies by Bourdieu and Jean-Claude Passeron (1979) and by Paul Willis (1977) document how cultural capital acquired in the family or neighborhood interacts with the internal organization of schooling to contribute to the reproduction of class structures. Kathryn Neckerman and Joleen Kirschenman (1991) show how new entrants into the labor market are sorted not only by their individual level of achievement but by the identity of their school. Finally, there is great potential to use cross-national comparisons, drawing on the growing number of ethnographies of *both* work and schooling, to think more generally about how schools do or do not aid students in making transitions to other forms of social activity.

These concerns bring us full circle, returning to Meyer and Rowan's observation of the lack of articulation between formal institutional structures designed to regulate and evaluate schooling and day-to-day activities in classrooms. It is worthwhile to reexamine this question through a wider lens, asking whether other institutions inform the organization of schooling or, from the vantage of formulating educational policy, whether it is possible to realign schooling with the organization of other realms of social life such as a changing economy or the modern polity.

The initial orienting questions for this chapter reflect a sense that current developments in sociological theory and practice represent an important opportunity for rethinking what is meant by the conjunction of school and society. To the extent that these lines of inquiry prove fruitful, each will have implications for the future development of education research and the training of education researchers. The guiding framework for the acquisition of sociological knowledge has been organized around separate institutions: the sociology of

work, the sociology of science, the sociology of family, the sociology of education. This framework has distanced education research from other areas of
inquiry and has also suppressed a fundamental theoretical question for current
debates over schooling: How does what is learned in one institution (the school)
influence a student's future in work? in family? in civic society? To begin to
address these questions adequately, we must build bridges between education
research and other specialties, facilitating a two-way exchange of more robust
models of learning processes for analyses of the organizationally complex world
in which we learn.

Work in organizational analysis and the sociology of science suggests three
lines of inquiry. First, if the process of learning is fundamentally local, for children and adults alike, then we need to know more about how knowledge is
organized into more general frameworks. Second, once knowledge is linked to
generalizable templates or narratives, how is it then relocated in response to
new challenges? Finally, social ties link individuals to others in diverse social
settings. How do such networks aid learners of all ages in learning and making
use of what they know in new situations?

References

Barley, S. R. "Technology as an Occasion for Structuring: Evidence from Observations
of CT Scanners and the Social Order of Radiology Departments." *Administrative Science Quarterly*, 1986, *31*(1), 78–108.

Bourdieu, P. *Distinction: A Social Critique of the Judgment of Taste* (R. Nice, trans.).
Cambridge, Mass.: Harvard University Press, 1984.

Bourdieu, P., and Passeron, J. C. *The Inheritors: French Students and Their Relation to
Culture.* Chicago: University of Chicago Press, 1979. (Originally published 1964.)

Bowles, S., and Gintis, H. *Schooling in Capitalist America.* New York: Basic Books,
1976.

Bruner, J. *The Culture of Education.* Cambridge, Mass.: Harvard University Press, 1996.

Bryk, A. S., Lee, V. E., and Holland, P. B. *Catholic Schools and the Common Good.*
Cambridge, Mass.: Harvard University Press, 1993.

Clark, A. E., and Fujimura, J. H. *The Right Tools for the Job: At Work in the Twentieth-
Century Life Sciences.* Princeton, N.J.: Princeton University Press, 1992.

Clemens, E. S. "Of Asteroids and Dinosaurs: The Role of the Press in the Shaping of
Scientific Debate." In *Social Studies of Science*, 1986, *16*(3), 421–456.

Clemens, E. S. *The People's Lobby: Organizational Innovation and the Rise of Interest
Group Politics, 1890–1925.* Chicago: University of Chicago Press, 1997.

Coleman, J. S., Hoffer, T., and Kilgore, S. *High School Achievement: Public, Catholic,
and Private Schools Compared.* New York: Basic Books, 1982.

Collins, H. M. "Tacit Knowledge and Scientific Networks." In B. Barnes and D. Edge (eds.), *Science in Context: Readings in the Sociology of Science*. Cambridge, Mass.: MIT Press, 1982.

Corcoran, E. "Learning Companies: Educating Corporations About How People Learn." *Scientific American*, February 1993, 105–108.

DiMaggio, P. "Classification in Art." *American Sociological Review*, 1987, *52*(4), 440–455.

Dobbin, F. *Forging Industrial Policy: The United States, Britain, and France in the Railway Age*. New York: Cambridge University Press, 1994.

Doyle, D. P. "Does It Matter What We Teach Our Children?" In S. B. Bacharach (ed.), *Education Reform: Making Sense of It All*. Needham Heights, Mass.: Allyn & Bacon, 1990.

Engeström, Y. "Developmental Studies of Work as a Testbench of Activity Theory: The Case of Primary Care Medical Practice." In S. Chaiklin and J. Lave (eds.), *Understanding Practice: Perspectives on Activity and Context*. New York: Cambridge University Press, 1993.

Fujimura, J. H. "The Molecular Biological Bandwagon in Cancer Research: Where Social Worlds Meet." *Social Problems*, 1988, *35*(3), 261–283.

Granovetter, M. "The Strength of Weak Ties." *American Journal of Sociology*, 1973, *78*, 1360–1380.

Heilbrun, C. G. *Writing a Woman's Life*. New York: Ballantine, 1988.

Hirsch, E. D., Jr. *The Schools We Need and Why We Don't Have Them*. New York: Doubleday, 1996.

Knorr-Cetina, K. *The Manufacture of Knowledge: An Essay on the Constructivist and Contextual Nature of Science*. New York: Pergamon Press, 1981.

Kuhn, D., Garcia-Mila, M., Zohar, A., and Anderson, C. *Strategies of Knowledge Acquisition*. Monographs of the Society for Research in Child Development, *60*(4). 1995.

Kuhn, T. S. *The Essential Tension: Selected Studies in Scientific Tradition and Change*. Chicago: University of Chicago Press, 1977.

Lamont, M. *Money, Morals, and Manners: The Culture of the French and the American Upper-Middle Class*. Chicago: University of Chicago Press, 1992.

Latour, B. *Science in Action: How to Follow Scientists and Engineers Through Society*. Cambridge, Mass.: Harvard University Press, 1987.

Latour, B. *The Pasteurization of France*. Cambridge, Mass.: Harvard University Press, 1988.

Latour, B., and Woolgar, S. *Laboratory Life: The Construction of Scientific Facts*. Princeton, N.J.: Princeton University Press, 1986. (Originally published 1979.)

Lave, J., and Wenger, E. *Situated Learning: Legitimate Peripheral Participation*. New York: Cambridge University Press, 1991.

Levitt, B., and March, J. G. "Organizational Learning." *Annual Review of Sociology,* 1988, *14,* 319–340.

March, J. G. *Decisions and Organizations.* Cambridge, Mass.: Basil Blackwell, 1988.

Martin, D. T. "A Critique of the Concept of Work and Education in the School Reform Reports." In C. M. Shea, E. Kahane, and P. Sola (eds.), *The Servants of Power: A Critique of the 1980s School Reform Movement.* Westport, Conn.: Greenwood Press, 1989.

Meyer, J. W., and Rowan, B. "Institutionalized Organizations: Formal Structure as Myth and Ceremony." *American Journal of Sociology,* 1977, *83*(2), 340–363.

Morin, R. "Who's in Control? Many Don't Know or Care." *Washington Post,* January 29, 1996, p. A1.

Neckerman, K. M., and Kirschenman, J. "Hiring Strategies, Racial Bias, and Inner-City Workers." *Social Problems,* 1991, *38*(4).

Paley, V. G. *Boys and Girls: Superheroes in the Doll Corner.* Chicago: University of Chicago Press, 1984.

Postman, N. *The End of Education: Redefining the Value of School.* New York: Knopf, 1995.

Powell, W. W., and DiMaggio, P. J. (eds.). *The New Institutionalism in Organizational Analysis.* Chicago: University of Chicago Press, 1991.

Powell, W. W., Koput, K. W., and Smith-Doerr, L. "Interorganizational Collaboration and the Locus of Innovation: Networks of Learning in Biotechnology." *Administrative Science Quarterly,* 1996, *41,* 1–145.

Reich, R. B. *The Work of Nations: Preparing Ourselves for 21st-Century Capitalism.* New York: Vintage Books, 1991.

Rheem, H. "The Learning Organization." *Harvard Business Review,* March 4, 1995, p. 10.

Rogoff, B., and Lave, J. (eds.). *Everyday Cognition: Its Development in Social Context.* Cambridge, Mass.: Harvard University Press, 1984.

Scribner, S. "Studying Working Intelligence." In B. Rogoff and J. Lave (eds.), *Everyday Cognition: Its Development in Social Context.* Cambridge, Mass.: Harvard University Press, 1984.

Sewell, W. H., Jr. "A Theory of Structure: Duality, Agency, and Transformation." *American Journal of Sociology,* 1992, *98*(1), 1–29.

Stinchcombe, A. L. *Information and Organizations.* Berkeley, Calif.: University of California Press, 1990.

Tilly, C. *Popular Contention in Great Britain, 1758–1834.* Cambridge, Mass.: Harvard University Press, 1995.

Toulmin, S. *Human Understanding: The Collective Use and Evolution of Concepts.* Princeton, N.J.: Princeton University Press, 1972.

Willis, P. *Learning to Labor: How Working Class Kids Get Working Class Jobs.* New York: Columbia University Press, 1977.

CHAPTER SEVEN

Understanding Educational Processes in an Era of Globalization

The View from Anthropology and Cultural Studies

Kathleen Hall

I think that one of the primary difficulties in communication may be that the anthropologists will tend to look at processes, concepts, and data from the viewpoint of research and theory-building. I think that the educators may be more inclined to look at the same things from the viewpoint of "what can be done now to improve education?" But I think that both groups have the ultimate improvement of society in mind. The anthropologist's goal of ultimate improvement is somewhat more delayed. But it is sometimes difficult for us to communicate, because the anthropologists are talking in the direction of understanding at the theoretical level, while the educator will be saying, "Well, so what?"
—G. D. Spindler, Education and Anthropology

In *The Culture of Education*, Jerome Bruner (1996) provides a persuasive argument for the centrality of the study of culture in education research, for psychologists as well as for anthropologists. It is becoming increasingly clear, he argues, "that education is not just about conventional school matters like curriculum or standards or testing. What we resolve to do in school only makes sense when considered in the broader context of what society intends to accomplish through its educational investment in the young" (p. ix). This question logically implies a prior set of issues: What should schools do in relation to any given social order? And, indeed, what can schools do as one force among many in what Lawrence Cremin (1989) called "the cacophony of teaching"? These dilemmas are inherently cultural. Education always has been, and certainly is increasingly today, at the center of debates about what our national culture can and should be and how we should prepare our youth (and adults) for their lives in this society.

These questions are hardly new, for in the words of Tyack and Cuban (1995), the history of public schools has been marked by various social projects aimed at "tinkering toward Utopia." For nearly two centuries, the citizens of modern nations have possessed a "secular faith" in the power of educational institutions to bring about increasingly "better" societies through the "improvement" of their young. These projects have been riveted with profound contradictions and philosophical conflicts, ensuring that education has remained a contested terrain (Lagemann, 1996). Yet after each ensuing battle over the direction of social

121

change, the public school has maintained its authority and legitimacy as a central institution for achieving social progress. Citizens may have disagreed over what type of society and citizen educational institutions should be shaping, but they have not lost faith, fundamentally, in the potential of pedagogy to produce this imagined future.

The modern system of mass public education from the beginning has been deeply interconnected with processes of nation building and state formation. In the modern industrial era, education systems have served the needs of the nation-state. Educational purposes and processes have been directed toward ensuring national unity and social integration through passing on a purportedly shared national culture, transmitting democratic values and ideals, and providing the skills and credentials required by the economic structure of each nation-state, capitalist or socialist. In capitalist societies in particular, the goals of advancing equality and democracy have often conflicted with the demands placed on education institutions by the requirements of the economy (Carnoy and Levin, 1985). Yet however deep the contradictions between the forces of capitalism and the ideals of social democracy and equality, emergent debates and controversies have been framed within an overarching concern for achieving what is best for the nation as a whole.

Debates about educational purposes and practices, however, are taking on new meaning and significance in this era of globalization. Forces related to globalization have contributed to the weakening of the power and centrality of the nation-state. Transnational corporations and international market forces have undermined the ability of national governments to control, protect, and regulate their own economies. The emergence of supranational political bodies and relations has weakened the basis of national political sovereignty and autonomy (Sassen, 1996). Advances in communications technology and media production, as well as the expansion of commodity markets, have contributed to the spread of a culture of global capitalism—a culture of images, icons, and representations that often has a decidedly American face. As supranational forces threaten the nation from without, the rise of localism and of social movements and policies emphasizing local control and decentralization have shifted political and economic relations within nation-states.

We are, in short, living in an age in which national cultures and social boundaries are being radically transformed and redrawn in the face of the expanding global capitalist labor markets, shifts in the geopolitical order, and the increasingly fast-paced transnational movements of people and commodities, ideas, and media images. A great deal of social science writing has been devoted to capturing the complex social, political-economic, and cultural dynamics of this era, resulting in debates about "the postmodern condition" (Lyotard, 1984), "the condition of postmodernity" (Harvey, 1989), the period of "reflexive modernization" (Beck, Giddens, and Lash, 1994), or multiple modernities in the context of globalization (Appadurai, 1996). These frameworks vary considerably in their assessments of the character and the magnitude of the changes the world is undergoing, yet all agree that tensions between global and local forces are a critical component of change within global capitalism.

Global–local tensions are driving two countervailing processes of change, each of which is fundamentally cultural. The global circulation of ideas and information, commodities, and media culture has, on the one hand, contributed to the emergence of what some refer to as a global culture, to an increase in cultural homogeneity. At the same time, global flows of diverse cultures, together with shifts in international power relations, have served to undermine the dominance of Western culture and increase opportunities for both the assertion of local "cultures" and the production of new hybrid cultural forms. It is these developments that lie at the heart of the postmodern condition—the historic juncture in which universalist ideals conflict with particularist visions, unity is challenged by diversity, and imagined national communities are crosscut by the politics of culture and calls to recognize collective forms of identity and difference.

In the era of globalization the contested terrain of education finds itself the site in which the politics of culture is being framed and often fought. Educational institutions are deeply implicated in postmodern debates and dilemmas concerning the politics of knowledge, culture, and identity. Consequently traditional educational purposes, frequently tied to projects aimed at protecting national unity—transmitting a national culture, perpetuating moral order and social solidarity, and preparing future citizens and productive workers to contribute to these ends—are increasingly questioned and challenged. To understand these developments and their implications for future educational policies and processes, education researchers will need to develop new analytic tools and theoretical formulations for addressing the role of education institutions in relation to the politics of culture and identity stimulated in the wake of global capitalism (Greene, 1994).

Anthropology and cultural studies are uniquely positioned to provide such analytic tools. Anthropology itself, over the past decades, has been in the midst of a struggle to expand its own conceptual capacity to address the types of cultural complexity generated by processes of globalization and local responses to such forces. Critical to the study of globalization and shifts in global dynamics of power are concerns with the interrelationships among power, knowledge, and identity.

In this age of postcolonialism there has arisen a major shift in the politics of knowledge and of knowledge production worldwide. At a foundational level, the very basis of what counts as authoritative knowledge, as valued forms of knowledge, is being questioned. Anthropology, as the discipline most closely engaged with studying other cultures, has been hard hit by these controversies over the politics of representation. As a result, a great deal of thought has been directed toward understanding power relations between a researcher and those who find themselves objects of research, as well as toward what constitutes a valid claim to understand cultures, ways of life, and experiences different from one's own. While these methodological and epistemological issues lie at the heart of the anthropological project, they can be seen to have much broader relevance, particularly for scholars, like education researchers, who seek to understand the experiences of groups of people differently situated within the structure of inequality within capitalist societies. Questions about how issues of power and identity influence researcher-researched relations and roles, how research problems are framed, and what voices and perspectives are represented in what form are of great concern within education research. The first section of this chapter, which explores challenges raised by postmodern critiques of ethnographic authority, seeks to lend insight into the politics of knowledge production in research into educational problems in multiracial, culturally plural, class-stratified societies.

Educational institutions find themselves at the center of the politics of culture and identity, whether the issue is multiculturalism, bilingual education policies, or providing for the particular needs of culturally and socially diverse students. Schools and college campuses are the battlefields of "culture wars" (Levine, 1996; Gitlin, 1995a). As "culture" and "identity" are invoked in educational debates, controversies, and reform initiatives, education researchers have increasingly turned to anthropology and cultural studies for theoretical frameworks to apply in their analyses. The second and third sections of this chapter provide an overview of some of the central theories of power and identity that education researchers are drawing from in their attempts to understand forms of social stratification in relation to the growing centrality of the politics of identity in educational contexts.

The challenges of studying processes of globalization have also required social scientists, particularly anthropologists, to develop analytic frameworks that can capture the dynamic interplay of global forces within local societies. The final section of this chapter introduces theoretical innovations and insights into global-local relations that may be of use to education researchers and practitioners in their consideration of how local educational projects, practices, and processes are influenced by globalization.

POWER AND THE PRODUCTION
OF ANTHROPOLOGICAL KNOWLEDGE

Postmodern, poststructural, postcolonial, and feminist analyses of knowledge have brought to the forefront a recognition of the play of power and identity in assigning social value and legitimacy to different forms of knowledge. These intellectual movements have contributed to the epistemological uncertainty in anthropology and within the human sciences generally. They themselves have arisen within, and in response to, a number of twentieth-century historical developments, shifts represented by, in Anthony Giddens's (1990) words, "modernity coming to understand itself" (p. 48). A central component of these movements is an appreciation for the "highly charged relationships between knowledge, identity, and power" (Moore, 1996, p. 1). Increasingly anthropologists, historians, literary critics, and cultural studies researchers have turned their attention to exploring social knowledge and ways of knowing as plural and political, local and positional. The questioning of scholarly authority has been tied to postcolonial shifts in global political and economic relations as well as to what Aihwa Ong (1996) has referred to as "the changing political economy of knowledge." With these shifts have come challenges to the authority of "the West," which have given rise to questions addressing the knowledge–power configuration on which this authority has in part been based. In the postcolonial era, it has become possible to challenge claims to intellectual authority and to universal truth: the unquestioned dominance of Western epistemology has been undermined. This is creating the space for the reassertion of forms of knowledge defined by Western science as illegitimate.

This challenge to intellectual authority and to the "master narratives" of the human sciences led in the 1980s to a "crisis of ethnographic authority" within the discipline of anthropology. Anthropologists have become more reflective about their role in knowledge production and the purpose and relevance of the knowledge they produce. This reflexive turn in anthropology more specifically has raised questions about traditional methods of ethnographic research and "writing culture" (Clifford and Marcus, 1986; Marcus and Fischer, 1986; Behar and Gordon, 1995). It has brought into focus a number of research issues, including claims to authority in ethnographic writing; relations between the researcher and those the researcher studies; the politics of representing and interpreting other cultures and perspectives; how an ethnographer can come to understand the subjectivity of another; the relationship between local knowledge and anthropological knowledge; and ethical and political concerns about the use and relevance of anthropological research.

The "postmodern turn" in anthropology has stimulated deeply opposed reactions across the discipline (Sangren, 1988; Jarvie, 1988). Yet regardless of where anthropologists have positioned themselves in these debates, these critiques have focused constructive attention on important and sometimes controversial aspects of ethnographic approaches to research. Amid the controversies has arisen a commitment to increased methodological rigor and an openness to creative experimentation. William Rosenberry, for example, reflects this in arguing that ethnographic authority should be founded on "the constant and sustained engagement with ethnographic subjects and the requirement that one embed one's observations, inferences, and interpretations within that engagement" (1989, pp. x–xi).

A great deal of attention is being paid to how researchers construct ethno-graphic accounts. Anthropologists have become much more cognizant of the ways in which knowledge claims are advanced in ethnographic writing through particular types of literary conventions. As Richard Fox (1991) has argued,

> Writing ethnography is always "an assertion of power, a claim to 'authority,' that, when successful, becomes an authorization." We are now much more aware—and wary—of the conventions by which we convince our readers that we were really there and faithfully got the native point of view. We are much more suspi-cious of ethnography's claim to provide a tidy picture of the Other [p. 6].

Central to concerns about the nature of ethnographic authority are questions about how an anthropologist can enter into and come to understand epistemo-logical orientations that are different from her own. Anthropologists learn about other cultural orientations and practices through developing intersubjectivity. *Verstehen*, or understanding, is assumed to develop over time as an anthropol-ogist coexists with—as well as observes and questions—"others" in a shared experiential world. Intersubjectivity, particularly when arrived at dialogically or through discussions between observer and observed aimed at collaboratively constructing interpretations, is what in part is thought to give ethnographic interpretations their validity.

Informants over the years have become more involved in crafting the answers anthropologists seek, yet rarely have they formulated the questions. Anthropo-logical research has tended to transform "others" into objects—beings in the world waiting to be discovered, to be placed under the anthropologist's gaze (Hobart, 1995). As Edward Said (1993) has noted, a Western "structure of atti-tude and referencing" has appropriated Third World cultures and peoples as sources of materials for the production of knowledge, as "cases" to explicate social theory. Anthropologists have been the source of the analytic frames, inter-pretive approaches, and critical perspectives that give structure and coherence or narrative shape to ethnographic accounts. They too have made decisions about the purposes for and relevance of these "thick descriptions" of other cultures.

Anthropological thinking about issues of representation has moved in the past decade from a primary focus on problems of interpretation to questions concerning the relationship between local and anthropological epistemologies. The British-based Association of Social Anthropologists, for example, during the past few years has sponsored a series of edited volumes with the theme, "The Uses of Knowledge: Global and Local Relations" (Fardon, 1995; Moore, 1996). Anthropologists have long been concerned with understanding culture from "the native's point of view." Yet as Ong (1996) recently pointed out, anthropological projects have too often involved gathering data about "others" the better to understand Western issues and social problems. What she and others are calling for is a "decolonization" of anthropology's research perspectives:

As late twentieth-century analysts, we must also execute a political decentering away from seeing everything from the Western vantage point. The decolonization of anthropology requires that we cease colonizing other parts of the world simply to validate Western theories of modernity, Marxism, feminism, socialism, or capitalism. If we continue to use pre-articulated categories of Western knowledge, we are merely redeploying our particular vision in transnational descriptive narratives. The Third World and other "interstitial places" will continue to be places where we gather field data to add to anthropological knowledge but are not themselves considered producers of knowledge and critiques that can change anthropological understanding of the world. We may change our language and the places we are studying, but nothing has changed if anthropological knowledge refuses to consider non-Western societies as producers of cultural knowledge about their own worlds [1996, pp. 84–85].

Debates about the politics and poetics of ethnographic fieldwork and representation have infused creative energy and innovation as well as conflict and tension into the discipline of anthropology. Several of these developments have converged to encourage a renewed interest among mainstream anthropologists in studying educational discourse and processes. Critiques of traditional anthropology's near-exclusive focus on "exotic others" has opened the way for broader interest in and acceptance of studying the West as well as Western institutions, such as schools. Increased interest in globalization, the politics of culture, and issues of knowledge, power, and identity are informing the development of innovative approaches to the study of discourses of science and technology, the cultural politics of international human rights or environmental movements and policies, tourism, and the production of "heritage" as well as the politics and power of different types of pedagogy. Intellectual uncertainty about the purpose and politics of producing anthropological knowledge has led many in the field to question the significance of our research—to reflect on, as the title of an edited volume addressing these concerns puts it, *The Future of Anthropology: Its Relevance to the Contemporary World* (Ahmed and Shore, 1995).

As anthropologists have become more concerned about issues of "public interest," education researchers have turned to anthropology and to ethnographic methods in their efforts to find more powerful tools for understanding and improving educational processes. In the context of research on schooling, concern with the politics of knowledge production has led to a good deal of discussion of issues of power and method (Gitlin, 1994) and to the emergence of a wide range of methodological innovations. Although the methodological approaches differ widely in ideological orientation and views about the role of the research and researchers in bringing about change, they have emerged in response to many of the same dilemmas anthropologists are struggling with in relation to the politics of knowledge production, both conceptually and methodologically.

Teacher-practitioner research (Cochran-Smith and Lytle, 1993), feminist methodologies (Olesen, 1994; Lather, 1991), critical ethnography (Anderson, 1993; Carspecken, 1996), and various collaborative approaches are concerned with relations between researchers and those researched. In the case of education research, however, researchers struggle with these issues not simply out of concern about epistemology, the validity of interpretations, or the politics of representing "others." The politics of knowledge production takes on added significance in education research as it is seen to influence the value and relevance of knowledge for improving schools and bringing about social change. Each of these orientations supports a more interactive or dialogic approach to knowledge building, one in which the subjects of research are involved to differing degrees in various aspects of the research process. The assumption is that knowledge acquired will be more relevant and therefore useful if subjects of change—teachers, administrators, parents, or students—are actively engaged with education research and become more involved in reflecting on the research and its findings.

EDUCATION, POWER, AND GLOBAL CAPITALISM

The recent conceptual and methodological innovation in ethnography has greatly enriched and expanded its potential as a vehicle for studying and better understanding social life in the era of globalization. From the perspective of education research, ethnography provides a particularly powerful methodology for considering the interrelationships among education, culture, and society.

Anthropological research on education—whether in the context of colonial histories, studies of nationalist projects, or analyses of experiences of minority students in American schools—has tended to emphasize the contradictory role of schooling, as both a path for personal and collective advancement and a powerful and subtle instrument of domination and control (Comaroff and Comaroff, 1991; Mitchell, 1988; Levinson, Foley, and Holland, 1996; Hall, 1995, n.d.a.). Frequently forging their analyses around the central question of power, this line of research has tended to question a central tenet of modern nation-states: the belief that schools are neutral institutions providing equal opportunities for achieving social mobility and increased prosperity. In the United States, ethnographic research in schools, classrooms, and other sites where young people "learn" has provided important information about how forms of inequality—racial, class, cultural, and gender inequities—are reproduced as well as challenged in everyday life, within and outside school. Recent developments in culture theory have provided yet more powerful analytic tools for understanding how forms of power and cultural difference influence student engagement in school as well as processes of teaching and instruction (Erickson, 1997; Eisenhart, forth-coming; Heath, forthcoming; Levinson and Holland, 1996).

Advances in technology, changes in the labor market due to the shift to service industries, and the remapping of ethnic and race relations with the arrival of the new immigrants from Asian and Latin American countries are giving increased weight and adding complexity to age-old problems of how to bring about greater equality in educational outcomes. Relationships of power, identity, and cultural difference remain central aspects of these dilemmas. Therefore, education researchers, reformers, and practitioners continue to have a need for theoretical formulations to help them understand and address the role that schools can play in bringing about greater equity, broader opportunity, and social integration.

In this section I discuss three theoretical approaches to culture and power that have contributed to the way anthropological and sociological researchers have come to conceive of relations between schools and broader processes of social stratification: Pierre Bourdieu's theory of cultural reproduction; British Cultural Studies and Paul Willis's formulation of cultural production, resistance, and subjectivity; and Foucault's work on power, discourse, and the making of subjects. Each of these theories in distinctive ways provides a window to examining the interrelations among culture, power, and educational processes. Each suggests avenues for framing future research into the contradictory nature of educational purposes and practices in advanced capitalist societies.

Bourdieu's Formulation of Culture, Power, and Educational Processes

Education holds a central position within Bourdieu's formulation of power and culture; he argues that in class-stratified societies, schools are the primary institutional site in which systems of classification and the symbolic power they express are legitimated and reinforced (see Swartz, 1997, pp. 189–192). Schools are the central settings for cultural reproduction. The critical issue for social scientists concerned with exploring how forms of social inequality persist, he argues, is to "determine the contribution made by the education system to the reproduction of the structure of power relationship and symbolic relationships between social classes" (Bourdieu, 1973, p. 71).

Bourdieu's work challenges Bowles and Gintis's (1976) Marxist explanation of social reproduction as based in the "correspondence" between schools and the social relations of production in the workplace. Bourdieu argues that in capitalist societies, an education system's relationship to the labor market is one of "relative autonomy." As Swartz (1997) explains, "Bourdieu's particular contribution is to show that schools are neither neutral nor merely reflective of broader sets of power relations, but play a complex, indirect, mediating role in maintaining and enhancing them" (p. 191).

Similar to other reproduction theories, Bourdieu's work provides a critique of the modern ideal of meritocracy: the vision that schools provide a direct path along which able individuals through their academic efforts can achieve class mobility. In France, as elsewhere, statistics on university attendance and completion painted a different picture. Bourdieu and Jean-Claude Passeron (1979, 1994) sought to understand the cultural processes that contribute to the unequal representation of students from the lower classes in French universities. How do universities, they asked, go about reinforcing class divisions by granting degrees to "the inheritors" of class privileges? Education institutions contribute to the reproduction of class relations not simply through the allocation of forms of cultural knowledge, but rather by selecting and honoring students who already possess cultural capital (see also Bourdieu, 1984). Universities "select the elect," those who have "inherited" cultural capital—a cultivated "taste" for "high culture," familiarity with and possession of manners, style, attitudes, habits—knowledge acquired through growing up within a particular class environment.

Access to educational opportunities, according to Bourdieu, provides neither equality of opportunity nor a clear path to social mobility. For children from "disadvantaged" class backgrounds, "the acquisition of culture is an acculturation" (Bourdieu and Passeron, p. 22). Learning through books what others learn in everyday life lessens one's familiarity, and therein facility, with forms of cultural capital. Their use of this knowledge, from the perspective of those who really know, will demonstrate their lack of inheritance, showing signs of the effort a student has to make to acquire these tastes, social skills, and types of cultural knowledge. Educational institutions may provide access to cultural knowledge, but it is access to other sites of cultural learning and to inheriting cultural capital that ensures cultural reproduction and the perpetuation of class relations and privileges.

British Cultural Studies: Understanding Student Responses to Schooling

British Cultural Studies has been another significant source of conceptual tools for analyzing the relationship of education, culture, and society in capitalist societies. Michael Apple (1993) has credited the work of Raymond Williams in particular with providing concepts and frameworks that have helped free educational theory from dependence on overly psychologistic and economistic approaches to educational processes. His work has been central to our understanding of how power works through culture.

The innovative contributions of the early pioneers of British Cultural Studies, Richard Hoggart, Raymond Williams, E. P. Thompson, and, later, Stuart Hall and Paul Willis, are rooted in the unique political and economic circumstances of postwar Britain. The early work sought to understand the ways British working-class culture and consciousness had been transformed in the 1950s and 1960s by changes brought about by postwar economic prosperity, the increasing influence of the mass media, and the beginnings of what was feared to be an Americanization of British culture (Dworkin, 1993, pp. 40–41).

British Cultural Studies has perhaps had its most direct impact on anthropological approaches to education through the influence of Paul Willis's ethnographic study, *Learning to Labor* (1977). In his analysis, Willis draws from and develops many of the insights within the early work of British Cultural Studies, particularly the emphasis placed on culture and agency in the making of subjectivity in everyday practice. As he puts it, "The difficult thing to explain about how working-class kids get working-class jobs is why they let themselves" do so (p. 1).

Willis shares with Bowles and Gintis (1976) a concern to situate research on schooling within a broader concern with the relationship between education and the economy. His neo-Marxist approach is founded on a view that schools are instruments of social reproduction—vehicles through which the existing structure of inequality is reinforced and perpetuated. Yet Willis's (1977, 1981, 1990) work emphasizes what he calls "the cultural level," showing how culture mediates this process of social reproduction. In this way, his work—like that of Bourdieu and Passeron's (1994) theory of cultural reproduction—avoids the problem of structural determinism implicit in earlier studies of schooling and social reproduction (Willis, 1981; Levinson and Holland, 1996).

Willis's most significant contribution is the notion of cultural production. He uses this concept to capture the ways in which culture, social structural forces (such as class relations), and human agency (in this sense, action in the form of "resistance") all contribute to the reproduction of social inequality across the generations. Willis's work builds on the theme of youth resistance addressed by a number of his colleagues associated in the 1970s with the Birmingham Center for Contemporary Cultural Studies (Hall and Jefferson, 1976; Hebdige, 1979). He provides a powerful critique of cultural reproduction or of traditional theories of socialization generally, theories that implicitly assume that students passively absorb forms of culture handed down to them (Lave, Duguid, and Fernandez, 1992). Willis's ethnographic account depicts a group of working-class "lads" who recognize their class situation and come to terms with it by creating an oppositional culture, one that draws on a particular working-class construction of masculinity. This counterculture provides a vehicle for challenging the ideology of equality in the school. Yet in resisting and choosing not to succeed, these "lads" reproduce themselves as working-class laborers.

The subcultures young people produce through such acts of resistance are infused with cultural meanings, signs, and symbols—markers that express or signify a shared or collective identity. This theory of youth resistance—of the cultural production of subcultural orientations and collective identities—has been adopted by education researchers wishing to move beyond the limitations of deterministic theories of the school's role in reproducing the status and class positions of particular groups of people. Resistance theory and formulations that focus on how social actors creatively produce cultural orientations in everyday practice provide a more powerful vantage point from which to consider the range of ways "disadvantaged" youth choose to engage with schools and schooling. This theoretical approach is quite widespread across ethnographic studies that consider the complex response of "minority" and working-class youth to multiple forms of "learning," both inside and outside school walls (Foley, 1990; Weis, 1990; Wexler, 1992; MacLeod, 1995).

Yet Willis's account, along with other studies of male youth subcultural resistance, has attracted a fair amount of criticism. Feminist cultural studies scholars have noted the absence of women in early studies of youth subcultures, as well as the nearly celebratory depictions of sexist forms of working-class masculinity (McRobbie, 1980). Critics have also argued that greater consideration needs to be given to the dark side of subcultural solidarities, to the racist nationalist sentiments that often infuse these social ties. Other critics have found the concept of resistance to be constrained by its philosophical roots. Founded on neo-Marxist assumptions, it bears the imprint of the "immanent core" of Marxism—the necessity to find in capitalist social formations "revolutionary agents" effectively posed to bring about radical social change (Davies, 1995). Martin Carnoy, among others, has also noted the problem of overapplying the concept of resistance as a label for all types of antischool behaviors, rather than reserving the term for actions that are directly political in nature:

> A number of analysts have called such conflict "resistance." "Acting out against or dropping out from the school" without political engagement is not resistance.
> Rather, it is essentially a personal attempt to escape from a costly, painful situation.
> And the only way that such exit becomes political is when the larger community—
> either the dominant business class or subordinate groups themselves—make school frustrations and dropouts a political issue [1989, pp. 20–21].

Whatever the limitations of resistance theory, the work of Willis and others has demonstrated that to understand the role of schooling in society, one has to consider the way social actors interpret and respond to race, class, cultural, and gender inequality, as well as to opportunities for contesting these forces in everyday practice.

Poststructuralism and the Making of Subjects in Schools

During the past ten years, a central intellectual frame that supported much of the work of British Cultural Studies has been undermined. Marxist theory has faced serious challenges from history—as it has played out in Eastern Europe and the former Soviet Union—as well as from postmodern criticisms of its tele-ological propositions: essentialism, Eurocentrism, and its general status as a totalizing master narrative (McRobbie, 1994, p. 44). Concerns with ideology and hegemony within the Marxist analyses of the mid-1970s to mid-1980s were displaced in the late 1980s and early 1990s by issues of modernity and post-modernity (which themselves have been overshadowed in certain circles recently by interests in globalization and the local). The "neo-Marxism" of the early British Cultural Studies has been followed by what is referred to as "post-Marxism"—a Marxism strongly influenced by postmodern critiques and theoretical orientations (Laclau, 1991).

A distinctive approach to understanding schooling and power derives from postmodern and poststructuralist formulations. These theories consider power as it is located not simply in traditional centers of political or economic influence, such as the economy, the state, or patriarchy, but on what are defined as discursive sites of power—sites where power is produced in contexts ranging from classrooms to policy centers and mental institutions to prisons. The work of Michel Foucault in particular has contributed to the development of post-structuralist formulations of the role of education institutions and processes in modern social orders. Foucault's analysis diverges from neo-Marxist formula-tions that locate power within the state-economy-school nexus. He argues that power is more diffuse or "capillary," working throughout the social body. Fou-cault's ideas about knowledge, power, and truth counter traditional formula-tions of power as repressive, coercive, constraining, negative, and linked to false consciousness, suppressed desire, and ignorance. Rather, truth and knowledge are assumed to have liberating potential as instruments for opposing repressive forms of power. In contrast, Foucault argues that truth and knowledge are central to the workings of disciplinary power. Power, for Foucault, is not negative and coercive but productive and regulative; it is not a quality or quantity possessed by particular groups within a social hierarchy.

In *Discipline and Punish* (1979), Foucault characterizes our modern form of power as "bio-power." Foucault is not concerned with the origin or source of power, but rather with understanding how rituals or techniques of power work. Foucault seeks to illuminate the interrelations of power, knowledge, and the body by locating the mechanisms through which power "is actually articulated on the body" (Dreyfus and Rabinow, 1982, p. 113). His work emphasizes how power relations have come to work on and through the discipline of the body. "Power relations," he writes, "have an immediate hold upon [the body]; they invest it, mark it, train it, torture it, force it to carry out tasks, to perform cere-monies, to emit signs" (1979, p. 25).

"Bio-power is the increasing ordering in all realms under the guise of improv-ing the welfare of the individual and the population" (Dreyfus and Rabinow, 1982, p. xxvi). It involves the social ordering and individuating of subjects and groups and is exercised on the dominant and subordinate alike. "Bio-power" operates through technologies of discipline—material practices that take different forms across institutional contexts. The application of particular techniques of discipline works on the body to produce what Foucault refers to as "docile bodies." Bio-power disciplines bodies and "makes" individuals. Through "correct training" it produces subjects in order that they may be subjected, ordered, transformed, improved, and therein used efficiently.

Schools, in Foucault's work, represent one among many institutions—along with hospitals, workshops, and prisons—in which disciplinary power is exercised. Schools produce modern subjects or "useful individuals." They exercise techniques of correct training and systems of gratification and punishment that divide, rank, and normalize individuals. Knowledge is power as it is used in the service of exercising normalizing judgments. Knowledge, acquired through such techniques as surveillance and the examination, or what Foucault calls "the normalizing gaze," "makes it possible to qualify, to classify, and to punish. It establishes over individuals a visibility through which one differentiates them and judges them" (Foucault, 1979, p. 184).

The ordering of individuals within hierarchies of normalization involves techniques of discipline and regulation that penetrate into the smallest details of everyday life. This is the basis of power's "capillary" functioning. Power is exercised through numerous surveillance and ordering techniques, including the organization of space, the distribution of individuals within architectural spaces, and the structuring of time. Foucault explains,

> The workshop, the school, the army were subject to a whole micro-penalty of time (lateness, absences, interruptions of tasks), and of activity (inattention, negligence, lack of zeal), of behavior (impoliteness, disobedience), of speech (idle chatter, insolence), of the body ("incorrect" attitudes, irregular gestures, lack of cleanliness), of sexuality (impurity, indecency) [1977, p. 178].

Schools achieve order not through repression or prohibition but through "the means of correct training." Schools are, in Philip Corrigan's words, "productive—differentially productive of subjectivities, or social identities." Schools attempt to fix subjectivities, to regulate, normalize, stratify, punish, reward, and, thereby, marginalize possible forms of human diversity: "to make difference equal disadvantage" (1987, p. 31).

Subjects are formed in discourse, or power–knowledge configurations, systems of ideas, and practices that form the objects of which they speak. Discourses are not about objects but rather constitute them, "and in the practice of doing so conceal their own invention" (Foucault, 1974, p. 49). Discourse, according to Foucault, "in its distribution, in what it permits and what it prevents, it follows the lines laid down by social differences, conflicts, and struggles. Every education system is a political means of maintaining or modifying the appropriateness of discourses with the knowledge and power they bring with them" (quoted in Ball, 1990, p. 3).

As recent work in the field of education has begun to suggest (Popkewitz and Brennan, 1998; Ball, 1990), Foucault's methodologies provide useful tools for considering power–knowledge configurations across a range of educational processes. His "genealogical approach" has been applied in studies of historical frameworks underlying educational discourse, to consider, for example, the historical construction of discourse and positions in debates over school reform policies (Kenway, 1990). Poststructuralist discourse analysis highlights the way policies and practices set limits on what can be said and thought, by and about whom, and with what authority (Ball, 1990, p. 2).

Education researchers are also applying Foucault's formulations to studies of social positioning within curricula as well as classroom discourse. Innovative applications include investigations of how students are positioned as subjects —as "boys" or "girls," "black" or "white"—in stories they read or discussions that take place. Social positioning in texts and classroom interaction influences how students respond to learning, as well as what they learn about themselves and the world they live in. In another vein, work such as David Schaafsma's (1998) considers how students themselves construct narrative formulations of a self or selves in writing stories. Narrative approaches to subject positioning and self formation, like Schaafsma's as well as Valerie Walkerdine's (1990) analysis of the production of "schoolgirl fictions," overcome an aspect of Foucault's formation that has received a great deal of criticism. Feminists in particular have brought Foucault to task for not giving adequate attention to resistance or to mechanisms through which individuals may "maneuver against" or contest the productive power of discourse. Individuals, they insist, rather than being molded into "unitary subjects uniquely positioned," "are produced at a nexus of subjectivities, in relations of power that are constantly shifting, rendering them at one moment powerful and at another powerless" (Walkerdine, 1990, p. 3). Individuals are produced as subjects differentially within a variety of discursive practices and multiple discourses. This provides "room for maneuver" (Chambers, 1990), for negotiating, performing, and playing with multiple identities. In this way, then, power is seen as always partial; "the discursive production of self as the unified coherent, humanist whole is always incomplete and fragmented because of the multiple and contradictory discourses to which each person is subject" (Davies, 1990, p. 346).

POSTMODERNITY, EDUCATION, AND THE POLITICS OF IDENTITY

Whether one views the current predicament as representing a transition from modernity to a new postmodern condition or simply as the emergence of a new, reflexive stage of modernity, it is clear that a number of historical developments have converged in ways that make questions of identity and identification increasingly salient. The decentering of the nation-state and a decline in the geopolitical dominance of the West have created spaces for new forms of cultural identifications and politics to emerge. In addition, the advances in global communication and media technology, together with the expanding forces of commodification and consumerism, have created new environments for and influences on processes of self-identity formation.

In the field of education, questions of identity, identification, and culture figure centrally within a range of debates, controversies, and innovations. I will discuss three foci within education research in which issues of group and self-identity, identification, and cultural difference are playing a particularly significant role: identity politics and issues of group inclusion and exclusion, recognition, and representation; the "culture wars" over epistemological issues and curricular content; and the role of forms of collective identification and processes of identity making in the social and academic experiences of students in schools. Within each of these areas of educational debate and innovation, a central tension underlies the ways in which concepts of identity and culture are being invoked—a tension that also lies at the heart of the postmodern condition. This tension informs the contrasts between essentialist and postmodern formulations of identity and culture. It corresponds to a widespread tendency, in politics and academic discourse alike, to objectify difference, view identities and cultural traditions as discrete and clearly delineated, and assert claims to cultural homogeneity and authenticity in the context of globalization—a world of increasing cultural fragmentation, heterogeneity, and hybridity. The phenomenon, I will argue, is not simply an academic issue. Educational policies and practices are being designed, debated, and implemented in relation to particular assumptions about the role of identity and culture in the schooling experiences of young people. The ability to understand the social, political, and cultural dynamics underlying educational policy debates, as well as the success or failure of various pedagogical approaches, is dependent on the adequacy of the frameworks for understanding the complex interplay of identity, culture, and education in the postmodern condition.

Group-based identities have long been central to concerns with representation and rights in the political tradition of the United States (Dunn, 1998, p. 19; Calhoun, 1994). The social transformations of the 1960s brought about the politicization of group identification as a basis for mobilizing and claiming rights within struggles against oppression and inequality. A turning point in the history of American political culture was the civil rights movement, which reflected a deeper set of social and cultural transformations in the United States related to the decline of social class as the primary basis of identity and political action. In the context of "identity politics," forms of group identity and difference—in place of class position—have come to be seen as the basis of oppression and inequality, of social exclusion and a lack of representation. "Identity politics," according to Robert Dunn (1998), "refers to a strategy whereby individuals define themselves through identification with or membership in groups or categories regarded as the source of distinct feelings and experiences of marginalization and subordination" (p. 20). Concepts of group identity and culture are increasingly invoked in both arguments explaining oppression and inequality and in collective efforts to mobilize against forms of injustice.

More recently, the end of the cold war and the collapse of Soviet communism have served to solidify the hegemony of capitalism globally. These developments within the "postsocialist condition" have further reinforced this transformation in political discourse, one that Nancy Fraser (1997) characterizes as a shift from the politics of redistribution to the politics of recognition. This change in discourse signifies a shift in our assumptions about justice. Within the postsocialist condition, the decentering of issues of class corresponds to a movement away from concern with socioeconomic injustices—forms of inequality assumed to be rooted in the political-economic structure of society. Struggles to achieve greater social justice no longer focus exclusively on manifestations of socioeconomic inequity, such as exploitation (wherein one's labor is appropriated for the benefit, or profit, of others), economic marginalization (being confined to low-paying labor), as well as disadvantage and deprivation (being deprived of an adequate standard of living) (Fraser, 1997, p. 13). This orientation to social injustice, Fraser argues, has been eclipsed by the rise of a new "political imagery" centered on "identity," "difference," "cultural domination," and "recognition" (p. 11). What Fraser calls "cultural injustice" is assumed to be rooted in sociocultural processes of representation, interpretation, and communication (p. 14). A concern with forms of cultural injustice informs claims for recognition, for the increased validation and valorization of diversity in general and the identities of "others" more particularly. Similar assumptions, I would argue, also underlie political action aimed at achieving greater inclusion, access, and representation on the basis of group identification.

In the era of identity politics, culture has taken on new significance. Liberal discourse and debates about "minority cultural rights" and political integration are infused with assumptions about the nature of "culture" and language as bases of collective identity. Within contemporary liberal debates, questions of equality have increasingly come to revolve around issues of nondiscrimination against, versus recognition of, difference. Some argue that equal treatment can be provided only by neutral public institutions, while others insist that citizens can be represented as equal only if agencies and institutions recognize and accommodate particular cultural identities and differences (Taylor and Gutmann, 1994, p. 4).

The creation of policies directed toward protecting the "rights" of "minorities" to "equal" educational opportunities generates a unique form of cultural politics. Policy debates concerning the educational rights of "cultural minorities" frequently are reconfigured as dilemmas about how to meet minority educational "needs." Fraser (1988) has referred to this form of cultural politics as "needs talk" or, more precisely, the "politics of needs interpretation." As she explains, "In advanced-capitalist welfare-state societies, talk about people's needs is an important species of political discourse . . . needs-talk functions as a medium for the making and contesting of political claims. It is an idiom in which political conflict is played out and through which inequalities are symbolically elaborated and challenged" (p. 39). Needs talk in educational policy creates the possibility for groups so targeted to mobilize to achieve political ends. The politics of needs interpretation opens channels for discourse about cultural differences. It prompts the invocation of objectified cultural forms in struggles over the distribution of resources and justice and against the cultural devaluation of ethnic and racial "others."

"The politics of needs interpretation" often masks more complex and contradictory forms of cultural politics, power struggles, and processes of cultural change (Hall, n.d.b.). To understand the cultural politics stimulated by local democratic approaches to resolving dilemmas of cultural diversity, one must look more closely at the nature of the political struggles being fought through the politics of needs interpretation. What are subordinate groups attempting to achieve in their struggles to reconfigure the way their "needs" are defined and their political claims legitimated? How are their claims subverted and their potential power defused by dominant and authoritative definitions of the "needs" of minority students? How do the "needs" and "problems" constituted in the politics of needs interpretation correspond, if at all, to the nuanced and contradictory ways people make sense of and experience these "problems" in their everyday lives? And what does this say about the potential for, as well as the limitations of, using welfare rights discourse to achieve social justice and greater equality, particularly in the public sphere that surrounds education? As educational institutions become ever more deeply embedded within the contested terrain of cultural and identity politics, further research will be needed to answer questions such as these about the subtle dynamics of power that underlie educational policy debates within the public sphere.

A second site in the field of education in which a distinctive form of identity politics is at work is the battle zone of the "culture wars." Here assumptions about the nature of "culture" and its relationship to group identities inform debates over questions of epistemology and what criteria should be used to assess the value of divergent forms of knowledge as well as what types of knowledge should be taught, and to whom and for what purposes. The rise of identity politics has generated a unique set of critiques directed toward the universalist "grand narratives" of Western modernity and the assumption that knowledge can be separated from values and politics. Identity politics, in the most general sense, has involved struggles to shift the balance of intellectual authority within institutions of higher education (Gitlin, 1995a, 1995b; Levine, 1996). The "forgotten people of modernity" (Wallerstein and others, 1996, p. 65)—subaltern, African American, feminist, and gay and lesbian scholars—have demanded and won recognition. Their efforts have stimulated profound transformations in the empirical and epistemological bases of scholarship. Histories have been rewritten to reflect the voices, perspectives, and experiences that have until now been excluded, denigrated, or silenced. Yet projects of rewriting history have not simply involved adding forgotten voices to existing historical narratives. Society, literature, and history have had to be rethought, new areas of inquiry have been created, and many of the age-old canonical master narratives produced at the center have been displaced, challenged by the often contradictory or incommensurable versions emerging from the increasingly powerful peripheries. These scholarly perspectives implicitly and explicitly bring into doubt the possibility of finding a single transhistorical truth, an Archimedean standpoint in relation to which the validity of knowledge claims can be determined. Postmodern approaches more generally view forms of knowledge, including scientific understandings, as always partial, positioned, and perspectival. What is called for is a replacement of "master" or "meta-narratives" with local, contextualized, and pragmatic conceptual strategies—strategies for assessing the value of knowledge from different standpoints and in relation to distinctive purposes.

Standpoint epistemologies are constructed by people living, at least partially, outside the dominant power structures. They are the "outsiders within" (Collins, 1991), living in the "borderlands" (Anzaldua, 1987), moving from the margins to the center (Hooks, 1983), or in the "lines of fault" that create "bifurcated consciousnesses." Their knowledge potentially reveals "'what is not supposed to exist,' the interested, 'subjective,' local, ethnocentric character of dominant knowledge systems that claim to be disinterested, maximally objective, universally valid, and speaking from no particular social location at all . . . that modern European science, too, is an 'ethnoscience'"(Harding, 1996, p. 447).

A critical tension crosscuts the various approaches to understanding identity-based epistemologies. This corresponds to differences between essentialist and constructivist (including postmodern) conceptions of social identity. Feminist formulations, among others, have frequently assumed that members of particular social groups share "essential attributes"—biological or cultural predispositions to view and to respond to the world in a similar way. Postmodern theorists, in turn, have sought to rid theories of identity and difference of the vestiges of essentialist thought. Social identities from a postmodern viewpoint are assumed to be multiple, fragmented, situationally contingent, and often contradictory.

Patricia Hill Collins (1991), Moleki Asante (1987), and other proponents of Afrocentric perspectives have been challenged for overextending the notion of an essential, unitary, and uniform transhistorical black culture and consciousness (Appiah, 1992). Identity-based theories of positional knowledge and ways of knowing, whether gay, feminist, ethnic, or racially oriented, all run the risk of assuming that individuals presumed to "belong" to a social group will share the same relationship to, and consciousness of, that identity and thereby will possess a common perspective. This is obviously not the case. For while oppression may work in part through the imposition of unifying categories—"black," "Asian," "gay," "female"—this does not mean that ascribed categories reflect the existence of unified groups. Nor do people so defined all identify, or identify in the same way, with a group label. While essentializing categories of identity are often useful for purposes of political mobilization, they gloss, under the guise of a unifying cultural essence, what is often a rich heterogeneity of historical traditions, cultural orientations, and individual experiences (McCarthy, 1995; Gitlin, 1995a, 1995b; Dyson, 1994). As Kwame Appiah (1992) argues in relation to the notion of an essential African American culture, "Whatever Africans share, we do not have a common traditional culture, common languages, a common religious or conceptual vocabulary [and] we do not even belong to a common race" (p. 26).

Categories of identity and difference, whether they signify gendered, racial, class, cultural, or sexual differences, are social-historical categories; they do not refer to stable groups possessing invariant characteristics, affiliated in the same way through time and across space. Yet essentialist assumptions are widespread within education research. This is evident in "origins-oriented" explanations of "minority" schooling experiences. These analyses attribute differences in student achievement levels to what are represented as indelible, shared characteristics of culture, linguistic style, cognitive capacity, or social organizational factors such as family structures or migration patterns. What needs to be acknowledged and attended to instead, argues Cameron McCarthy (1995), is "contradiction, discontinuity, and nuance within and between embattled social groups," as well as "the contradictory interests, needs, and desires that inform minority education [and] cultural and political behavior, and that define minority encounters with majority whites in educational settings in society" (p. 331). What is required are analyses that do not assume that collective or self-identities, orientations, or experiences are homogeneous, stable, or shared across different social contexts or over time.

The sustained challenge of postcolonial, black, gay, and feminist scholars has brought attention to the cultural politics underlying dominant Western forms of knowledge and ways of knowing; it has paved the way for a greater appreciation for and consideration of local, culturally distinctive epistemologies. These scholars have sparked greater interest in and realization of the importance of the local and the specific and the politics of positionality and location (Moore, 1996, p. 2). The focus on questions of identity and epistemology highlights the complex relationship between local cultural conceptions of knowledge and knowing and orientations to formal education. Implicit in these analyses are important lessons for Western educators—insights into how local beliefs about knowledge inform the way different cultural groups assess the value, or lack thereof, of formal education.

Educational anthropologists have been concerned for decades now with the question of how cultural differences influence the way students and their parents engage with schools and other sites of socialization and learning. Research into "minority" educational experiences and academic performance has typically ranged from micro to macro perpectives on group achievement. (For an insightful discussion of studies of "school failure," see McDermott, 1997; and for an alternative approach to the construction of "school success," see Mehan, Villaneueva, Hubbard, and Lintz, 1996). Rigorous sociolinguistics-based "microanalyses" of classroom interactions have described the forms of miscommunication that can occur due to differences in communication styles between teachers and students (Erickson, 1993; Philips, 1983). In contrast, broad-based macro studies have focused on how a group's migration history shapes perceptions of, and responses to, educational opportunities (Ogbu, 1987). Yet as Margaret Eisenhart (n.d.; see also Gibson, 1997) suggests, each approach has been limited by its use of traditional theories of culture—formulations that couple a notion of a fairly static, homogeneous, and shared culture to a social group. As Eisenhart and others (Levinson and Holland, 1996) have pointed out, a focus on processes of identify formation—on the production and negotiation of cultural identities by social actors within and across social settings—provides a more powerful analytic framework for addressing the influences of culture on the schooling experiences of students.

More recent research into processes of identity formation in schools draws from what has become a vast literature on issues of subjectivity and the cultural politics of identity and difference. These influences are evident in a number of ethnographic studies of the "making of" gender, race, sexual, and ethnic identities in schools, communities, and families (Walkerdine, 1990; Mac an Ghaill, 1994; Hall, 1995, n.d.a.; Davidson, 1996; and Proweller, 1998). Identity formation is described as a process requiring young people to negotiate multiple forms of identification whose meanings vary across social contexts, involving what Renato Rosaldo (1989) has referred to as "cultural improvisation" and Willis (1990) as "symbolic play."

Analyses of the cultural production of identity and difference also are increasingly emphasizing the "dialogic" nature of collective identity formation. As many have argued (Barth, 1969; Comaroff, 1987; Omi and Winant, 1994), processes of minority group identity formation are always relational and historically specific to the sociopolitical context in which these groups are interrelating. Minority groups may "invent" or "improvise" new cultural forms, practices, traditions, and identifications, but they do so within the context of ongoing cross-cultural dialogues about difference (Marcus and Fischer, 1986, pp. 104–106).

Dialogues about difference, moreover, are taking on an increasingly global or transnational character (Appadurai, 1996; Basch, Schiller, and Blanc, 1994). Local processes of identity formation are shaped by what Appadurai refers to as "global cultural flows"—transnational connections created in part by the increasing movement of people, media images, and commodities across national boundaries. The impact of these global forces on local processes of cultural learning and identity formation reflects additional dimensions of cultural production that theoretical formations increasingly will need to address.

In our age of global expansion in communications technology, the media increasingly mediate processes of socialization and acculturation. The media play a critical role in "mediating" processes of cultural learning. Mediated cultural learning, following from Thompson's (1995) formulation of mediated culture or symbolic forms, can refer to a number of diverse "media-mediated" cultural processes. The images, ideas, commodities, and narratives that circulate via television, music styles, and other popular culture mediums shape the subjectivities of those who consume these media products. Yet the influence of media messages is not in any way deterministic, for the messages are complex and contradictory, and those who receive these images read them, or actively construct their specific meanings. Television, music culture, and magazines provide resources that young people use "in making sense of their experiences, in relating to others, and in organizing their daily lives" (Buckingham, 1993, p. 13). The notion of the media as a vehicle for cultural transmission or social learning is hardly new. More work is needed, however, to clarify the ways in which mass-mediated processes of cultural transmission enter into the lives of young people and the different types of cultural engagement or learning these entail. Recognition of the power of the media and of "common culture" has led some, like Willis (1990) and Peter McLaren and Rhonda Hammer (1996), to call for the development—in the words of the latter—of "critical media literacies."

Teenagers are consumers of the cultural styles, symbols, and tastes embodied in, and expressed through, youth cultural forms and commodities. Many also seek out the relatively new hybrid forms of popular culture and music. These media messages and representations and popular culture styles and images provide potential cultural identifications—"identity formation materials" (McRobbie, 1994)—that young people use in making sense of what it means to be a teenager. Their understandings, in turn, influence how they respond to other forms of cultural learning in their lives, such as socializing forces encountered at home, in school, within their peer groups, and in their communities.

Mass-mediated cultural learning is a critical component of processes of identity formation for all youth, but in the lives of minority youth it provides a context for cross-cultural reflection. In fashioning their sense of what it means to be a member of an "ethnic" or "racial" minority, young people draw from a range of media productions, including the objectified images and representations of their culture, religion, history, and traditions depicted on television and in films. "Their culture" is invoked in what are implicitly cross-cultural dialogues about difference—dialogues that give young people the opportunity to reflect on how they and others socially construct and view "their culture" and "their place" in society. These media representations have a powerful influence on how young people come to understand what it means to be defined as "different" or as "other."

The focus on processes of identity formation in education research provides a greater appreciation of the complex role that culture as well as various cultural influences play in informing how students and their parents make sense of and engage with schools and forms of schooling. Research into processes of identity formation and transformation, then, is providing critical insight into student response to schooling. Recent studies have benefited from developments in theories of culture and identity. Anthropologists of education are developing theories of culture and identity that provide greater explanatory power as they give attention to both the multiplicity of individual paths through schools and the fragmented and often contradictory perspectives students defined as "other" hold toward schools and their schooling experiences. At the center of these accounts is an appreciation for human creativity—for the myriad ways that students react to forms of social inequality, make, resist, and play with cultural identities, and interpret and respond to educational opportunities.

UNDERSTANDING "THE LOCAL" IN THE CONTEXT OF GLOBALIZATION

The postmodern turn in anthropology and cultural studies has directed attention to the multiple and positional, local and political nature of social knowledge, ways of knowing, and forms of knowledge production as well as processes of identity formation. This postmodern emphasis on things local has emerged in tandem with another major shift within the social sciences: the growing concern with the impact of globalization. The field of globalization studies is vast, diverse, and highly interdisciplinary. Anthropological studies tend to center on two major foci: first, research into the production of global cultures, institutions, and cultural forms; and second, the local articulation of global processes.

This parallel concern with the local is hardly an accident of academic history. Postmodern skepticism about the meta-narratives of modernity along with the widespread (and largely nonpostmodernist) interest in the dialectics of the global must each be viewed in the context of the developments of capitalism or, more precisely, of global capitalism and the emergence of a global division of labor. The shifts in the geopolitics of knowledge, identity, and power that I have highlighted are directly tied to transformations in the global economy and the traditional divisions between the center and the periphery. As nations and regions formally known as "Third World" have achieved economic success, questions have been raised not only about Western knowledge but also about the assumptions of traditional Eurocentric models of development and "progress" (Dirlik, 1996).

The impact of Western cultural forces and forms—under the auspices of colonialism, "modernization" projects (including education and literacy programs), or "the world system"—has long been a central focus of anthropological research. Accounts of cultural contact have been dominated by two distinctive yet equally Eurocentric models of cultural continuity and change. The first theoretical perspective has presumed that Western cultural forces and forms—religion, commodities, and "school knowledge"—would erode local cultures and eventually transform them in the image of Europe. Local traditions would vanish as casualties of global (Western) homogenization. A second theoretical perspective has been just as pessimistic about and dismissive of local initiative and contributions to social change. What Ulf Hannerz (1997) has labeled "the peripheral corruption scenario" depicts cultures at the periphery as drawing from Western ideals and knowledge, only to corrupt them (pp. 108–109). In each case, cultural change is viewed as a one-way process of penetration of the center into the periphery. Perceiving global transformations from a decidedly Western vantage point, these formulations have implied, as Marshall Sahlins puts it, "that Western hegemony is human destiny" (1994, p. 378).

Over the past decade, a great deal of conceptual innovation has resulted from attempts to develop theories of culture to meet the conceptual challenges of analyzing the global–local dynamics of social change (Cvetkovich and Kellner, 1997). These efforts have stimulated a range of debates about the nature of culture and forms of "cultural complexity" in a world crosscut by networks of transnational connections (Sahlins, 1992; Appadurai, 1996; Hannerz, 1992, 1996; King, 1997; Kearney, 1995). What is evident on each side of these debates, however, is that theories of global-local articulations are moving beyond the Eurocentric and unidirectional models of change exemplified by traditional modernization and world-systems theories.

From across the debates and controversies over theorizing local processes of social change, a number of general themes have emerged. First, the concern with understanding local responses to globalization has encouraged anthropologists to give closer and more systematic attention to the range of cultural practices and material conditions that are being produced under the conditions of late modernity (Comaroff and Comaroff, 1993). There is greater appreciation for the culturally and historically specific nature of the multiple modernities and "cosmologies of capitalism" (Sahlins, 1992) that are being created at the intersection of global-local transactions. Anthropologists are also examining the interrelationships among processes of cultural production at different levels of the social scale (within global organizations, national policies, institutional contexts, and everyday practices) as well as across the parameters of time and space. To capture these multidimensional processes, anthropologists are design-ing analytic frameworks that make use of multiple concepts of culture. Culture increasingly works in the world as both a folk and an analytic construct. It is something that people who are studied invoke within the discursive practices of cultural politics, commodify or consume as "heritage" or "style," and take for granted or simply live as "habitus." What the culture concept lacks in clar-ity (and, therefore, some argue, utility) has certainly gained in complexity.

Finally, attempts to come to terms with the transnational aspects of cultural processes in the context of globalization have prompted anthropologists to reflect in creative ways on the relationship between culture and space. Concerns with global cultural and economic forces and forms are leading researchers to question many of the traditional ways that social scientists have considered social life in spatial terms. Recent anthropological research has called for the uncoupling of notions of society, culture, and territory and has problematized taken-for-granted assumptions that "locality and community are obvious, that their recognition and affective power flow automatically out of direct sensory experience and face-to-face encounters." This has paved the way for innovative research exploring "how understandings of locality, community, and region are formed and lived" (Gupta and Ferguson, 1997, pp. 6–7).

Education institutions have served as one of the primary vehicles of mod-ernization. Hence, developments in theories of local-global connections promise to stimulate new ways of thinking about local responses to the educational proj-ects in what is referred to as the global age. As yet, there has not been a great deal of anthropological research into the impact of globalization on local edu-cational projects, practices, or purposes. There are a few exemplary examples of promising lines of research, however. These ethnographic approaches once again demonstrate quite powerfully that one must look beyond the school itself to understand the local meanings and impact of schooling.

Over the years, the concern to understand the contextual meanings and use of literacy practices has led to the development of innovative ethnographic approaches to studying knowledge and knowledge acquisition (Goody, 1968; Heath, 1983; Street, 1984; see Collins, 1995). Research under the auspices of the "New Literacy Studies" (Street, 1993) has furthered this tradition, situating ethnographic descriptions of the "richness and variety" of literacy practices within analyses of their significance to relations of power and authority.

Don Kulick and Christopher Stroud (1993), among others, have noted a prob-lem in the way literacy researchers have tended to construct "the local." Local people, they argue, are too often represented as "passive objects who become affected by literacy in ways they are neither fully aware of or able to control." Literacy programs do not simply have local "impact"; rather, local people "affect literacy." Their approach to literacy learning, in keeping with anthropological theories of learning more generally, focuses on the active agency of learners, or how people in everyday practice "actively and creatively apply literacy skills to suit their own purposes and needs" (p. 31). The acquisition of literacy clearly has social consequences, yet these effects cannot be explained without considering how local people respond to and choose to make use of the skills that programs seek to provide.

Maurice Bloch (1993), addressing issues of cross-cultural literacy, stresses the continued significance of a fundamental anthropological principle: local responses to schooling, to be understood, must be viewed through a wide ethnographic lens. His study poses a basic question: Why do the Zafimaniry, a people living in a small, remote village in rural Madagascar, value so highly the education they receive from a local Catholic church school? In exploring this question, Bloch moves beyond the school itself to consider the organization and valuation of local forms of knowledge—the knowledge and orientations to knowing that people bring with them when they enter the schoolroom door. The meaning and purpose people give to schooling and school knowledge, he argues, can be understood only from the perspective of the broader sociocultural context within which this schooling takes place. As he explains,

> When we put school knowledge within that context it becomes possible to understand somewhat better both why villagers should value school knowledge, and how they use it. The strength of the explanation depends on the fact that . . . the schooling villagers receive does not seem to affect their organisation and philosophy of knowledge; instead school knowledge is itself interpreted within the terms of the village home culture. . . . *The strength of home culture, in Mamolena, at least, is not surprising to an anthropologist who has carried out field work in the traditional manner, noting daily life as it occurs, not focusing on a pre-defined problem, while it might escape the research approach of those who have focused on education even when thinking of themselves principally as anthropologists.* . . . In other words, it is by understanding things which at first appear totally remote from education and literacy that their meaning for the Zafimaniry can finally be grasped. . . . The Zafimaniry . . . have a meta theory about different kinds of knowledge which is associated with different styles of communication and which is itself part and parcel of much more general concerns such as the maturation of the body and the person, the nature of human society and its relation to the non-human world of plants, animals and places [1993, p. 95; emphasis mine].

The Zafimaniry interpret school knowledge in relation to their beliefs about different types of knowledge. School knowledge, explains Bloch, is seen as similar to the "wisdom" of elders. Hence, "it also comes from an absolutely authoritative beyond, which one respects but does not want to come too close to." Like wisdom, school knowledge is believed to be categorically true, though not of practical relevance in the empirical world. The association of school knowledge with wisdom, however, also produces expectations for its proper transmission —expectations that are not met by the school's teaching practices:

School knowledge cannot in every way be that simply assimilated into the preexisting system. This is because Zafimaniry theories of knowledge assume a heterogeneity between the type of knowledge and the kind of person who professes it. If school knowledge is a form of wisdom it is being transmitted by the wrong kind of people to the wrong kind of people since it is taught by the young to the very young. Furthermore, the problem is made worse by the fact that the type of communicative code that is appropriate for the transmission of "wisdom" is inappropriate for either pupils or schoolteachers [1993, p. 101].

For the Zafimaniry, then, schooling creates anomalies that can be problematic. On the one hand, the association of school knowledge with wisdom predisposes them to accept the value of schooling. Yet on the other hand, when students and teachers, neither of whom are elders, teach or use literacy, they implicitly challenge principles supporting the local social order and traditional authority relations. Hence, "since communicative style, person, and knowledge are totally welded together for the Zafimaniry, the use of literacy in the village presents the same problems" (1993, p. 102). Villagers do find ways to make use of literacy in ways that do not disrupt authority relations, however, such as making young writers appear to act as scribes who record the wisdom of the elders.

The ethnographic case studies included in another recent book (Levinson, Foley, and Holland, 1996) provide examples of analytic frameworks that educational anthropologists are developing to study more effectively the location of schooling within broader national and local cultural politics. This line of research represents an important point of synergy between research in education, anthropology, and cultural studies. The studies give critical ethnographic attention to the complex cultural politics informing the production of educational purposes and educated persons. They bring together concepts of cultural production and human agency to consider "the way people actively confront the ideological and material conditions presented by schooling." Bradley Levinson and Dorothy Holland (1996) describe their approach to "the cultural production of the educated person" as providing a window to the ways social actors navigate the multiple forms and forces of cultural learning within any social order. Becoming an educated person, they argue, creates forms of subjectivity and ways of being in the world that in turn generate "understandings and strategies which may in fact move well beyond the school, transforming aspirations, household relations, local knowledges and structures of power." Moreover, formal schooling, they remind us, is not the only path to becoming an "educated person." To understand the role of formal schooling in any society, they argue, researchers have to consider that "outside the school, in diverse spaces of street, home, and family, other kinds of educated persons are culturally produced as well" (pp. 14–15).

These studies mark an important transition in anthropological approaches to understanding the place and purpose of modern education within a globalizing world. Increasingly the anthropologist's attention has shifted from traditional concerns with the local impact of Western schooling or with cross-cultural differences in how schooling is conducted, to research focusing on interactive processes of cultural production. This presents significant methodological and conceptual challenges. Considering education from this perspective requires that anthropologists do justice to local conditions and contingencies, as well as to the dynamics and dialectics of local and global processes of change. For although Bloch's argument for studying the local context of schooling is fundamental, local cultural knowledges seldom exist in the deceptively simple and systematic form he describes in representing Zafimaniry meta-theory. Anthropologists, including Bloch, have largely abandoned traditional assumptions about bounded autonomous cultural systems. Formulations of conflicts between encountering cultures are dismissed because they fail to account for the role of human agency and, as Appadurai suggests, "internal cultural debates" (1996, p. 48).

CONCLUSION

In this era of globalization and the rise of identity politics, "culture" has taken on new meta-cultural meanings, connotations, and relevance. It has become a source or locus of collective rights and a resource for political mobilization. Meta-cultural politics emerge from the historical conjuncture of the global organization of capital and the concomitant surpassing or decentering of the power of the nation-state, as influenced as well by the increasing transnational flows of labor migration and media forms, capital and commodities. As the centrality of the nation-state has declined and, correspondingly, as the hegemony of national cultures has eroded, "culture" has become a focal point of contestation over group interests, aims, and rights. In the context of these forms of cultural politics, "culture" becomes reified—converted into a political asset to be used to forge and mobilize group solidarity and assert collective claims (Turner, 1994, p. 420; Dominguez, p. 1992). Education, from the politics of multiculturalism to the projects of modernization, continues to be a central site for what are increasingly globalized local contests over culture, identity, and power. It is in the contexts of these cultural politics that educational purposes are being produced.

Historically, national publics have designated educational purposes in struggles to invent national cultures, create ideal citizens, and fight for imagined futures—often to contradictory ends. As I have argued in this chapter, the displacement of modern centers, national as well as Western, has provided opportunities for thinking anew about relationships among power, knowledge, and identity. The cultural politics of education are becoming ever more plural yet perspectival, situationally contingent yet played out on increasingly globalized-local terrains.

As is evident across the educational landscape in the United States, the cultural politics of education holds more than purely academic significance. The paradox of pluralism is fueling heated debates and controversies, claims and counterclaims about what schools should be teaching, how different students should be taught, and who should be their teachers and where they should teach (at school or in the home). Education remains a contested terrain, and the contests are inherently cultural and frequently contradictory. The dilemmas that underlie debates over standards, bilingual education, multicultural curriculum, and home schooling are far from resolved. New forms of cultural politics, in other words, are at the heart of many of the practical challenges our modern system of public education is facing today. To unravel these controversies—to imagine new educational purposes, institutional structures, and instructional practices to meet these often paradoxical public demands—we as researchers and practitioners need a broader vision and greater conceptual clarity.

What this suggests is that the synergistic connections between education and anthropology appear destined to expand in density and deepen in significance. Educational researchers and practitioners are recognizing increasingly that underlying current debates over educational purposes and practices are complex dilemmas associated with the paradox of pluralism and the politics of identity in an era of globalization. Anthropologists, in their desire to understand the shifting relationships of knowledge, power, and identity, are being drawn in greater numbers to the study of educational processes. Standing at the border of both worlds, as an anthropologist teaching in a school of education, I feel I am witnessing a period producing particularly fruitful cultural encounters. I hope that the conceptual clarification I have provided will contribute to enriching these conversations.

References

Ahmed, A., and Shore, C. (eds.). *The Future of Anthropology: Its Relevance to the Contemporary World.* London: Athlone, 1995.

Anderson, G. L. "Critical Ethnography in Education: Origins, Current Status, and New Directions." In C. Conrad and others (eds.), *Qualitative Research in Higher Education.* New York: Ginn Press, 1993.

Anzaldua, G. (1987). *Borderlands/La Frontera: The New Mestiza.* San Francisco: Spinsters/Aunt Lute, 1987.

Appadurai, A. *Modernity at Large: Cultural Dimensions of Globalization.* Minneapolis: University of Minnesota Press, 1996.

Appiah, K. A. *In My Father's House.* New York: Oxford University Press, 1992.

Apple, M. W. "Rebuilding Hegemony: Education, Equality, and the New Right." In D. Dworkin and L. G. Roman (eds.), *Views Beyond the Border Country: Raymond Williams and Cultural Politics.* New York: Routledge, 1993.

Asante, M. K. *The Afrocentric Idea.* Philadelphia: Temple University Press, 1987.

Ball, S. J. "Introducing Monsieur Foucault." In *Foucault and Education.* London: Routledge, 1990.

Barth, F. *Ethnic Groups and Boundaries: The Social Organization of Culture Difference.* London: Allen & Unwin, 1969.

Basch, L., Schiller, N. G., and Blanc, C. S. *Nations Unbound: Transnational Projects, Postcolonial Predicaments and Deterritorialized Nation-States.* Langhorne, Pa.: Gordon & Breach, 1994.

Beck, U., Giddens, A., and Lash, S. *Reflexive Modernization: Politics, Tradition and Aesthetics in the Modern Social Order.* Cambridge, England: Polity Press, 1994.

Behar, R., and Gordon, D. (eds.). *Women Writing Culture.* Berkeley, Calif.: University of California Press, 1995.

Bloch, M. (1993). "The Uses of Schooling and Literacy in a Zafimaniry Village." In B. V. Street (ed.), *Cross-cultural Approaches to Literacy.* New York: Cambridge University Press, 1993.

Bourdieu, P. "Cultural Reproduction and Social Reproduction." In R. Brown (ed.), *Knowledge, Education, and Cultural Change.* London: Tavistock, 1973.

Bourdieu, P. *Distinction: A Social Critique of the Judgement of Taste.* Cambridge, Mass.: Harvard University Press, 1984.

Bourdieu, P., and Passeron, J. C. *The Inheritors.* Chicago: University of Chicago Press, 1979. (Originally published 1964.)

Bourdieu, P., and Passeron, J. C. *Reproduction in Education, Society, and Culture.* Thousand Oaks, Calif.: Sage, 1994. (Originally published 1970.)

Bowles, S., and Gintis, H. *Schooling in Capitalist America: Educational Reform and the Contradictions of Economic Life.* New York: Basic Books, 1976.

Bruner, J. *The Culture of Education.* Cambridge, Mass.: Harvard University Press, 1996.

Buckingham, D. (ed.). *Reading Audiences.* Manchester, England: Manchester University Press, 1993.

Calhoun, C. "Social Theory and the Politics of Identity." In C. Calhoun (ed.), *Social Theory and the Politics of Identity.* Cambridge, Mass.: Blackwell, 1994.

Carnoy, M. (1989). "Education, State, and Culture in American Society." In H. Giroux and P. McLaren (eds.), *Critical Pedagogy, the State, and Cultural Struggle.* Albany: State University of New York Press, 1989.

Carnoy, M., and Levin, H. M. *Schooling and Work in the Democratic State.* Stanford, Calif.: Stanford University Press, 1985.

Carspecken, P. F. *Critical Ethnography in Educational Research: A Theoretical and Practical Guide.* New York: Routledge, 1996.

Chambers, R. *Room for Maneuver.* Chicago: University of Chicago Press, 1990.

Clifford, J., and Marcus, G. E. (eds.). *Writing Culture: The Poetics and Politics of Ethnography.* Berkeley, Calif.: University of California Press, 1986.

Cochran-Smith, M., and Lytle, S. L. *Inside/Outside: Teacher Research and Knowledge.* New York: Teachers College Press, 1993.

Collins, J. "Literacy and Literacies." *Annual Review of Anthropology,* 1995, *24,* 75–95.

Collins, P. H. *Black Feminist Thought: Knowledge, Consciousness, and the Politics of Empowerment.* New York: Routledge, 1991.

Comaroff, J. L. "Of Totemism and Ethnicity: Consciousness, Practice and the Signs of Inequality." *Ethnos,* 1987, *52,* 301–323.

Comaroff, J., and Comaroff, J. L. *Of Revelation and Revolution: Christianity and Colonialism in South Africa,* Vol. 1. Chicago: University of Chicago Press, 1991.

Comaroff, J., and Comaroff, J. L. Introduction to J. Comaroff and J. L. Comaroff (eds.), *Modernity and Its Malcontents: Ritual and Power in Postcolonial Africa.* Chicago: University of Chicago Press, 1993.

Comaroff, J., and Comaroff, J. L. *Of Revelation and Revolution: Reading, Rioting and Arithmetic.* Vol. 3. Chicago: University of Chicago Press, forthcoming.

Corrigan, P. "In/forming Schooling." In D. W. Livingstone (ed.), *Critical Pedagogy and Cultural Power.* New York: Bergin & Garvey, 1987.

Cremin, L. "The Cacophony of Teaching." In *Popular Education and Its Discontents.* New York: HarperCollins, 1989.

Cvetkovich, A., and Kellner, D. (eds.). *Articulating the Global and the Local: Globalization and Cultural Studies.* Boulder, Colo.: Westview, 1997.

Davidson, A. L. *Making and Molding Identity in Schools.* Albany: State University of New York Press, 1996.

Davies, B. "Agency as a Form of Discursive Practice: A Classroom Scene Observed." *British Journal of Sociology of Education,* 1990, *11*(3), 341–361.

Davies, S. "Leaps of Faith: Shifting Currents in Critical Sociology of Education." *American Journal of Sociology,* 1995, *100*(6), 1448–1478.

Dirlik, A. "The Global in the Local." In R. Wilson and W. Dissanayake (eds.), *Global/ Local: Cultural Production and the Transnational Imaginary.* Durham, N.C.: Duke University Press, 1996.

Dominguez, V. "Invoking Culture: The Messy Side of 'Cultural Politics.'" *South Atlantic Quarterly,* 1992, *91*(1), 19–42.

Dreyfus, H. L., and Rabinow, P. *Michel Foucault: Beyond Structuralism and Hermeneutics.* (2nd ed.) Chicago: University of Chicago Press, 1982.

Dunn, R. G. *Identity Crisis: A Critique of Postmodernity.* Minneapolis: University of Minnesota Press, 1998.

Dworkin, D. L. "Cultural Studies and the Crisis in British Radical Thought." In D. Dworkin and L. G. Roman (eds.), *Views Beyond the Border Country: Raymond Williams and Cultural Politics.* New York: Routledge, 1993.

Dyson, M. E. "Essentialism and the Complexities of Racial Identity." In D. T. Goldberg (ed.), *Multiculturalism: A Critical Reader.* Cambridge, Mass.: Blackwell, 1994.

Eisenhart, M. "Changing Conceptions of Culture and Ethnographic Methodology: Recent Thematic Shifts and Their Implications for Research on Teaching." In V. Richardson (ed.), *The Handbook of Research on Teaching.* (4th ed.) New York: Macmillan, 19xx.

Erickson, F. "Culture in Society and in Educational Practices." In J. A. Banks and C. A. McGee Banks (eds.), *Multicultural Education: Issues and Perspectives.* (3rd ed.) Needham Heights, Mass.: Allyn & Bacon, 1997.

Erickson, F. "Transformation and School Success: The Politics and Culture of Educational Achievement." In E. Jacob and C. Jordan (eds.), *Minority Education: Anthropological Perspectives.* Norwood, N.J.: Ablex, 1993.

Fardon, R. (ed.). *Counterworks: Managing the Diversity of Knowledge.* New York: Routledge, 1995.

Foley, D. E. *Learning Capitalist Culture, Deep in the Heart of Tejas.* Philadelphia: University of Pennsylvania Press, 1990.

Foucault, M. *The Archeology of Knowledge.* London: Tavistock, 1974.

Foucault, M. *Discipline and Punish.* New York: Random House, 1979.

Foucault, M. "Prison Talk." In C. Gordon (ed. and trans.), *Power/Knowledge: Selected Interviews and Other Writings by Michel Foucault, 1972–1977.* New York: Pantheon, 1980.

Fox, R. G. "Introduction: Writing in the Present." In *Recapturing Anthropology.* Santa Fe, N.M.: School of American Research Press, 1991.

Fraser, N. *Justice Interruptus: Critical Reflections on the "Postsocialist" Condition.* New York: Routledge, 1997.

Fraser, N. *Unruly Practices: Power, Discourse, and Gender in Contemporary Social Theory.* Minneapolis: University of Minnesota Press, 1988.

Gibson, M. "Complicating the Immigrant/Involuntary Minority Typology." *Anthropology and Education Quarterly,* 1997, *28*(3), 431–454.

Giddens, A. *The Consequences of Modernity.* Stanford, Calif.: Stanford University Press, 1990.

Gitlin, A. (ed.). *Power and Method: Political Activism and Educational Research.* New York: Routledge, 1994.

Gitlin, T. *The Twilight of Common Dreams: Why America Is Wracked by Culture Wars.* New York: Henry Holt, 1995a.

Gitlin, T. "The Rise of 'Identity Politics': An Examination and a Critique." In M. Berube and C. Nelson (eds.), *Higher Education Under Fire.* New York: Routledge, 1995b.

Goody, J. (ed.). *Literacy in Traditional Society.* New York: Cambridge University Press, 1968.

Greene, M. "Epistemology and Educational Research: The Influence of Recent Approaches to Knowledge." In L. Darling-Hammond (ed.), *Review of Research in Education.* Washington, D.C.: American Educational Research Association, 1994.

Gupta, A., and Ferguson, J. "Culture, Power, Place: Ethnography at the End of an Era." *Introduction to Culture, Power, Place: Explorations in Critical Anthropology.* Durham, N.C.: Duke University Press, 1997.

Hall, K. "There's a Time to Act English and a Time to Act Indian": The Politics of Identity Among British-Sikh Teenagers." In S. Stephens (ed.), *Children and the Politics of Culture.* Princeton, N.J.: Princeton University Press, 1995.

Hall, K. (n.d.a.). *Battling the boundaries of belonging: Education and the politics of culture in England.* Unpublished manuscript.

Hall, K. (n.d.b.). "Asserting 'Needs' and Claiming 'Rights': The Cultural Politics of 'Minority' Language Education Policy in Britain." In J. L. Comaroff and J. Comaroff (eds.), *Anthropology and Education: New Perspectives.* Unpublished manuscript.

Hall, S., and Jefferson, T. (eds.). *Resistance Through Rituals: Youth Subcultures in Post-War Britain.* London: Hutchinson, 1976.

Hannerz, U. *Cultural Complexity: Studies in the Social Organization of Meaning.* New York: Columbia University Press, 1992.

Hannerz, U. *Transnational Connections: Culture, People, Places.* London: Routledge, 1996.

Hannerz, U. "Scenarios for Peripheral Cultures." In A. D. King (ed.), *Culture, Globalization and the World-System: Contemporary Conditions for the Representation of Identity.* Minneapolis: University of Minnesota Press, 1997.

Harding, S. "Gendered Ways of Knowing and the Epistemological Crisis of the West." In N. R. Goldberger and others (eds.), *Knowledge, Difference, and Power.* New York: Basic Books, 1996.

Harvey, D. *The Condition of Postmodernity.* Cambridge, Mass.: Basil Blackwell, 1989.

Heath, S. B. *Ways with Words: Language, Life, and Work in Communities and Classrooms.* New York: Cambridge University Press, 1983.

Heath, S. B. "Culture: Contested Realm in Research on Children and Youth." *Journal of Applied Developmental Science,* forthcoming.

Hebdige, D. *Subculture: The Meaning of Style.* London: Routledge, 1979.

Hobart, M. "As I Lay Laughing: Encountering Global Knowledge in Bali." In R. Fardon (ed.), *Counterworks: Managing the Diversity of Knowledge.* New York: Routledge, 1995.

Hooks, Bell. *Feminist Theory from Margin to Center.* Boston: South End Press, 1983.

Jarvie, I. "Reply to Sangren, S. P. Rhetoric and the Authority of Ethnography: 'Postmodernism' and the Social Reproduction of Texts." *Current Anthropology,* 1988, *29*(3), 427–428.

Kearney, M. "The Local and the Global: The Anthropology of Globalization and Transnationalism." *Annual Review of Anthropology,* 1995, *24*, 547–565.

Kenway, J. "Education and the Right's Discursive Politics." In S. J. Ball (ed.), *Foucault and Education: Disciplines and Knowledge.* New York: Routledge, 1990.

King, A. D. (ed.). *Culture, Globalization and the World-System: Contemporary Conditions for the Representation of Identity.* Minneapolis: University of Minnesota Press, 1997.

Kulick, D., and Stroud, C. "Conceptions and Uses of Literacy in a Papua New Guinean Village." In B. Street (ed.), *Cross-Cultural Approaches to Literacy.* New York: Cambridge University Press, 1993.

Laclau, E. *Reflections on the New Revolution of Our Times.* London: Verso, 1991.

Lagemann, E. C. *Contested Terrain: A History of Education Research in the United States, 1890–1990.* Chicago: Spencer Foundation, 1996.

Lather, P. *Getting Smart: Feminist Research and Pedagogy With/in the Postmodern.* New York: Routledge, 1991.

Lave, J., Duguid, P., and Fernandez, N. "Coming of Age in Birmingham." *Annual Review of Anthropology,* 1992, *21,* 257–282.

Levine, L. W. *The Opening of the American Mind: Canons, Culture and History.* Boston: Beacon Press, 1996.

Levinson, B. A., Foley, D. E., and Holland, D. C. (eds.). *The Cultural Production of the Educated Person.* Albany: State University of New York Press, 1996.

Levinson, B. A., and Holland, D. C. "The Cultural Production of the Educated Person: An Introduction." In B. A. Levinson, D. E. Foley, and D. C. Holland (eds.), *The Cultural Production of the Educated Person.* Albany: State University of New York Press, 1996.

Lyotard, J. F. *The Postmodern Condition: A Report on Knowledge.* Manchester, England: Manchester University Press, 1984.

McCarthy, C. "Contradictions of Existence: Identity and Essentialism." In M. Berube and C. Nelson (eds.), *Higher Education Under Fire.* New York: Routledge, 1995.

McDermott, R. P. "Achieving School Failure 1972–1997." In G. D. Spindler (ed.), *Education and Cultural Process: Anthropological Approaches.* Prospect Heights, Ill.: Waveland Press, 1997.

McLaren, P., and Hammer, R. "Media Knowledges, Warrior Citizenry, and Postmodern Literacies." In H. Giroux and others (eds.), *Counternarratives: Cultural Studies and Critical Pedagogies in Postmodern Spaces.* New York: Routledge, 1996.

McRobbie, A. "Settling Accounts with Subcultures: A Feminist Critique." *Screen,* 1980, *34,* 37–39.

McRobbie, A. *Postmodernism and Popular Culture.* New York: Routledge, 1994.

Mac an Ghaill, M. *The Making of Men: Masculinities, Sexualities and Schooling.* Buckingham, England: Open University Press, 1994.

MacLeod, J. *Ain't No Makin' It: Leveled Aspirations in a Low-Income Neighborhood.* Boulder, Colo.: Westview Press, 1995. (Originally published 1987.)

Marcus, G. E., and Fischer, M. M. J. *Anthropology as Cultural Critique.* Chicago: University of Chicago Press, 1986.

Mehan, H., Villaneueva, I., Hubbard, L., and Lintz, A. *Constructing School Success*. New York: Cambridge University Press, 1996.

Mitchell, T. *Colonising Egypt*. Berkeley: University of California Press, 1988.

Moore, H. L. (ed.). "The Changing Nature of Anthropological Knowledge." In H. L. Moore (ed.), *The Future of Anthropological Knowledge*. New York: Routledge, 1996.

Ogbu, J. U. "Variability in Minority Responses to Schooling: Nonimmigrants vs. Immigrants." In G. Spindler and L. Spindler (eds.), *Interpretive Ethnography of Education at Home and Abroad*. Hillsdale, N.J.: Erlbaum, 1987.

Olesen, V. (1994). "Feminism and Models of Qualitative Research." In N. K. Denzin and Y. S. Lincoln (eds.), *Handbook of Qualitative Research*. Thousand Oaks, Calif.: Sage, 1994.

Omi, M., and Winant, H. *Racial Formation in the United States*. (2nd ed.) New York: Routledge, 1994.

Ong, A. "Anthropology, China and the Modernities: The Geopolitics of Cultural Knowledge." In H. Moore (ed.), *The Future of Anthropological Knowledge*. New York: Routledge, 1996.

Philips, S. U. *The Invisible Culture: Communication in Classroom and Community on the Warm Springs Indian Reservation*. New York: Longman, 1983.

Popkewitz, T. S., and Brennan, M. (eds.). *Foucault's Challenge: Discourse, Knowledge, and Power in Education*. New York: Teachers College Press, 1988.

Proweller, A. *Contrasting Female Identities: Meaning Making in an Upper Middle Class Youth Culture*. Albany: State University of New York Press, 1998.

Rosaldo, R. *Culture and Truth: The Remaking of Social Analysis*. Boston: Beacon Press, 1989.

Rosenberry, W. *Anthropology and Histories: Essays in Culture, History, and Political Economy*. New Brunswick, N.J.: Rutgers University Press, 1989.

Sahlins, M. "Cosmologies of Capitalism: The Trans-Pacific Sector of the World System." In *Proceedings of the British Academy*, 1992, *74*, 1–51.

Sahlins, M. "Goodbye to Tristes Tropes: Ethnography in the Context of Modern World History." In R. Borofsky (ed.), *Assessing Cultural Anthropology*. New York: McGraw-Hill, 1994.

Said, E. *Culture and Imperialism*. London: Chatto & Windus, 1993.

Sangren, P. S. "Rhetoric and the Authority of Ethnography: 'Postmodernism' and the Social Reproduction of Texts." *Current Anthropology*, 1988, *29*(3), 415–424.

Sassen, S. *Losing Control? Sovereignty in an Age of Globalization*. New York: Columbia University Press, 1996.

Schaafsma, D. "Performing the Self: Constructing Written and Curricular Fictions." In T. S. Popkewitz and M. Brennan (eds.), *Foucault's Challenge: Discourse, Knowledge, and Power in Education*. New York: Teachers College Press, 1988.

Spindler, G. D. (ed.). *Education and Anthropology.* Stanford, Calif.: Stanford University Press, 1955.

Street, B. V. *Literacy in Theory and Practice.* New York: Cambridge University Press, 1984.

Street, B. V. "Introduction: The New Literacy Studies." In B. V. Street (ed.), *Cross-Cultural Perspectives on Literacy.* New York: Cambridge University Press, 1993.

Swartz, D. *Culture and Power: The Sociology of Pierre Bourdieu.* Chicago: University of Chicago Press, 1997.

Taylor, C., and Gutmann, A. (eds.). *Multiculturalism.* Princeton, N.J.: Princeton University Press, 1994.

Thompson, J. B. *The Media and Modernity: A Social Theory of the Media.* Stanford, Calif.: Stanford University Press, 1995.

Turner, T. "Anthropology and Multiculturalism: What Is Anthropology That Multiculturalists Should Be Mindful of It?" In D. T. Goldberg (ed.), *Multiculturalism: A Critical Reader.* Cambridge, Mass.: Blackwell, 1994.

Tyack, D., and Cuban, L. *Tinkering Toward Utopia: A Century of Public School Reform.* Cambridge, Mass.: Harvard University Press, 1995.

Walkerdine, V. *Schoolgirl Fictions.* London: Verso, 1990.

Wallerstein, I., and others. *Open the Social Sciences: Report of the Gulbenkian Commission on the Structuring of the Social Sciences.* Stanford, Calif.: Stanford University Press, 1996.

Weis, L. *Working Class Without Work: High School Students in a De-Industrializing Economy.* New York: Routledge, 1990.

Wexler, P. *Becoming Somebody.* Bristol, Pa.: Falmer, 1992.

Willis, P. *Learning to Labor.* New York: Columbia University Press, 1977.

Willis, P. "Cultural Production Is Different from Social Reproduction Is Different from Reproduction." *Interchange,* 1981, *12*(2), 48–67.

Willis, P. *Common Culture.* London: Open University Press, 1990.

PART THREE

EDUCATION
RESEARCH AS A VOCATION

CHAPTER EIGHT

Professing Educational Scholarship

Lee S. Shulman

The chapters in this part, and indeed in the entire book, explore the ideal qualities of education research as a form of scholarship, the manner in which such work ought to be conducted, and the means by which scholars who conduct that work should be prepared. All the chapters take account of the ferment that currently characterizes our field. As Ellen Lagemann and I observed in the Introduction to this book, scholarship in education is undergoing change in many areas, much of it moving from the laboratory to the classroom and school. Much research not only documents attempts at reform; it stimulates precisely the kinds of reform it then intends to study. This interaction of research and practice creates new occasions for both methodological problems and ethical dilemmas. The number of disciplines whose ideas and methods shape educational inquiry has increased dramatically, and the challenge of drawing on these disciplines, their interactions and applications, has become formidable. At the same time, our technological tools for capturing educational practice and archiving and distributing both data and reports of findings have matured rapidly, affording our field opportunities that never existed earlier.

In this chapter, I outline a few of the issues that underlie our call for the improvement of education research. What do we mean when we designate any human activity as a form of scholarship? How does scholarship change when it is an activity associated with a profession of scholarship? What are the special responsibilities associated with conducting a scholarship of practice?

DEFINING SCHOLARSHIP

No scholar is an island. No scholar can work alone. The essential feature of all scholarship is that it is an activity or form of work that cannot be pursued in total isolation. Scholars engage in their work with a sense of modest inadequacy. Every scholar understands that he or she cannot solve all the significant problems of any field alone. Therefore scholarship must be pursued in ways that others can understand, critique, and use. Moreover, since it is unreasonable to expect fellow scholars to reproduce all the steps one has taken in arriving at particular conclusions, there is a necessary combination of factors that accompanies good scholarship: trust that the investigator has collected and managed the "data" in a careful and reasonable manner, has employed well-understood methods to gather and make interpretations of the data, and has presented the research in forms that can be readily understood, appropriately criticized relative to community standards, and then used by colleagues in the pursuit of their own inquiries.

Even that most proverbially isolated of all forms of scholarship, theoretical mathematics, is shaped by membership in scholarly communities. The Princeton mathematician Andrew Wiles, who came up with the proof to Fermat's Last Theorem, was portrayed in the popular media as an isolate, but his account of the discovery repeatedly acknowledged his dependence on the contributions of peers. He devised the strategy that proved necessary for the proof while reading the work of other mathematicians from around the world. After completing his proof, he wrote it up and submitted an article to a refereed journal. Another mathematician who reviewed his article spotted a flaw in the proof, and so reported it to the journal editor. The editor sent the article back for revision. Only then did Wiles recognize the error, attempt to work on it by himself for a few months, and then invite a British algebraist to help him work out the correct solution.

Scholarship thus involves acts of the mind or spirit that are undertaken in disciplined ways and subsequently made public so that members of one's intellectual community can judge their worth and then use them to support the more general program of the community. Scholarship can be identified by four features: the "discipline" with which the work is conducted, the variety of ways in which the work is made public, the manner in which an identifiable intellectual community examines and attests to its quality, and the ways in which the work is displayed, exchanged, aggregated, and shared that render it widely useful and generative. Each of these attributes—discipline, publication and display, peer review, and generativity for others—has undergone change in the world of education scholarship and contributes to the analyses found in this volume.

Discipline

Scholarship must be disciplined. It must be engaged in a systematic manner that permits other members of one's community to place trust in the sources of the investigator's claims. If a historian claims to have discovered a new archive and quotes extensively from it, readers must trust that he or she has indeed treated the evidence as reported and that the claimed quotations are authentic. Readers may disagree with the sufficiency of the sources or with the interpretations that are offered, but no questions will be raised about the evidence itself. History as a discipline has rules and standards for working with historical sources, and it is assumed that historians play by those rules. One of the reasons that the quality of education research is perennially contested is that education draws from many disciplinary sources, each with its own rules, standards, and conventions. Moreover, as several of the chapter authors point out, education researchers are not always adequately trained or socialized in the norms of any one discipline to use its standards consistently. Yet to compress one's education research into forms that fit any one discipline may corrupt the inquiry by distorting its questions into forms that more readily fit a particular disciplinary template. Education research must be disciplined if it strives to be credible and useful, but what standards or rules should it follow?

The Public Face of Scholarship

Scholarship must be public. To be useful and credible, it must become "community property." But one does not normally need access to the raw data of an investigator. If a biochemist has spent three years in the laboratory conducting careful experiments, with observations and interpretations recorded in thousands of pages of lab notebooks, no one wants to spend three years learning about the work. Research is about the compressions, transformations, and reconstitutions of experience into forms that can be readily assimilated and understood by one's peers. Articles and monographs are conventional means for summarizing the complexities of an investigation and reporting them to peers in a cogent form.

Several of the chapter authors address the question of how the complex data of educational scholarship can be more readily stored, displayed, and exchanged using new technologies. For example, the multidimensional complexity of classrooms has been captured in the past by observational rating scales, questionnaires, narrative descriptions, teacher logs, and the like. New ways of using videotape, digitizing, and coding episodes for rapid retrieval and analysis can open utterly new vistas for research on classroom teaching and learning. Moreover, the databases themselves can become available to other investigators, much as survey data have been available for years from the National Center for Educational Statistics and similar sources. If the capacity to "go public" with one's evidence is a hallmark of a more mature form of scholarship, education research may be moving in that direction.

Peer Review

The problem of standards of review remains significant in education research. Once one leaves the relative safety of disciplinary inquiry, quality assurance is up for grabs. (I do not claim that in the traditional disciplines, controversies over quality are nonexistent. They are just different.) Should tight rules of procedure be stipulated as the criteria for judgment, much as one critically examines the adequacy of a statistical procedure and a test of significance? Or is educational inquiry a form of knowing that resists such judgmental procedures? There are two very different jurisprudential traditions at odds in American legal discourse —a preference for rules versus a preference for standards.

Legal directives can take either of two forms: clear-cut rules ("drive no faster than 65 MPH") or flexible standards ("drive safely for existing highway conditions"). Those who favor rules stress their advantages of certainty, predictability, formal equality of treatment, and clear notice; those who favor standards counter that their approach is more substantively fair and accurate and more practical because capable of flexible adaptation.

Most research in education requires a search for reasonable standards rather than strict rules. With so much of the research falling into the interstices among the disciplines, it has been a frustrating challenge to find reasonable and stable bases for those standards and the judgments of quality they frame. Nevertheless, absent such standards, any possibility of building significant understandings from aggregating and exchanging pieces of scholarship is seriously compromised.

Building on One Another's Work: Generativity

The key rationale for insisting on disciplined, public, and peer-reviewed work is to provide a sound basis for others to build atop one's efforts, even as each of us strives to stand on the shoulders of our peers. If the edifice of education scholarship is to achieve integrity, then the investigations that constitute that corpus of work must themselves have integrity. They must inspire trust and be seen as faithful representations of the educational phenomena they depict, analyze, and interpret. Those who seek to understand and to improve education through better scholarship value the generalizability of research. They value the potential of any study or program of studies to be generalized beyond the particular circumstances or sample that was investigated. Scholars wish to infer general rules from the special conditions of an experiment, a survey, or a classroom analysis. Policymakers strive to scale up the experience of a single school or a small number of sites into a general school reform that will make a difference for many children.

Most education research must be situated—framed locally by the conditions of class, community, program, local history, gender, teacher, and many other factors even while employing disciplined, trust-inducing approaches. How can one generalize from a local narrative? How do you scale up a family? The interstitial character of such inquiries (falling between disciplinary cracks) creates challenges for the community that are daunting but not paralyzing. Other fields, such as medicine, law, and architecture, have managed to grapple with such issues, with modest success. By and large they have done so by creating significant professional communities that have established working standards and then applied them conscientiously. It would appear that a similar approach is needed in education.

EDUCATION SCHOLARSHIP AS A PROFESSION

Educational scholars form a professional community whose members must support one another's work through actively preparing the next generation of scholars and through the exchange of methods and findings as well as in monitoring and maintaining the quality of the work. Membership in a professional community is defined by shared obligations, standards, and methods. Indeed classic professions such as medicine, law, and architecture are characterized by the inherent uncertainty of their fields of practice and by the centrality of judgment (rather than knowledge) as the dominant feature of accomplished practice. They draw heavily on scholarships of carefully considered histories and cases of practice. In that way research in support of professional practice is not expected to confer certain knowledge but rather to offer guides to practice. Research offers ways of reducing uncertainty but not removing it. It offers precedents and examples more often than clear rules. It informs judgment but rarely relieves the professional of his burdens. It contributes to standards of practice rather than rules of procedure.

When moving from disciplinary knowledge to the grounding of professional practice, one moves from the purely intellectual to a realm in which theoretical, practical, and moral principles connect, collide, and merge endlessly. Educational judgments, whether at the level of policy or practice, rarely derive from theoretical understanding alone or from a single compelling experiment. Ever more credible evidence from research on the conditions for achieving mathematical excellence mixes with moral dilemmas about the impact of certain pedagogies on equality of opportunity, even as teachers' practical experience may offer particular insights into how the history of this school in this community suggests an entirely different perspective.

What forms of education scholarship will inform such situations? What forms of scholarship will provide the most useful theoretical generalizations? The most credible cases of reflective experience? The most useful evaluations of the outcomes of judgments rendered, decisions made, and programs enacted? And how can such scholarships be disciplined, displayed, reviewed, and exchanged? These are the responsibilities of an education research and practice community, a professional community that does not yet exist, much less exercise its legitimate responsibility to set standards for research, for training, and for informing practice and policy.

In addition to its responsibilities in vetting education research through peer review, professional communities teach. They determine how the next generation of scholars will be prepared, how continuing professional education for the current crop is organized, and what will be treated as normal scholarship in any one generation. In *The Structure of Scientific Revolutions*, the late Thomas Kuhn wrote so dashingly about paradigm-busting examples of scientific revolution, in contrast to the drably described persistence of "normal science," that readers were inclined to underappreciate the necessity of every field of study or profession's establishing some commonly understood norms of inquiry.

The academic preparation of scholars is where these norms are conceived and conveyed, modeled and sanctioned. There are few other domains of scholarly work more demanding in this regard than education. Finding the appropriate balance of disciplinary rigor and adequate field experience can be defined as a problem of graduate admissions, graduate education, or both. Moreover, for those who plan to study teaching and learning in a particular subject matter domain, yet another imperative is introduced. How shall the young scholar intending to investigate the psychology of mathematics learning in secondary schools divide herself up among preparation in mathematics, psychology, and studies of schooling? The problem is exacerbated when expectations grow from "knowing" these fields to experience in actually "doing" them.

Perhaps concepts like "distributed expertise" and "communities of practice" invite application in this arena, as well as in other aspects of social organization. The image of education scholars as powerful polymaths is probably unrealistic. In that case, graduate education (as well as the organization of education research at all levels) should be inherently a collaborative enterprise. Should the individual project or dissertation remain the defining experience of graduate accomplishment? These are among the core problems facing our emerging scholarly communities. There are yet others that are peculiar to the scholarships of practice.

SCHOLARSHIPS OF PRACTICE

Special responsibilities attach to a scholarship of practice. These are associated with the reactivity of the work, since those whom it studies often participate in the inquiries themselves and are typically either the beneficiaries or the victims of its conduct. Research on educational practice is inherently consequential. It is often cross-cultural, carried on when the social class, language, ethnicity, or commitments of those conducting the research are incongruent with those whom they study. Moreover, rarely do scholars have the same stake in the outcomes of the research as do those being studied. Repeatedly we ask, Whose research is it? Who ought to have the last review, the final say in how evidence is interpreted and sense is made?

For more than a generation, sociologists and anthropologists have argued about the relative advantages and liabilities of insiders and outsiders in social research—of those who study phenomena from the perspective of those who experience them directly as against those who stand outside and more dispassionately observe and reflect. These problems are magnified in studies of education, whether historical or ethnographic, experimental or descriptive. Here again the questions apply to both the conditions of graduate education and admissions as well as to the conduct of the research itself.

As in any other profession, the challenges to accomplishing a significant body of education research lie at the intersection of the intellectual, the practical, and the moral. That is the task that the chapter authors have taken on. That is the challenge for the National Academy of Education's Commission on the Improvement of Education Research. And that will be the challenge for a vital community of educational scholarship.

REFERENCE

Comaroff, J., and Comaroff, J. I. *Of Revelation and Revolution: Christianity and Colonialism in South Africa*. Chicago: University of Chicago Press, 1991.

Kuhns, T. *The Structure of Scientific Revolution*. Chicago: University of Chicago Press, 1970.

CHAPTER NINE

The Core, the Canon, and
the Development of Research Skills

Issues in the Preparation of Education Researchers

Alan H. Schoenfeld

The charge for this chapter was as follows: given a reconception of locus, methods, media, agents, and standards for education research, researchers and mentors of researchers in education are confronted with the challenge to outline approaches for preparing the next generation of education scholars. What should graduate work in education scholarship entail?

On reflection, I have concluded that this charge is impossible. There is good reason to believe there is no straightforward solution to either of what I consider to be the two main problems of research preparation in education: the definition of core knowledge (the "canon") and the development of research competency in beginning researchers.

Consider core knowledge, or the question of "what every good education scholar should know." It is a commonplace that "education" is not a discipline in the sense of mathematics or anthropology. One need only look at the list of the American Educational Research Association (AERA) divisions (Administration; Curriculum Studies; Learning and Instruction; Measurement and Research Methodology; History and Historiography; Social Context of Education; School Evaluation and Program Development; Education in the Professions; Postsecondary Education; Teaching and Teacher Education; Policy and Politics) to see scope and diversity that matches or exceeds that of any college of letters and science. As to three recent AERA handbooks—*Research on Curriculum* (Jackson, 1992), *Research on Mathematics Teaching and Learning* (Grouws, 1992), and *Research on Teaching* (Wittrock, 1986)—despite their ostensible common ground, the overlap between any two of them is small; and among the three, it is very small. The canon just does not seem to be there.

The problem of the core manifests itself in two ways. On the one hand, the intersection of various perspectives represented in education is near null. On the other hand, the union is immense—far larger than can be dealt with in a short time in a meaningful way. I note, for example, that my career in education research and practice has, in essence, been a lifelong tutorial aimed at uncovering and remediating my own ignorance. As my interests or responsibilities have grown and my work has taken me into new arenas, I have continually been confronted by my ignorance—of the fundamentals of assessment, of issues in teacher preparation, of school cultures and what shapes them, and of the major political forces that influence the contexts within which schooling takes place, to name just a few of the issues I have grappled with recently. If a long-term professional has such lacunae in his background, how can anyone have reasonable expectations of solid knowledge bases among those who are just entering the field?

Thus far my comments have focused on knowledge as classically defined— what the researcher "knows." When it comes to what the researcher is prepared to *do*—produce research—the situation is far worse. Each of the constituent fields of education (anthropology, economics, history, philosophy, psychology, and more) has its own paradigms. The multiplicity and diversity of methods are problems enough. But that is just the start, because, as the other chapters of this book make clear, those paradigms are for the most part inadequate for addressing education issues. As an evolving interdisciplinary field, education does not yet have relevant methods to approach many of the problems we need to understand. In Thomas Kuhn's terms (1970), ours is not a period of "normal science"; the methods currently available, even if mastered, will soon be eclipsed. Professionals need to be prepared for change.

Beyond these considerations, there is a huge diversity of productive models from which to choose when it comes to the nuts and bolts of research training. Recently the Spencer Foundation brought together a collection of scholars who had been identified for their ability to nurture young researchers in education. One of the most interesting aspects of the foundation's Mentor Network meetings was the wide diversity of mentoring styles revealed—from students apprenticing individually with a faculty member and laboring together in private to the kind that takes place in the heart of a large research community and is largely "public" within that community. There is no common denominator of mentoring.

To sum it up, there is no canon, there are no core methods, this is not a time of normal science, and there are myriad models of mentoring, even among those especially talented in it. Should we give it up? Of course not: the job is too important. In fact, I shall argue that, first, education research is not really worse off than are many other fields—the other disciplines do not have it right either; and, second, there are ways to think productively about the problem.

It goes without saying that "solutions" cannot and will not be prescriptive. But there will be a set of constraints that, when honored, will increase the likelihood that students will emerge from graduate programs better prepared to engage in meaningful and important education research. There will be many and very different ways to honor those constraints—ways shaped by institutional history, context, and the characteristics of the faculty.

It is important to understand how our field stands relative to other fields, so that researchers and teachers do not browbeat themselves unduly for their inadequacies or look elsewhere for inappropriate models. For the purposes of comparison it may be helpful to take a quick look at how well research preparation is conducted in a very different field, mathematics.

Trained as a mathematician, I grew up within the professional norms of one of our "mature" disciplines—one with well-established paradigms and methods. The field is healthy and growing, with the periodic development of new areas for exploration (chaos and fractals, exploratory data analysis), the resolution of old problems, and fertile new ground being plowed (the solution of Fermat's Last Theorem). Although new tools and methods have emerged—for example, computer-assisted proofs and explorations that have extended the ways in which mathematics is an empirical discipline—the basic forms of argument and of student preparation remain the same. There is a stable base on which to build. So how well does the mathematical community fare in preparing new researchers?

It is generally accepted within the field that less than 3 percent of those who earn Ph.D.s in mathematics go on to publish any mathematics research beyond the direct content of their dissertations. This strikes me as hardly evidence of success in research preparation. If anything, it seems evidence of rather significant failure. A tiny fraction of certified researchers are actually able to produce the academic coin of the realm on their own—and, of course, only some of those people go on to have productive careers as research mathematicians.

The reason is, to obtain a Ph.D. in mathematics, or in other fields, but particularly in the sciences, one has to solve a problem deemed by the research community to be sufficiently difficult or important to merit the degree. Accomplishing this is not trivial, and the attrition rate is pretty high. But however difficult, it pales beside what is involved in becoming a research mathematician. The hard part of being a mathematician is not solving problems; it is finding problems that one can solve and whose solution the mathematical community will recognize as significant enough to constitute an advance in the field. For most students, *problem identification* is not part of the research apprenticeship process. Typically the selection and shaping of the problem that the student will work on is done by the adviser. Yet that is the hard part of doing research. Is it any wonder that when they are set loose, so few students can do it on their own?

Make no mistake, there is a consensually agreed body of core knowledge in mathematics. All around the country, first-year graduate students take courses and then qualifying examinations on real analysis, complex analysis, and algebra, or something very closely related. What is the purpose of this professional preparation? I think a case can be made that its major purpose is not preparation for research. Mastering the core does, of course, play some role in that regard; graduate students in their first year develop a knowledge base of facts and techniques, a shared vocabulary, and some shared perspectives. But many mathematicians will tell you that they began to learn what research is only when they began to do research—typically after passing their qualifying exams.

What, then, is the role of the canon in a discipline? I think it is twofold. First, it is to develop the knowledge base and provide a certain level of literacy. (Could any English Ph.D. not be familiar with Shakespeare or Donne? Could any mathematician not be knowledgeable about Dedekind cuts or the Sylow theorems?) Second, it is to provide the mathematician with a broad enough background of knowledge to be able to teach significant chunks of the undergraduate curriculum. The one thing the canon does not do is prepare mathematicians to be researchers.

There is, I think, good news in this bad news. In terms of the canon, one should not hope to "cover" everything in the field. In education, the focus of mentors should be on helping students develop deep understandings of what constitutes good research, of the contributions that come from the disciplines, and of perspectives that inform their work. In education research, the fact that this is not a period of normal science may not be that much of a problem.

In any *real* research, the first bottleneck issue is that of problem identification: being able to focus on problems that are difficult and meaningful but on which progress can be made. There is every reason to believe that education scholars and professors can deal with this at least as effectively as do their counterparts in other disciplines. Beyond that point, our field faces some more interesting and complex issues than does mathematics, in which the standards of validity are known. In mathematics a proof is a proof, period. In education claims are not proved; they are substantiated with evidence. The central question for research in education is, What constitutes a robust and valid finding, and what warrants are needed to justify it? This, of course, is the central question for research in all of the social sciences. In sum, the challenge we face in preparing the next generation of researchers is in principle no more difficult for us than it is for anyone else, save perhaps for the complexity of some of the problems we seek to understand.

This chapter considers two dimensions of research training in education: the canon and the preparation for research careers. Taking them in reverse order, I begin with a series of assertions regarding the kinds of core knowledge and skills that beginning researchers in education need. Then I follow with a series of examples, for the most part brief cases in point. The section closes with a more extended discussion of the assertions that began it. In the two subsequent sections I describe some ways of addressing the needs of developing researchers, focusing on core courses and providing a brief description of constraints that such courses must satisfy. Then I move on to pragmatics, describing a variety of institutional mechanisms ("action-oriented" courses, first- and second-year projects, and research groups) that can nurture the desired skills in beginning researchers. The goal is most emphatically not to say, "This is how to do it." Rather, it is to illustrate ways that some of the particular needs of young researchers can be met within the organized structure of a doctoral program. If the ideas resonate, readers might consider if and how they might be adapted to their own circumstances.

CORE KNOWLEDGE AND NECESSARY COMPETENCIES FOR BEGINNING RESEARCHERS

What are the kinds of core knowledge and skills that beginning researchers in education need to acquire? First, they need to guard against the dangers of compartmentalization. It is all too easy to focus narrowly and ignore or dismiss work in, or perspectives from, areas not clearly related to one's own. Beginning researchers need a sense of the big picture and how things fit together. Part of this involves understanding the different ways of viewing educational phenomena and the kinds of insights available from various perspectives. I argue below that a major purpose of the core is to provide such knowledge.

Second, apprentice researchers need to guard against the dangers of being superficial. Superficial knowledge of information or methods is likely to yield trivial research. Generally high-quality research comes when one has deep understanding of the area being examined and extended experience mulling over the issues under question. Focus is essential, especially for researchers at the start of their careers.

Third, and perhaps most important, researchers need to develop deep understanding of what it means to make and justify claims about educational phenomena. What is a defensible claim? What is the scope of that claim? What kinds of evidence can be taken as legitimate warrants for that claim? Such considerations will be at the core of researchers' work throughout their careers.

Fourth, beginning researchers need to learn how to identify and frame workable problems—meaningful problems on which legitimate progress can be made in a reasonable amount of time.

From my perspective, the third and fourth assertions identify the fundamental "life skills" that a researcher must have today. The contexts within which we work, our knowledge base, and our available methods are all changing dramatically. Two decades ago studies of thinking and problem solving were usually done in the laboratory; those of teaching typically involved the search for correlations between teacher behaviors and student outcomes based on a limited number of variables. Increasingly, research studies take place in the midst of complex educational interventions, with the researcher trying to make sense of what is taking place within the chaos of classrooms. To put it starkly, yesterday's tools, techniques, and perspectives are valuable, but they are inadequate to cope with today's challenges, just as today's tools, techniques, and methods will be inadequate in just a few years. The one underlying constant for doing good work is, and will continue to be, having a coherent intellectual frame for exploring the issues of interest—a frame in which to identify important phenomena, formulate central questions about them, decide what appropriate evidence is, and provide defensible rationales for the claims one makes using that evidence appropriately. With that as a base, the field (and individuals) can continue to grow.

Knowledge and Skills Researchers Must Have

Following are seven short anecdotes and a slightly more extended one, having the dual purpose of providing some substantiation for the assertions made above and some grist for discussion.

Example One: The Life of a Principal. One of the presenters at the Spencer Fellows Forum during the 1996 fall meeting of the National Academy of Education was Arlene Holtz, whose presentation, "The Urban Principal as Moral Decision Maker," provided compelling descriptions of issues she faced as a principal in an urban middle school: How does one deal with the fact that one student in the school has shot another to death? How does one respond when confronted with the fact that the student who was accused of the shooting has the right to return to school until his guilt is established in the courts? Holtz's presentation was riveting. In the question-and-answer period that followed it, she was asked about academics: How does she deal with curricular reform, standards, professional development? Holtz's response was a plaintive cry: "I don't *do* education. I don't *do* education. I just don't have the time."

Example Two: Where Is the Content in School Reform? There was an eerie echo of Holtz's presentation the same afternoon in a symposium devoted to Chicago school reform. Chicago's was one of the many school systems named by former U.S. Secretary of Education William Bennett as "the worst in the country," and it has undergone significant reforms. It was transformed from a highly centralized (and some say highly corrupt) system run through city hall to a decentralized system with local schools run by governing boards that typically have parent majorities and whose principals no longer have tenure but fixed-term contracts. Recently the system moved slightly toward centralization, with the imposition of regulations saying that schools "in trouble" could once again be taken over by the city. The symposium was fascinating, with descriptions of finance and governance, of political excesses (the day before the symposium the principal of a school "in trouble" had been forcibly removed from his office by twenty armed police officers in full riot gear), of plans for having standardized test scores go up. But there was no mention of reform of any kind. I could not help thinking, Do they have the time to *do* education?

Example Three: Where Is the Content in Curriculum Reform? "School-to-work" is a hot topic, and a range of schools and curricula is focusing on it. One member of my research group was recently employed to examine exemplary new vocational programs that teach mathematics within vocational schools. Her job was to see what the programs did. Her preliminary analysis, in the form of a 2 × 2 matrix, looked at whether the curriculum had high or low mathematical content and high or low vocational content. Never mind that the "high, high" box was empty. What was dismaying was the fact that this kind of analytic frame was itself seen as a significant contribution. "Content" had not previously been on the table for discussion in a plausible way.

We see here, as in the preceding examples, a disconnect between top-level policy goals and what takes place in classrooms. One might well ask how the authors of these curricula thought they could "fix the mathematics instruction problem" in vocational education when they lacked solid desiderata for the fix and means for finding out whether these had been met.

Example Four: The Role of Knowledge and Epistemology in Teacher Change. My research group's curricular efforts in schools, and the ways that teachers have dealt with them, have hinged to a critical degree on the details of our, and their, understandings of mathematics. We had a particular view of mathematics content that was grounded in an extensive research program on mathematical thinking. We took a particular epistemological stance, which was reflected in the materials and the ways they were intended to be used. What happened at times was that a teacher's underlying sense of the discipline was different from ours—and as the teacher adapted our materials to his understandings, the materials were transformed in a way that made their purposes radically different from what we had intended. Our failure to understand the teacher's sense of the mathematics meant we were unprepared to deal with the ways he would use the materials. Such understanding of the teacher's knowledge and epistemology is essential in curriculum reform.

There are potentially such disconnects, with similarly problematic consequences, at the systemic level. Recent studies of school culture (Little, 1993) provide rich descriptions of the collegial contexts that can support reform. However, the connections to what the content of that reform is, and what kinds of knowledge growth take place when the right support structures are in place, have not been made. They need to be.

Example Five: Understanding Master Teachers. In our studies of teaching, my research group has looked at some extraordinary teachers—those who are widely acknowledged as pioneers in their profession. What they do in their classrooms goes far beyond dealing with content. Building learning communities is at the core of their efforts. If researchers do not understand a teacher's understandings of what they are teaching (and those understandings are *deep*), then they cannot get a real sense of what the classes are all about. If researchers do not understand teachers' conceptions of (and goals for) learning communities, their understandings of their classrooms will be equally impoverished.

Example Six: The Knowledge Base for Teaching. I spend Tuesday mornings doing mathematics with a class of third graders. The Berkeley Unified School District has recently adopted some new curriculum materials, and much of what I do is explore the mathematical possibilities of these materials. Frequently I take the activities proposed as a starting point and then explore extensions or variations with members of the class. We often go off into territory not explicitly suggested by the materials and unfamiliar to the teachers in whose classrooms I work. One needs to know a fair amount of mathematics to make judgments about where the students' explorations might lead. This being the case, there are serious questions about the kinds of mathematical preparation and understandings that must be faced if classroom teachers are to explore the latent potential of those materials.

Example Seven: The "Problems of "Disciplinary" versus Nondisciplinary Research Training. When the Spencer Foundation conducted a review of its program of predoctoral research fellowships for "research related to education" a few years ago, the data indicated that students coming from schools of education were at a disadvantage. A high proportion of successful fellowship applications came from students in departments outside education, like anthropology, psychology, history, sociology, and philosophy. One reason, presumably, was that those disciplines offered more clearly defined paradigms, resulting in proposals of more recognizably high quality. Interestingly, the advantage to those in related fields seemed to vanish by the time scholars with doctorates were competing for Spencer postdoctoral fellowships. A possible explanation for these findings will be offered further on.

Example Eight: School-to-Work and the Issue of "Theories of Competence." From the examples I have given, it is clear that I am a content person. My focus is on what it is that students learn and how schooling can be arranged so that they do learn. In the broadest sense, I think that schools are places where students should develop the skills and attributes that will enable them to be powerful, productive, and contributing members of our ever-changing society and culture. I shall illustrate my viewpoint with regard to the school-to-work issue and then draw some morals from that story and the examples given above.

The school-to-work issue is largely concerned with the roles of schools in preparing America's youth for productive work lives. One mainstream approach to such vocational preparation is direct skills building: examine the workplace, identify productive workplace skills, and teach students those skills. Another offers a more contextual solution, with suggestions that students engage in apprenticeships or that curricula be designed to reflect workplace demands, or both, thus providing nurturing contexts for the development of work-related skills.

Putting aside the narrowness of focus—schools should be about much more than learning job-related skills—both of these forms share some fundamental flaws. On the pragmatic side, building particular workplace skills is bound to fail because the skills set is a moving target. Many of today's useful skills will be irrelevant a decade or three from now. (Can you change a typewriter ribbon? Who cares?) But this is only symptomatic of a deeper problem: we do not yet have a decent theoretical understanding of what comprises workplace competency, and until we do we are shooting in the dark. I believe vocationalism is precisely the wrong solution to the school-to-work problem and that the kinds of vocational approaches being suggested are the result of serious misconceptions about the nature of competence—misconceptions that apply to literacy and mathematics as well as to workplace training.

Here the analogy to mathematics learning is directly relevant and appropriate. Over the past two decades we have come to understand that the skills orientation in mathematics instruction misses the boat, not because skills are unnecessary but because they tell only a small part of the story. We now understand that having access to strategies, being effectively meta-cognitive, possessing a productive belief structure, and knowing how to engage, and actively engaging, in particular disciplinary practices are all part and parcel of "being mathematical." An emerging theory of mathematical practice is that competence along these lines has serious ramifications for instruction. After all, if "being able to engage in certain mathematical practices as a member of a mathematical community" is important, then instructional environments must be shaped to foster the development of such competencies and practices. Note that this reconceptualization of competence, although not neglecting skills, results in very different instructional emphases: skills are put in their proper place, as part of what a person good at mathematics uses when appropriate.

Similarly, in school-to-work, the skills approach, whether in the form of teaching skills in the classroom or "apprenticeships" of various sorts, is the direct intellectual descendant of skills-related curriculum approaches in the content domains (mathematics, science, history, and the like), and it is doomed to fail for the same reasons. We lack, and desperately need, theories of competence. What enables people to be functional in the workplace—or literate, or historically knowledgeable, or good citizens? And how do we foster such competencies in the classroom, in the preparation of teachers, in our institutional arrangements, and in the societal structures that shape those arrangements? Below, I offer a more extended discussion of the assertions that began this section.

Knowledge in Practice: Difficulties and Dilemmas

Assertion One:
Researchers need to guard against the dangers of compartmentalization.

The first three examples given above are all cases of the danger of compartmentalization. In the first example, compartmentalization was forced on the principal. Her life was so crisis-laden that she had no time to focus on what students actually learned in her school. But if she does not or cannot do this, then who does, and how? The issue is structural and systemic, and that is the point of the second and third examples. Where in the Chicago school system is the focus on what actually gets learned if the systemic emphasis is on structural changes that will result in local control, raise test scores, and so forth? Across the nation, how can one even think about judging the effectiveness of vocational curricula in mathematics unless the vocational and mathematical desiderata for those curricula are clear? My point is not to highlight the neglect of content considerations in policy discussions, but to illustrate the potential for difficulty when these considerations are not taken into account.

The counterpoint—that considerations of context are equally essential—is every bit as important, as illustrated by the fourth and fifth examples. The moral is that it does not matter how well one knows the content or how well it is embedded in curriculum materials; unless the instructional context supports their use in ways that are consonant with one's intentions, the whole effort may be undermined—and often is. In short, understanding of both content *and* context is essential.

The difficulty is that there is an all-too-natural tendency for people to focus on issues within the sphere of their interests, discounting the "other" as not very important. It is not uncommon for researchers on cognition to make suggestions that fly in the face of current classroom realities or, conversely, for policy researchers to ponder questions, such as, "How can we retrain surplus social studies teachers into mathematics teachers over the summer?" that drive subject matter specialists crazy. I have a vivid memory of a comment made nearly fifteen years ago by a colleague whose focus was policy analysis. I had just moved to the University of California, Berkeley, to help build the Division of

Education in Mathematics, Science, and Technology. Referring to our intention to focus on cognitive science analyses of thinking and learning, my colleague said bluntly, "Fads and fashions in educational psychology come and go, and they're all irrelevant to what counts in schools. What you folks do doesn't matter at all." (This, I should note, was the faculty member who was exploring the possibility of having social studies teachers become mathematics teachers with a summer's training.) My unspoken reply would have been unprintable—a polite version of it being, "If you don't know squat about kids or what they're supposed to learn, how can you pretend to know anything about what's important in schooling?" The point is that we were both right in some ways, and we were both very wrong in others. You have to be utterly blind to think that teaching is so content free that anyone can be trained to teach anything on a summer's notice. But you are almost as blind to think you can have an impact on what happens in classrooms by focusing solely on thinking and learning. The picture is much more complex. Like a jigsaw puzzle, it is dreadfully incomplete unless all the pieces are in place.

The following paragraphs sketch some of the things that need to be understood if the research community is to have a decent chance of influencing practice in a reasonable way. The issues are listed in order of grain size, from individual factors to societal ones. They are *all* important:

- One can start with knowledge—about content, about development, about what is to be learned and the attributes of those who will be learning it. If one does not have these right, the enterprise is hobbled from the very beginning.

- One needs to worry about curricula. A series of National Science Foundation (NSF)–financed studies in the mid-1970s indicated that the vast majority of secondary mathematics and science teachers depended almost exclusively on the materials in their texts and that their students experienced a subset of what is in those texts. I am sure this is equally true today—and in all subjects, not just mathematics and science.

- As the saying goes, there is the *intended* curriculum and the *implemented* curriculum. What is implemented depends on the teachers and the instructional context; hence one must be concerned with the nature of teaching and teacher preparation and the conditions under which teachers find themselves trying to teach.

Indeed, in these days of curriculum reform, novel curricula are placing increased content and pedagogical demands on teachers. Some require engagement with new content, explorations of new classroom norms (such as collaborative work), and "delivery" of the content in the absence of student textbooks. As the literature shows (see Cohen, 1990), teachers' understandings of what they teach are fundamental shaping variables of what their students experience. Of necessity in times of curricular change, issues of teacher knowledge are of paramount importance, in both preservice and in-service education.

- At the level of the building and the district there are issues of leadership and school culture, as documented by McLaughlin and Talbert (1990), among others. While the teacher is in some sense autonomous ("nobody peeks behind the closed classroom door"), it is also the case that school, department, and district culture shape what is possible (or what the teacher thinks is possible, which is often functionally the same thing).

But all this, so far, is tied to what takes place inside the schoolhouse walls.

- As Jonathan Kozol documents eloquently in *Savage Inequalities* (1992), what is possible inside the classroom is shaped in myriad ways by what happens outside it. Kozol's focus is on resources—the fact that significant numbers of this nation's children are routinely deprived of the opportunities to learn, while other students, often a short distance away, attend schools rich with amenities. No matter what one's theory of teaching and learning, simple material resources make a huge difference. They cannot be ignored.

Beyond those issues, there are constraints that go far beyond the school building and the locality. States adopt curriculum frameworks and assessment systems, and those shape instruction in powerful ways. And then—

- There is politics, of which my adopted home state has of late provided a seemingly unending series of pathological examples. California's assessment system was scuttled a few years ago after attacks on it were mounted by the religious right. The attacks were mounted because some controversial books were chosen as part of the curriculum, because the science standards taught evolution, and because some items on statewide assessments asked students about their thoughts and feelings.

The fact is that what was once a matter of professional judgment is now often a matter of politics. The battle over mathematics reform, attacked as the "new new math" and "fuzzy crap" by a particularly vehement antireform columnist, is as much a public relations battle as it is a substantive intellectual one, independent of the intellectual merits of various stances. Similarly, the conflict over whole language versus phonics has been polarized to the point where rational dialogue is difficult.

Politics have become overt and nasty. When I was writing the first draft of this chapter, the California State Board of Education had just rejected many of the state Curriculum Commission's recommendations for members of the new

Mathematics Framework Committee, replacing them with representatives of the far mathematical right. I wrote then, "This portends a return to 'basics' and a reversal of the directions of reform." My prediction was accurate in anticipating the results, but almost no one could have predicted how dramatic they would be. In late 1997 California's Mathematics Standards Commission, appointed by the State Board of Education, submitted its recommended mathematics standards to the board. These standards had taken a year and a half to produce, with many public hearings and revision cycles along the way. The state board, which contains no members with expertise in mathematics education, rewrote half the standards in less than two weeks and commissioned some mathematicians with little knowledge of education issues to rewrite the other half in the same amount of time. Despite strenuous protests from their own standards commission, which repudiated the changes, and from a wide range of national experts, including the head of the National Research Council's Mathematical Sciences Education Board and the U.S. director of the Third International Mathematics and Science Study, the state board unanimously adopted the altered version.

In short, politics counts. If one does not understand this, one's work may be to no effect. Although my examples have been at the state level, they could occur at all levels of the system. At the national level, national standards and voluntary national tests in reading and mathematics are now being debated. If such accountability measures are put in place they will, as they trickle down through the system, have profound effects on what is possible in individual classrooms.

Let me repeat: it does not matter which issues are discussed or at what level of grain size. If any of the various factors just described are ignored, there is a significant chance that one's work, while fine on its own (narrow) terms, may ultimately have no impact. Indeed the work may be seriously flawed despite being fine on its own (narrow) terms. The bottom line is that it is clearly impossible for aspiring researchers to develop deep understandings of all the issues I have highlighted, yet they must know a fair amount or they risk the consequences just described.

Assertion Two:
Researchers need to guard against the dangers of being superficial.

In an important way, Examples Three through Six all deal with this issue. As I have already made clear, I am content-oriented. My first professional training was in mathematics, and one of my major goals is that all students have the opportunities to derive the kinds of pleasure and power from engaging in mathematics that I do. I have spent much of my career delineating the richness of mathematical understanding, a kind of understanding that goes far beyond the traditional focus on facts and procedures. That perspective shapes my view of what should take place in classrooms, what should happen in curricula, how teachers need to be prepared, what should be assessed, and so on.

The point is that absent such deep understandings, instructional design, teacher preparation, and assessment are each likely to be *very* problematic. Through the years, for example, psychologists with little understanding of mathematics have made recommendations regarding curricula and instruction that, in essence, have helped to teach the "wrong stuff" effectively! Example Three shows that vocational curricula in mathematics can be nearly mathematics free. Example four suggests that unless one understands teachers' understandings of mathematics and deals with those understandings head on, curricula and instruction may be implemented in ways that barely resemble the original intentions. Examples Four and Six suggest that going off the beaten track in mathematics lessons requires a relatively rich map of the terrain to be explored. I could provide many more examples. In short, I worry about anyone doing education research that touches on mathematics if that person does not have—or collaborate with someone who has—a solid grasp of mathematics. What I have just written applies equally well to *any* content domain. It is the reason I do not do research on physics learning, much less on the learning of social studies.

The preceding examples focus on one kind of depth—depth of content knowledge and what counts. The next issue to consider is that of methods and the question of how one gets at what counts, introduced by the final short example, on disciplinary versus nondisciplinary research training. The data from the Spencer Foundation indicate that predoctoral students who come equipped with standard paradigms from allied fields, which are known and describable, tend to have an advantage over those students who come from within education, where the paradigms are not as well formed. Hence, according to the most optimistic interpretation of this finding, they can write proposals that appear more cogent or methodologically competent.

In contrast, students' first attempts from within education may seem clumsier, since there is not a clean disciplinary scaffolding on which to rely. One might hypothesize that the advantages to those coming from outside education would wither away over time and perhaps even turn into disadvantages. After all (see the elaboration of Assertion Three below), education issues transcend the capacity of methods from the allied disciplines to solve them. The scholar who has learned to grapple with new problems may ultimately be in a better position to do research in education than the scholar who merely has a disciplinary tool kit. And indeed, the Spencer Foundation's data on postdoctoral fellowship applications indicate that, at that level, scholars from allied fields no longer have a competitive advantage.

Shirley Brice Heath's chapter in this book, however, suggests that there is a deeper problem: that of researchers in education using methods from other fields without really understanding them. Her particular example is *discourse analysis,* a term as frequently and as ill used in education circles as *gourmet* is in the frozen food sections of supermarkets. Heath writes that there are various types of discourse analysis, each with its own tradition and entailments; moreover, each type makes particular kinds of contributions, takes a fair amount of time to learn, and should not be used cavalierly by amateurs. Researchers in education who call their ad hoc attempts to make sense of dialogue "discourse analysis" are not only bad scholars; they are giving education a bad name. The same could be said for those who make cavalier use of "clinical interviews," "protocol analysis," and so on.

The examples in the preceding paragraph were all drawn from qualitative research, but it is easy to find similar abuses in the quantitative domain as well (let me count the ways!). Various misuses of statistical methods are discussed in the following elaboration of Assertion Three. There are the obvious errors where, for example, the wrong test is used. But there are more subtle and fundamental errors, such as using statistical tests when the conditions of the situation being analyzed do not fit the assumptions underlying the statistical tests. I characterize the tradition of such abuse as a form of scientism; put bluntly, it is slovenly work. Neither individuals nor the field as a whole can afford it. The bottom line is that it is all too easy to trivialize tools and techniques from allied fields when they are borrowed for educational use. Education research students should be inoculated against this particular disease.

Assertion Three:
**Researchers need to develop a deep understanding
of what it means to make and justify claims about educational phenomena.**

What is a defensible claim? What is the scope of that claim? What kinds of evidence can be taken as a legitimate warrant for that claim? Such considerations will be at the core of researchers' work throughout their careers. Doctoral training of historians prepares them to produce what "sells" to the community of historians. There are standard forms of narrative, standard types of claims, and standard ways of making a case for those claims. The same goes for philosophers, linguists, sociologists, economists, anthropologists, psychologists, and cognitive scientists, to name a few of those who contribute regularly to education. But attached to each paradigm are its "applicability conditions"—the set of circumstances to which the set of associated methods provides robust and meaningful results. The application of any research method is only as good as the match between the assumptions underlying the method and the set of circumstances being explored. If there is a mismatch, the findings may well be either meaningless or wrong. And that can lead to big problems when one is doing work in education.

Let me start with some uncontroversial examples framed somewhat provocatively. A case can be made that following the conclusion of World War II, American academia fell under the spell of "science"—that in many fields there was a large-scale adoption of the trappings of the scientific method in an attempt to emulate the kinds of approaches (and successes) of the hard sciences. It is no accident, after all, that sociology, anthropology, and psychology came to march under the banner of the "social sciences." Yet the rush to adopt scientific methods resulted, quite often, in abuses of those methods. In the use of controlled experiments, for example, there is a well-established set of methods for the analysis of "Treatment A versus Treatment B" comparisons, under the assumption that the two treatments are identical save for a small number of variables whose values are carefully controlled. Studies of this type work well in agriculture, where two adjacent fields of a particular crop can be subjected to almost identical treatments, with the differences in treatment controlled and measured. But students are not as simple as corn or alfalfa, instructional materials are not as consistent as measured doses of particular chemicals, and adjacent classrooms cannot be made as uniformly consistent as adjacent plots of land can be made. Consider a simple experiment that compares these two "treatments": having students read a body of text by itself and having them read the same text preceded by an "advance organizer," a brief introduction designed to place the text in context (Ausubel, 1963). The comparison sounds straightforward, but—and this example is far from atypical—it turns out that the construct of advance organizers was ill defined. What are now called meta-analyses of the literature on the topic showed mixed results, in large measure because advance organizers had not been defined carefully enough so that two people working independently would generate similar findings for any particular body of text. The literature contains myriad studies for which experimenters, with inadequate guidance, put together what they thought were advance organizers and tried to see if they worked. Some did; some did not. It is hardly surprising that the cumulative findings are not clear.

But even when treatments were reasonably well defined (such as prepackaged instructional materials), the application of statistical methods was often dubious at best. If the two treatments were given at the same time, then different teachers were teaching them—and thus the most important variable may not have been officially part of the experimental design. If the same teacher taught both treatments, it was most likely at different times—and whether the materials were studied before or after lunch may have been the most important variable. The outcome measures—say, scores on particular tests—may have been idiosyncratic and not easily generalizable to the broad issue being studied.

In sum, I do not think it overly harsh to say that the wholesale and inappropriate adoption of statistical methods into small-scale education studies was, in

large measure, a triumph of scientism over common sense. There are few findings of any lasting significance emerging from such statistics-dominated small-
scale work in education over more than the quarter-century from the 1950s and
1960s through the 1970s.

My intention is not to disparage the use of statistics in education—indeed,
quantitative work may be underrepresented today—but to point out that the
substance of the methods has to match details of the problem being studied and
that when it does not the conclusions drawn are not to be trusted. The same
could be said of various econometric analyses that have been concerned with
the "educational effects of class size." In many such studies, districts' total staff-
to-student ratios were used as proxies for teacher–student ratios, because data
about the latter were unavailable. This methodological convenience, which
lumps together teaching and administrative staff as the independent variable,
results in the conflation of administratively bloated districts that have relatively
low teacher–student ratios with those districts that have lean administrative
staffs and high teacher–student ratios. Add to this the fact that standardized
tests (or some other such measures) may not be consistent with the curricula
in the various schools, and one now has reason to doubt both the inputs *and*
the outputs of the models. Is it any wonder that the findings of multiple studies turn out to be contradictory?

One can find similar difficulties in the application of almost any disciplinary
paradigm to education. Although the econometric analyses just mentioned are
of the macro type, there are numerous analogues at the micro level. Consider,
for example, the decades-long history of complaints from educators about the
irrelevance of psychological laboratory studies to "real-world" issues in education. Indeed, the very coining of the term *ecological validity* within the psychological community in the 1970s represented the explicit recognition that there
had been a consistent mismatch between the methods and conditions of psychological research and the situations to which the conclusions from such
research were being applied. Similarly, it would not be hard to find educational
analyses stemming from the methods and perspectives of other social sciences
that just miss the point.

I need to be clear about the moral of these stories. In none of the cases above
have I questioned the intellectual solidity of the affiliated fields, the robustness
of their methods, or the potential utility of their perspectives and findings. All
I am saying is that there needs to be a match between the methods and perspectives being used and the contexts to which they are applied. Whenever
there is a mismatch, there is potential for serious difficulty.

This observation bears directly on the preparation of researchers in education. Most of the meaningful problems that scholars in education face are not
neatly formulated and do not come with relevant paradigms attached. This puts

us in a much more problematic position than other researchers with respect to the big issues. For apprentice researchers in fields where the methods match the problems, there is a simple path to the development of research competence. Mastering the paradigms while working on tractable but meaningful problems provides the emerging researcher with ready-made ways to answer questions and at the same time meet the discipline's standards of evidence. In doing so, he or she can begin to develop the ability to come to grips with complex phenomena necessary for good scholarship. Business as usual within standard disciplinary boundaries makes it easier to develop research competencies.

In some corners of the education enterprise it may well be the case that business can and should proceed as usual. Where that is so, things are straightforward. As the charge for this chapter indicates, however, teachers of young scholars in education are undergoing "a reconception of locus, methods, media, agents, and standards for education research." What is one to do?

Some rather extended musings on this question may be found in a special issue of the *Journal of the Learning Sciences*, entitled *Research Methods in and for the Learning Sciences* (Schoenfeld, 1992). In it, Ann Brown, Geoff Saxe, and I each published articles discussing the kinds of problems we have faced when confronting new phenomena. Mine had to do with making sense of what students did during extended problem-solving sessions. The data were phenomenological —videotapes of students working on mathematical problems, sometimes for extended periods of time. The questions were, What seems to account for the students' success or failure in solving the problems? and What is the nature of their knowledge, and how does it change over time? The task was to figure out what was important and make a good case for it. This was exploratory research, which would produce hypotheses and methods for exploring those hypotheses. The contexts of Brown's and Saxe's work were radically different, but the issues were the same. Brown's work took place amid the glorious chaos of an experimental classroom. Her research team was "engineering a working environment" and trying to figure out and document what was happening in it. What were students learning? How were they learning it? What story did the instructional data tell? Saxe's data were both "naturalistic" (changing patterns of arithmetic among the Oksapmin people of Papua New Guinea) and interventionist (studies of an educational game in inner-city Los Angeles). In both cases, the key problem was the "sociogenesis of cognitive change"—understanding how the intellectual tools that people used were modified as a result of social needs and interactions.

From one perspective, our three articles are quite distinct: they deal with different problems, different theoretical frames, different kinds of data. Yet they all share a property that is increasingly common, given the state of the field as it moves away from its dependence on the paradigms of its constituent disciplines.

In each of these studies, part of the problem was defining the problem—framing ways to think about it, crafting methods for gathering data and forms of argument that would use those data, and weaving all data and argument together to make a compelling case.

And there we have it: What makes a compelling case? Speaking personally, I think that researchers in the field of education have been less than diligent in addressing this question. Terms like *theory* and *model* are bandied about casually, and we rarely worry in depth about the warrants that are produced for the claims we make. This is, I must emphasize, a mainstream concern. Given the state of flux referred to in the initial charge, any researcher's current tool kit will be obsolete within a few years. Individually and collectively researchers will have to refurbish the tool kit. That can be done only if they have clear standards for the methods proposed and clear statements about the range of applicability of those methods, about what can legitimately be taken as substantiation for conclusions drawn using them, and about how and why findings in particular settings can or cannot be generalized to other settings. (For a more extended discussion of standards, including issues of explanatory power, predictive power, and scope, see Schoenfeld, forthcoming.) Below I discuss ways in which beginning researchers can deal with such issues.

Assertion Four:
Beginning researchers should learn how to identify
and frame workable problems—meaningful problems on which
legitimate progress can be made in a reasonable amount of time.

Two independent lines of reasoning provide warrants for this assertion. The first was discussed in the first section. The dismal postdissertation publication rate of Ph.D. mathematicians provides the strong suggestion, for which there is ample support in the mathematical community, that problem *finding* is the hard part of problem solving. The difficulty is to find a problem that is hard enough so that its solution merits publication but not so hard that it cannot be solved. Learning to do this should be part of all doctoral training.

The second line of reasoning is, in essence, the one given in the elaboration of Assertion Three concerning the three articles that Brown, Saxe, and I wrote. Problem framing, along with the adaptation or invention of appropriate methods, is really a core competency in education research. As the field of education scholarship matures, researchers are increasingly able to grapple with complex behavior in relatively uncontrolled social settings—with cognition "in the wild" rather than in the laboratory. As they do so, they will continue to face new challenges. Can they adapt known methods to deal with a new situation? Will it be possible for them to focus on some aspect of the situation that is meaningful but tractable? Will they be able to invent relevant methods and provide warrants for them? The brief answer is that they had better be able to do all these things. That ability will be the education researcher's primary survival skill for the foreseeable future. Thus, the current generation of professionals has an obligation to help new researchers develop that skill.

THOUGHTS ON THE CORE

Earlier in this chapter I argued that there is no canon in education—no agreed-on core of work that every educator should know. There are certainly important papers, both classic and contemporary, but the fractionalization of the discipline precludes the possibility of "coverage." Furthermore, although there are important research methods in education, the multiplicity of relevant methods precludes the possibility of in-depth, across-the-board training. I also argued that the core in education plays a different role from the core in, say, mathematics or sociology. In those fields and many others the expectation is that all faculty members will be familiar with the same core—ignorance of it is unthinkable—and they will be prepared to teach large chunks of it.

In short, there is a functional form of literacy in education, but it is not the kind provided by a canon. What the core can provide is knowledge and appreciation of the main dimensions of the education enterprise—results and methods —and a sense of their interconnectedness. Students who have had productive experiences in their core courses will appreciate the myriad factors that shape education issues and have a sense of what it means to think deeply in various areas of education. They will not be prepared to do serious research, for much of that demands on-the-job training, as I discuss further on. They will, however, have a sense of the degree to which they understand various issues and of some of the basic ones they will need to confront in order to do good research.

Assertion Five:
Core courses should provide students with opportunities
to engage with some major education issues in such a way that they
come to grips with differing perspectives on them and a wide range
of methods to address them. In core courses students should learn
to become critical readers and thinkers. Part of this includes being able
to recognize the strengths, weaknesses, and range of applicability of the
different perspectives and methods that can be brought to bear on education.

This simple assertion imposes some fairly strong constraints on core course design, if not content. For example, narrowly focused courses are unlikely to provide intellectual handholds for a wide range of students or to support the kind of cross-fertilization of different perspectives that I argue for here. Some degree of breadth of coverage is necessary. At the same time, superficial survey courses will not achieve the desired ends. Depth and coherence are more important than coverage: students need to get enmeshed in the topics studied and work them through from different perspectives. One way is through sampling: choosing a small subset of issues that can be used toward desired ends. Indeed, which of these to choose and which examples are worked through may be less important than the ways they are explored.

I have seen enough attempts at solving the "core course problem" through the years to believe there is no permanent solution to it. There is certainly no general solution; even well-designed institution-specific solutions are unlikely to last very long. Good core courses are demanding, requiring a significant amount of energy and commitment from the individuals or teams who develop and teach them. The courses tend to go stale after some time and need to be rejuvenated—typically with new instructors—or replaced. Nonetheless, there are somewhat standard ways to proceed with reasonable short-term measures. I shall first address content and then methods, albeit briefly.

Assuming that a school of education is organized into some small number of units, there are two generic ways to organize the content core: (1) into courses that are consistent with the basic thrusts of individual units or clusters of them, or (2) into courses that deal with "crosscutting" topics deliberately chosen because they are relevant to all of the units. A mix of some of each is healthy. Again, local circumstances should determine the shape and number of such courses.

Along the lines of the first way, the School of Education at the University of California, Berkeley, is now moving toward an organization that has three overarching academic units: Cognition and Development; Policy, Organization, and Measurement; and Language, Literacy, and Culture. Each of these areas, which represents an amalgam of smaller units from our previous organizational structure, covers a fair amount of territory. Faculty members in one area are encouraged to propose core courses that give a taste of the mainstream issues, perspectives, and methods in that area, while highlighting connections with, and perspectives and methods from, the others.

As to crosscutting issues, one might consider such topics as assessment, diversity, the preparation of teachers, school-to-work, or any of a dozen others as the vehicles for courses that could draw contributions from the whole faculty. Such courses would come and go as the interests of the faculty wax and wane, but any course on such topics that draws the active participation of faculty members with complementary perspectives has the potential to be tremendously exciting, for the professors as well as for the students.

Methods courses are a quagmire. I make the same assertions with regard to methods that I do with regard to content. Simply put, it is impossible in a few introductory courses to provide the depth and breadth of coverage that will result in students' being adequately prepared for the research they will do. We can prepare students to be knowledgeable and skeptical consumers, and we can help engender in them an understanding of the fundamental issues. We can, in the best of all possible worlds, help them develop the right kinds of questioning attitudes—asking, as they proceed with their work, what they can say with justification and how best to approach issues so they can make strongly warranted claims. But we should not make the mistake of thinking that methods courses will prepare students adequately for conducting research. If students emerge from their methods courses with a sense of how to approach a problem, how to select methods that seem reasonable, and where to go for help when they realize the limits of those methods, then the core will have been quite successful.

This set of assertions, like those regarding content, imposes some serious constraints on course design. For example, a quantitative methods survey course that zips through descriptive statistics, hypothesis testing, regression analysis, and the like is likely to leave students with a thoroughly inadequate sense of relevant methods—especially if, as is typically the case, the approach is to present the methods (t-tests, z-tests, and so on) in the abstract and then apply them post hoc to problems. If the students are to make any sense of research methods, they must have some experience in problem formulation and methods selection. Moreover, they should have substantial experience "going meta"—determining the degree to which the methods chosen actually help address the problems they seek to address. The same is perhaps even more strongly the case with regard to qualitative methods. These are far less codified than their quantitative counterparts. Moreover, it is very easy to do superficial work under the banner of techniques that are subtle and take a long time to learn—for example, participant observation, ethnographic analysis, protocol analysis, or discourse analysis. Students must have enough in-depth experience with at least a small number of methods so that they themselves can tell the difference between superficial and serious work. Here too they must go meta, and here, too, they must have some experience in problem formulation and methods selection.

I have focused on constraints, pointing to features of core courses that might be either problematic or useful. There are multiple ways to honor those constraints, and the choice of how one goes about it should depend on local circumstances. It may be worth offering an artifact, however, as an indication of how one constraint might be met. As I have indicated, a major goal of core courses should be to help students become critical thinkers in education. Typically in my own course I hand out a general list of questions for students to consider when they do their readings. These questions, set out in Exhibit 9.1, provide an explicit structure for class discussions of readings the first few weeks of the course. The class does not rely on the explicit list for very long, but the questions remain in the air the entire term—and I return to them when I feel the students have not been appropriately thoughtful in dealing with the papers they have read. They are an illustration of what I mean by "going meta."

A. The Authors' "Bottom Line"
- What are the authors' goals? (There may be an overt *and* a hidden agenda.)
- What is the problem the authors address?
- What is the scope they
  1) claim to address?
  2) actually address?
- Does the paper actually address what the authors claim to address?
- In a few phrases, what are the major "punch lines" of the paper? What major claims are made?
- What background assumptions do the authors make? Are those assumptions reasonable and justifiable? If not, how does that affect the conclusions they draw? Does the context within which the authors work affect the way you should read the paper?
- What evidence do the authors find for their claims? Is that evidence
  1) adequate?
  2) coherent?
- Suppose you were assigned to argue either pro or con? Pro, could you find more support? Con, could you find the holes in the argument, flaws in the data, and so on?

B. More Global Questions
- What about the authors' conception of the task or issue addressed? Is that conception too broad, too narrow, properly defined? Does the paper deal with the whole issue as described? How does the authors' conceptualization compare with others? How should that affect the way you interpret the findings in the paper?
- Given your sense of the issue (as they did or should have defined it), is the authors' conceptualization reasonable? Did they leave out anything important? And if so, does consideration of that issue affect your conceptualization of the paper and its solidity?

Exhibit 9.1. Questions Designed to Help Students Become Critical Readers

LEARNING TO BECOME A RESEARCHER

It must be clear that prescribing any kind of research program is out of the question: the research preparation that takes place at any institution must fit naturally within the research culture of that institution. Moreover, there are diverse mentoring styles, from "the single disciple learning at the feet of the master" to apprenticeship that takes place mainly in the context of large research groups.

What works in any teaching relationship is very much a function of the style and disposition of the teacher and the students; what works for one faculty member may not work for another, and what works for some students may not work for others. All comments made here should be interpreted accordingly.

Apart from these general caveats, I should stress the limits of my knowledge and experience. My initiation into mathematics research was in the "single disciple" mode, and (not in any form of reaction; my mentor's style was ideal for me) my advising these days depends very much on my research group and community. I thus have some familiarity with both kinds of mentoring. I have spent some time in large scientific research groups as well. But I am not familiar with the norms of doctoral preparation in history or economics; what I say may or may not therefore be germane to research with strong historical or economic paradigmatic underpinnings (though I suspect it may be, as my experience with sociological-anthropological work suggests). *Caveat lector*: one should try to wear these shoes only if they seem to fit.

Having issued these warnings, I lay out some desiderata for a research preparation program in education. After that, I describe some pragmatic ways in which students can be provided with the desired kinds of intellectual support in their research preparation.

Some Assertions and Warrants for Them: Research Preparation in Education

Assertion Six:
Students should have the opportunity to engage in research as early as possible in their careers, and they should be continually involved in various aspects of research—problem definition, data gathering, data analysis.

Students should be encouraged early on to formulate problems and try to solve them, even if their first attempts are as awkward as a baby's first steps. The reason is simple. Research is not a spectator sport, and people will not develop a sense of it until they start doing it. This is the case even when learning to master standard techniques. It is especially the case when the research calls for the kinds of problem framing and methods development that I have argued are now part and parcel of our ongoing work. One colleague has summarized the issue succinctly: "The best way to succeed is to fail early and often—with the appropriate support and guidance, of course."

There are myriad places where one can go wrong when doing research. Fundamental errors can occur in the ways one conceptualizes a problem, selects data, or analyzes them, to name just a few. Mistakes are unavoidable, but with the proper feedback and reflectiveness, one will learn from them. It makes sense, I believe, to start this process as early as possible. To put things in very direct terms, would we rather have a student make a major conceptual error in a course project or in pilot work for a thesis?

Assertion Seven:
Multiple perspectives and multiple sources of feedback are good things.

Students are likely to learn more if their work is commented on by more than one faculty member—especially if the expertise each possesses overlaps and complements the other's. This is, I hope, self-evident.

Assertion Eight:
Living in a research culture makes a difference—that is where habits of mind get shaped.

There may well be "independent scholars," in the sense of those whose ideas have sprung almost completely from within, but I suspect they are relatively few in number and that most scholars profit from sustained membership in a congenial intellectual community. My experience has been that there is no better way to have one's ideas shaped than to be a member of a community in which one's own and related ideas are discussed. Sometimes the shaping is obvious: one walks out of a discussion with new or different thoughts as a result of the exchange. Sometimes the shaping is extremely subtle: I have realized, after the fact, that some of my ideas were, in important ways, the product of my environment. That is, I was most unlikely to have come up with some of my ideas had I not been engaged in long-term conversations with particular colleagues and been influenced by their thinking (see Schoenfeld, 1989). Moreover, there are a lot of skills that students can pick up through discussions of each other's work before they contend with big problems on their own.

Assertion Nine:
Passion helps, when appropriately harnessed.

People do their best work when they care about what they do. A program that allows students to pursue their interests is likely to foster a higher degree of commitment and higher-quality work than a program that does not. This too should be self-evident.

Pragmatics: Institutional Mechanisms

"What works" is often context dependent. I can say, however, that the institutional mechanisms described here have proved to be remarkably robust in my home environment. They have been implemented for more than a decade in the Education in Mathematics, Science, and Technology (EMST) program at Berkeley, and I am deeply wedded to them. I describe three separate aspects of the program: action-oriented courses, first- and second-year projects, and research groups.

Action-Oriented Courses. Roughly half of the courses in our program require students to conduct an empirical project of some significant scope. In such courses, there is usually a heavy reading load up front. In the middle of the term, the reading load lightens as students design and implement projects related to the course content. At the end of the course, the projects are used as vehicles to reflect on that content.

Course projects come in all shapes and sizes. The default option, which actually very few students exercise, is to replicate a study discussed in the course. Another option is to make a minor modification or extension of a study examined in the course. A third, and the one most frequently taken, is to find a phenomenon of interest and try to make sense of it. The data examined might be videotapes of a classroom or school, students' work on particular instructional materials or a computer program, people's "out-loud" thoughts as they try to solve chemistry problems, or just about anything else. Pretty much anything related to the general content of a course is fair game.

For example, this past semester I taught a course entitled The Nature of Mathematical Thinking and Problem Solving. Most of the students in the course were first- and second-year graduate students. We did a substantial amount of reading, covering much of the content of two books and a fair number of papers in depth. But the class's attention midsemester turned to student projects.

One student had been working for some time as part of a team developing a test of "mathematical ability" that was being administered to thousands of students and analyzed using statistical measures. For her course project she selected some people at various points on the spectrum from "ordinary beginner" to "talented expert" (a faculty member in mathematics). She hypothesized the kinds of performance that people with different levels of mathematical ability would display when they worked the problems and then videotaped the people solving the problems. The reality of people's performance was an eye-opener. Some novices displayed much more effective problem-solving practices than she expected, and her "expert" engaged in rather sloppy reasoning in places. This experience led her to question some of the assumptions she had been making about the problems and about what people's test scores really meant.

A second student hypothesized that girls and boys would act differently in same-sex problem-solving groups from the way they would if some or all the other students in the group were of the opposite sex. As it happened, the people she chose (somewhat randomly) as the main subjects in her study tended to have robust character traits (shyness in some cases, aggressiveness in others), and there was not much apparent difference in their performance. In reviewing the tapes, however, the student became interested in how collaborative the various groups were. She began to develop a coding scheme that looked at comments from students that invited reaction versus those that were neutral or that closed off conversation. This was a legitimate first step toward the quantification of collaborativeness and a good example of problem definition and method creation.

A third student analyzed some videotapes of an experimental course on mathematical representations that had been taught as part of a colleague's research and development work the previous summer. He looked at a student's beliefs about "what counts" as being mathematical and then tried to correlate her beliefs with her behavior. This particular student tended to disparage successful qualitative reasoning as "mere" common sense, while giving high praise to mathematical behavior that included writing and solving equations—even though the equations she praised were, from our perspective, pretty much nonsense. Such beliefs seemed to play out in her actions during the course as well, though the evidence for this claim was tenuous at best.

Other projects dealt with student and teacher perceptions of a "reform" mathematics course, an attempt to analyze the teaching of a master teacher, and use of artifacts such as white boards (instead of individual sheets of paper) to catalyze interactions during group problem solving, and more.

How good were the projects? The truth is that when beginning students try to carry out such projects, their attempts tend to be half-baked. They come to realize that they did not see the things they expected to see, that they cannot make the arguments they thought they would be able to make, and sometimes that there are interesting and unexpected leads in what they did see, which provide pointers to issues they would like to pursue. Almost all of the papers were flawed in some way or other. That is no surprise, since the students did not yet have the background to design or carry out near-perfect studies. I think what happened is quite healthy. What the course offered was an institutionally supported way to make mistakes in the process of trying to define and work on a nontrivial research problem. Of course, this is profitable only if the students have the opportunity to learn from their mistakes. As part of their projects, students are asked to say how they would do things differently if they had them to do over again. Then, in class discussion of the projects, which are presented formally as though in an AERA session, and in my evaluations of them, there is extended discussion of what worked, what did not, and what might be done about it.

Before I discuss our required first- and second-year projects, I want to mention one important way that the program encourages multiple lines of feedback. In any given semester a student may be enrolled in two or three courses or research groups that require projects—for example, a course in instructional design and a course on mathematical cognition. Rather than considering it cheating, we encourage that student to design one project for both courses—say, a project that includes the design of some instructional materials in mathematics, followed by the analysis of what students do with those materials (or, if the student is taking a course in qualitative methods and is also part of a research group working in schools, a project for the group and the course that might be to analyze some part of what is happening in the schools using some of the techniques studied in the methods course). Since the project is to be submitted for credit in two courses, it will, of course, be larger than a project for either course alone would be. But the development of this larger project is then facilitated by two or more faculty members and commented on by two or more as well. Typically students take a number of courses each year that have such projects. In that way, the program offers an institutionalized mechanism for failing early and often—and for learning from those failures.

First- and Second-Year Projects. Although students can and often do combine course projects, their efforts are usually limited to what can be done in one semester. For this reason such course projects often have the character of a pilot study, where an idea is explored but without enough time to work it out fully. To allow for more scope and quality, in the summer following the first year of the program, and again in the summer following the second, students are required to conduct and write up more extensive studies. Typically, at Berkeley, these first- and second-year projects are extensions of course projects. A course project may have yielded some tantalizing results, so the student goes back to gather more (or better) data to explore the issue in greater depth. With some frequency, the work is cumulative: a second-year project is an outgrowth or modification of the first year's and may itself evolve into a dissertation project. These projects are expected to meet rather stringent standards, in which they are written up as though for publication and judged accordingly. The resulting report is read by two members of the faculty, and the discussion of the student's project is a major component of our annual student evaluation.

Even though they come on the heels of course work, first-year projects can turn out to be seriously flawed, in which case the students are told to revise them and try again. Many are respectable, however, and need only minor revisions. Either way, it is healthy to establish the standard for judgment and provide rigorous feedback. Second-year projects tend to be of uniformly high quality, and a fair number of them have been published. Indeed, my favorite datum regarding the success of the project requirement is that a few years back, 63 percent of our third-year and above students were first or sole authors of papers accepted for presentation on that year's AERA annual program. That year the acceptance rate for the program was about 50 percent—and since EMST was young and very few students were nearing completion of their dissertations, almost all of the positively reviewed work was not from dissertations but from second-year projects. Our students consistently beat the average percentage rate for the profession as a whole with regard to acceptance on the AERA annual program. I have no doubt that their success is attributable to the fact that we provided them with consistent opportunities to do independent work and to receive solid critical feedback on it.

Research Groups. I now move from the discussion of institutional constraints to more idiosyncratic issues of research mentoring and apprenticeship. I have already stated my belief that students are more likely to become productive researchers, and to develop useful habits and perspectives more rapidly, if they are members of a research community. When one is constantly engaged with people who live and breathe research, participating at least vicariously and sometimes actively in the development of their ideas and in their successes and failures, one is much more likely to pick up what counts than one would working in isolation.

As a matter of policy, no student is admitted to our program unless she or he has a faculty sponsor and a cosponsor. Each faculty member has one or more research groups, and students are expected to participate in their sponsor's research groups. Many students attend two or more research groups, because they find the complementary perspectives and expertise of value. Although there is tremendous variation, certain properties tend to be present if a research group or community is functioning well. Four of those properties are as follows:

- Much of the work done really matters to the people involved. There is a sense of purpose and meaningfulness in the work; it is not seen as busy-work but as part of what needs to get done to advance the enterprise.

- Much of the work being done is *visible*—the processes of doing research, including mulling through problems, are public property in the sense that dilemmas are shared and community input is valued as a way of solving them.

- There is a culture of reflectiveness, where the expectation is that problematic issues will be raised and members of the community will consider contributing to their solution—even problems whose solution does not contribute to their own progress, as one of their communal responsibilities. The culture is such that there is room for the work and the contributions of all members to be taken seriously.

- The work and interactions of the group provide a series of handholds that allow individuals at various levels of knowledge and expertise to contribute meaningfully to the enterprise and make parts of it their own. Newcomers' contributions may consist of routine work in the service of the cause—for example, first-year students have helped develop homework problems for a curriculum unit we were building or helped videotape lessons. At the same time, those students were present for the theoretical discussions and were invited to contribute whenever they felt comfortable doing so. Typically early contributions consist of occasional comments or questions, as beginners try to sort out the spirit or the details of what is being done. As they become more central members of the community, the character of their questions and contributions tends to evolve. They are likely to take on larger tasks, individually or in collaboration, and they increasingly take on ownership of tasks and ideas.

A way to describe this process in somewhat more theoretical terms is that a functioning research community provides multiple opportunities for legitimate peripheral participation. As once-peripheral members become more central to the enterprise, they find more means of achieving centrality, and there is room and access for new members at the periphery. (A detailed examination of this process would be a most welcome study.)

There is, it should be stressed, no one model of a productive research group or community, any more than there is of an effective school of education. Such communities may be very small, consisting of one senior researcher and a few students, or they may be rather large, with a substantial number of people with varied levels of skill and expertise. Moreover, no group is static. Depending on the people involved and the tasks at hand—for example, to conceptualize a new project, build a collaboration, "engineer change," design or implement materials, gather data, analyze data, write papers or proposals and revise them—the day-to-day transactions of the group and its level of activity will vary. What follows should be interpreted in that light. It describes the operation of one research group whose modus operandi seems to support the four properties.

The functions group began at Berkeley in 1985 pretty much as a historical accident. We had obtained NSF funding for an ambitious project, and the small group of people present had to figure out how to get the work done. The group evolved in various ways over the ensuing decade. When there was a major influx of funding, group meetings could involve up to two dozen postdoctoral students, visitors, collaborating teachers, and students. At one point when we were developing and implementing instructional materials in a local school, there were, in addition to the weekly general meetings of the group, regularly scheduled meetings of four research and development subgroups. These days the group is smaller, with two main streams of activity: a set of general umbrella meetings and a set of meetings focused on a particular research agenda. It is worth discussing the characteristics of both, for they serve different and important roles.

The Umbrella Group. The research group as a whole has regularly scheduled weekly meetings. Its explicit agenda is to serve the needs of the members of the group. Group meetings fall into several equivalence classes:

- *Providing group members feedback on issues of importance to them.* Any member of the group may request time for a discussion of his or her work. What is brought to the group can vary substantially. A student may have a vague idea for a project and ask for the group's help in honing that idea. He or she may have some data and want to see the group's reactions or may want to run an explanation by us and see if we buy it. The student may have a draft piece of work—a course project, a master's thesis, a dissertation proposal, a chapter of a dissertation, a proposal for a conference presentation, or a paper for submission—and want our feedback. These sessions are scheduled with enough lead time so that group members are expected to go through the relevant materials and serve as colleagues in providing help to the presenter.

Since one misconception about research groups is that they function well only if everybody is working on more or less the "same thing," I should highlight the diversity of interests and foci in the work of group members. As cases in point, I shall briefly describe the work and work trajectories of three of my advisees who finished their dissertations within the past two years and of one who is close to finishing.

Thanks to the NSF funding, many of my students were involved in a major project that included the development of curricular materials to help students understand the topics of functions and graphs. JL was one of our main curriculum designers. Her second-year project had been on the topic of approximation, the area in which she expected to write her dissertation. It was clear to me, however, that JL was deeply interested in issues related to curriculum design—in, specifically, what sense students made of the materials she had designed. JL had tried to follow the National Council of Teachers of Mathematics *Standards* (1989), introducing mathematical concepts through the use of real-world contexts. The intuition that drove the curriculum was that students would develop more robust understandings of notions such as slope if they learned them meaningfully in various contexts, rather than through the standard formal symbolic approach. The curriculum included some laboratory activities, such as finding the slope of a conical pile of sand, that, it was hoped, would provide the basis for transfer. At one point I observed that JL was captivated by trying to figure out what the students had actually learned, and I suggested that figuring out in a rigorous way what the students had understood from the materials could well be the subject of a dissertation. She took to the suggestion immediately, and her dissertation, grounded in the data from our classroom efforts, wound up providing a reconceptualization of the concept of transfer.

MG's trajectory was somewhat different. From the day she entered our program, MG knew she was interested in the study of teacher knowledge. As it happened, our R&D efforts provided a lovely context within which to study the issue. The curriculum we had developed made strong pedagogical and content demands on the teachers who were

THE CORE, THE CANON, AND THE DEVELOPMENT OF RESEARCH SKILLS 197

using it. Observations of our lessons raised some interesting issues, for, based on their understandings of the mathematics involved, teachers sometimes made very different use of the curricular materials from what was intended. This raised a significant question regarding the influence of teachers' knowledge on their teaching practices: How did their knowledge shape and constrain the ways in which they could adopt or adapt to the materials? MG's dissertation provides a finely grained analysis of the various ways in which teachers engage in dialectic with the materials, transforming or adapting them as they make them their own.

DM entered our program with a strong interest in providing access to mathematics to minority students, in particular African American students. His original plan was to explore the development of "mathematical culture" in a highly regarded national reform project being implemented in a local school that has a very large proportion of African American students. Unfortunately the project failed to take hold, so DM had to modify his plans significantly. He went on to study the various community, classroom, and individual forces that shape the ways that novel curricula can take hold in schools and the factors that enable some African American students to succeed in mathematics despite strong countervailing pressures.

SM came to our research group with experience as a teacher and curriculum designer. Along with MG and JL, she was one of the major contributors to our curriculum. During her early years in the program, SM had used various tasks related to our curriculum for course and other projects. She came to realize the various and subtle ways in which her understandings—as designer of curriculum materials and tasks, as classroom teacher who was implementing these tasks, and as researcher developing a deeper understanding of student cognition—all interacted. The nature of those interactions, and the contributions that the communities of researchers, teachers, and curriculum developers can make to each other, is the subject of her dissertation.

In sum, the main topics of these students' work could be labeled as transfer, teacher knowledge, multilevel analyses of cultural forces and individual agency, and reflection on professional growth and integration. This is hardly a homogeneous collection of topics. Three of the four dissertations grew out of our NSF-funded project, though going in very different directions, while the fourth flourished independent of it. Yet discussions of these students' ongoing work—from the early stages of problem formulation through the stage of selecting data, agonizing over what the data meant, and then writing things up in ways that were cogent and compelling—all proceeded in parallel and in comfort.

What made the group function effectively was a common interest in helping each other work things through and an understanding that at some fundamental level we were all grappling with the same questions. No matter whose work was being discussed, our conversations were all grounded in the same kinds of questions: What are you trying to say (What are the "punch lines")? Why would anyone think this is important? What kinds of evidence will convince people that what you are saying is justified? What are counter-interpretations? What position will you be in if the data do not tell the story you would like? What are the implications of your expected results, and why should anyone believe them? We tried not only to raise the questions but also to help answer them.

In these conversations everyone profits. The presenter gets feedback that is useful. The others hone their skills in understanding and critiquing research and in learning to ask others the kinds of questions they will have to ask themselves as independent researchers. A major factor in the quality of the students' work was that the project was a labor of love for each one of them. They really cared about what they were trying to explain, and that means a lot.

- *Dealing with topics or readings of interest.* When desired, the group serves as a reading or discussion group. We have, at various times, decided to "go to school" on various theoretical perspectives (constructivism, situated cognition), to explore the strengths and limitations of particular research methods, or to discuss papers on topics that just plain seemed interesting.

- *Dealing with issues raised by collaborating partners.* When our group has been involved in schools, membership in the group automatically extends to all of our collaborating partners. Collaborating teachers are given e-mail accounts and linked electronically to the group; just like any other group members, they initiate conversations about topics of interest.

- *Providing a critical but friendly audience for practice talks.* In the period preceding the annual AERA meeting, there is often a need to schedule extra group meetings so that members of the group can practice their presentations. This is most likely the second time they will have worked on the topic with the group; their proposals would probably have been previously discussed as well. Typically members rehearse any presentations before the group before they go "public." Last year we had a series of "job talk" rehearsals. One of the most gratifying aspects of the group meetings was watching students who were sometimes literally in competition with each other (being finalists for the same faculty positions) helping each other hone their presentations.

In short, the umbrella group works in response to the needs of its members. It may well advance my own research agenda—after all, the students are working on topics of interest to me, and in some cases the students are funded directly to work on my projects. But any advancement of my agenda is a happy by-product of the interactions. Another happy by-product is that since the discussions are public, many of the issues that would typically get dealt with one-on-one in a faculty member's office—how one picks a research problem; the kinds of data one needs to collect; the appropriate form for a dissertation proposal and how much evidence one has to offer in it—are now the subject of community discourse. The group meetings hardly supplant individual meetings with students. They do, however, cut down substantially on what needs to be said in one-on-one conversations, and they allow the individual meetings to be more focused and productive.

Focused Research Subgroups. In addition to weekly umbrella group meetings, we have much more focused meetings that pursue a particular research agenda. In its current incarnation, the research group has one set of such meetings a week, devoted to exploring and modeling teachers' knowledge and behavior. In this "teacher model" group, our agenda is much more constrained than it is in the general functions group meetings. The arena for inquiry is agreed on, and we engage in short- and long-term planning regarding goals for the research and ways to meet them.

The more focused nature of the subgroup's agenda means that its workings are more continuous and intense than are those of the larger group. Depending on the timing of their tenure as graduate students, some students have lived through the entire life cycle of a particular project, from its conceptualization through its instantiation. What the focused group offers is the possibility of experiencing the nitty-gritty of such research from beginning to end, whether as core player or legitimate peripheral participant. Having this experience is an important part of living in the research environment—for those who intend to be teachers and those who intend to be researchers. Currently about half of the regular attendees of the teacher model group are students in our master's-plus-teaching-credential program. This embedding in the research culture is by design an important part of the teacher preparation program. As members of the research group, these student teachers are learning about research and reflecting on the teaching process. Theirs is far from a token role; they participate fully and have made significant contributions to our analyses.

As in the case of the umbrella group, there is a self-conscious attempt to make sure that there are opportunities for all group members to participate in ways they find comfortable and to make sure that the work is meaningful and visible. For instance, there are many discussions about how and why we are doing what we are doing, and we work things out together. (To digress a moment, I cannot resist telling one story about the consequences of making the process of doing research visible. Some years ago our group was in the early stages of a new project. As we got down to work, one of the new students asked what our research plan was. I told her I did not know yet; we needed to make more sense of the data before we could lay out anything resembling a coherent agenda. She persisted, insisting that I *must* have a plan. I persisted in saying I did not and said we should get on with our work. We did. She told me later she had decided at that point I must have had a plan; I simply did not want to tell her because it was important for her to discover it by herself. Be that as it may, we proceeded with the work, and she became a major contributor to it. The following fall I began the academic year as usual, introducing new students to the group and describing our modus operandi. When I got to the point about much of our work being exploratory in nature, the student—by now a core member of the group—announced to the newcomers: "And let me tell you: When Alan says he doesn't know what he's doing, you can really believe him!")

What Is Flexible? What Generalizes? In bringing this section to a close I comment on the notion of apprenticeship through membership in a research community and discuss how much of the preceding discussion is generalizable, as opposed to depending on the idiosyncrasies of the research group leader. I have argued that it is extremely valuable for beginning researchers to live in communities where basic research issues are worked out "in public" and where the nature of the community is such that it supports their easy entry and facilitates their moves toward centrality. Beyond that, almost all of the features discussed in the previous section are optional. The functions group is run primarily by one person (me), but research groups with a number of core members of the faculty are equally viable and might even be preferable in some ways. The group's modus operandi has varied through the years as a function of funding and its members' interests. Again, I should stress that there need not be one coherent focus for the group's work: there is large variation within our umbrella group meetings, and a colleague who is an anthropologist of education tells me that her group works similarly. What really counts is providing a supportive environment that lives and breathes research issues, is open and reflective, allows people to pursue ideas that they really care about, and provides them with many opportunities to learn, early on, from the mistakes they will inevitably make.

SUMMARY AND CONCLUSION

Established researchers in education face serious challenges in the preparation of the next generation of education researchers. As the charge at the beginning of this chapter recognizes, the very conditions under which researchers conduct their work are undergoing radical change: they are exploring new phenomena with new perspectives and developing new methods as they proceed. What, then, can we offer those who wish to enter the field?

We must help beginning researchers develop a broad view and an appreciation of multiple perspectives on education issues, for the dangers of compartmentalization and narrow focus cannot be overstated. We must provide them with the opportunity to develop significant depth as well as breadth, for the dangers of superficiality are every bit as serious as those of narrow focus. We must prepare them for change. They should learn how to identify and frame workable problems and to adapt or invent methods suitable to deal with those problems. Most important, we should prepare them to think deeply about the nature of the claims that can be made in education research and the warrants that constitute valid support for such claims.

This is a daunting but not an impossible task. There are institutional mechanisms for moving in the right direction. A reconceptualization of core courses can provide the basis for offering new researchers a kind of functional literacy, which at least focuses them on the right issues. Action-oriented courses and major projects can provide the theoretical-empirical mix that is appropriate for professional growth. Strong research communities can provide good models of professionalism, a base of support, and ways for beginning researchers to reflect on and profit from their mistakes.

This is not a period of normal science. That makes our job that much more challenging—and that much more fun.

References

Ausubel, D. *The Psychology of Meaningful Verbal Learning.* New York: Grune & Stratton, 1963.

Cohen, D. "A Revolution in One Classroom: The Case of Mrs. Oublier." *Education Evaluation and Policy Analysis,* 1990, *12*(3), 311–329.

Grouws, D. A. (ed.). *Handbook of Research on Mathematics Teaching and Learning.* New York: Macmillan, 1992.

Jackson, P. W. (ed.). *Handbook of Research on Curriculum.* New York: Macmillan, 1992.

Kozol, J. *Savage Inequalities.* New York: Harper, 1992.

Kuhn, T. *The Structure of Scientific Revolutions.* Chicago: University of Chicago Press, 1970.

Little, J. W. "Teachers' Professional Development in a Climate of Educational Reform." *Educational Evaluation and Policy Analysis,* 1993, *15*(2), 129–151.

McLaughlin, M. W., Talbert, J. E., and Bascia, N. *The Contexts of Teaching in Secondary Schools: Teachers' Realities.* New York: Teachers College Press, 1990.

Schoenfeld, A. H. "Ideas in the Air: Speculations on Small Group Learning, Peer Inter-actions, Cognitive Apprenticeship, Quasi-Vygotsean Notions of Internalization, Cre-ativity, Problem Solving, and Mathematical Practice." *International Journal of Educational Research,* 1989, *13*(1), 71–88.

Schoenfeld, A. H. (ed.). "Research Methods in and for the Learning Sciences." *Journal of the Learning Sciences,* 1992, *2*(special issue 2).

Schoenfeld, A. H. (in press). "Toward a Theory of Teaching-in-Context." *Issues in Education.*

Wittrock, M. (ed.). *Handbook of Research on Teaching.* (3rd ed.) New York: Macmil-lan, 1986.

CHAPTER TEN

Discipline and
Disciplines in Education Research

Elusive Goals?

Shirley Brice Heath

In the field of education research, the end of the century has brought with it a paradox. As research has gained prominence with public calls for evidence justifying the reward or punishment of students, teachers, administrators, school reformers, and schools, professional confidence in research on education has declined. Education researchers, particularly those located exclusively within higher education institutions, are being edged out by evaluators and political analysts, independent or attached to laboratories, in battles over the terms of school reform.

Perhaps under this pressure, education researchers in the final two decades of the twentieth century have increasingly asserted the relevance of their findings to specific reform efforts. They struggle for ways to become more visible in the collective national endeavor to do more than tinker with classroom environments, teaching, governance, curricula, school finance, assessments, and standards. They wrestle also with the fact that much of what absorbs them is what keen observers with commonsense insights already know about learning and teaching. Findings from research show the strong learning outcomes from small group inquiry projects, adequate time for student-initiated questions, authentic tasks and audiences, and caring teachers who hold consistently high expectations for performance. But in their efforts to be both relevant and responsible, and in competing with this new class of evaluators, education researchers see their work too often judged on narrow grounds: the promises it can make for practice or the proof it can offer of specific, quantifiable positive effects of one reform or another.

Within the ranks of education research, disquiet lurks. Gatekeepers of the fenced reserves of theory (critical, feminist, neo-Marxist, whole language) stand ready to pounce on studies that fail to argue from within specific theoretical boundaries or give due consideration to personalities linked to a specific "ism." More and more, education researchers hear from postmodernists that they should reflect as much on their own role in studying subjects and in claiming objective stances as they do on their collection and analysis of data.

Where education research now sits with respect to the disciplines and to time-honored frames for judging such research is the subject of this chapter. I examine four major trends affecting the field in recent decades and their ramifications in the training of education researchers. The first of these—the push for positive results—dominates coverage of the remaining three, because, it seems to me, it shapes the other trends in inestimable ways. My comments show all the biases of one who has trained in anthropology and linguistics and has chosen to work across different social groups on language acquisition, socialization, and cultural influences and on the values that surround what counts as learning and as communication. I close with some speculative proposals concerning the responsibilities of schools of education for education research.

Here, briefly, are the four trends I examine:

1. **The positive and familiar imperative.** There has been a growing habit, particularly within education research heavily influenced by the social sciences, to emphasize only positive results from research. This pattern, which began to take hold in the 1970s, has been influenced by the inclusion of cultural difference theory within education studies.

2. **The quest for institutional reform.** In the squeeze on education research coming from public cries for school reform, centuries of consideration of education as far more than schooling have been nearly forgotten. The rush was on in the early 1980s for panacea, quick fix, proof, and remedy for schools, with little attention given to socialization and learning experiences outside of formal education settings.

3. **The punishing influence of psychology.** During the 1970s, the discipline of psychology, with its attendant concepts of controls, variables, and quantifiable indicators, increasingly dominated estimations of sound research as well as billets in schools of education and mandated courses for doctoral students. The focus on individual learners and their accumulation of factual knowledge was manifested strongly in courses in methods of teaching for preservice teachers, giving impetus to techniques for measuring achievement through quantifiable evidence of students' mastery of discrete points of information. In this period, human development courses perpetuated the idea of a universal pattern of learning, with primary focus on a transmission model of

socialization that flowed from parents to teachers in the individual's movement from the institution of family to that of school.

4. **Living with expectations.** Two groups stand out as holding expectations that have come increasingly to shape education research. The first is that group looking to such research for practical reform and restructuring of schools. As the federal government and states have taken up education and schools as major political issues, researchers have been looked to as supporters for particular policy directions or programmatic decisions. Hence what might in an earlier era have been termed evaluation has come to be called research or proof of the efficacy of one solution or policy over another. The second group comprises theorists from particular camps who began in the late 1970s to hammer away at the shortcomings of essentialist and universalist ideas. They did so largely by deriving their critiques from philosophers and sociopolitical theorists and from persons speaking for minority groups and for the power of linguistic and cultural variation. Much of this work moved away from a focus on the individual learner to the centrality of sociocultural groups, of environments of learning and discourse, and of the uses of language in institutional contexts for specific purposes. Brought into the arena of education research were anthropologists, sociolinguists, political scientists, historians, and economists, who began to detail just what happens through discourse and what is in a context and to offer revisions of broad societal phenomena related to public schooling.

Scholars from these disciplines who joined psychologists in a serious commitment to education research two to three decades ago have been the majority within groups such as the National Academy of Education, the National Research Council, and the American Educational Research Association (AERA). Many of them came to schools of education, and hence to education research, with one or more of their degrees in specific disciplines and often none in education. Most came with no elementary or secondary school classroom teaching experience prior to their positions in postsecondary institutions. Their knowledge of the methods and theories of their fields came directly from their disciplinary training and not, as is increasingly the case today, from derivative fashion-driven courses around topics or problems related to formal education. Their disciplinary bases stood as firm supports for their studies in education. This separation from education as both practice and field of study has made it especially difficult for them to respond to expectations from policymakers and practitioners with recommendations for action—for example, to develop performance standards and to promote national norms of learning. Their disciplinary background led them instead to prefer to develop theories, understand group behaviors, and challenge earlier empirical work and its ideological bases.

THE POSITIVE AND FAMILIAR IMPERATIVE

Sir Francis Bacon, sometime scientist and philosopher and an always eager essayist, reminds us in *The Advancement of Learning* (1900, p. 156), which was originally published in 1605, of the researcher's tendency to publish positive scientific results that fit well into a progressively accumulating body of knowledge. As he observed, "The nature of the understanding is more affected with affirmatives and actives than with negatives and privatives." Bacon terms the preference for positive results in scientific inquiry "a kind of contract of error" that results from the desire of writers to have their knowledge more believed than examined.

Bacon's caution reminds us that scholars tend to state outcomes in positive or negative terms, and the preference for the positive has long been dominant. Recent consideration of this point began in 1986 when a meta-analysis of papers published by the clinical and psychotherapy divisions of the American Psychological Association revealed a selective bias for positive articles (Coursol and Wagner, 1986). Scientists often acknowledge that overturning past positive reports is difficult, even when strong new evidence negates these results.

Perhaps even more difficult is the task of dislodging accepted conceptual systems that stand guard around certain folk theories lying deep within value systems. Abundant illustrations of this point come from scholarship on language learning. For example, more than four decades of research have shown that teaching spelling and grammar will not have nearly the positive long-term effects that many English teachers and key persons have claimed. Instead, immersing students in rich reading experiences will more likely produce careful writers and thoughtful readers. Teaching grammar rules will not produce improvements in composition that are commensurate with embedding extensive writing within substantial reading requirements, and yet the teaching of spelling and of grammar and vocabulary in isolated formats still dominates both belief and practice around what is good for students (Weaver, 1996).

Beliefs about language and culture resist displacement in large part because everyone knows what language and culture are and is therefore sure that research can only confirm conventional wisdom. Several such unyielding conceptual systems encircle the study of language acquisition (how humans learn to speak and to understand communication) and language socialization (how those humans responsible for nurturing the young use language to shape their development to conform with surrounding social groups and cultural habits). In studies of language, certain seemingly undeniable truths still stand firm:

- Caregivers are generally biological parents, expected to know about communication, behaviors, and values of the surrounding society because of their own experience as recipients of a transmitted culture.

- Language, like most other behaviors in the early years, lays open for study a developmental trajectory common to human beings around the world.

- The bulk of language learning takes place before entry to school, and therefore the primary task of formal education is to teach reading and writing, develop vocabulary according to a developmental continuum, and impress on students the primacy of displaying learning through written means.

- Language, like the brain, can be used to study itself. Asking questions and answering them are perceived as normal within early childhood, a process that may be expected to continue to yield the most useful information on what individuals know in formal education.

These concepts, stemming primarily from psychology and content areas (especially reading), have effectively silenced most research that springs from distant and different premises regarding learning and learners. Anthropologists have, for a century or more, documented the extent of caregiving by peers and older siblings and relatives within families. They have illustrated that fundamental notions such as attachment, mother–child talk, and question-answer sessions between the old and the young occur relatively infrequently among societies of the world. Linguistic anthropologists have demonstrated further that expected trajectories of language development will not play themselves out in societies that place heavy emphasis among the young on tactile manipulation and that value silence and deeds rather than words as ways of showing what one knows and can do. Gender distinctions in space usage, time of exposure to particular kinds of language, and types of tasks undertaken shape in many ways the path of language use the young follow and their willingness to accept possible risks in displaying what they know by writing or by talking. (Summaries of this research appear in Schieffelin and Ochs, 1986; Ochs, 1988; and Eckert and McConnell-Ginet, 1992.) Nevertheless, psychologists and psycholinguists continue to discount—in the vast majority of articles published in such journals as *Child Language*, *Developmental Psychology*, and *Verbal Language and Behavior* —cases of socialization that do not fit transmission models and that reflect not-so-straight situations fitting clumsily, if at all, into their required methods or conceptual frames.

Education researchers who study learning in content areas and reading follow the lead of psychologists and tend not to challenge the focus of psycholinguists and child language researchers on parent-child interaction. In addition, education researchers do not themselves study the role of language as a medium for displaying knowledge in school or how use of this medium differs beyond the classroom. Social scientists who do challenge the dominant body of language development work (see especially Hoyle and Adger, 1998) ask: How can scholars claim to understand language learning when they study only the small percentage of speakers available to laboratories in their preschool years and leave the vast array of speakers—bilingual and multilingual as well as monolingual—out of consideration? What we do know about the language development of school-age children centers on testing the grammatical development of children and their understanding of a small range of complex syntactic structures. Carol Chomsky (1969), for example, studied five- to ten-year-old children's understanding of verbs such as *promise, tell, order,* and *want.* A surprising finding in this study was the late and individual patterns of acquisition among some children of the syntactic structures necessary to understand concepts such as go in sentences of the type, "John promised Bill to go." Contrary to the general view that children have mastered their native tongue by the time they go to school, Chomsky found that structures commonly associated with the verbs named above were still being acquired by children as old as nine years of age. In essence, older children were still acquiring what may be regarded as the "adult linguistic system" much later than educators and linguists believed them to be.

A second study by Walter Loban (1963, 1976) includes a cross-section of children between the ages of five and eighteen and lays out both the stages and velocity of language development over these years. This work again shows a considerable amount of individual variation among children in the acquisition of longer communication units and in the elaboration of subject and predicate, adjectival-dependent clauses, variety and depth of vocabulary, and clause-embedding techniques. Particularly notable is the variability in children's expressions of conditionality and tentativeness: statements of supposition, hypothetical reasoning, and conjecture follow much later than the language of labeling and categorizing. In comparing, contrasting, conjecturing, clarifying, and communicating feelings and emotions, the children show variability in their facility in production (that is, in what they say as distinct from what they can understand), a variability that is not consistently associated with social class and occupation or educational level of parents.

But Loban's study was done well before bilingual educators and multiculturalists began asking questions about why non-native English speakers have not been considered in studies such as this. In any case, the few tests reported today of language proficiency among non-English speakers focus predominantly on the production and reception of particular morphemes (smallest units of meaning within a given language, such as "-ed" to mark past tense in English), vocabulary recognition, and storytelling abilities. In essence, education researchers have done almost nothing to follow up Loban's study—for example, to see whether his conclusions hold up for other groups of children or to explore the implications of his findings for assessing students' abilities to master certain subject areas at specific grade levels. Education researchers still have few careful studies of the achievement effects of curricular adaptations for students from differing linguistic, cultural, and economic backgrounds that do not fit the mainstream norms and value orientations of middle-class, school-literate populations.

Relatively few long-term studies situated in a wide range of environments and at different age and status levels of interaction exist. Also omitted from scholarly attention are ways that students' language changes in relation to different kinds of arrangements for classroom discussion, small group work, and project-based assignments. In essence, the development of language abilities recedes in importance to researchers once children enter school, when, in reality, expressive abilities and capacities for understanding information increase in importance as individuals move through formal education and when their background of language socialization differs from that of the mainstream.

Schooling relies almost exclusively on assessment of the abilities of individuals on written forms of display, which are not only equated in formal education with knowing and doing but are also strongly related to competency in reading to learn. Other means of demonstrating understanding and skill level, such as visual or dramatic arts, go untutored and unrewarded and often prompt derision and contempt. Visual literacies other than the written word, and all the modes of showing achievement through music and dance, drama, and other oral forms—and through media technology—receive little notice in formal education or education research. Yet competencies with these forms of representation matter greatly in the larger society and within many of the increasingly heterogeneous populations in formal schooling (Flood, Heath, and Lapp, 1997).

In the 1980s, the slim amount of discipline-based research that focused on language and learning in everyday contexts brought education researchers to cultural difference theory, prompting questionable responses from practitioners and curriculum developers. Research among working-class whites and blacks showed evidence of strong, clear differences in the socialization of children to the use of oral and written language (Heath, 1983). Numerous scholars from the Kamehameha Early Education Project in Hawaii made similar points, suggesting the need for psychologists to step back from their views about universal paths of development and forms of knowledge display (Tharp and Gallimore, 1988). Amy Shuman (1986) followed urban adolescents from an inner-city school into their homes and neighborhoods to consider ways they conceal and withhold as well as reveal and celebrate information, while also adeptly using language to adjust relationships, often sending different messages to various members of the audience. Shuman showed how the young people she studied outside of school use both writing and speaking across a variety of roles and text types, while within school their competence was judged as poor. Marjorie Goodwin (1990) studied the sidewalk life of urban African American boys and girls, illustrating ways they use language to build and maintain as well as break and mend social relations. Critical here was the centrality of talk in play and work: the youngsters argue, give directives, gossip, pretend, and complain as they align and realign their knowledge of one another in relation to the resources and spaces in their neighborhood that permit them to accomplish the work of play. All of these researchers showed how the language of the children they studied reflects complex understandings and productive competence in a broader range of genres than those used in classrooms.

In response to these and a few similar studies, education researchers embraced "cultural difference, not cultural deficit" as the basis for introducing multicultural texts into curricula. Versions of classroom adaptations to perceived cultural differences followed and were widely reported by liberal education researchers eager to show just what the children of others could do. Their reports in turn led to conclusions that, when carefully considered, lacked common sense: African American culture is oral, and thus oral performance by African American students amounts to natural achievement, or, Latino children prefer group work over individual achievement and should therefore gain academically with the use of group projects. Conclusions such as these ignored the power of socioeconomic differences, length and place of residence in the United States, and individual differences, leaving many educators with strong tendencies to standardize their expectations of children regarded as nonmainstream. Only superficial understandings of language and its links to cognition entered into many multicultural programs, which administrators often felt forced to grab as quick fixes to cultural differences. For example, schools outside Hawaii adopted talk story; classrooms adopted African American folktales as reading material in the hope of raising children's scores in reading and on standardized tests (for further discussion of these points, see Rickford and Rickford, 1995).

Education researchers meanwhile moved to embrace ethnographic methods, but with little understanding of the grounding they needed in anthropology before launching into fieldwork involving participant observation, close analysis of discourse, or comparative analyses of learning under different circumstances. Courses in ethnography-as-method sprang up in education schools throughout the 1980s, and many were taught by instructors who had never studied anthropology. Moreover, many methods courses viewed ethnography and qualitative methods as more appropriate in the study of minority groups than procedures that came to be oppositionally lumped together as quantitative. The results for education research of lifting methods out of any discipline-based contexts can be felt in numerous ways. Some journals embrace qualitative research but do not explicate the standards of judgment that would enable articles to be refereed in any predictable or reliable way. Judgments on tenure or reappointment cases similarly float without agreed-on norms for appropriate references or comparison sets for faculties. A dichotomy between quantitative and qualitative methods has grown, seemingly ignoring the time-honored view that research questions and a conceptual framework determine relevant methods and analytical approaches and that methods do sit outside these. The halls of the majority of education schools preparing future researchers echo with announcements by students that they are either qualitative or quantitative; professors align with one or the other of these, as indicated by their warmth or coolness toward requiring statistics courses for their students.

Meanwhile, the pressure increases on journals that are seen as major organs of professional associations, not only to publish work from minority scholars who hold a particular position with regard to education policy and practice, but also to publish this work in formats and genres that deviate from the norm. Prestigious journals published by AERA have recently been identified by special interest constituencies as critical barriers to overcome in getting their work out in front and past the gatekeepers.

An additional fallout from the power of the positive imperative is widespread blind endorsement of multiculturalism, without due attention paid to the fact that multicultural has come to be synonymous with other. This dichotomy of we-they clearly reifies the color boundary and reinforces racist views, particularly through the mandatory study in school curricula of certain literary works from writers of color. For example, teachers and administrators often unwittingly choose *The Bluest Eye* by Toni Morrison for secondary students. The story is of a young black girl who wants to be white, who is raped by her father, and whose family drives her mad. In the hands of teachers without adequate background in African American literature, the work could easily convince a naive young reader that self-loathing marks young blacks and confirm stereotypes about dysfunctionalism within African American families. Also frequently chosen for secondary readers is the Latina novel *The House on Mango Street,* by Sandra Cisneros. On the surface, the book exhibits extremely simple writing, with short sentences and accessible vocabulary; yet it needs informed analysis and substantial background to help readers see beyond its appearance of simplicity to the complexity of its intertextual weavings. Novels such as these need considerable study and more sensitive treatment than they are likely to gain in the hands of those accustomed to teaching from basal readers or textbooks with teachers' manuals.

Ironically the classroom use of many writings most often selected by authors of color can reinforce the notion of orality as somehow more basic to African Americans or immigrants than to any other group. With this push to attend to the oral side of language has come a celebration of story. Students throughout the elementary years and well into middle school now write more and more personal stories in what is often put forward as a culturally sensitive way to be multicultural and meet the needs of diverse students. Narrative as story is often presented as both universal and simple—known and therefore easier to grasp than other genres. Educator Lisa Delpit (1995) and others have repeatedly pointed out the harm that such practices do to all children, not just those of other people. In addition, anthropologists and linguists have shown that the personal story offers considerable challenge to all students whose early socialization has not included immersion in either children's literature or familial exchanges in which they recount events in their lives (Wolf and Heath, 1992). Story carries strong ideological biases that insist on individual agency, problem, and resolution and cause-and-effect consequences across time. Many students come from families where none or only some of these notions have high value. In any case, adolescents have come to view narrative as having only certain relevance or purpose within their talk—primarily to address interpersonal difficulties or to display a facility for hyperbole and exaggeration (Heath, 1994). Thus, the use of narrative forms within, or as a substitute for other, academic genres or forms carries special risks for those students who have become accustomed to conventional textbook discourse forms.

During the early 1990s, goals of being politically correct fed the use of both multicultural materials and the opening up of research in education to qualitative methods. Those studying minorities, learners (or students) of color, or members of any other group historically disenfranchised by socioeconomics and politics often seemed compelled to represent only the positive aspects of their lives. Researchers from these groups especially came to see themselves as speaking for historically disadvantaged groups whose voices have been marginalized, silenced, or shouted over. Epistemological and ethical foundations of basic research often lay neglected in this work. It became risky to publish research suggesting findings such as: 1) parents in poverty do not offer their children highly interactive language environments characteristic of parents who have leisure and resources to spend with their young; 2) teachers fail to engage verbally or nonverbally with a certain percentage of their students daily; or 3) adults of a certain sociocultural group instruct their children primarily by demonstration and other nonverbal means. Such work following a positive imperative appeared to come out of the belief that governmental intervention in education, at either the federal or state level, is needed to right injustices. If only enough evidence could be marshaled to convince those with power of the merits or the equal abilities of the disenfranchised, then all would be set right again. Education researchers came to avoid giving serious detailed attention to the effects on children's learning of racism, socioeconomic deprivation, stop-and-start life within homes marred by the violence of mental illness or local group tensions, or harsh exclusions based on class, location, or length of residence.

It is not difficult to discern the blatant hazards of continuing to allow the positive imperative to dominate education research about historically disenfranchised groups. These pitfalls arise in part from the push and pull of sources of funding, private and governmental. Fads and fashions prevail in both, and program officers rarely match the background knowledge or experience of scholars to the research being monitored. Several other latent hazards may not, however, come easily to mind. For example, problematic work, some of it done by minority scholars, has come to cluster around particular causes in education (parental involvement; bilingual education; whole language instruction; open classrooms; experienced-based learning). Throughout most of the 1990s, this kind of research rarely carried pervasive or persuasive force in the programs of national professional organizations. Only occasionally did such groups give any substantial attention to these topics in relation to learning and academic achievement. Most of such sessions included as both presenters and attendees minority scholars and others already convinced of the importance of the topics under discussion. Federal and state policymakers throughout the 1980s and 1990s convened conferences to address topics having to do with minority issues, while often giving only cursory or token attention to such substantial matters as how these might influence funding priorities or peer review.

As the 1990s draw to a close, individuals who are known for their research as a member of a minority group or who conduct research on such groups are coming to hold office in national professional education organizations. If this trend continues, these individuals will no doubt urge more substantial assessments of research on language and culture issues and the more frequent inclusion of this research in conferences and publications.

THE QUEST FOR INSTITUTIONAL REFORM

Since the publication of *A Nation at Risk* (National Commission on Excellence in Education, 1983), professionals in education research have responded with amazing speed to reshape research, their roles, and their postsecondary institutions in order to position themselves well within the reform movement. By the mid-1980s prominent schools of education had moved to squeeze out or downsize areas related to international or comparative education. In the spotlight now were American classrooms from kindergarten through grade 12. Graduate students in such programs soon found figures such as Comenius, Rousseau, and Locke omitted from courses in the history of education, with greater attention given not only to particular American stellars, such as John Dewey, but also to patterns or trends, such as caring, often seen as particularly relevant to women in the teaching force (Noddings, 1984). Similar shifts came in other courses, where topics or problems courses in education allowed faculty members to draw students' attention to specific current issues: the professionalization of teachers, the standards movement, recent developments in literacy (or social studies or mathematics education or science and technology).

Such courses almost invariably pull in one or two theorists from outside education to offer a perspective. Rarely do students read either the original works of the theorist(s) being studied or those of their key predecessors; instead they read excerpts and secondary summations or research articles written from the theoretical perspective of so-and-so. Students in education are heard using bundles of interrelated terms, starting with *culture* but extending to others such as *hybridity, praxis, action, interaction, activity, performance, agency, appropriate,* and *subjective,* showing little understanding of their grounding in any one of several fields or of key differences in meanings among theorists. Perhaps more than at any other time in recent history, the 1980s and 1990s have brought special pressures on particular words, so that use of key terms for those in the know is meant to trigger not only certain background knowledge but also assurances of particular ideological alignments.

The loss of grounded and historical work on theories from philosophy coincides with the equation of *education* with *schooling* that has emerged out of the quest for reform. Gone in most programs are courses in comparative human development or courses that offer broad perspectives on learning as distinct from methods of teaching, testing, and restructuring. The primary comparative perspective of the past decade has concerned student achievement and test scores in subject areas across nations. Learning throughout the life span or even in a day or week in the life of a school-age child receives less attention than what happens through particular pedagogical strategies, curricula, technologies, or programs of in-service teacher training. Even the social foundations of education courses have greatly decreased in number in schools of education, replaced by topics courses or introductory survey courses around particular subject areas or major current issues in education. Particularly lamentable is the almost total absence of courses that examine models of social change or compare the ways that institutions from other fields engage in formative evaluations. Every effort to tinker with curricula of schools of education seems calculated to prepare future education researchers to address specific audiences with highly defined and restricted goals related to reform.

Discipline-based researchers in schools of education who do focus on out-of-school learning or other topics viewed as unrelated to reform increasingly receive the label antischool. Several examples stand out. One is the work of anthropologist Jean Lave at the School of Education, University of California, Berkeley, which derives from both her fieldwork in Africa on everyday cognition and her research at the Institute for Research on Learning in Palo Alto. Coauthored with Etienne Wenger (Lave and Wenger, 1991), *Situated Learning: Legitimate Peripheral Participation* appeared to many scholars not to support teaching and to focus too much on learning and on the individual in a community of practice. Another example concerns scholars who worked in the 1970s and 1980s in the fields of artificial intelligence and cognitive psychology, who have increasingly come to situate their studies within classrooms as though to prove their work has relevance for the reform of school practices. Currently a continuum of learning with interlinking ties from everyday cognition to specific school subjects seems capable of examination from only within schools and not in the traffic of learning elsewhere. In this connection, the work of Shirley Brice Heath and Milbrey McLaughlin (1993) on optimal learning environments in youth-based organizations has met with resistance or, at the very least, strong questions about the relevance of this work for schools. Again, clear evidence abounds that the word *education* has lost its essential meaning in the minds of researchers, no longer signifying learning or leading out as it has since pre-Enlightenment days. *Education* now has the narrow connotation of formal learning prescribed and transmitted by adults and their chosen artifacts and sites.

THE PUNISHING INFLUENCE OF PSYCHOLOGY

Not surprisingly, within education research, especially research on human behavior, categories and research methods from psychology remain dominant, although occasionally they receive support from sociology, historically grounded in the study of mainstream middle-class groups and their institutions. A focus on *individual subject* with particular labels such as socioeconomic status, national origin, and family type still prevails in descriptions of research subjects. Behind these terms rests a host of assumptions about what is and is not normative. Experimental and control groups remain highly desired, as do procedures or trials that can produce reliability. One legacy of the reliance on given and largely unexamined categories and research methods is the difficulty scholars have in legitimizing their studies of nonmainstream groups and of learning environments beyond the control of adults. The field of psychology has only recently begun to address the issue of its own culture boundedness within Euro-American contexts (see Kagitcibasi, 1996). For example, when only a diminishing portion of families reflects two-parent households with one parent working outside the household, retention of this family type as the norm stigmatizes the increasing variety of household units that have responsibility for socializing the young.

To address some of the limiting influences of psychology on education research, I offer here several broad recommendations for consideration. The accompanying examples come from research centered on language (for a fuller treatment of these issues, see Heath, 1997):

- The definitions of data must expand to include situations not within the control of researchers and to incorporate the reflections of individuals studied by researchers. Similarly, certain attributes, such as formal, antisocial, or individualistic, cannot be taken as givens or as similarly understood by researcher and subject. For example, it is common for child language researchers expecting to collect data on mother-child interactions in a laboratory setting to define as data only that information collected within the experiment. A notable exception to this pattern came in the early 1970s when Catherine Snow (1972), who was studying the language learning of children, first noted the importance of attending to the way that mothers and children interacted in the lobby or on the way to the experiment. The behaviors she observed there either paralleled or contradicted behaviors manifested during laboratory interactions. Clearly the mothers who entered the laboratory saw this setting as formal and therefore as requiring behaviors that differed from ordinary interactions with their children. Similar assumptions regarding adult-child interactions carry over to classroom studies of language, where education researchers inevitably focus on the talk of the teacher to the student(s) rather than on student-initiated talk or covert or even group-sanctioned interactions among students only. The latter type of work is increasing, but much of it carries a similar burden of assuming the existence of a leader and of focusing on the talk of students to and with that individual.

- Methods of data collection must take into account varieties of ways that individuals and groups use symbol systems, handle relationships, display knowledge, and talk about specific topics. For example, it is customary to assume that responding to interviews is normal and that factual information will be given by respondents. Yet in some cultures— for example, Mexican-origin groups in New Mexico (Briggs, 1986)—and professional groups such as literary writers (see issues of *Paris Review*), interviews may be treated as occasions for willful deceit, imaginary invention, or inside entertainment for all except the unsuspecting interviewer. Even when cultural differences, an intent to deceive, or a desire for humor are not involved, responses given at different times may reflect the current mood, whims, and recency of experience of the individual being interviewed. Hence, usual expectations of reliability cannot be taken as a given or as having been fulfilled.

- Claims of universality must give way to acknowledgments of particularities of institutions and of groups in activities and contexts of learning within or beyond these. For example, it is far more common (and easier) for researchers to study the acquisition of certain behaviors (ranging from language learning to reading) than the retention, development, or transfer, adaptive or otherwise, of these behaviors. In so doing, researchers tend to focus on universal patterns of acquisition assumed to be common to the human learner rather than on the variations in these patterns. Relatively few studies have been carried out of what happens to reading once it is initially acquired or is beyond the point of initial language learning, because at these levels particularities overwhelm patterns of what can be accounted for as universal. There are numerous illustrations of the dangers of universalist claims about the developmental patterns of learners in work conducted by scholars working within traditions that flow from Mikhail Bakhtin and Lev Vygotsky (Tharp and Gallimore, 1988; Chaiklin and Lave, 1993; and numerous authors in the journal *Cognition and Instruction*).

- The abandonment or sharp reconsideration of linear or monotonic patterns of influence will allow us to consider the orderly disorder that marks both human development and learning. Most research in education springs from an assumption of linear factors of influence at work on individual learners, events, items, or other phenomena. The expectation that this linear order will create predictability or regularity confirms belief in cause and effect. Such false or simplified precedents are often argued. As a consequence, unexamined realities that do not fit these precedents can be dropped from conscious equations. Education researchers persist in the expectation that evidence mounted toward one course of behavior more rational or effective than another will lead to a change in attitude, belief, or behavior. Similarly education researchers hold generally to the belief that an effect is proportional to a cause and that an effective program at a local level can be taken to scale and still maintain central identifying features. These universalizing, totalizing perspectives need strong and severe reconsideration in the light of cross-disciplinary work toward local, fractured systems and modes of analysis. The philosophical push from Ilya Prigogine (1984, 1997), the nonlinear dynamics of Mitchell Feigenbaum (1987), and much recent work in neuro fields (neurolinguistics, neuropsychology) and in epidemiology, especially with regard to "tipping points," those pivotal moments when a social situation shows evidence of shifting from one pattern to another (Crane, 1991), should lead education researchers to work much harder to see chaotic or apparently random events as partner or precursor to order and also to acknowledge that chaotic systems generate new information. Of course, all variants of chaos theory are marked by nonlinearity, which means that small causes can give rise to large effects—and often suddenly. Moreover, the complexity of chaotic systems means that new attention must be given to the importance of scale, to recursive symmetries between scale levels, and to the sensitivity of any chaotic system to initial conditions and feedback mechanisms.

LIVING WITH EXPECTATIONS

Behind many of the problems laid out here is education researchers' strong belief that they work in the service of others—the public, schools, peers, and discipline-based scholars, especially theorists. This view may lead to work that seeks a common denominator (in a particular theory, for specific audiences, or with expected policies or outcomes in mind). In other words, education research, to achieve its goals, cannot deviate too radically from that which is expected or that which is likely to be already known by potential readers. Thus, radical departures, such as nonlinear theories and highly particularistic perspectives, risk losing audience. Much of education research seems compelled to work off of dichotomies (order-disorder, different-deficit, mainstream-nonmainstream, minority-majority, standard-nonstandard, effective-ineffective) that promise ready answers and quick fixes.

Working to change long-standing underlying expectations and conditions of education research will require strong alterations in fundamental principles, reconsideration of what local means, and some serious thought about the role of disciplines. Now that psychology no longer holds the foundational place it once did in education, and other disciplines are having greater influence, what will the training of education researchers entail? Will education return to preface titles such as *anthropologist, linguist, policy analyst,* or *historian,* just as it did *psychologist* for so long? Will sharp assessment of the state of education research lead to a withering away of programs with titles such as "language, literacy, and culture" or "curriculum and instruction" from which doctoral students graduate with little or no solid understanding of the intellectual history of disciplines relevant to these topics? Will core questions, such as how we understand human learning (whether of individuals or of institutions undergoing change) and how systems, technologies, and structures respond under constant pressure to reform, emerge to require new approaches to research? Will education researchers find it necessary to consider the extent to which their work should be proactive, and answer basic questions about human learning, or reactive, and address public concerns and immediate or pending institutional needs?

If any of these questions is to receive serious attention, certain epistemological premises will need to be far more widely acknowledged than they are. The principles that follow are offered to challenge much of education research as currently conceived, implemented, and evaluated:

- Structures and meanings, socially constructed through interpretation and practice, lie embedded in their situations and therefore are highly subject to both initial conditions and feedback mechanisms. Consequently effects will vary with projected outcomes, audiences, power relations, and the like.

- Historical dimensions—memories of the past and myths built around events and people—shape ways in which knowledge is displayed, encoded, and applied and may operate in spite of all rational or empirical evidence to the contrary.

- The unitary rational self is not the central knower or interpreter, as has often tacitly been assumed in much laboratory research. Instead, meanings and knowledge multiply across situations, places, persons, and combinations of these.

- The social dynamics of power constantly shape and reshape knowledge and meanings, since relations of power shape particular interests, determine saliency, and reconfigure the extent of fullness or partial coverage of information and its contexts.

In short, research that has the intention of taking into account dimensions of diversity, variability, and particularities across cultures, situations, and their institutions must pay attention to what may seem to be admittedly chaotic, but nevertheless socially realistic, situations.

The foregoing points obviously carry my bias as a researcher whose work in learning and using language and culture across a variety of societies and institutions has, since the early 1980s, heavily influenced both research and practice in education. Comments here bear the influence of my own disciplinary training in linguistics and anthropology and my orientation toward lessons learned from anthropology's strong push to have its scholars work in cultures other than their own. My concerns therefore relate primarily to what I see as the derivative position of education research and the weakening of the disciplinary base or epistemological frame that relates to basic research.

It seems to me that key pointers for education research rest in both the transformation of macrostructural elements and microstructural transactions, intentions, and interactions and the forces vibrating between the macro and micro. These levels and their connections need to enter education research in ways that reintroduce a much more holistic view of learning and much stronger ties to the disciplines. Rather than the cursory lip service that many graduate schools of education pay to either a disciplinary minor or focus, solid connections to departments or to discipline-grounded faculties within schools of education must be brought about. Increasingly in the 1990s, however, schools of education have mandated more courses in education, leaving students little opportunity for meaningful discipline-based study.

In addition, graduate schools of education have rushed to embrace former teachers among their graduate students, without giving serious attention to what teachers bring with them. On the one hand, many programs ignore teachers' expertise and case-based knowledge in the required courses that teachers need to take. On the other, many programs ignore in teacher choices of thesis topics the fact that most teachers bring to their graduate study strong notions of what is right and wrong in classrooms. Therefore, more and more education research for dissertations allows teachers to go out and prove that their methods of teaching bring results, rather than socializing teachers-turned-researchers to address differences between basic research and advocacy. If education research is to continue to claim pursuit of original ideas, development of theories of explanation, and discovery of unknowns, then drastic changes must be made in the preparation of education researchers.

Pedagogy and concern about recognizing teachers as professionals often come as the reason for celebrating teachers within graduate programs of education. This view lifts pedagogy onto its own shaky platform, having neither the structural underpinnings of content nor the necessary cross-bracing of pedagogy with an understanding of human learning and the mediating forces of technology, assessment, and organizational structures (such as special interest groups, school boards, and teacher unions).

CONCLUSION

Teaching and learning, inextricably tied, must never become a duo that leaves behind the recognition that, more often than not, what is taught is not what is learned, that what is said is not what is heard. Just as there is no absolute ground for language, there can be no absolute ground for pedagogy. If schooling is to survive within the United States as anything more than one (if not the) major employer in most regions and therefore primarily a taken-for-granted economic entity as well as public service agency, then it must come to grips with the fact that currents of history, language, and culture make pedagogy neither deterministic nor predictable in the linear fashion in which it has been conceived by practitioners and researchers alike.

Education research must find ways to bring the disciplines much more centrally back into the preparation of scholars, standards of quality in research, and public forums presenting findings. Such a move means initially careful consideration of the meaning of education as something far more than schooling. Following this redefinition must come hard-nosed recognition that neither interdisciplinarity nor theory-grounded research emerges with any validity from quick-and-easy doses of this theory in derivative form or from that discipline in methodological guise. In addition, schools of education have to decide whether they wish basic research, as distinct from action research, to be the marker of their identity. If the choice goes to the latter, then these schools must determine the bases of such work. Within the United States, much of it has recently carried strong influence from particular ideologies or reform programs—neither of which is consistently called on to justify or clarify research premises. If the choice is the former—basic research —then this research, particularly under postmodernist influences, must increasingly not only clarify its epistemological grounds and their origins, but also the researcher's role (Brettell, 1993). Basic research, when it is solidly grounded, will inevitably carry strong resonance with prior work in particular disciplines and subfields, helping ensure that the research does not rest on the persuasive powers of author-as-celebrity or ideology-as-fashion.

Nearly a decade ago, Patricia Graham, from within her position as leader of the National Institute of Education, wrote of basic research and its differences from applied or clinical studies. She stated then, as she has exemplified in her leadership of the Spencer Foundation (the major foundation committed in the 1980s and 1990s to the support of basic research in education), her faith in what basic research, unfettered by a sense of immediacy of practice or reform, can do to increase knowledge. Many journals and spokespersons in education, however, seem to practice lexical avoidance behavior with regard to the adjective *basic*. It is time to bring the term back into the vocabulary of education research. Basic research in any field must stand apart in its fundamental procedures, standards, and audience from those on which journalism, advocacy, policy analysis, evaluation, and public service depend. This is not to say that it cannot and should not be of use to the latter groups. On the contrary, decisions, recommendations, and applications of these groups stand to carry more weight and merit when linked to basic research. When basic research figures in action, elements of consistency, fairness, and predictability increase for those who are pursuing careers that are embedded in practice, policy, service, and philanthropy.

It may be that if changes that are indicated here as necessary are to take place, many involved in education will have to reject Hamlet's notion that conscience makes us cowards. The armor of the brave will be necessary for us to accept negative findings and to recognize that the maps we have made of education research of late do not reflect the territory. We need instead to rechart old territories and explore new ones carefully, find new ways of preparing travelers to go there, and know that those who follow will be the better surveyors, architects, and builders for the charting work of our basic research.

References

Bacon, F. *Advancement of Learning.* London: Colonial Press, 1900. (Originally published 1605).

Brettell, C. (ed.). *When They Read What We Write: The Politics of Ethnography.* New York: Bergin & Garvey, 1993.

Briggs, C. *Learning How to Ask: A Sociolingual Appraisal of the Role of the Interview in Social Science Research.* New York: Cambridge University Press, 1986.

Chaiklin, S., and Lave, J. (eds.). *Understanding Practice: Perspectives on Activity and Context.* New York: Cambridge University Press, 1993.

Chomsky, C. *The Acquisition of Syntax in Children from 5 to 10.* Cambridge, Mass.: MIT Press, 1969.

Coursol, A., and Wagner, E. "Effect of Positive Findings on Submission and Acceptance Rates: A Note on Meta-Analysis Bias." *Professional Psychology: Research and Practice,* 1986, *17*(2), 136–137.

Crane, J. "The Epidemic Theory of Ghettos and Neighborhood Effects on Dropping Out and Teenage Childbearing." *American Journal of Sociology,* 1991, *96*(5), 1226–1259.

Delpit, L. *Other People's Children: Cultural Conflict in the Classroom.* New York: New Press, 1995.

Eckert, P., and McConnell-Ginet, S. "Think Practically and Look Locally: Language and Gender as Community-Based Practice." *Annual Review of Anthropology,* 1992, *21*, 461–490.

Feigenbaum, M. *Report of the Research Briefing Panel on Order, Chaos, and Patterns: Aspects of Nonlinearity.* Washington, D.C.: National Academy Press, 1987.

Flood, J., Heath, S. B., and Lapp, D. (eds.). *Research on Teaching Literacy Through the Communicative and Visual Arts.* New York: Macmillan, 1997.

Goodwin, M. H. *He-Said-She-Said: Talk as Social Organization Among Black Children.* Bloomington: Indiana University Press, 1990.

Heath, S. B. *Ways with Words: Language, Life, and Work in Communities and Classrooms.* New York: Cambridge University Press, 1983.

Heath, S. B. "Stories as Ways of Acting Together." In A. H. Dyson and C. Genishi (eds.), *The Need for Story: Cultural Diversity in Classroom and Community,* pp. 206–221. Urbana, Ill.: National Council of Teachers of English, 1994.

Heath, S. B. "Culture: Contested Realm in Research on Children and Youth." *Applied Developmental Science,* 1997, *1*(3), 113–123.

Heath, S. B., and McLaughlin, M. W. (eds). *Identity and Inner-City Youth: Beyond Ethnicity and Gender.* New York: Teachers College Press, 1993.

Hoyle, S., and Adger, C. (eds.). *Kids Talk: Strategic Language Use in Later Childhood.* New York: Oxford University Press, 1998.

Kagitcibasi, C. *Family and Human Development Across Cultures: A View from the Other Side.* Hillsdale, N.J.: Erlbaum, 1996.

Lave, J., and Wenger, E. *Situated Learning: Legitimate Peripheral Participation.* New York: Cambridge University Press, 1991.

Loban, W. D. *The Language of Elementary School Children.* Champaign, Ill.: National Council of Teachers of English, 1963.

Loban, W. D. *Language Development: Kindergarten Through Grade Twelve.* Urbana, Ill.: National Council of Teachers of English, 1976.

National Commission on Excellence in Education. *A Nation at Risk: The Imperative for Educational Reform.* Washington, D.C.: U.S. Department of Education, 1983.

Noddings, N. *Caring: A Feminine Approach to Ethics and More Education.* Berkeley: University of California Press, 1984.

Ochs, E. *Culture and Language Development.* New York: Cambridge University Press, 1988.

Prigogine, I. "Order out of Chaos." In *Stanford Literature Studies* (Vol. 1, pp. 41–60), 1984.

Prigogine, I. *The End of Certainty: Time, Chaos, and New Laws of Nature.* New York: Free Press, 1997.

Rickford, J., and Rickford, A. "Dialect Readers Revisited." *Linguistics and Education,* 1995, *7,* 107–128.

Schieffelin, B. B., and Ochs, E. "Language Socialization." In *Annual Review of Anthropology* (Vol. 15, pp. 163–192), 1986.

Shuman, A. *Storytelling Rights: The Uses of Oral and Written Texts by Urban Adolescents.* New York: Cambridge University Press, 1986.

Snow, C. E. "Mothers' Speech to Children Learning Language." *Child Development,* 1972, *43,* 549–565.

Tharp, R. G., and Gallimore, R.. *Rousing Minds to Life: Teaching, Learning, and Schooling in Social Context.* New York: Cambridge University Press, 1988.

Weaver, C. *Teaching Grammar in Context.* Portsmouth, N.H.: Heinemann, 1996.

Wolf, S. A., and Heath, S. B. *The Braid of Literature: Children's Worlds.* Cambridge, Mass.: Harvard University Press, 1992.

CHAPTER ELEVEN

Culture and Commitment

Challenges for the Future Training of Education Researchers

Vanessa Siddle Walker

For faculty members in schools of education who would produce researchers interested in and capable of addressing the pressing educational issues of the next century, the challenges are daunting. Children of European descent continue to score higher than most other ethnic groups on tests of academic achievement at the elementary and secondary levels; they tend to be more involved in extracurricular activities and to attend schools with better-trained teachers and more orderly environments. In contrast, African American children, who begin school with comparable verbal memory scores, find themselves outperformed in tests of academic achievement through high school; they are more likely to be disciplined within their school and to be disproportionately represented among special education enrollments. The schools they attend are likely to be less comfortable and secure than those attended primarily by non–African American children, and they are often taught by less experienced teachers (Nettles and Perna, 1997).

Other ethnic minority groups suffer similar disparities. For example, Latinos are often considered "one of the most undereducated groups in the United States" (Nieto and Rolan, 1997, p. 911). Their school dropout rate is 29.4 percent. Those who are retained are located in schools with little access to high-quality programs and are taught by teachers who know little of their cultural background. Sonia Nieto and Carmen Rolan write that "the educational portrait of Latinos in the U.S. schools . . . points to a number of disturbing trends that, left unattended, will continue to doom a great number of students to educational failure" (p. 93).

Even where ethnic minority children excel, as among members of Asian Pacific groups, other difficulties in school are encountered. Often victims of "model minority" myths, many such students are isolated; they often feel invisible and forgotten by teachers who see them as needing no special attention. The lack of academic success of some members of these groups in a subject area such as English, or the diversity of performance by those within a group, is masked by the popular perception that all such members are high achievers (Pang, 1997).

Across the array of ethnic groups, the problems of inequitable educational achievement are pervasive and challenging. They suggest that schools have yet to become places of equal educational opportunity. As the year 2000 approaches, when more than half of the students in school are expected to be children of color (Hodgkinson, 1989; Dilworth, 1992), disparities discernible by ethnic identity offer a formidable challenge to scholars interested in creating supportive educational environments.

As they move into the next century, how will faculty members in schools of education respond to the difficulties ethnic minority children experience—particularly when many universities are accused of being disconnected from communities and the educational problems of ethnic groups? Can schools of education whose faculties are composed mainly of professors who are culturally, ethnically, and socially distanced from the problems provide and assume an efficacious role in addressing those difficulties? And for faculty members who choose to meet such a challenge, what might it take to prepare a new generation of scholars capable of producing the research and providing the leadership that would make the public schools places with outcomes not so directly correlated with ethnic power and privilege?

This chapter explores the complex question of culture and commitment in education research and suggests that these influences are related to both the production of quality research and the ability of research to influence educational change. Until recently this subject has been largely submerged by the more visible mechanisms of facilitating school change, such as consortia linking universities to schools and revised teacher education programs aimed at producing teachers better trained to handle diversity within their classrooms. While these and other initiatives are to be applauded, the influence of research on educational change should not be overlooked, for when research results do not accurately reflect the realities of the people researched, curricular efforts will be misguided, school interventions will be inappropriate, and the plans of would-be reformers will be ill informed.

A major premise of this chapter is that researchers today must see themselves as having a responsibility not only to research and report educational problems but to assist in solving them, and that researcher training must be changed accordingly. Current training of researchers to assume responsibility for connecting the purposes of research to the solution of real educational problems varies widely at individual institutions. In fact, if most texts of research methods provide any indication, the teaching of would-be researchers to take part in changing the educational terrain is not currently a high priority. Even a cursory review of research methods texts indicates that methodologists have a limited view of the relationship of researcher training to school problems. The methodology of data collection —design, sampling, data management, analysis, generalizability, reliability—continues to dominate researcher texts. "Subjects" are acultural and seldom situated in communities that are facing major challenges to their survival (Lancy, 1993). Ethical responsibility is phrased in terms of an individual's obligation to colleagues (Strauss and Corbin, 1990), not to communities. The intent toward communities is to do no harm rather than make an overt attempt to do them good; "data free from bias" means "data collection and statistical computation that do not vary in significant ways," thus allowing differences to be attributed to the independent variable, not to factors stemming from the bias of the researcher (Wieksma, 1995). In short, these texts suggest that a good researcher can be correlated with a set of methodological procedures that, if followed correctly, will produce good research, with "good" meaning technically pure. Except for the Ph.D. student trained in anthropological traditions, there is little indication that graduates will have any idea how cultural knowledge influences their ability to ask the right questions or to interpret results in ways that are culturally and socially responsible. Even less will be understood about the responsibility of researchers to connect the purposes of their work to the solution of children's problems in schools.

Yet in scattered articles and occasional texts, voices have been raised arguing that good research is more than a matter of manipulating methods. Over the past decade a chorus of researchers, frequently led by anthropologists, scholars of color, and feminist scholars, has begun to acknowledge the intimate connection of the researcher to the research and the researched. These scholars are addressing such issues as the influence of trust; the personality of the researcher; and the influences of access, relationship, ethnicity, gender, and class (Delamont, 1992; Gadsden and Irvine, 1994; Hammersley and Atkinson, 1995; Lather, 1991; Punch, 1994). Michelle Fine (1994) conceptualizes the problem as researchers learning to "work the hyphens," in that "researchers [must] probe how we are in relation with the contexts we study and with our informants." In a similar vein, Eisner and Peshkin (1990, p. 244) have called for research with two attributes: "the sensitivity to identify an ethical issue and the responsibility to feel committed to acting appropriately in regard to such issues."

The challenge will be to move these concerns from the periphery to the center of discussion about training education researchers for the next century. This is not to suggest that methods training should be diminished or forfeited. To be sure, any research will be jeopardized by inappropriate understanding of the methodological tools available within the scholar's research tradition. Tools, however, are just that: they have no meaning apart from the person who manipulates them. Thus, while tools in inquiry must continue to be carefully and systematically taught, they can no longer be all that is taught. Concurrent with the teaching of methodology there must be efforts to instill a broader understanding of the purposes of the research enterprise and of the influences that can defeat the accomplishment of those purposes.

In particular, I argue that two influences must be considered in any conversation about research training, if schools of education are to produce researchers who can address some of the educational inequities in schools. One is the influence of culture —the culture of both the researcher and the researched. I consider culture to be an underexplored area of education research. Amid the focus on independent and dependent variables and appropriate analytic tools, the influence of culture in the research enterprise is too often overlooked. In my view, culture does matter. Drawing heavily on anthropological research traditions, I argue that culture has the potential to influence the research process and the information disseminated.

The other influence relevant for schools of education that would produce researchers capable of stimulating change is the researcher's commitment to this view. Should the moral commitment of the researcher—a step beyond ethical responsibility—be part of the conversation on research training held in schools of education, and, if so, what might be the nature of the conversation that needs to be held? Finally I consider the barriers to change and explore the kinds of teaching and learning about research that might position faculties of schools of education to assist in the solution of educational problems, especially those of inequity.

CULTURE AS A MINIMIZED INFLUENCE IN THE TRAINING OF EDUCATION RESEARCHERS

Culture matters in conducting education research only if culture influences who all of us are, as both researchers and researched. If culture is defined by shared beliefs, values, and norms within a group, then all human beings belong to some form of cultural group. A cultural group may or may not be identified with a particular ethnic group, since ethnic groups are a particular kind of cultural group where members share an involuntary ancestral history and members may consciously choose to embrace or reject their ethnic identity. Cultural identification may be regional or ancestral, acknowledged or unacknowledged. As Jerome Bruner (1996) has argued, however, culture is the tool kit by which all of us construct our worlds.

The research enterprise is not immune to these human constructions and therefore is also culturally laden. As human beings, researchers construct meanings based on participation in cultural group(s); similarly, participants in the research are also constructors of their worlds based on cultural understandings. Bruner writes of the cultural nature of human encounters:

> Meaning making involves situating encounters with the world in their appropriate cultural contexts in order to "know what they are about." Although meanings are "in the mind," they have their origins and their significance in the culture in which they are created. It is this cultural situatedness of meanings that assures their negotiability and, ultimately, their communicability. . . . On this view, knowing and communicating are in their nature highly.interdependent, indeed virtually inseparable [1996, p. 3].

Bruner's conception of culture suggests that any meeting between a researcher and an informant, whether through the distribution of a survey instrument or through participation in an interview, is a cultural encounter; neither party is free from the cultural lens that will influence the nature of the interactions between them.

A concrete example of the influence of culture in research encounters is captured in the following description of a researcher's efforts to be cultural neutral—just a scientist—and the failure of this attempted neutral ground in a segregated, southern community:

> Early in his five-month stay in Southerntown, however, [the researcher] discovered that he could not work entirely on his own terms. His identities as a Northerner and as a white were neither completely overlooked nor always subordinated to his identity as a scientist, as he had hoped and requested they would be. Some of the local whites were suspicious of his motives and felt certain that, because he was a Northerner, he had come to Southerntown to foment trouble or to organize Negro labor. Other whites were uncertain about the ultimate utilization of any information [the researcher] might obtain. Would he write a book? If so, would their views be accurately and fairly represented? Because he was a Northerner, they could not be certain. It was also in his identity as a Northerner, rather than as a scientist, that blacks cooperated with and confided in [him].

In this example, the researcher's cultural identity both enhanced and inhibited his data collection. Ironically, the identity of the researcher enhanced his relationship with African Americans who attached more significance to his regional identity than to his ethnic identity. On the other hand, although the researcher shared an ethnic bond with whites, his regional identity was a liability, making them untrusting and suspicious of his motives. This example illustrates some of the difficulties that researchers have when they attempt to enter a cultural world divorced from the cultural self.

Added to this layer of cultural interaction is a second layer that also exists for researchers: the culture of the academy. Graduate school training requires learning new forms of interaction that are themselves a cultural form. For example, graduate school teaches that researchers should ask the questions and informants should answer them, that tape recorders are ways to achieve reliable data, and that researchers should listen and not reveal their true feelings.

But these cultural forms respected in academia may be in conflict with other cultural forms. One researcher, for example, reports that all her questions to gang members had to be indirect if she wanted to elicit responses. Moreover, the use of the tape recorder, a highly valued research tool, actually diminished the quality of the data. "I tried to interview one of the gang members with a small portable tape recorder," she reports (Horowitz, 1989, p. 152). "He was so concerned about how he said things and 'making a good story' that much of the material was so exaggerated and stilted that it was unusable" (pp. 51–52). Peruvian-born sociologist Edmundo Morales (1989, p. 20) describes his informants as very sensitive to direct questions about themselves and reports that informal conversations with indirect questions were necessary for data collection. Other researchers note that some respondents avoid their questions completely (Harper, 1989; Whyte, 1989). These illustrations provide examples of the ways the culture of the academy can conflict with the culture of individual informants.

A researcher thus enters a research setting with at least two cultural traditions: his or her own cultural self-identification, including the beliefs, values, and norms held, and the organizational traditions of the academy. In addition to cultural problematics related to the self and the organization, the researcher also meets informants who have their own cultural traditions and beliefs, many of which may be at odds with the cultures of the researcher:

> Researchers naively make a lot of assumptions about their level of knowledge about communities of color, particularly the African American community. . . . In a recently published study . . . participants were asked which racial or ethnic group they felt they had the most and least in common with. White Americans said they had the most in common with African Americans; conversely African Americans said that white Americans were the group they had the least in common with [Irvine, 1994, p. 2].

In the following paragraphs, I discuss the influence of these cultural complexities on the research process. Specifically I argue that the cultural self can directly affect the quality of the data collected and produce false findings and false interpretations. These findings and interpretations, unknown by other researchers to be false, can become part of a knowledge base that influences the questions that new researchers will ask and may unwittingly become a barrier to facilitating positive outcomes in communities, since the results disseminated could be erroneous or accurate only in part. Such inaccuracies can make it virtually impossible for researchers to provide the valid data needed to help reform schools.

Influence of Researcher's Cultural Self

An understanding of the role of culture is important because the researcher's cultural self sets in motion a series of cultural encounters with informants that can influence the quality of data collected. These encounters are significant, in that they may be the critical variable in distinguishing between having collected data and having collected "good" data. For purposes of this discussion, the contrast is represented as "authentic" findings versus "false" findings. By authentic findings, I mean that the data represent an informant's actual way of seeing and interpreting events; they represent truth at least as far as the informant understands and is able to communicate his or her truth. False findings occur when an informant provides a way of interpreting his or her world that is specifically designed for the researcher. When false findings occur, the informant may intentionally or unintentionally misrepresent or omit perspectives that would assist the researcher in understanding the phenomena being studied. Although data have been collected in both cases, the quality of the data is strikingly different. In one, the findings are valid, in that they represent an informant's actual way of viewing the world; in the other, the data constitute a misrepresentation and are false.

Several stages in the engagement process can influence whether the data collected are authentic or false: the cultural location of the encounter, the affective response of the informant to the researcher, the verbal response of the informant to the researcher, and the quality of the information exchange.

Cultural Location. Researchers and informants meet at a cultural location. Cultural location includes the physical location, for example, a meeting at the university or the informant's home. Cultural location, however, also includes decisions about whose cultural identity will be used during the interchange between researcher and informant and includes the ways in which cultural differences are negotiated. The resulting cultural location can be at the informant's comfort level or the researcher's. For example, language choices are indications of cultural location. In some African American communities, verbal feedback is frequently a sign of listening. The *uh-huhs, yeahs,* and so forth are ways in which the listener conveys to the speaker that he or she is being understood. Paralleling the African American church experience where audience members are expected to respond verbally to the minister or anyone else who is speaking, this pattern is also a common one in small groups and even one-to-one conversations. To fail to provide vocal response in these settings—as may be the case for a researcher taught not to interrupt—frequently sends a message that the listener is not really paying attention. Taken to its logical end, the informant will soon cease his or her remarks, as the message will have been communicated that he or she is not being heard.

In my seven years of conducting research in a southern African American community, I became very conscious of a second influence on cultural location, and that is the use of titles. As a people who have not historically been accorded titles, many older African Americans value the use of "Dr.," "Mrs.," or "Mr." and are offended by the use of first names. Thus, Katie Bowe can be "Mrs. Bowe," or she can be "Miss Katie," if she is well known to the interviewer. But she could never be "Katie" if the interviewer expected to elicit her full cooperation, because to do so would be a sign of disrespect. Ironically this emphasis on using titles among some members of the African American community is in direct contradiction to the tradition of many northern universities, where titles are omitted and first names used instead, ostensibly in order to minimize power relationships.

Morales (1989) notes that he "conducted the interviews in Quecha in order to make the people feel comfortable and to facilitate a better and more precise expression of their feelings, opinions, attitudes, and ideas." In addition, he notes the cultural norms he had to respect for beginning an interview as, for example, starting a conversation with a flattering statement or friendly argument. Morales reports that "this approach worked much better than just knocking on doors with a long questionnaire in hand and saying 'Hi, I am doing research on peasant economy and would like you to answer some questions'" (p. 119).

These examples of language choice indicate some of the nuances that determine the cultural location of an encounter. Where the comfort level is set is the cultural location of the encounter. Researchers who enter communities expecting the informants to meet them on their terms are placing their research in a different cultural location from one where researchers actively seek to meet informants on their terms. As described by Martyn Hammersley and Paul Atkinson (1995, p. 55), dress, personal characteristics, and other behaviors should all be taken into account in interactions with informants.

Affective Response of Informant. Either of two affective responses to a researcher is possible during an encounter: legitimization or suspicion. Legitimization means that the informant accepts and receives the researcher and trusts the researcher enough to provide access to his or her knowledge. Legitimization in this definition extends beyond textbook mandates of access, where a researcher is told to communicate the purpose of the research, receive permission from gatekeepers to conduct the research, or to protect the human subjects. Here, legitimization is an affective response of one individual to another. It assumes that research guidelines will be followed but acknowledges that access to an informant's presence does not presume access to his or her knowledge.

Anthropologists have identified several factors that influence legitimization. One of them is trust. Researchers who are trusted with the knowledge are more likely to be legitimized by the community than those who are not. Researchers report that trust can sometimes be given because of the researcher's membership, or perceived membership, within a cultural community. If, for example, the researcher is already known by the informant, or someone acquainted with the researcher is known by the informant, or if the researcher appears to exhibit the cultural norms of the community through appearance or interaction, legitimization may be automatically conferred. Informants seem to assume that membership means that their interests will not be betrayed, because to do so would be to betray one's own cultural group.

In cases where the researcher is unknown to those being researched, the most consistent form of gaining psychological access is through some form of sponsorship. The sponsor is someone who legitimates the researcher. Members of the community accept the researcher not on the basis of the researcher's abilities or training, or even interest in the topic, but as a result of a cultural member they respect saying that this person is "okay." Many well-known ethnographies provide evidence of the importance of sponsorship (Smith and Kornblum, 1989). Elliot Liebow (1989), in particular, provides examples of the mistrust he receives as a Jewish researcher in an African American community and contrasts their change in attitude when he had a sponsor.

Another influence on legitimization is friendship. Indeed many researchers report that informants share their lives because they have come to see the researcher as a friend (Liebow, 1989; Stack, 1989). In many of these reports, the term *friend* is frequently used by informants to explain the relationship they have with the researcher; not uncommon is that the "sponsor" is one who later lays claim to a friendship.

Friendship, sponsorship, and membership can all influence the degree to which an informant legitimates the researcher by giving his or her trust. Although trust is related to other variables (see Anderson, 1989; Sterk, 1989; Harper, 1989), researchers have argued that its presence is important and have reported problems in data collection that ensue when it is not present.

Opposing an informant's legitimization of a researcher is suspicion. Suspicion means the researcher has not been deemed meritorious by the informant and, though questions may be answered, the researcher is viewed as someone not to be trusted. This affective response will influence the verbal response. Ironically the expectation of the culture of the academy that dictates that researchers ought not to be too familiar (Kammer and Stouthamer-Loeber, 1998) may lead directly to suspicion and an unwillingness of some informants to respond in meaningful ways because the interaction incorporates none of the trust, friendship, and sponsorship that leads to legitimization.

Verbal Response of Informants. The affective response of an informant to a researcher is linked to the informant's verbal response. Again, an informant might respond in one of two different forms: retreating into public discourse or revealing private belief.

Public discourse is the response that an informant gives to those he or she believes do not fully understand the community, topic, or themselves. It represents a shallow response—one that may more accurately reflect what the informant believes the interviewer wants to hear. Many cultural and ethnic communities, particularly those that have been the victims of oppression and exploitation or are involved in activities or embrace attitudes they do not wish to make public, have no incentive to communicate private beliefs to researchers.

In contrast, private beliefs reflect what would be embraced as truth in a non-public setting. Here informants reveal the private part of themselves that explains their actual reason for engaging in an act, responding in a certain way, or making the decisions they do. Especially in cases where the power relationship between the researcher and informant is unequal or when societal pressures frown on a particular response, the discussion of private beliefs may be seen as more of a threat and therefore more difficult to obtain. The following description provides a good example of the difficulty of eliciting private beliefs versus public discourse:

> The real problem lay in [the informal] replies, which were evasive, avoiding any relevant discussion of the slave system. . . . A full evening had already passed and all I had heard were superficial reminiscences about slavery "times," but no extended accounts about specific events or occurrences. I suddenly realized I had struck a solid wall of resistance. But why? I knew the slave experience is very much a part of Black oral tradition, so why wouldn't they talk to me— really talk, not just politely parry questions?

This is an example of a researcher who has achieved physical access to the informant's presence but not access to the informant's knowledge. The former slaves are reported to have avoided "any relevant discussion of the slave system." They provided "superficial reminiscences . . . but no extended accounts." The researcher reports recognizing a "solid wall of resistance." What the researcher has encountered is public discourse. Fine (1994) provides a more contemporary example. She notes that some informants regularly referred to members of other cultural groups in derogatory terms, ostensibly because they felt they were in the presence of researchers they could trust with the references.

The point is that it may not always be in the community's best interest to be forthcoming about private beliefs. When it is not, the informant may participate only by engaging the researcher and the topic at the level of public discourse. His or her responses may not contradict what is commonly known, but neither do they extend the knowledge by providing any new insights. For all researchers to be aware of the variance in types of responses is critical because the authenticity of the data relies on access to informants' knowledge, not just on access to their presence.

Level of Engagement Between Researcher and Informant

The cultural location of the encounter and the affective and verbal response of the informant to the researcher each influence the level of engagement. When real engagement occurs between a researcher and an informant, the researcher has been accepted and has tapped an informant's willingness to share private beliefs. Presumably during such an encounter, the informant is providing information deemed to be true, at least as far as the informant understands that truth. In other words, the informant has placed himself or herself physically in a position to be queried and has psychologically opened himself or herself to an engaging encounter with the researcher. The researcher thus has access to both the informant's presence and his or her knowledge.

When an encounter does not produce real engagement, only polite response, the researcher has physical access to the informant but has not been given psychological access. Polite response can be deceptive because an informant can be physically present with the researcher and provide answers to all of the questions, thus giving the appearance of real engagement, but never move beyond perfunctory replies. The responses may be lies, exaggerations, or omissions that intentionally distort or mask the informant's real opinions about the issue being raised; they may be what the informant thinks the researcher wants to hear; they may even be what the informant actually believes but so little elaborated as to make it impossible to interpret accurately the meaning of what has been said.

The well-known ethnography *Tally's Corner* provides an often overlooked example of the move from polite response to real engagement on the part of Tally:

> On one occasion . . . all of us left Tally's room together. Tally grabbed my arm and pulled me aside near the storefront church and said, "I want to talks to you." With no further introduction, he looked me straight in the eye and started talking. "I'm a liar. I been lying to you all along now and I want to set it straight, even if it means we can't be friends no more. . . . You remember when you first came around here, I told you. . . . Well, it was a lie." [Liebow, 1989, p. 43].

In this description, Tally's informant talked to the researcher but by his own admission did not completely reveal his private self. Arguably, he so effectively masked his polite response that it had the appearance of real engagement.

The several cultural influences on the research process suggest two possible paths that will have different outcomes for the quality of data collected. In one, authentic findings are possible because of real engagement with its accompanying values of trust and shared private beliefs. In the other, researchers find themselves in conflict with the culture of their informant, arousing suspicion, public discourse, and polite response, with false findings the likely result.

Although this description suggests a linear pattern, it does not have to be so. For example, an initial gaining of trust does not automatically mean that authentic findings will be the outcome. At any point during the involvement of the researcher with an informant, trust can be replaced with suspicion, which will send the researcher on an alternate trajectory. Similarly, public discourse may be replaced at any time with private beliefs if some event, behavior, or conversation causes the informant's response to move from suspicion to trust. This shift can lead to authentic findings even though the earlier interactions may not have suggested that authentic findings would be a likely outcome.

I note as well that the description of levels of engagement between researcher and informant does not consider shaded or mixed responses. An informant may be merely hesitant before a researcher—not overtly suspicious but not trusting either. In that case the encounter may produce some real engagement and some public discourse. Unfortunately the way an informant weights responses is individually constructed, making it impossible to predict how much of the response will constitute authentic findings or how much false or some unknown combination of the two.

The Influence of Culture on How Data Are Interpreted

Culture is also present in the interpretive phase of research. With the exception of some recent research traditions (such as teacher–researcher collaboratives), researchers have historically been given the power to attribute meaning to the findings that emerge from research. Thus, after data are collected, researchers are the ones who will bring meaning to the data. Researchers decide which points will be significant in the discussion and which will be minimized. They decide what informants meant in what was said and how what was said relates to what is known. The decisions are all influenced by the symbols, beliefs, traditions, experiences, and knowledge about the informants that researchers have.

The cultural orientations that researchers bring to their work make the task of constructing an interpretation of the informant's knowledge more difficult. According to Jackie Irvine (1994), "Taking another's story carries a great deal of responsibility and raises a lot of questions." Among the questions she poses are whether the researcher is telling the story correctly, what has been lost in the translation, and whether informants have the right and power to veto the story. Fine and Lois Weiss (1996) also pose the dilemma as they reflect on their research on the lives of poor women and question the extent to which they insert their "relatively privileged lives . . . into essays when [they] chronicle lives under assault from the economy, the state, and within communities and even homes" (p. 265). The influence of the cultural self on interpretation is also disclosed by these researchers:

> As theorists, we refrain from the naive belief that these vices should stand on their own or that voices should survive without theorizing. We also find ourselves differentially theorizing and contextualizing voices, however. That is, those voices that have been historically smothered—voices of white women, and men and women of color—we typically present on their own terms, perhaps reluctant, as white academic women, to surround them with much of our theory. And yet, when we present the voices of white men who seem eminently expert at blaming African American men for all their pain and plight, we theorize generously, contextualize wildly, rudely interrupting them or reframe them [p. 266].

Interpretation then, like portions of research, is not culturally neutral but is influenced by the beliefs, values, knowledge, and experiences of the researchers who do the interpreting.

Ironically the interpretations that researchers produce become the disseminated results, since seldom are the voices of the researched presented with regard to the conclusions rendered. While we sometimes hear the voices of the researched in the data analysis sections of the work, those voices are missing when the researcher moves to the section that imposes meaning. Thus, readers do not know how the school resounded to the portrait painted of itself or what the teacher believed about the researcher's analysis. The result is that authority is given to the researcher to impose all meaning. Researchers' last words are the ones made public and become the common understanding that is held about a place or topic.

The disseminated results, whether or not they are accurately interpreted or based on authentic data or false findings, become part of the body of academic knowledge that now influences the literature that new researchers will read as they create new research questions. Unaware of the influence that culture may have had on the accuracy or inaccuracy of the findings, new researchers will assume that truth has been found, especially if the work is methodologically sound. Thus, the cycle of lack of understanding about the ability of culture to jeopardize findings and interpretations will begin again.

COMMITMENT AS A MINIMIZED INFLUENCE ON EDUCATION RESEARCH

A second area important in the training of education researchers is to move questions of commitment to the center of the conversation about educational inequities. This section draws primarily on my own experiences as a researcher and as a member of one of the ethnic groups that have been underserved.

As a graduate student at an elite private institution, I was taught to live in the realm of possibilities. In spite of having come from a rural world of practical concerns, I soon learned to theorize about problems and, perhaps of my own making, see research as a distinct enterprise unconnected to solving educational problems in a complex world. Not until I had made a trip back to my home and conversed with an African American woman who had lived over one hundred years was I forced to reconcile the worlds of the privileged elite and the rural poor and reflect on my responsibilities to both.

At the end of the interview in 1991 with this frail, forceful-speaking figure of the past, a former teacher, I found that she had asked the most significant question of the day and, in so doing, had prompted me to redefine my thinking about research and its purposes. With some difficulty, Miss Elsie Green Palmer, who in 1926 used her influence to raise funds so that African American children could have a new school, now raised herself on a pillow and with a piercing, almost haunting look said to me, "Miss Vanessa, what are *you* gonna do?" Stunned silence. She was not talking about the book I was writing. She did not appear to be interested in my prestigious funding sources. She was asking something greater, and it did not have to do with lectures or publications. Rather, this woman who had given of her meager resources for the common good seemed to be asking what *I* was going to give. Silence. Fumbled response. The look of resignation on her face at my ineptness to articulate what I would do is a solid mental image that has remained with me long since her death.

What is it that I was going to do? What is it that *researchers* set out to do? More important, does the purpose of research have any connection to the practical improvement of people's lives? Informants, after all, are the ones who move researchers from ignorance to understanding. Informants know their worlds; researchers are the ones who are ignorant of them. Having been granted passage from ignorance to knowledge, what should be our response? Do we have the responsibility to make sure that informants have any returns for the investment they made in teaching us?

Some would argue that these questions are addressed by the ethical guidelines that prescribe the conduct of the researcher during the research process. But ethical guidelines are frequently aimed at being certain that the researcher does the community no harm. For example, following ethical guidelines, the concept of reciprocity—if it is engaged at all—can then be handled with flowers, small amounts of money, or some other token or gift that masks the larger responsibility of the researcher to the community in which inquiry has been carried out.

But the issue posed here is deeper than one of doing communities no harm, as important as that is, or even of providing some token of thanks. It directly asks whether researchers should attempt to do the community good, moving beyond ethical reciprocity to moral questions about responsibility. Vivian Gadsden and Jackie Irvine (1994) ask how truth is related to advancement of the common good and the betterment of society. Quoting earlier works, they argue that

> research has sometimes confounded the possibilities for social change by ignoring the consequences of research. Because political agendas often dictate the nature of research and conduct of studies, issues that would advance knowledge, improve the life chances of children and families, and influence policy sometimes are sacrificed [p. 19].

This view of education research as having a larger purpose accords with the view of some participants at a recent conference in Bath, England (Reason, 1996). Questions about the transformative purpose of inquiry and the need for research to make a difference in the lives of the researched were among the issues raised. Some even argued that "the Western world view [of science as pure, distant, and objective] is coming to the end of its useful life" (p. 25).

With Miss Palmer as a specter, the questions resound for me. To enter communities with only our own purposes in mind and no sense of responsibility beyond the publication of results is to victimize—no, rape—communities for our own gain. We gain in professional reputation, grant moneys, and books and articles published, while the lives of those who have made the research findings possible remain the same. Ann Lieberman (1992) has argued that researchers have the responsibility to change lives, not just describe them. Steiner Kvale (1996) suggests that, ethically, researchers at the outset should ask themselves what will be the "beneficial consequences of the study" (p. 119). Similarly, Ann Brown (1997) declares, "If the children with whom I and my partners work did not learn, understand, and achieve better as a result of their experiences in our research, I would find it morally unacceptable to continue" (p. 31).

To be sure, many researchers have linked their research to a commitment to change the communities they study for the better (Brown, 1997; Comer and others, 1996; Hale-Benson, 1982; Irvine, 1990; Ladson-Billings, 1994; Slavin, 1990). In each of these cases, research results are used to build programs designed to help children succeed. The research then directly addresses the problems identified in the community and ostensibly exemplify the researcher's commitment to change. As David Flinders (1992) writes, however, such linkages are not the norm, and few researchers would say that they were motivated by the training they received.

TEACHING CULTURE AND COMMITMENT: CHALLENGES FOR FUTURE TRAINING

How then might schools of education operationalize the ideology that reflection on the importance of culture and commitment should be part of the training of education researchers? This final section offers several possibilities for implementing the arguments and calls on journal editors, professional organizations, and grant agencies to assume the roles they are capable of playing in changing research practice.

First, those who serve as gatekeepers for article publication and funded research should revise guidelines so that researchers are forced to be explicit about their own role in the research and their view of the research. In the 1995 volume of the *American Educational Research Association Journal,* of the twenty-nine articles that appeared, only one made this information available. The articles all presented detailed methodologies but, save for the one, did not address the way culture may have influenced the questions posed, data authenticity, or interpretation. In these articles, the researcher was unknown, except by name. Such a role allows the researcher to be a shadowy, lurking figure who wields the power to impose meaning but is not expected to make the nature of his or her power or bias explicit. This stance could be eliminated if the gatekeepers for journals and granting agencies required the researchers, both quantitative and qualitative, to include this perspective in their research proposals and publications. Although the inclusion of the perspective does not in itself solve cultural bias, it at least makes the nature of the bias public.

Journals and granting agencies might also require researchers to address the ways in which they methodologically attempted to counter the influence of the "self" on the process. For example, if I am an African American woman conducting research in an African American community, I am challenged to use methodological approaches in data collection and analysis that avoid the risk of making false connections and presuming special understanding because of the similarity of my own cultural or ethnic background to that of my research subjects. Similarly, I am challenged to create a design that will force me to disconnect beliefs based on shared understandings and assume an objectivity distant enough to provide a reasoned interpretation of events.

If I am a white researcher exploring questions in a Latino community, I am confronted by questions of cultural distance. How will I connect with informants in such a way as to have a basis for interpreting their responses in ways that reflect their own meanings? How will I be sure that I have not imposed my cultural paradigm on the interpretations, particularly in deciding what is appropriate and inappropriate behavior? If I rely only on the theory of other white researchers who have studied the community, how will I be certain they have not ignored the community's ways of knowing in their own theoretical understandings? As a white researcher, I will be challenged to reflect on how being white affects my thinking, behaviors, and attitudes and then methodologically to consider the influence of this identity on my intellectual product (Scheurich, 1993). The same questions are relevant if I am a white male researcher conducting research with white female teachers. Here I will be confronted by differing perspectives on race, gender, ethnicity, and class (Lather, 1991).

Gatekeepers can require researchers to provide the evidence of methodological attention to these areas. What methods did I use to distance myself? to connect myself? Did I consider the inclusion of a coprincipal investigator or research team members whose cultural backgrounds differ from my own but who can assume powerful roles in data collection and analysis, so that I can produce authentic findings? Such questions should be methodologically addressed and perhaps included in validity or other relevant sections, and researchers should be routinely expected to do so.

Requiring researchers to serve in an internship capacity in an unfamiliar community is also a possible solution to some of the problems that occur when research is cross-cultural. An elderly Jewish man captures vividly the need for researchers to familiarize themselves with the communities when he responded to one researcher:

> You don't understand. How could you expect to understand? You ask me all these things, but you know nothing. You don't know Yiddish. You don't know Hebrew. You don't know Aramaic. You don't know Russian and not Polish. You have not set your eyes on any part of the places we lived in. How can you expect to understand? [Myerhoff, 1989, p. 88].

Although limits should be placed on the expectations about what a researcher is required to learn in cultural communities, internships in research settings as part of a doctoral program would prohibit researchers from graduating with a näiveté toward the people who are informants. Instead researchers would have opportunities to explore the complexities of the problems they seek to research from a real-life view, not just the view of other researchers in an established literature.

The idea is not so far-fetched. An internship does not have to be designed to give the graduate student all the experiences he or she will ever need in a lifetime of conducting research in similar or different cultural areas. The internship can, however, place a student in the setting similar to that where dissertation work is to be conducted and allow the student to begin by learning how the cultural self and the cultural other may influence the research process. This opportunity to reflect on what was understood and misunderstood about cultural influences and to attempt to account for this understanding in the construction and completion of the research projects can provide students a powerful tool for future thinking about research. Thus, the learning about how cultural settings should be approached will be the significant outcome of the endeavor, rather than the learning about any particular cultural setting.

A reward structure among granting agencies that gave the greatest rewards to scholars who have demonstrated commitment to correlating research and service could also provide the impetus for closer connections between research and improving the lives of schoolchildren. For example, the current university model assigns the roles of teaching, service, and research to the faculty member. In universities, these responsibilities often operate independently and, when correlated, are more likely to link research and teaching. Service is left ill defined and disconnected to the other components of scholarly activity unless the scholar individually chooses to make connections with the other areas. Granting agencies, however, could encourage a greater correlation between research and service by providing rewards for researchers who link service activities with their research practices. This connection has the potential to produce much better work in both domains and make a much greater impact on the lives of children than when the scholarly activities are allowed to remain distinct. A change in reward structures might encourage some researchers to become motivated to link research and improved practice in ways that they have not heretofore considered.

Making commitment an acceptable form of academic discourse is another mechanism for enhancing the training that educational researchers receive. As long as dialogue about commitment is viewed as being oppositional to good research, students will speak little of commitments. On the other hand, if environments are created in schools of education where professors teaching research classes can speak openly about commitments, even while they insist on the maintenance of intellectually rigorous designs, their example would set the stage for new researchers to talk about the same issues. Talk in itself will not improve results. Open dialogue, however, will communicate different messages to graduate students about the expectations faculty members hold for them.

Finally, the change in the training of education researchers must begin with practicing researchers like myself acknowledging the current limitations of research training and committing ourselves to change. As long as we deify methodology and overlook issues that can jeopardize the careful methodological designs we have constructed, prevailing practices cannot be expected to change. And as long as graduate students see education professors isolated in their offices without any connection to solving the complex educational problems before us, they will assume that the model of isolation from problem solving is the one to emulate.

I understand that the difficulties for those who embrace the need for changed research practices will be great. Indeed, change will require new ways of thinking about research, new and bold forms of leadership, and new models of scholarly activity. Change will also require making explicit the broad assumption on which this argument rests: that training researchers to do work that attempts to improve the lives of poorly served children is an important value. For people who do not hold that value, little progress toward change can be made. For those who do hold similar values and commitments, I encourage us to move the conversation forward. Current and future graduate students will inherit the complex educational problems we have not solved. Let us hope that we can begin to teach in ways that will allow them to do a better job than we have yet done.

References

Anderson, E. "Jelly's Place." In C. Smith and W. Kornblum (eds.), *In the Field: Readings on the Field Research Experience*. New York: Praeger, 1989.

Brown, A. *Annual Report of the Harvard Graduate School of Education*. Cambridge, Mass.: Harvard University Press, 1997.

Bruner, J. *The Culture of Education*. Cambridge, Mass.: Harvard University Press, 1996.

Comer, J., and others. *Rallying the Whole Village: The Comer Process for Reforming Education*. New York: Teachers College Press, 1996.

Delamont, S. *Fieldwork in Educational Settings*. Bristol, Pa.: Falmer, 1992.

Dilworth, M. *Diversity in Teacher Education*. San Francisco: Jossey-Bass, 1992.

Eisner, E., and Peshkin, A. (eds.). *Qualitative Inquiry in Education*. New York: Teachers College Press, 1990.

Fine, M. "Working the Hyphens: Reinventing Self and Other in Qualitative Research." In K. Denzin and Y. Lincoln (eds.), *Handbook of Qualitative Research*. Thousand Oaks, Calif.: Sage, 1994.

Fine, M., and Weiss, L. "Writing the 'Wrongs' of Fieldwork: Confronting Our Own Research/Writing Dilemmas in Urban Ethnographies." *Qualitative Inquiry*, 1996, *2*(3), 251–274.

Flinders, D. "In Search of Ethical Guidance: Constructing a Basis for Dialogue." *Qualitative Studies in Education*, 1992, *5*(2), 101–111. 1992.

Gadsden, V., and Irvine, J. "Private Lives in Public Conversations: The Ethics of Research Across Cultural Communities." Paper presented at the Annual Meeting of the American Educational Research Association, New Orleans, 1994.

Hale-Benson, J. *Black Children: Their Roots, Culture, and Learning Styles*. Baltimore: Johns Hopkins University Press, 1982.

Hammersley, M., and Atkinson, P. (1995). *Ethnography: Principles in Practice*. (2nd ed.) New York: Routledge, 1995.

Harper, D. "Relations of the Road." In C. Smith and W. Kornblum (eds.), *In the Field: Readings on the Field Research Experience*. New York: Praeger, 1989.

Hodgkinson, H. (1989). *The Same Client: The Demographics of Education and Service Delivery Systems*. Washington, D.C.: Institute for Educational Leadership.

Horowitz, E. "Getting In." In C. Smith and K. Kornblum (eds.), *In the Field: Readings on the Field Research Experience*. New York: Praeger, 1989.

Irvine, J. *Black Students and School Failure*. Westport, Conn.: Greenwood Press, 1990.

Irvine, J. "Private Lives in Public Conversation." Paper presented at the Annual Meeting of the American Educational Research Association, New Orleans, 1994.

Irvine, J. *Cultures*. Unpublished program description, 1994.

Kammer, W., and Stouthamer-Loeber, M. "Practical Aspects of Interview Data Collection and Data Management." In L. Bickman and D. Rog (eds.), *Handbook of Applied Social Science Methods*. Thousand Oaks, Calif.: Sage, 1998.

Kvale, S. *InterViews: An Introduction to Qualitative Research Interviewing.* Thousand Oaks, Calif.: Sage, 1996.

Ladson-Billings, G. *The Dreamkeepers: Successful Teachers of African American Schoolchildren.* San Francisco: Jossey-Bass, 1994.

Lancy, D. *Qualitative Research in Education.* New York: Longman, 1993.

Lather, P. *Getting Smart.* New York: Routledge, 1991.

Lieberman, A. "The Meaning of Scholarly Activity and the Building of Community." *Educational Researcher,* 1992, *21*(6), 5–12.

Liebow, E. "A Field Experience in Retrospect." In C. Smith and W. Kornblum (eds.), *In the Field: Readings on the Field Research Experience.* New York: Praeger, 1989.

Morales, E. "Researching Peasants and Drug Producers." In C. Smith and W. Kornblum (eds.), *In the Field: Readings on the Field Research Experience.* New York: Praeger, 1989.

Myerhoff, B. "So What Do You Want from Us Here." In C. Smith and W. Kornblum (eds.), *In the Field: Readings on the Field Research Experience.* New York: Praeger, 1989.

Nettles, M., and Perna, W. *African American Education Data Book.* Fairfax, Va.: Frederick D. Patterson Research Institute of the College Fund/United Negro College Fund, 1997.

Nieto, S., and Rolan, C. "Preparation and Professional Development of Teachers: A Perspective from Two Latinas." In J. Irvine (ed.), *Critical Knowledge for Diverse Teachers and Learners.* Washington, D.C.: AACTE Publications, 1997.

Pang, V. "Caring for the Whole Child: Asian Pacific American Students." In J. Irvine (ed.), *Critical Knowledge for Diverse Teachers and Learners.* Washington, D.C.: AACTE Publications, 1997.

Punch, M. "Politics and Ethics in Qualitative Research." In N. Denzin and Y. Lincoln (eds.), *Handbook of Qualitative Research.* Thousand Oaks, Calif.: Sage, 1994.

Reason, P. "Reflections on the Purposes of Human Inquiry." *Qualitative Inquiry,* 1996, *2*(1), 15–18.

Scheurich, J. J. "Toward a White Discourse on White Reason." *Educational Researcher,* 1993, *22*(8), 5–10.

Slavin, R. *Cooperative Learning: Theory, Research, and Practice.* Englewood Cliffs, N.J.: Prentice-Hall, 1990.

Smith, C., and Kornblum, W. *In the Field: Readings on the Field Research Experience.* New York: Praeger, 1989.

Stack, C. "Doing Research in the Flats." In C. Smith and W. Kornblum (eds.), *In the Field: Readings on the Field Research Experience.* New York: Praeger, 1989.

Stanfield, J. "The Myth of Race and the Human Sciences." *Journal of Negro Education,* 1994, *64*(3), 223.

Sterk, C. "Prostitution, Drug Use, and AIDS." In C. Smith and W. Kornblum (eds.), *In the Field: Readings on the Field Research Experience.* New York: Praeger, 1989.

Strauss, A., and Corbin, J. *Basics of Qualitative Research.* Thousand Oaks, Calif.: Sage, 1990.

Whyte, W. "Doing Research in Cornerville." In C. Smith and K. Kornblum (eds.) *In the Field: Readings on Field Research Experience.* New York: Praeger, 1989.

Wieksma, W. *Research Methods in Education: An Introduction.* Needham Heights, Mass.: Allyn & Bacon, 1995.

PART FOUR

THE ORGANIZATION AND COMMUNICATION OF EDUCATION RESEARCH

CHAPTER TWELVE

Preparing Education
Practitioners to Practice Education Research

Anna Neumann
Aaron M. Pallas
Penelope L. Peterson

Unlike the disciplines, education is a field centered on professional practice, whereas education research derives from and contributes to both theory and practice. This dialectic between research and practice has been a major theme in education for over a century (Lagemann, 1996). It is reflected in ongoing debates about how to improve the quality of research in education and about the qualities and educational experiences desired in graduate students who are being groomed to become the next generation of education scholars.

In times past, practitioners have not been welcomed into the leading doctoral research training programs, or they have often been tracked into separate, and decidedly unequal, curricula (Cronbach and Suppes, 1969). Our assumption is that they have much to offer education as researchers. Experienced teachers entering graduate programs in education bring to those programs not only the wisdom of practice but a wealth of knowledge about the political, social, and

Devon Brenner was a participant in a study that Aaron M. Pallas, Penelope L. Peterson, and Anna Neumann carried out in 1995 and that Pallas and Neumann conducted in a follow-up in 1997. The quotations throughout the chapter from Brenner are data culled from the 1995 interviews, 1995 class reflections, and 1997 interviews. We have inserted brief descriptors in parentheses or brackets after each major quotation from Brenner. In January 1997 Penelope Peterson conducted an interview with Gloria Ladson-Billings; the quotations in the chapter from the interview are so noted.

247

cultural contexts of schooling. Such knowledge cannot be gleaned from books. It derives from the lived experiences of teachers struggling day by day to teach group after group of squirming children who seem to be learning more amidst the confusion of our information-rich, fast-changing society than in the local and comparatively less hectic and less exciting classroom. Teachers must do all this amid ongoing national, state, and local questioning about curricula and about the goals and values of our education system: What shall be taught and learned? For what purpose? And to whom? Who will be advantaged and who disadvantaged within the various educational configurations associated with diverse reform efforts? Where shall the control of education lie? With teachers? Parents? Policymakers? Or among all of these working in collaboration? Might control lie within the learner himself or herself? These and other questions confront educators daily. By extension, they confront researchers seeking to construct and articulate knowledge addressing the problems of educational practice.

An analysis of previous attempts to improve the quality of education research suggests that, historically, graduate schools have not taken seriously the wisdom of practice that teachers and other educators who desire to become researchers bring with them to the disciplines. Conceivably, much could be learned if graduate education were adapted to address the unique needs, experiences, understandings, and questions of these practitioners. The challenge is how to frame and develop meaningful learning and teaching experiences for them—experiences that will lead them to become full-fledged researchers in education.

We address these questions here not by considering graduate programs themselves or by looking at aggregate data on students' characteristics or preferences (though we make some reference to trends in such data), but by exploring the interview-based reflections of a current doctoral student, Devon Brenner, and the autobiographical accounts of an established researcher, Gloria Ladson-Billings. Neither is by any means typical. Rather than extrapolating from their lives and experiences to those of doctoral students in general, we have used their respective situations to address central issues concerning the doctoral preparation of teachers desiring to become education researchers.

We chose their two cases for a particular reason. Although both Brenner and Ladson-Billings entered graduate school from the profession of teaching, they arrived there from widely divergent cultural contexts and communities and, as graduate students, participated in markedly different environments. How they negotiated these contexts and communities and struggled to make sense of them is the story of this chapter. The lessons to be learned for improving the graduate education of education researchers constitute the moral.

We first met Devon Brenner a few years ago when she enrolled in Educational Inquiry, an introductory research course required of all entering doctoral students in Michigan State University's (MSU) College of Education. Anna Neumann and

Aaron M. Pallas were teaching the course, and Penelope L. Peterson was engaged with them in a study of graduate students' learning in the course. Brenner, a participant in the 1995 study and in a follow-up that Neumann and Pallas conducted in 1997, is a white, middle-class woman in her twenties. An alumnus of the teacher education program at MSU, she had taught fourth grade for three years in the rural Michigan Paxton Elementary School (a pseudonym). She then left teaching to commute to Lansing, intending to work on a master's degree in literacy, but was persuaded to enter the doctoral program by her former undergraduate adviser.

In their course, Pallas and Neumann periodically ask their students to provide informal written reflections, similar to journal entries, describing their reactions to readings and discussions. Students often have used these reflective papers as opportunities to connect their learning experiences to others in their lives. In her own written reflections early in the Inquiry course, Brenner told a story about Adam, a student in one of her fourth-grade classes at Paxton. For several years prior to entering graduate school, she had taught both writing and reading workshops, following the guidelines presented in Nancie Atwell's *In the Middle* (1987). In so doing, she came to understand that "the writing workshop was not the romantic writing miracle" that she had imagined. For Brenner, Adam was a case in point. "Commonly referred to as one of the two smartest boys ever to hit fourth grade," "Adam wrote long (hundreds of hand-written pages) complex stories" during writing time. Yet much to Brenner's chagrin, "one thing remained consistent in all of Adam's writing—violence. Characters regularly maimed and killed each other with excruciating detail and very little remorse." Even when Brenner outlawed the use of weapons in any writing done in her classroom, Adam found ways to include violence. In one of her reflective papers, she wrote:

> I was always very troubled about how to proceed with Adam. His spelling and grammar were impeccable, his stories were detailed and complex. They were just horrible to read. And morally troubling. And so I walked a fine line all that year, between respecting Adam's voice and freedom of choice, and pushing Adam to find a different, more humane voice. My only consolation was that Adam's parents seemed more embarrassed than I was at his choice of topics. They understood it as a phase, a way to "be ten years old in a pacifist family." While this soothed me, I still wish I could have shaped the workshop in some ways that would have helped Adam grow as a writer, and not just a ten year old [Brenner, class reflection, 1995].

From her experience with the writing workshop, Brenner became aware of her lack of content-area knowledge. She admitted in interviews that she had not had a clear conception of good writing, so she did not know what to push for in terms of content and story structure, nor did she know how to push.

Brenner returned to graduate school after earning the teaching degree because she wanted to join a community of learners with whom she could discuss the problems of practice that intrigued her and among whom she might learn to be a better teacher. In having sought such knowledge and community among her teaching colleagues she had become frustrated. She had failed in efforts to draw the teachers in her school into a critical examination of their teaching of writing and literature.

Gloria Ladson-Billings is currently a professor of education at the University of Wisconsin at Madison. We first met her four years ago when Neumann and Peterson invited her to write an autobiographical chapter detailing the personal story that lay behind her research on teachers with culturally relevant practices. The chapter was to be included in a book on the personal meaning of research that Neumann and Peterson were coediting (Neumann and Peterson, 1997). Ladson-Billings described how throughout her life she had sought to improve the educational achievement of African American children and youth who often have not fared well in school. Her book, *The Dreamkeepers: Successful Teachers of African American Schoolchildren* (1994), draws strongly on her own experiences as a learner in the classes of her teachers years back. To provide a sense of the power of these teachers in her life, and concomitantly in her work, we quote directly from what she has written about them:

> In fifth grade I met the teacher who I think is most responsible for my belief that some teachers truly motivate students to be their very best. This was Mrs. Benn. At first, I didn't want her to become my teacher. She was an African American woman and she was old: in her late 50s. She was also heavy set and had large breasts. . . . But it took only a short time for me to discover that I had been wrong about Mrs. Benn. . . . There was no aspect of working with children that seemed boring or routine to Mrs. Benn. . . . And she instilled in us a sense of responsibility by requiring us to take home the classroom house plants on weekends or long vacations. She expected those plants to come back thriving—and they did. She was a proud woman who demanded excellence at every task we undertook. We were required to write with precise handwriting and perfect spelling. She taught every subject—from reading to physical education—and she warned us that playing around in her class meant that we did not value ourselves. "This is your chance, don't let it slip away," she urged. . . . Most importantly for me, Mrs. Benn opened us to the world of U.S. history. She told glorious tales of exploration and invention. She was a great storyteller and, unlike any teacher I had ever known before, she made a point of telling us about what "the colored folks" contributed to this story [Ladson-Billings, 1994, pp. 10–19].

Ladson-Billings was inspired not only by teachers who gave of themselves but also by those who withheld themselves (and withheld authentic teaching):

My fourth-grade teacher, Mrs. Powell, seemed out of place in our largely African American school. She was a middle-aged white teacher who rarely smiled. I cannot remember her ever touching any of us. I do recall her saying that nobody could get an A in her class because an A would mean that we were as smart as she was. "What a bizarre notion," I thought. I worked hard to earn the A's she did not intend to give. Despite my perfect spelling, reading, and math papers, she only gave me a B+. My mother went to see her about the discrepancy between the papers I brought home and the grades on my report card. And from the second reporting period until the time I left her room, I received A's from Mrs. Powell. I don't think she thought I was particularly deserving of those A's, but I don't think she wanted to try to explain her unjust grading system to my mother again [Ladson-Billings, 1994, pp. 44–45].

In her book, Ladson-Billings moves quickly to the personal sources of her research interests: her appreciation of truly good teaching in her own life and her unwillingness to accept anything less, initially for herself and now for the children of her communities. Today she looks back to teachers like Mrs. Benn as the touchstone for her research on successful teachers of African American youth. As she writes, "Memories of those [teachers] I knew well could be the subject of a book itself." But in the shadow of the successful teachers are those like Mrs. Powell who seemed less concerned that she succeed in life. "Memories of the [those] others," she notes, "provoke a series of questions for me. Who were you really? What did you care about? What did you think of me? Did you even know who I was?" Ladson-Billings's recollections of and reflections on her experiences as a young learner among teachers with varying degrees of commitment to teaching are the source of her research today on what it means to teach well.

In the following sections we, as teachers of future education researchers, consider our own question: How might we think generatively about the creation of meaningful doctoral programs for teachers like Brenner and Ladson-Billings? We begin by using accounts of their experience in graduate school as tools to help us frame the interplay between doctoral students' epistemologies and the varied contexts and communities they encounter during graduate study. We then use each case to explore three tensions in the research preparation of practitioners. One is the *tension of agenda*, which bears on whose questions get asked: researchers' or practitioners'. Another is the *tension of perspective*, which considers the ways in which the understanding of educational phenomena flows from the academic disciplines and from educators. The third is the *tension of response* (and responsibility) to primary stakeholders in the education enterprise, which examines the interplay of researchers' public and intellectual stakes in the study of educational phenomena. Throughout, we attempt to develop implications for the preparation of researchers that flow from our analyses of these tensions and attendant issues.

THE MULTIPLE CONTEXTS AND
COMMUNITIES OF GRADUATE STUDENT LEARNING

In this section we explore doctoral education as but one (admittedly elaborate and complex) experience cast in an array of diverse life experiences. We consider what the learning of research might entail and what it might mean in lives within which significant learning has already occurred, both professionally and personally. We give particular attention to what happens when the knowledge and ways of knowing that doctoral students of education bring with them from their previous lives mix and meld with the knowledge and ways of knowing that they encounter in graduate school. Beginning with Brenner's and Ladson-Billings's early doctoral study in very different graduate school settings, we consider how each crafted her experience in relation to her own schooling, teaching, and personal aspirations for further learning.

Brenner's Initial Experiences in Graduate School

Brenner saw herself as a teacher—an identity forged in her B.A. teacher preparation program at Michigan State and her early years of elementary school teaching at Paxton. Her experiences there produced and amplified her core beliefs and questions about the nature of teaching and learning. We saw this in her account of her efforts to teach Adam.

Through her struggles with Adam, Brenner began to realize what she wanted to do as a teacher—and also what she did not yet know how to do. For example, her interactions with Adam confirmed her central assumptions about teaching as a profession *and* as a social and human activity. First, Brenner viewed the classroom as a social context in which she, as teacher, strove to communicate with a learner, in this case, Adam. But her approach went beyond simply responding to what Adam wrote. She also sought to achieve a meeting of minds—what she referred to as "consensus"—between herself and Adam regarding subject matter (writing) and how it is to be rendered (in nonviolent terms). To Brenner, creating shared understandings through discourse was at the heart of the teaching enterprise. Her work with Adam also pointed up her conception of teaching as fundamentally a moral activity that interacts with the values of her students. In Adam's case, Brenner recognized that her teaching and his learning brought two sets of values and attitudes toward violence into conflict with each other, a situation with which she struggled all year. Brenner's account indicates her belief that a teacher's choice of curricula and assessments is ultimately an act of "valuing" and that teachers make judgments about these on a daily basis.

Brenner as a Member of Professional and Local Communities. In addition to the context represented by her classroom interactions with students, Brenner forged beliefs about teaching and learning through her work with colleagues, both locally at Paxton and as part of a more dispersed professional community of teachers, including teachers fostering literacy. As a teacher, Brenner had looked to this larger community of educators for insights and support in her understanding of what it means to teach literacy. She joined the National Council of Teachers of English (NCTE) and read professional periodicals and books on teaching and learning.

Although Brenner also saw herself as part of a community of language teachers at Paxton, she sensed a discontinuity between the national and the local professional community. The broader community reinforced her natural propensity to inquire into her own and others' practices, but her local colleagues had little inclination to do this: "They were dedicated teachers for the most part, and they, you know, they weren't really questioning what they were doing and why they were doing it."

Interestingly, Brenner's beliefs about developing a shared language between teachers and learners also applied to her relationship to the professional research community. Teachers, she believed, need to learn about their practice as they engage in it; conversely, the research community has an obligation to facilitate teachers' learning through a teaching–learning relationship founded on communication and on the forging of "consensus" between those who would teach the teachers (the researchers) and those who would learn (the teachers). Given this view, Brenner pointed quickly to what she saw as the problem in current conceptions of professional development: researchers are not concerned enough with whether consensus ever takes hold; they are not concerned enough with whether the subject matter they teach teachers is accessible and meaningful to them or whether teachers can make use of it in their work. She told us:

> And I think a lot of writing about education and about learning is inaccessible to most teachers, in the language, the vocabulary that's in it. Through my classes, through a lot of my coursework, I've come to understand why the research articles are written the way they are, but it doesn't change the fact that they're inaccessible to the people who, you know, they really are inaccessible to a person who wants to just jump in and start thinking about their own teaching for the first time in twenty years [Interview, 1995].

The failure of teachers and researchers to forge a shared understanding stems, she believes, from the inability of either to converse in meaningful ways and value one another:

> Well, I just think that most teachers don't really value what goes on at the university and they'll take their master's courses and see them as hoops to jump through and when they're done, they're done, and that allows the teachers from Paxton to conclude that it would be a really good idea, since their language arts isn't working, to buy *Hooked on Phonics,* which is what they did, which was

scary to me. And so they don't value the educational research, and academia, I think, doesn't value oftentimes, or doesn't come across as valuing the real world of teachers and students [Interview, 1995].

Brenner thought in similar ways across two teaching-related settings: in the elementary classroom, where she struggled to teach students like Adam, and in the larger setting of her developing professional practice, where she struggled to learn from teacher colleagues and understand why they are not, for the most part, able to learn in meaningful ways from researchers. In both cases, interpersonal communication is critical.

Brenner was drawn to ideas of language and literacy (specifically to issues of reading, writing, and speaking) for all facets of her learning, from how to be a teacher in the classroom to how to be an education researcher concerned with teachers in classrooms. She saw literacy practices as central to both teaching and research. Those practices that she developed as a classroom teacher simultaneously led her to imagine that they might be the same in research. She thus selected herself into settings in graduate school that reinforced what she had already learned.

Brenner's Initial Assumptions About Research. When Brenner entered graduate school, she did not at first perceive herself as a member of the research community. Ironically, although she saw research as something exotic and all-too-often unconnected to practice and practitioners, she proceeded to construct a view of research that was grounded in the same principles and ideas undergirding her conception of teaching—that it was a social, communicative, and moral activity involving the valuing of others. In her mind, research and teaching were similarly devoted to a process of coming to consensus, a term she used repeatedly in describing both professions. She described *Ways with Words* (Heath, 1983) as good research "because it seems to be something that helps people agree on ideas or at least get started talking about ideas in order to come to agreement. It's somehow being used to form consensus, to construct a body of knowledge that's agreed upon." At this point, she imagined herself as engaged in research that seeks, as she put it, to "construct what I believe and what others might believe about the world and come to some sort of agreement," as opposed to "discovering sort of the truth that's out there and digging for the final answer." Once again the parallel between her conception of research practice and her conception of teaching practice is striking.

Bringing Past and Present Learning Together. As she moved through graduate school, Brenner saw a substantial divide between the communities of teachers and researchers, evidenced by the absence of a common language and of mutual valuing. Her struggles to make sense of the absence of communication and consensus between these communities paralleled her struggles to teach students like Adam. In time she came to believe that the primary purpose of education research was to improve teaching practice, a stance rooted in her own struggles as a beginning teacher and emerging from her awareness that these struggles were shared by many others in the teaching community, at Paxton and beyond.

In a sense, then, Brenner as a researcher sought to do for the practitioner community what she had earlier sought to do with students like Adam: to bridge two sets of understandings, bringing them together in relation to a common set of values. But both tasks—the teacher working to educate her pupils and the researcher to educate teachers in ways that are meaningful to them— are formidable. Brenner had experience with the first of these, but the latter was uncharted territory: "I wouldn't even know how to start at this point to bridge the gap between teachers and researchers," she told us, "except to try and have my writing readable, that is where I would start and then I don't know where you go from there."

Further into her graduate career, she began to see herself as shifting among multiple communities—that of teaching practitioners with a commitment to literacy and teaching and that of scholars with a commitment to research on teaching and literacy. She saw the act of bridging these communities as part and parcel of a larger process of inquiry that would guide research and teaching practice. Becoming an inquirer, however, would require Brenner to carry on a conversation, not only with communities existing outside herself but within herself. Externally Brenner evoked images of herself as building bridges; internally she envisioned an epistemic conversation between the different ways of knowing, both of them inscribed within herself, each scrutinizing and learning from the other. To develop this view, Brenner turned to one of the later readings in the Inquiry course, Timothy J. Lensmire's *When Children Write* (1994).

In Lensmire's book, which originated as a dissertation in the doctoral program in which she is currently enrolled, Brenner found a way to connect the knowing of her former community of teachers and teaching and the knowing of her new community of researchers and research. Lensmire's text is a teacher–researcher's study of peer relations among the students in his writing classroom. In reading his work, Brenner first found voice for her teacherly beliefs as these might be reconstituted in her emerging conceptions of research. Her discovery of teacher research, an activity that allowed her to build an internal conversation between the community of teachers and researchers, was, to use her term, "empowering." In sum, without clearly realizing it at the time, Brenner was deriving her conceptions of research from her reflections on the multiple communities in her life. She was able to identify with teacher research, which legitimated what she already knew, based on her teaching practice.

Brenner used her experience in graduate school to construct images and metaphors that made connections between teaching and research. As we shall argue later, her learning was doubtless made easier by the fit between her commitments and the institutional culture of her doctoral program, which was a powerful socializing force given the high status of the program in the field. The College of Education at Michigan State is supportive of students with commitments and interests like those of Brenner, as Lensmire's book demonstrated. But what happens when the fit between a student's commitments and ways of knowing and those of the doctoral institution is more tenuous? We turn to the experiences of Gloria Ladson-Billings to consider this question.

Ladson-Billings's Recollections of Her Early Years of Doctoral Study

Born into a working-class African American family, Ladson-Billings grew up during the second phase of the civil rights movement in the United States. She has written:

> My own coming of age was inextricably linked to the larger changing consciousness of African Americans who were challenging the existing social order in new ways. Rather than a cry of "let us in," which had seemed to shape the discourse of the early civil rights struggle for school desegregation and public accommodation, there were increasing calls for self-definition and self-determination among African Americans and other people of color. This confluence of social change, my interests in intellectual and political activity, and my reawakened sense of myself as an African American woman, all pointed me toward finding ways to make a closer fit between my "work life" and my "real life" [Ladson-Billings, 1997, p. 54].

Although she had strived to connect the intellectual and the political throughout her life, she found that especially difficult over the ten years she spent as a teacher and teacher consultant in Philadelphia. "There was less intellectual activity and more work involved than I imagined," she said.

"I didn't kid myself about what I did. I was a firefighter. I did damage control." Seeking something more intellectually satisfying, she decided in 1978 to undertake graduate study in the School of Education at Stanford University. "Still," she writes, "I lacked a clear notion of what I would 'do' as a result of graduate study."

Ladson-Billings entered the School of Education with an agenda to promote social change through intellectual and political activity, an agenda grounded in her experience as an African American woman and as a teacher of African American students. She sought to locate her work in a community that she could claim as her own: "What I research is . . . intricately linked to the life I have lived and continue to live," she wrote. Shaped by the political activism of the late civil rights movement, she wanted to join her doctoral study to her commitment to improving the education of African American schoolchildren. She had not yet articulated a view of how research, cast as an intellectual and political activity, could help her to do this.

Ladson-Billings's early years at Stanford only succeeded in widening the gap that she had hoped to close between her "work life" and her "real life." The faculty members and students with whom she interacted had little interest in advancing the education of African American children: "The whole experience seemed surreal. People were speaking an alien language and arguing over seemingly meaningless problems at the same time *real* people were struggling with *real* problems." Although she saw herself as "relatively well liked" by peers and professors, there was little support at the school for her intellectual interests in the African American community.

These interests were reinforced by Ladson-Billings's decision to live in an African American neighborhood near the university. "While my days were spent in the 'unreal' world of graduate school, my nights and evenings were spent in the real world of a struggling, largely African American and Latino school district geographically located near a prestigious university and alongside a predominantly white school system that was reputedly among the best in the state." As a parent of a school-aged child, she shared the concerns of other parents she met:

> Sitting in the shadow of a "great" university, they wondered why the fact that their children were failing at unprecedented rates seemed not to be an issue for scholarly inquiry. Their questions were my questions and became the principal way for me to merge my personal interests and community politics with my professional goals. Their struggles helped me articulate the meaning that education and educational research could have in the lives of African American people [Ladson-Billings, 1997, p. 55].

With respect to the questions, language, and purposes of each, Ladson-Billings struggled with the disjuncture between graduate school and the ethnic community where she resided, to which she was passionately committed. She was unable to find faculty members who could model ways to bridge this gap or were even willing to support her efforts. "I had no mentors who were interested in the issues of race and racism in the same way I was," she explained. Nor did she find support in her graduate school cohort, recalling that she "could not imagine being interested in the things they were busy researching." She summed up her quandary by writing, "Even though I regarded my work as relatively easy, I was not prepared for the sense of alienation I would feel as an African American woman"—an alienation she describes as stemming from "intellectual segregation."

Ladson-Billings looked beyond the school of education, finding, as she wrote, "some intellectual stimulation in my minor department, anthropology. Culture was a real thing in the anthro department." But it was the Afro-American Studies Program that brought "salvation." "Three times a week, I would be in an all-Black intellectual space," an experience that she described as providing "a comforting feeling." The class in "Afro-Am," along with other experiences in the anthropology department, were less escapes from the "whiteness" of her graduate studies than "opportunit[ies] to rethink and re-envision the relationships between and among race, culture, and education."

From this base, Ladson-Billings developed a set of theoretical tools that allowed her to articulate research questions about the education of African American children. "If I could read Ellison and Douglass in a new way, perhaps I could read education and anthropology in new ways. In what ways were these disciplines 'socially constructed' and how did these social constructions intersect with race and gender? What were the implications of these constructions for the educational lives of African American children?" The connections that she crafted in the course enabled her to develop a research question that was at once personally meaningful and intellectually defensible. "In my circuitous route from the ed school to the anthropology department, to Afro-Am, I was beginning to formulate a question—a question I do not think I would have gotten to in the narrow confines of the school of education. Taking the long way around may have saved my (intellectual) life."

Implications for Doctoral Programs in Education

So far we have examined the ways in which Brenner and Ladson-Billings struggled as doctoral students to make sense of the purposes of education research and the kinds of questions they believed were legitimate subjects of inquiry. We now consider the implications of their experiences for the design of doctoral programs in education. In particular, we take up the problem of how doctoral programs, and the faculty members who staff them, can give meaningful attention to the epistemologies of novice researchers.

We view an epistemology as a conception of knowledge, of knowledge creation, and of knowing and learning, that reflects assumptions about the "nature, validity, and limits of inquiry" as well as "ontological dimensions such as the nature of reality" (Rosenau, 1992, p. 109). We suggest that epistemologies are created through personal and social interactions attuned to the nature of thought. We also suggest that epistemologies represent knowledge (expressed symbolically) and ways of knowing (including ways of constructing and invoking symbols) that, formed and re-formed over time, become the foundations of continuously regenerated cultures. Clifford Geertz, in *The Interpretation of Cultures* (1973, p. 89), defines culture as "an historically transmitted pattern of meanings embodied in symbols, a system of inherited conceptions expressed in symbolic forms by means of which [people] communicate, perpetuate, and develop their knowledge about and attitudes toward life." We view that "system of inherited conceptions" as well as its symbolic encodements as the elements of epistemology. Thus an epistemology is socially and culturally rooted; it is learned—internalized in unique personal form—by participating members of a culture.

Ladson-Billings's doctoral program at Stanford, whose members (both professors and students) interacted in bounded spaces over extended periods of time and sought to create disciplinary or field-based knowledge, represented a culture that was enacted in unique epistemological forms. The community of teachers within which Brenner first encountered a particular orientation to teaching also represented a culture and a unique epistemological stance with regard to what it means to teach and to be taught, to learn, and to support the learning of others. The local community within which an entering doctoral student first learns what it means to learn, or simply to be a person, thus reflects a culturally inscribed way of knowing oneself among others (Kondo, 1990). In addition, the community to which a doctoral student departs after completion of graduate school is likely to reflect particular epistemologies, as is the community in which the doctoral student might study in conducting dissertation research.

What all this suggests is that doctoral study is likely to be a time when students shift among the epistemologies associated with diverse communities. Among these are their regional or ethnic communities of origin, families, professional communities, communities within graduate school itself and their associated professional associations, communities in which they engage in research, and communities to which they go upon completing doctoral study. For some students, such shifts may be more dramatic and personally trying than for others, in that they entail forms of learning that are likely to reshape students' fundamental conceptions of knowledge, self, and community.

In graduate school, a doctoral student may experience, perhaps for the first time, an epistemological confrontation, the resolution of which will, of necessity, require her or him to make sense of newly acquired academic ways of knowing in the context of a previous life constructed through very different ways of knowing. The confrontation may be especially acute, as in Ladson-Billings's case, if the doctoral student attended graduate school because of a commitment to the community—and perhaps to the epistemology—that defined her life and work before graduate school and if she wishes to explore and perhaps deepen that commitment in her emerging program of research. Our framing suggests that such an epistemological confrontation exemplifies a larger clash of cultures or communities. Initially it may occur among individuals who are interacting with each other. But a person-to-person clash among conceptions of knowledge and ways of knowing may eventually be internalized within the person struggling to make sense of epistemic diversity.

To explore the confrontation further, it is helpful to consider longitudinal changes in the communities in which doctoral students have lived and learned prior to entering graduate school. Doctoral programs in education today are more likely than ever before to be populated by women, racial and ethnic minorities, international students, and middle-aged adults. Many of them have participated in communities that are different from those of previous generations, and they therefore have different epistemologies.

The composition of the faculties of such institutions, however, have not changed as quickly as the composition of doctoral students. Because of this gap, we believe that many students entering graduate school today bring with them well-developed conceptions of knowledge, derived from their social experiences, that differ markedly from the conceptions of knowledge that have been institutionalized in doctoral study. The epistemologies of the graduate schools of education in which these students are enrolled, particularly the epistemologies characteristic of elite institutions like Stanford and Michigan State, need to be better understood, since such institutions can have powerful effects on the thinking of their students and on the field.

What happens when the epistemology that underpins a program faculty's conception of research is poorly aligned with the epistemology of a doctoral student's home community and his or her way of life, especially if what the student wishes to research is life and learning in that home community? What happens to beginning researchers who are well versed in multiple ways of knowing and who can examine (and critique) academic cultures through the lenses of cultures existing well beyond academe with as much facility as they can examine nonacademic cultures through traditional academic lenses? What happens if these doctoral students decline to give primacy to traditional academic epistemologies, turning instead to culture-based critiques of those epistemologies? To what extent, and how, can program faculty members help these students bring such diverse epistemologies into conversation with each other, thereby improving their explorations of the ways of knowing that prevail in both their home communities and the academic communities they have just joined?

We suggest that education doctoral programs take graduate students' epistemologies, and biographies, into consideration at the point of entrance to doctoral study and throughout the program. Students' memberships and ways of knowing developed in communities outside graduate school should be acknowledged and considered in the mapping out of their program of study. Such mapping might include efforts to deepen graduate students' understanding of their own cultural roots and to diversify knowledge of culture itself, exploring its implications for human development—one's own and others'. Faculty mentors with their students should consider the personal and social origins of students' research interests in charting the substance and methodological needs of their programs of study and help to create supportive environments for students' learning throughout graduate school.

Further, we wonder how, through the course of graduate school, program faculty members and others might help students come to terms with the idea of epistemology itself and how professors might help them realize, and come to terms with, the idea that their own perspectives and epistemologies may differ from those of others around them. To this end, historically and culturally situated biographical and autobiographical writings that promote conversations such as these could become central to the teaching and learning of research.

We believe that doctoral students' opportunities to explore multiple inquiry-based communities—and the stances toward inquiry that these communities represent—should be enlarged over what is currently available. Such explorations should be supported, guided, and mediated in meaningful ways. It seems that with the expansion of technologies, students today have more opportunities than ever before to explore alternative communities, including those of which their advisers may be but dimly aware or to which they might not subscribe. Beyond this, they should have the opportunity to talk through their explorations and consider them in analytical and supportive ways with other faculty members and students within their graduate programs—that is, built into the structured discourses of doctoral study, whether in office-based conversations with advisers, in classroom discussions, or in other forums. These might go hand in hand with instructor-initiated inquiries, perhaps in the context of a seminar that examines different ways of thinking about research, including feminist, poststructuralist, postmodernist, and critical perspectives and epistemologies (Moss and others, 1997).

At the dissertation stage, doctoral students could be assisted in negotiating membership in multiple communities, especially when those communities differ in a significant way from the ones in which they have lived and learned. Novice researchers may also need assistance in reentering the communities they have left and in intertwining previous ways of knowing with those developed in the context of the graduate school experience, as a means of reflecting on a variety of educational phenomena. This might require, as in the case of Brenner, the assumption of a blended role, a blended stance, a blended epistemology. In contrast, as in the case of Ladson-Billings, such blending is not always possible, so that new research agendas, strategies, and stances must be devised. At such moments, professors, advisers, mentors, and guides stand to learn as much from their novice researchers as the researchers from them and should view their work with "students" as opportunities for their own learning and that of the field.

THE MULTIPLE TENSIONS IN GRADUATE STUDENT LEARNING

We followed some of Brenner's learning experiences in "real time," in the context of research we were conducting when she took the course, and we traced Ladson-Billings's learning through her autobiographical writing about a decade after she completed graduate school. Although each was anchored in different educational concerns, both of these women had (and continue to have) in common a belief in the power of teaching and teachers and a commitment to the study of teaching and teachers.

Each also sensed (and, in the case of Brenner, continues to sense) a deep divide between the knowledge of practice developed prior to coming to graduate school and the image of research that she brought to her doctoral program. Brenner directly experienced the gulf between the respective discourses of teachers and researchers and the absence of bridges between the two communities. Ladson-Billings saw and felt the lack of attention to practice-related issues of diversity and the death of education research on issues meaningful to African American communities.

Ironically, missing for both these individuals in their early graduate school years was the commitment that had led them there in the first place. Brenner wanted to write research articles that teachers could read and from which they could learn how to teach reading to young children. But rather than finding guides for meaningful discourse between researchers and practitioners, she encountered only distance, at least initially. Ladson-Billings wanted to conduct research on education issues of concern to the African American community. But as she looked around her school of education, she saw no such opportunities. Instead she saw her peers researching topics with which she, as an African American woman, could not identify as truly "problematic" and encountered silence around those questions that she felt most deserving of exploration in the context of the educational needs of African American students. As we noted, graduate school for both Brenner and Ladson-Billings encompassed a search for ways to bring practice and research together—ways that made sense to each of them personally.

How to bridge the divide between research and practice—what we call the tension of agenda—is not the only tension concerning doctoral students' learning of research. In the next section we consider two other tensions: the tension of perspective and the tension of response (and responsibility) to primary stakeholders in the education enterprise.

The Tension of Agenda: Bridging Research and Practice

How to fashion research that will improve current educational practices or result in the creation of new practices and how to devise practices that are responsive to research knowledge are long-standing concerns in education. Intellectual leaders in the field have asked repeatedly, Should we educate students aspiring to careers of educational practice and those aspiring to careers of research separately or together? Should future researchers be required to have solid experience in practice before proceeding too far into their doctoral programs, or should they be shielded from it? How much research preparation should future educational practitioners have, and what role will research have in their practice (Cronbach and Suppes, 1969; Guba and Elam, 1965; Sieber and Lazarsfeld, 1966; Harnqvist, 1994)?

Although many scholars of education have considered the question of how close research and researchers should stand to practice and practitioners (or how far from it), few until recently have asked the still more challenging question of how to bring these together in meaningful and helpful ways. To what extent might we imagine a research practice that is focused purposefully on diverse teaching practices or on specific aspects of such practices? To what extent might we imagine a research practice that exists within teaching or other educational practices that are open to improvement as part of the research process? Such questions have grown from, and yielded, a new generation of educators—practitioner-researchers, in particular, teacher–researchers—who are slowly remaking the meaning of both teaching practice and research on teaching in education. Such questions have also grown from and yielded new contexts where teachers and researchers find themselves freer than ever before to experiment with ways to bridge the historical practice-research divide. These new contexts include professional development schools (PDS), where researchers can work in classrooms as teachers and alongside teachers who may themselves engage in some research on their own (Howes, 1997; Yerrick, 1994; Rosaen, 1995; Cochran-Smith and Lytle, 1993; Goswami and Stillman, 1987).

We have already referred to one of the members of this new cohort of teacher–researchers, Lensmire, in our exploration of Brenner's struggles to bring teachers and researchers into meaningful conversation. To illuminate an effort to bridge these traditional tensions, we will next discuss the mathematics teaching, and learning from teaching, that Deborah Ball has developed through her classroom-based research in PDS settings. We will follow with discussions of professional development schools as an example of sites conducive to teacher research and other efforts to bridge the worlds and the learnings of teachers and researchers in education. We close with a discussion of how Ladson-Billings and Brenner addressed the research-practice tension (or not) in the context of their graduate school experience.

New Practices for Bridging Teaching and Research: Teaching-Research. Through her work as a practicing mathematics teacher and as a researcher of teaching and learning, Ball has invented new pedagogies showing that it is possible to "practice what we preach" and to enact in our own teaching what we espouse in our research and scholarship. For several years, Ball, in collaboration with Magdalene Lampert, has used National Science Foundation support to study her own mathematics teaching and to develop videodisc materials for teacher education. In an article published in the *Elementary School Journal*, Ball

(1993) describes a student named Shea in her third-grade mathematics class. Shea conjectured that some numbers, such as 6, can be "both odd and even." As the classroom discourse unfolded, Shea explained what he meant in response to queries from his fellow students. Reading the classroom discourse, we learn, as Ball did at the time, that Shea had discovered that some numbers have factors that are both odd and even (for example, 6 has a factor that is an odd number—3—and a factor that is an even number—2). (See also Chapter Sixteen, this volume.)

Respecting Shea's thinking and the conjecture he was sharing with the class, Ball pointed out that Shea had invented another kind of number that they had not thought about before, and she suggested that the class call these "Shea numbers." Although Ball herself had never before thought about "Shea numbers"— numbers composed of an odd number of groups of two—she subsequently learned from reading D. E. Smith's *History of Mathematics* (1925, p. 18) that "Euclid [studied] 'even-times-even numbers,' 'even-times-odd numbers,' and 'odd-times-odd numbers.' His definitions of the first two differ from those given by Nicomachus (*c.* 100) and other writers. . . . How far back these ideas go in Greek arithmetic is unknown, for they were doubtless transmitted orally long before they were committed to writing." Professor Harvey Davis of the mathematics department at Michigan State confirmed this finding and indicated further that both Plato and the neo-Pythagoreans had also worked with 'Shea-type' numbers.

The example of Shea numbers and their invention by a child working within a mathematical community in the classroom is important because it represents an "existence proof" of the kind of mathematical knowing and learning within which children can engage in the social context of a classroom. Until recently studies of children's mathematical knowledge have focused on individuals being interviewed one at a time in laboratory-like contexts. We are just beginning to learn the kinds of mathematics that children are capable of inventing in the social context of their own classroom communities. What we learn from the Shea numbers example in Ball's classroom is that researchers' earlier studies may radically have underestimated what children know and understand and what they can ask and pursue when knowledge is created and shared within a community of learners. What we see in the case of Shea numbers is a "research" discovery so compelling that it has been cited repeatedly by other education researchers (see Peterson and Knapp, 1993; Shulman and Quinlan, 1996).

Along with other researchers exploring this genre, including Lampert, Lensmire, Kathy Roth, and Suzanne Wilson, Ball offers a new image of the education scholar: the researcher-practitioner. In their work as teachers and through their expertise as researchers, these scholars are able to engage in research on teaching from within teachers' experiences. Thus they need not carry the lessons derived from their research *to* practice—which exists at some distance, substantively and conceptually, from the locus of their research—or to communities of practitioners, because these findings are already situated, substantively and conceptually, within practice and within communities of practitioners. As both teachers and researchers of their own practices, Ball, Lampert, Lensmire, Roth, and Wilson blur the boundaries between research and practice in ways that Dewey himself might have envisioned but did not achieve.

Although educational practice often refers only to pedagogical practices, in actuality education incorporates learning, leading, counseling, testing, and policymaking as well as many other "practices." Moreover, these practices extend beyond the boundaries of K–12 schools to include preschools, institutions of higher education, and other educating institutions. We suggest that the boundaries between research and practice, much as Ball's teaching example shows, might be blurred in the various fields represented by these diverse practices— teacher education, educational psychology, administration and policy studies, counseling—and in settings beyond K–12 schools. Although we now have examples of scholars who are researchers and teachers, we will in the near future need similar images of scholars who see themselves as researchers of their own practices of learning, leading, counseling, testing, and policymaking in diverse settings (for example, Cooper, 1996).

Earlier we saw the significance of such cases of teacher–researchers for the learning of research by former teachers. By reading of teacher–researcher work, graduate students may come to envision ways in which research can connect with teaching and also consider some of the dilemmas and difficulties of this work. We suggest that such models would be helpful in other educational domains—for example, in giving graduate students who are former teachers ways to connect their already-developed knowledge of their practice with their developing knowledge of research.

New Sites for Linking Teaching and Research: The Professional Development School. We view the professional development school as a unique context for learning about the relationship between research and practice. How might one think about the PDS as a context for doctoral students' learning about research? To what extent do PDS sites present opportunities for learning research that are not available in other settings? What are the disadvantages or risks associated with incorporating PDS-based research into doctoral students' research preparation?

To address these questions, we first define a professional development school. This is no simple matter, as virtually every PDS is unique. Nevertheless, there do appear to be some common elements that might guide our thinking. First, the PDS is an organizational configuration that connects schools of education with K–12 schools in a partnership built on a set of common objectives. One is the professional development of K–12 educators (both preservice and inservice), in which the PDS draws on the resources of the partner school of education. Another is the improvement of educational practice (sometimes phrased as the development of exemplary practice)—for example, through insights developed through teacher–research and related practices. Another is the conduct of collaborative inquiry on practice—for example, between schoolteachers and university researchers working in schools. Although this tripartite mission is central to the Holmes Group's (1990, 1995) conceptualization of the PDS, most PDSs have more completely realized the objective of preparing teachers than they have other objectives, especially the conduct of collaborative inquiry (Holmes Group, 1995). The PDS represents a continuing commitment among all parties (teachers, administrators, parents, researchers) to work together on problems of common interest. There is therefore a kind of social capital that inheres in the social fabric of the PDS, in the form of trust and norms of reciprocity and fairness. The PDS is, by design, a democratic institution in which the various parties have some control over what happens to them.

To what extent is the PDS a distinctive setting for doctoral students' learning about education research devoted to the improvement of educational practices? In *Tomorrow's Schools of Education,* the Holmes Group argues that

> the PDS, in effect, redefines the relationship between researcher and practitioner, bringing the latter closer to the scholarly investigation while easing the way for researchers to tie their investigations more readily to actual situations. . . . The PDS approach sets the stage for research to be a collaborative activity, combining the experience of the university-based investigator and the savvy of the classroom practitioner [1995, p. 82].

We believe that such kinds of collaborative inquiry as teaching-research are more likely to take place in the PDS than in other settings. One of the distinctive features of the PDS is that it brings university faculty, graduate students, teacher interns, and classroom teachers into dense interactions with one another around concrete problems of educational practice. These networks form a rich context for research on classroom practice and teacher learning and development. Thus, the PDS may have a comparative advantage over other settings for carrying out this research and therefore may be especially well suited as a site for graduate students to observe or participate in research.

Although such collaborative arrangements can exist in schools other than PDSs (Brown, 1992; Collins, Hawkins, and Carver, 1991), the reservoir of trust and goodwill built up in the PDS may facilitate the negotiation of research activities and spur the participation of school staff members who might otherwise be indifferent or, worse, hostile to the notion of school-based inquiry. In this sense, the PDS may also be an unusually good site for doctoral students to learn about education research.

If the PDS becomes institutionalized as a site for education research, then it will be worthwhile for a substantial number of doctoral students to gain exposure to the distinctive rewards and challenges of such work. Novice researchers and their advisers might consider which kinds of research are appropriate for the PDS and which are not; the ways that PDS-based research might either solidify or weaken the social bonds of trust, reciprocity, and fairness on which the PDS as an institution depends; differences in the process of negotiating access to the PDS as a research site and other sites; and how the participation of the full range of PDS members (university faculty members, graduate students, interns, and building-level practitioners) in a research project changes the dynamics of that project.

Beyond these caveats, we recognize that there are many types of research in which doctoral students might participate that are indifferent to whether the site is a PDS or some other school. School-based inquiry is not limited to the PDS, and collaborative inquiry between classroom teachers and university-based faculty members and doctoral students predates the PDS era. Moreover, some kinds of research might not be properly situated in a PDS at all, and we caution against the Holmes Group's (1995, p. 86) recommendation that university researchers be obliged to "focus more of their investigations through the PDS prism" (Labaree and Pallas, 1996a, 1996b).

Renewing Efforts to Bridge Practice and Research: Individual Perspectives.
We now return to Brenner and Ladson-Billings to consider in what ways the tension between education research and education practice (in their case, teaching) manifested itself in their lives and in their development as education researchers in two very different doctoral programs, institutional cultures, and learning experiences and at two different times.

Brenner's institution, MSU's College of Education, for years has been at the center of field-based efforts to bridge education research and practice through teaching-research and through related efforts situated within professional development schools. The teacher–researchers whom we cited in the preceding subsection (Ball, Lampert, Lensmire, Roth, and Wilson) all have been professors or doctoral students at the college, contributing to (and learning from) its cultural ethos of "research-on-practice" and, concomitantly, "research-in-practice." MSU has also been a national leader in the development of the PDS as a site for research-based teaching and teacher development. Thus Brenner entered a site of doctoral study with a long tradition of addressing the very questions that most interested her, though it took her some time to realize how the "place of MSU" connected to her personal concerns. Brenner's reading of Lensmire's research about his students' learning to write in the context of his teaching was a turning point in her efforts to make sense of how the teacher–researcher conversations might proceed through the channel of teacher–research as a scholarly genre. During her career at MSU, Brenner has held two assistantships related to PDS research. In one job she interviewed teacher interns learning to teach (Peterson, Pallas, and Neumann, 1996). In a second job she worked more directly and more closely with teachers in the development of classroom materials and processes intended to support students learning to read (Neumann and Pallas, 1997). We have few doubts that the research-in-practice context in which Brenner is situated as a doctoral student at MSU has helped her to articulate, elaborate, and pursue her personal questions about what meaningful researcher-practitioner relationships might entail and what these might yield in the form of learning, for teachers and students alike.

Ladson-Billings undertook doctoral study in a very different graduate school setting, at a different time, and in the midst of a very different tradition for connecting (and separating) research and practice, particularly the kind of practice to which she was committed. Because her program did not provide her with a clear avenue for studying the practices that she most wanted to explore (teaching African American children), her "study," in a sense, effectively carved it out as a legitimate area for inquiry. Ladson-Billings has thus become a leading researcher—and a leading definer of research agendas—on the topic of how streams of research and practice come together (and how they might come together in improved ways) in the education of African American children. What she found missing in her doctoral program she created for herself as a researcher and thereby for others who would pursue research careers years later.

Moreover, although Ladson-Billings conceptualized this research, and the arguments for it, in graduate school, she has continued to pursue this work in her postgraduate career—for example, convening for regular conversation and reflection a group of outstanding teachers of African American youth. To begin to map the dimensions of teachers' developed practices, she has drawn on the black feminist epistemology of Patricia Hill Collins (1991) to create a research method that relies on dialogue anchored in concrete experience, caring, and personal accountability; teachers' narrative efforts to express their teaching experiences and their motivations; researchers' and teachers' close and careful listening to each other's efforts to make sense of such experiences; in-class observations of teaching practices in action; reflections on practices observed; and conversation as a research tool (Ladson-Billings, 1997). Ladson-Billings represents an education researcher who is crafting compelling new images of practice and research as these bear on the lives and learning of current and future generations of African American children and, ultimately, on their communities.

Brenner and Ladson-Billings share a determination to bridge research and practice that, though different in substance, is central to their lives and imbued with deep personal meaning. Their personal commitment to improve practice through research is why they committed themselves to become researchers. In fact, they care for their research as deeply as they do for their teaching-related practices, largely because the two are so closely intertwined in their minds and lives. The personal origins of their efforts are reason enough for the current generation of research professors and mentors to discern, articulate, support, and extend their own doctoral students' interest in bridging research and practice, particularly in the case of doctoral students whose past (and current) experiences in education practice are, like those of Brenner and Ladson-Billings, rooted in their personal and social commitments and values.

Implications for the Preparation of Researchers. Any discussion of the tension between research and practice must acknowledge both the diverse goals of education research and the diversity of individuals who pursue it. Here we are emphasizing the preparation of students who come to doctoral study with expertise as educational practitioners, for it is toward this group that our recommendations are directed. In so doing, we do not intend to slight those students whose journeys to graduate school have not taken them through way stations of practice. Nevertheless, we cannot state strongly enough that education researchers studying educational practice need a deep understanding of that practice. Although it is unlikely that all such knowledge can be acquired in the course of a doctoral program, we believe that graduate study can add conceptual depth to practitioners' understandings of their developed practice.

Our analyses of Brenner's and Ladson-Billings's development as researchers has led us to question the value of segregating students aspiring to careers as education researchers from students aspiring to expand their skills as educational practitioners. We encourage graduate schools of education to revise curricular structures and policies that reify a research-practice dualism, believing that the doctoral preparation of current and former educational practitioners would be enhanced by the development of course work, dissertation seminars, and doctoral advising based on the assumption that research originates *in* practice.

We also urge graduate schools of education to develop a broad array of milieus of practice so that students who so desire might engage in practice and, more important, observe and study practice. The professional development school is one possible model for such a practice milieu, but it is by no means the only one. An important agenda for the future will be to develop new milieus of practice in which doctoral students might participate.

Educational practice extends well beyond K–12 teaching, although this is at the center of many education schools. Although no education school can do everything, it is our hope that as practice moves to the fore in research preparation programs, the full range of practice and practitioners will be represented.

The Tension of Perspective: The Disciplines and the Study of Education

Alongside the theme of resolving tensions between practice and research in education is that of resolving tensions between disciplinary and educational perspectives for the study of education issues. Although others contributing to this book have much to say about the ways in which this tension—and its resolutions—might be construed, we focus in this section solely on what disciplinary study might mean for doctoral students whose backgrounds in educational practice inform their developing research agendas, theoretical stances, and methods. For this, we look once again to Brenner and Ladson-Billings for guidance and for corollaries to the views espoused historically by leaders and teachers of education research.

Disciplinary Study and the Preparation of Education Researchers. Traditionally the preparation of education researchers has relied heavily on disciplinary knowledge and methods of inquiry drawn from the disciplines. Education was not considered to be an academic discipline with a distinctive set of theoretical traditions and methods for studying either a particular or a more general clustering of social, psychological, political, or cultural phenomena. Education, rather, was viewed as a complex phenomenon to which researchers brought the perspectives and approaches of the social and behavioral sciences and other fields. Although education schools were often the locus of education research at the university, the leading scholars were themselves often educated in a discipline and regarded themselves as discipline-based scholars who studied education. Thus, when the National Academy of Education convened a number of scholars in the late 1960s to consider the future of disciplined inquiry in education, its resulting report, *Research for Tomorrow's Schools: Disciplined Inquiry for Education*, emphasized disciplinary knowledge. The report's authors, Lee J. Cronbach and Patrick Suppes, called for the preparation of researchers whose backgrounds reflect "a thorough grounding in at least one academic discipline, together with solid training in whatever technical skills that discipline employs" (Cronbach and Suppes, 1969, p. 212). These authors noted, "Our position is that the investigator should be a disciplined inquirer first and a topical specialist second; those with experience in his topical area have much to teach him" (p. 219). Other roughly contemporaneous reports made similar recommendations. Harnqvist (1994) notes that a Council of Europe Committee report on research preparation released a few years later called for a thorough knowledge of a social or behavioral science discipline. Sam D. Sieber and Paul F. Lazarsfeld's (1966, p. 348) federally funded report on the organization of education research in the United States also made reference to instruction in the established doctrines, claiming that "the 'grammar' or basic doctrines of research can generally be provided through lectures."

Of the reports issued during the mid- to late 1960s, the 1964 Phi Delta Kappa Symposium on Educational Research is the least prescriptive regarding the role of disciplinary study in the preparation of education researchers (Guba and Elam, 1965). In summarizing the symposium speakers, Egon Guba and Stanley Elam (1965) suggested that the research preparation of doctoral students in education could be enhanced by ensuring flexibility and breadth of exposure to related disciplines, indicating that education had a disciplinary status equal to other university-based fields of study, especially in the arts and sciences.

From the standpoint of curriculum and concerns about student learning, we might ask just what it is about discipline-based education that could be so important as to lead to recommendations that education doctoral students have, at the very least, access to disciplinary study or, alternatively, that they be required to engage in it prior to or during the course of doctoral study. As far as we can tell, the writers of this era saw disciplinary studies as providing students with theoretical lenses and research methods that might fruitfully be applied to the study of education problems. Although some writers may have argued, in the context of resource battles, for the elevation of the field of education to the status of a discipline, others indicated that education did not, in and of itself, reflect a distinctive set of theoretical stances or methodological approaches that would provide a base for the conduct of rigorous research. To generate new knowledge in education, they argued, researchers must look to the frames—to the modes of knowing and inquiring—of one or more disciplines. The topical areas that education researchers might examine, and the questions they might ask, were viewed as outgrowths of methods and theories native to arts and sciences disciplines.

Disciplinary Study and the Preparation of Education Researchers Today. The context for disciplinary study in the preparation of education researchers has changed to some extent over the past twenty years. Contemporary scholarly discourses in education suggest at least three different reasons to pursue disciplinary studies as part of the preparation of education researchers.

The first rationale is much the same as the historical commitment to bringing theoretical lenses and methodological approaches from the disciplines (for example, learning theory, organizational theory, and the methods of ethnography or historiography) to the study of education problems. Yet this view of how the disciplines may contribute to the framing of education research has not remained consistent over time; nor can it remain the same in the light of changes in the disciplines themselves. This is especially so in the humanities and social sciences, as the postmodern turn and diverse standpoint epistemologies redefine disciplinary terrains (Rosenau, 1992). Alongside this disciplinary and perspectival change, we see as well a change in the departmental structuring of the university, as some departments of sociology, geography, and others of the social sciences have been closed or merged with allied departments and as a number of disciplinary scholars have moved into applied areas subject to multidisciplinary study. Despite such changes, one continuing view of the relation of the disciplines to education is that of the "cognate." The requirement of cognate studies grew from the expectation that in order to ground their studies in meaningful theory, conceptual stances, or perspectives, students must first acquire such theories, concepts, and perspectives from disciplines outside education. In this view, then, the disciplines, however construed, are expected to provide an intellectual foundation for the scholarly study of education.

The second rationale for retaining disciplinary study as a core component of doctoral preparation programs in education speaks more broadly to the conceptualization of the social, historical, and cultural contexts that shape education and educational outcomes. This argument is built on the assumption that the disciplines can provide the necessary context for an understanding of educational phenomena. Disciplinary scholars do not study education qua education; they study it as a case of a more general phenomenon of interest to a discipline. For example, sociologists see education as one of several social institutions, and some of the most insightful sociological work has resulted from attempts to view education in relation to other social institutions, such as the family (Lareau, 1989), the economy (Kerckhoff, 1993), and the world polity (Meyer, Kamens, and Benavot, 1993). In similar fashion, education has been a fruitful venture for political scientists to study the policymaking process (Peterson, 1976) and the interplay of politics and markets (Chubb and Moe, 1990). Doctoral students are expected to enrich and broaden their substantive and conceptual understandings of educational phenomena by coming to view them in relation to larger social, cognitive, and philosophical issues.

The third rationale stems from the recent refinement of ideas about the teaching and learning of school subjects. In the 1980s, Lee Shulman and his colleagues (Shulman, 1987; Grossman, Wilson, and Shulman, 1989) put forth a conception of teachers' professional knowledge that distinguished among three different domains of knowledge: subject matter knowledge, general pedagogical knowledge, and pedagogical content knowledge. Subject matter knowledge represents the teacher's knowledge of the school subject to be taught. General pedagogical knowledge consists of fundamental knowledge and beliefs about learners in general—how they learn and how that learning can be fostered by teaching. Such knowledge also includes knowledge of strategies for creating learning environments, conducting lessons, and effectively managing the classroom. Finally, pedagogical content knowledge includes an overarching conception of how to teach a subject, knowledge of instructional strategies and representations in that subject, knowledge of students' understandings and potential misunderstandings of the subject matter, and knowledge of the curriculum and curricular materials available for that subject.

If these three domains capture the expanse of teachers' professional knowledge, then it may follow that a researcher attempting to study teachers and teaching will need to have a firm grasp of them, including how teachers acquire facility within them. Shulman and Kathleen Quinlan (1996, p. 412; recalling Leinhardt, Zaslavsky, and Stein, 1990) capture this point quite well: "The work of educational psychologists who are knowledgeable about the subject matters whose teaching and learning they study lends credence to the argument that psychologists can no longer conduct credible research on the educational process in a domain with which they have only passing acquaintance." A deep understanding of the teaching of school subjects can come only from sustained study of the discipline itself, for example, in biology, chemistry, physics, or astronomy.

A similar case can be made, we argue, for the study of learning (assuming, for the moment, that it is meaningful to talk of teaching and learning apart from one another). The study of young people's learning of school subjects may require deep understanding of those subjects by the researcher—a richer understanding than is likely to emerge from the morass of "instructional methods courses" historically foisted on preservice teachers.

Thus, close and sustained study in the disciplines may provide aspiring education researchers with particular lenses and perspectives for understanding educational phenomena. Disciplinary study also may provide future education researchers with enlarged views of the social, psychological, political, cultural, and related landscapes within which educational phenomena are situated and within which education assumes particular forms. Finally, study in one or more disciplines may provide future researchers with deep understanding of the substance of what teachers and students strive both to teach and learn; for without such understanding, and of the thinking that creates the subject matter, one has a very narrow view of how teaching and learning proceed.

The Contributions of the Disciplines to the Work of Two Learners

Brenner and Ladson-Billings, each in her own way, pursued the personal commitment to turn research toward the improvement of particular problems of practice. To what extent does disciplinary study frame or in any way connect to their conceptions of their work, and how does it do so?

Brenner provides one useful perspective on this question. Rather than leaving her school of education for disciplinary study in other corners of the university (as Ladson-Billings did in her flight to Afro-American Studies and anthropology), she joined a school of education–based community of anthropologists, psychologists, and teacher educators concerned with students' literacy learning in K–12 settings as well as in homes and communities. This community has been heavily influenced by the ideas of such psychologists, anthropologists, and sociolinguists as Vygotsky, Bakhtin, Cazden, Heath, Erickson, and Florio-Ruane. Although not representing a single discipline in the standard sense of the term, the community shares some common conceptual concerns—for example, about the crafting of intersubjectivity. Intersubjectivity, in several of these scholars' terms, implies the achievement of degrees of consensus (we borrow the term from Brenner herself) between at least two people around the meaning of a given word or thought. In this view, a person does not think alone but always in the company of others—for example, authors or peers and teachers sharing a common text. Reading a text, therefore, involves the creation of intersubjectivity, a conversation between reader and at least one other, namely, an author. In process writing (which Brenner has taught and which this community studies), the responses of others (a teacher or peer) to a child's writing play an important role in revision.

Brenner gravitates toward this community, perhaps as much for the new perspectives that it promises to offer her as for what is already familiar. As we noted in her relationship to Adam, the challenging student in her class, Brenner's conception of teaching, and hence research, requires the achievement of degrees of intersubjectivity. Like Ladson-Billings, Brenner appears to seek a community where she can speak, listen to, contemplate, and elaborate familiar sounds and meanings, perhaps at times by looking at them from unfamiliar perspectives. Thus, in relation to the first rationale for disciplinary study in education, it seems that rather than searching for new and untried lenses and perspectives, Brenner seeks to unearth and comprehend what she possesses already. She does so not in a disciplinary site outside her college of education but within it. In this spirit, her preparation has encompassed course work that has brought various disciplinary perspectives (history, psychology, literary criticism) to the study of literacy and the connections among reading, writing, speaking, thinking, and learning. She has brought the learning of reading and writing into all of her course work and used that course work to help her better understand literacy and literacy learning.

In terms of the second rationale for disciplinary study, we see that Brenner contextualizes educational ventures in a larger landscape of moral action. As her interactions with Adam indicate, her actions are based firmly in her personal and social values and commitments; she sees her job as a teacher to address the values of her students as they are expressed in their discourse. We know from later work with Brenner that this view has transferred as well to her conceptions of research on teaching. We know of no university-based "discipline" as such to which Brenner has gone for help in framing her views (much as Ladson-Billings did), only that she appears to have done something akin to this, perhaps building a conceptual platform for her own work by drawing on the multiple resources of her particular school of education, in particular, the literacy learning community.

Finally, and in relation to the third rationale for disciplinary study through the course of doctoral study, we see, from the case descriptions we have provided, that Brenner is well immersed in concerns about reading and writing as school subjects, work that she has pursued in her doctoral program since leaving the Educational Inquiry class.

As we have learned, Ladson-Billings was unable to find an agenda and a perspective that fit her intellectual questions and concerns within the confines of her school of education. Within the domain of teachings that the school offered, she sought a base of theory, concepts, and perspectives that connected meaningfully to her own values. Finding none, she turned to alternative sites, the anthropology department and an Afro-American Studies Program, where she found generative spaces to talk, think, and ask about education, race, and culture that connected authentically with her practice-based concerns. In a sense, the discourses that Ladson-Billings found in these locales were familiar to her, for they resonated with her life in schools and in African American communities.

In her work well beyond graduate school, Ladson-Billings has continued to develop the thinking that grew initially in these alternative graduate school spaces. She turns, for example, to the work of public intellectuals like Cornel West, bell hooks, and Patricia Hill Collins to help her pave her way:

> As an African American female, public intellectual, I struggle to do intellectual work that is politically significant and culturally grounded. I struggle to do this work as a way to acknowledge and revere those who have gone before me and as a way to pave the path for those who must come after. This struggle is grounded both in what I choose to study and how I choose to study it. . . . My academic struggle primarily has been one of methodology and theoretical grounding. . . . Patricia Hill Collins' work on Black feminist epistemology provides a *theoretical and conceptual platform* on which to rest my methodology [emphasis added] [Ladson-Billings, 1997, pp. 61–62].

If we consider Ladson-Billings's efforts in relation to the first rationale for disciplinary study through doctoral education—that disciplines provide aspiring researchers with theories, concepts, and perspectives for framing education issues and questions—we see that she has contributed to and relies on the conceptual platforms undergirding her research. Moreover, although earlier views addressed how students may learn to think in new and deeper ways through engagement in disciplinary study, what we glean from Ladson-Billings's experiences suggests that in her journey to anthropology and Afro-American studies, she was seeking modes of thinking that, in deepened and articulated form, made sense of the questions that *she* wished to pursue. She then gravitated toward a conceptual platform, grounded in the disciplines, that promised to help her speak in a familiar voice and to hear and decipher, in deepened ways, the familiar problems to which she wished to respond as a researcher.

If we then consider Ladson-Billings's efforts in relation to the second rationale for disciplinary study in doctoral work—that the disciplines help to place education issues in the context of a larger intellectual terrain—we see the possibility that her studies in anthropology and in social studies (writ large) provided her with a perspective that she continues to develop in her construction of herself today as a public intellectual.

Finally, looking at Ladson-Billings in relation to the third rationale for doctoral study, we see that her immersion in the study of social studies provides her with a subject to trace deeply the learning of the teachers and students whose lives are her primary concern. To the study of social issues she brings her understanding of the disciplines of history and anthropology.

Brenner and Ladson-Billings help us see that the three disciplinary study traditions are situated in the contexts of their lives before graduate school and in relation to their burning questions in graduate school and to the school's and university's resources. Brenner does not have to travel far to find kindred intellectual spirits, for they exist right in her school of education and in the course texts that her instructors assign (for example, Lensmire's book). Ladson-Billings, on the other hand, must venture much further, to anthropology and Afro-American studies. Although both of these women look to the disciplines for conceptual platforms that resonate with what they already know and with how, intuitively and naturally, they wish to pursue their inquiries, each in good part has constructed her own conceptual platform, drawing from the resources of her school of education (Brenner) or more broadly from her larger university setting (Ladson-Billings).

Implications for Preparing Researchers. In one sense, neither Brenner nor Ladson-Billings emphasized disciplinary study through her graduate school years, for the core of the course work was in schools of education rather than in a traditional discipline. But in another sense, both drew heavily on such study as a route toward developing the conceptual platforms that supported their initial forays into research. Brenner did this by connecting to the philosophical, psychological, and sociolinguistic concepts that anchored the literacy learning community found in her college of education. Ladson-Billings did this by connecting to concepts of culture in courses that she took selectively in Stanford's anthropology department and in its Afro-American Studies Program. Without formally committing themselves to membership in disciplinary communities beyond education (for example, by becoming anthropologists), they immersed themselves in these communities long enough and deeply enough to absorb, and learn to articulate, concepts and perspectives that would be helpful to them in their research. This is an essential point: relying heavily on their own sensibilities and interests, Brenner and Ladson-Billings took as much as they needed from the disciplines in order to create solid conceptual platforms for the study of their particular subjects.

We believe there is an important place for disciplinary study in the preparation of education researchers, including those whose imaginations are captured by the problems of education practice. In staking out this position, we emphasize that each of the three rationales for disciplinary study makes a distinctive contribution to the preparation of education researchers. Graduate schools of education should ensure that doctoral students have the opportunity to benefit from these three modes, but we do not wish to be prescriptive about how this should happen. Different institutions and programs have developed their own approaches for incorporating the disciplines into their doctoral programs in education, and this is as it should be. We do wish to acknowledge, however, that the expertise of a given institution's faculty will be influential in determining whether disciplinary preparation should be located primarily within the school of education or outward into the university.

Regardless of where such study is located, it is essential that doctoral students in education not be isolated from disciplinary discourse. Novice education researchers need to be able to converse intelligibly with disciplinary scholars in other corners of academia about topics in which they have common interests—much as they need to be able to converse with education researchers and education practitioners whose work bears on their own.

The Tension of Public Response and Responsibility

The third tension in education research and in the education of education researchers is located within the contradiction of education scholars' desires to be responsive and responsible simultaneously to both public needs and causes, on the one hand, and intellectual questions and norms, on the other. Although education is often cast as a public right and commodity and educators as public workers concerned about and responsive to public demands, the situatedness of education within academe, and the concomitant growth of communities of education scholars, indicate that education is also a field of study—an arena of intellectual thought. Although both domains of education—the public and the intellectual—are deemed valid, with few exceptions (Ladson-Billings, 1994; Peterson, 1998) we lack clear ways to think and talk about them together. We have few opportunities to experiment with and examine potential developments at the intersection of these two views, much less consider the implications of such developments for doctoral study.

The paucity of such work to serve as precedents or guides for public-oriented scholarship is surprising. "I would think in a field like education, that touches everybody, the call for public intellectuals is really important," commented Ladson-Billings to Peterson (Interview, January 1997). Even so, Ladson-Billings refers frequently in her autobiographical writings to her personal commitment to create and use knowledge at the intersection of the public and the intellectual domains of education. We therefore turn to an exploration of Ladson-Billings's public-intellectual stance as an exemplar of a possible future direction for the field of education generally.

"The term [public intellectual] is one that's been used by people like Cornel West and Skip Gates and bell hooks," said Ladson-Billings, "[people] who have essentially said that . . . African Americans in particular don't have the luxury of just being academics." Elaborating on the origins of this term in a recent autobiographical account, she commented:

African American and other scholars of color rarely have the luxury of considering only their personal sojourns. Rather, our position in the academy is typically the result of collective struggle and support. Thus our understanding of our roles includes an intertwining of the personal and the public, the intellectual and the emotional, the scholarly, and the political [Ladson-Billings, 1997, p. 59].

Her point, however, becomes especially clear when we view it in the context of her aspirations as a college student who was perhaps all too aware of what was possible—and impossible. For as she noted wryly, looking back on her undergraduate days, "In my secret life I was a writer, but just thinking about saying that aloud made me laugh" (Ladson-Billings, 1997, p. 53). Her "real life" —past, present, and future—as she saw it then had no room for this fantasy of academic life, distanced as it apparently was from the demands of everyday life on her family, on the African American community, and on herself:

I could see it all clearly. After earning a bachelor's degree I would return to the solitude of my room (in my parents' home) to think and write. Never mind that most of my family's resources had gone to secure my education. Never mind that there was an expectation that I would both take care of myself (financially) and contribute to the family. I merely would announce that I had returned home a "writer" and each morning while other family members marched off to work, I would retreat to my "study" and "write." The entire imagined scene was ludicrous [Ladson-Billings, 1997, p. 53].

Rather than seclude herself in an effort to research and write, Ladson-Billings constructs her research in the very midst of everyday life, purposefully reflecting it. In her view, an education researcher has no time, no opportunity, and no desire to ponder or create within quiet, contemplative escapes; the personal and public imperative for thought-in-action—now and in the midst of problems and crises—is too strong. Moreover, her image of "public" encompasses far more than academe and is far larger than the education profession itself. As she explained, "There are those of us who feel that the issues that concern us most need a wider hearing, and we're very deliberate in making sure that we write, speak, and listen to voices beyond the academy" (Interview, January 1997). Thus, Ladson-Billings's crafting of her life and career as a public intellectual permits her to use her intellect for the "social good." As she notes, "To me it's one of the ways in which I exercise my own citizenship" (Interview, January 1997).

What does being a public intellectual entail for Ladson-Billings? First and foremost, it entails speaking, to both academics and schoolteachers, and also to parents who send their children to school and to the larger public that derives general benefit from public education. A public intellectual is one who, in talking to parents and members of the public, departs from traditional academic discourses and interacts with them in alternative ways: "I cannot go over there to a talk with parents and give these people a list of citations," she said in her interview with Peterson. "I can't even go over there and give them handouts to read that are, you know, some journal article. I have to give them some strategies, some ideas for strategies, and I also have to go over there and listen."

Being a public intellectual in the African American community also means, in Ladson-Billings's words, "sharing with people my own struggles." She added, "Then they'll realize they're not stupid when they can't get what they want from schools. 'Well, here's this woman,' they might say, 'who should know better than anybody how schools operate, and she still has to fight.'" So for Ladson-Billings, being a public intellectual involves not only helping parents and the general public in instrumental ways, but also making a connection that they will find both encouraging and inspiring for its human qualities. "I think a part of being a teacher is helping kids helping students—who can be adults," she said, "helping learners understand that humanity in you. And so part of the way in which they see me as a human being is that I have the same kind of issues that they have." For Ladson-Billings, learning begins with the realization that one can learn, just as change begins with the realization that one can enact change and just as persistence and survival begin with the realization that one can persist and survive. In her role as a public intellectual, Ladson-Billings provides her audiences, which she sees as composed of learners, with images of such possibility.

In this view, Ladson-Billings's public-intellectual stance is as much an enactment of her teacher-self as it is of her political-and-citizen self. She inspires learning and the belief that the members of her community can learn in the classroom and well beyond it. Her research is less about the construction of knowledge than about the creation of meaning for particular people at particular times. As she notes, "I was less interested in the proliferation of my work than whether or not the work had meaning for those whom I intended to serve" (Interview, January 1997, p. 59).

Brenner is also grappling with the tension between intellectual commitments and public commitments in education. Like Ladson-Billings, her commitments to education as a public endeavor emanate from her concern for her own children's education but encompass the interests of other children and parents in her community. Brenner initially addressed these concerns by participating on the school improvement team in her daughter's elementary school. This foray into school governance and management was revealing, for it provided a window into life in schools that was not well represented in her graduate school curriculum and that spurred her to learn more about the politics of education and school leadership.

More recently, Brenner's joining of the intellectual and the public has taken a new turn. The large urban school district in which she and her family reside

is perceived to be in decline, losing students to neighboring districts and charter schools and raising fears within the local business community about the district's ability to provide employers with skilled graduates. In response, the mayor
organized a blue-ribbon panel joining university and school district officials,
business and civic leaders, and local politicians with a charge to develop and
implement recommendations to improve the schools. Brenner attended several
of the public meetings of this panel and read the reports it had issued. She
became uneasy about the direction the panel was headed, particularly with the
influence that one particular employer, long associated with the area, might
have. "What's good for business might not be good for the schools," she said.
She expressed her reservations to the school board president, but her offer of
assistance in implementing reforms was largely ignored.

As the panel moved into its implementation phase, Brenner had increasing
concerns about the diverging interests of the community and local employers,
fearing that the employers' interests in preparing students for the workforce
might be at odds with the community's interest in preparing students to be
thoughtful citizens. She expressed these concerns in a letter to the mayor and
again volunteered her services. She also sent the letter to the local newspaper,
which published it, with slight editing, as an op-ed piece.

The day the op-ed piece appeared, Brenner received a telephone call from
the business executive heading the implementation committee. In her words,
he asked her to "put her money where her mouth is" by serving on one of the
task forces. She joined the preschool and elementary education task force with
few illusions about her probable influence on the process but concluded that
voicing her concerns publicly was preferable to inaction.

There is one more piece of this story to recount. After her op-ed piece was published in the local paper, Brenner circulated an invitation to graduate students at
MSU's College of Education to become involved in the reform process. She volunteered to coordinate graduate student participation in the reform effort and to
be a conduit of information about the reform process to the college community.

It is too soon to know how Brenner's introduction into the public arena will
play out, but the parallel between the way that she and Ladson-Billings enacted
their dual intellectual and public commitments during graduate school is striking. Both sought to apply intellectual ideas to the improvement of educational
chances for children and youth in their community, and they did so by going outside their graduate school of education, which provided few structured opportunities for joining the public and the intellectual. The story of the potential
leadership role that Brenner has crafted is all the more remarkable when one recognizes that Michigan State's president chaired the blue-ribbon panel and that
the college of education has a long-standing presence in the district in question.

What can we learn from Ladson-Billings and Brenner about the traditional tensions between the intellectual and public commitments in education and about

approaches to resolving these, so that intellectual expertise can be powerfully joined to public need as a core educational endeavor? It appears that for Ladson-Billings, the public-intellectual tension circumscribes all others, and the role of public intellectual defines all others. What is clear from her writings is, first, that we do not yet have a well-developed language for discussing public-intellectual endeavors, and thus the work of writers in this genre is foundational. Second, the role of the public intellectual, though seemingly contradictory, is fruitful ground for educational thought and action, for it is public life that is perhaps most in need of the shaping that thoughtful intellectual and educational endeavor can provide. Third, managing the public-intellectual tension is not about lecturing or disseminating knowledge; it is about being in conversation with people who aspire to learn how to draw on and live by the meanings within themselves—for example, as they craft their own lives and the lives of their children and their communities. Fourth, being a public intellectual involves the forging of personal connections with others—links that make meaningful educational action possible by those historically shut out of it. Finally, the life of a public intellectual, though "public," is of necessity intensely personal, for without personal commitment neither the intellectual nor the public can take authentic form.

Implications for Preparing Researchers. What are the implications of this developing articulation for doctoral students and for the programs in which they study? We suggest that today's and tomorrow's doctoral students are more likely to frame public intellectualism as a legitimate educational endeavor than their teachers who, in their work, have largely positioned themselves as committed to either public endeavors *or* to intellectual activity, and only rarely to the two in meaningful conjunction. We suggest, however, that these teachers need to help doctoral students frame their unique relationships to potential public-intellectual stances, even as these teachers struggle within themselves to reconsider, and possibly reframe, their own past commitments. The public-intellectual tension, though real, is just now being articulated, explored, and created for life as we have created it (and are creating it) today.

The tension of public response and responsibility touches all students of education, although it has been especially prominent in the scholarly activities of members of subordinated communities. We believe that all preparation programs should provide novice researchers with structured opportunities to reflect on the personal and public in intellectual perspective and to engage the faculty in conversations about this tension. Precisely how this might occur is a matter we believe best left to the faculty at particular institutions. We do, however, offer a few suggestions that might be considered.

First, one way of casting this tension is as a problem in the representation of research to multiple audiences and through diverse media and diverse forms of articulation. Students need experience representing their research and their ideas to multiple audiences, including researchers, practitioners, and a broader public. They need experience in diverse forms of self-expression. As the case of Ladson-Billings suggests, they also need experience in listening and responding to what they hear in meaningful ways. We encourage graduate schools of education to design settings where such learning can take place.

Second, we believe that students can learn a great deal about this tension by reading the works of public intellectuals, past and present, within the field of education and beyond. Such writings might include biographical and autobiographical texts as well as more traditional treatments of education as a public good.

Finally, we note that we ourselves continue to work at understanding what it means to be a public intellectual. It strikes us that this concept, as it applies to the field of education, could benefit from further development. We therefore call on scholars struggling to make sense of the tension between public and intellectual stakes in the study of education to continue to write about their struggles, so that the field can draw on this discussion in designing opportunities for doctoral student development.

CONCLUSION

As we have explored the past and present conditions of how educational practitioners, especially teachers, who enter graduate school make sense of their learning of research, we have also explored its implications for the future practices of graduate schools of education. Rather than repeating these, we here make some observations about ways to conceive of the learning of research—especially about the experiences of educational practitioners' learning of research through doctoral study. We believe that it is helpful to consider these issues in the contexts, first, of the learning that these practitioners have gained, in diverse communities, about issues that matter deeply to them and that might someday become the subjects of their own research; second, of the cultures of the universities and schools of education that they enter; third, of the advising, mentoring, and teaching relationships that they encounter, purposefully or by chance, in graduate school; fourth, of the peer and professional relationships that they forge in classrooms, assistantships, and out-of-school settings that bear on their thought; fifth, of the communities in which they conduct their research; and, sixth, of the communities to which they hope someday to turn to work as intellectuals and as professionals. We believe that each of these contexts—and others—holds, shapes, and molds the thinking, values, concerns, and aspirations of these students and that students' thoughts are likely as well to shape and mold these contexts, perhaps in bits and pieces. We believe that the learning of research requires understanding of "the learning mind" in context but, more to the point, that research requires an understanding of how students learn as they move from context to context and as the contexts in which their lives are embedded ebb and flow—at times in understandable ways, at times in ways that are anything but understandable. It is impossible to map exactly what this means for all students; we can only point to how we, as mentors, might use the lens of context to explore our students' learning experiences and how we might assert our agency, and our students' own agency, to create contexts for generative learning.

We also believe that for practitioners striving to become researchers, it is neither helpful nor possible to strive to construct professional lives focused solely on research or solely on practice. To focus on research alone would deny the learning from practice that practitioners have gained and that have become intertwined with their lives and their identities. Alternatively, to focus on practice alone would deny the unique contribution to learning that graduate study can make: The conceptual deepening and substantive broadening of practitioners' understandings of practice—its sources, its contexts, its effects, its meanings, its values. Thus we call for the creation of a discipline of studied educational practice and practice-based study in schools of education. To do this we will need to continue inventing new mergers of research and practice, across diverse fields and educational settings, and new milieus in which this work can occur. We hope that schools of education will be able to take up this challenge.

The traditional disciplines could help in this effort in multiple ways: by providing discipline-based concepts and practices for the study of educational phenomena, enlarging educators' perspectives of the multiple contexts within which education is enacted in its particular forms, and fostering deep understanding of the subject matter that is at the core of teaching and learning in schools. But the common separation of disciplinary study from practice-based study is unhelpful in this regard, for even researchers with deep commitments to the improvement and development of practice seemingly have more to gain from disciplinary study. As we saw in the cases of Brenner and Ladson-Billings, the disciplines can be sites for practitioners selectively to absorb concepts, theories, and ideas that can then be used to build what Ladson-Billings calls the "conceptual platforms" on which they conduct their research. Although this can be done formally and in a structured way through cognate studies, it can also be accomplished more informally, through selective, self-directed study of disciplinary texts or affiliation with informal scholarly communities concerned with developing particular perspectives for the study of educational phenomena. Our point, however, is that learning from the disciplines does not require one to become a disciplinarian. It does, however, require sustained time and thought in disciplinary study toward building a meaningful and comprehensive conceptual platform on which to situate the study of educational practice.

Finally, we believe that the intersection represented by public intellectual efforts is a site ripe for thought and scholarly development. All educators—teachers, principals, counselors, other school and college staff, and especially those associated with public institutions (as all public schools and many college and universities are)—work on the boundary between what lies protected from the public eye and what lies directly in its view; and in this era more and more does fall into the public view and thereby into the public discourse. As such, the vast majority of teachers, principals, and other personnel in America's schools, and the majority of professors, administrators, and other staff persons in colleges and universities are, effectively, workers in the public domain. This does not necessarily mean they must bow to every public whim and message; it does mean they must know where they stand, they must attend to the public mind inasmuch as they attend to the minds of the children of that public, and they must attend to the learning of parents and members of the public, as well as to the learning of the children and adults who sit in their classrooms.

We believe that all educators must be teachers in addition to whatever else they may be doing; they must be prepared to educate the public, policymakers, parents, politicians, and others about educational needs and educational strategies deriving from their scholarly efforts. They must teach to expanded audiences what it means to educate. They must be prepared to help the members of these various audiences understand both the limits and possibilities of education, and they should encourage the members of these audiences to see not only their children but themselves as learners.

What does all this imply for the unique position of education scholars? If teachers, principals, and other education professionals are drawn into these public roles, it is hard to imagine that scholars of education will not be also. We recognize that assuming such roles will require much additional development, and we suggest that schools of education establish opportunities for doctoral students, professors, and local school staff to work together in the creation of public intellectual stances that will be meaningful in their communities.

How is all this to be done? We have several preliminary suggestions, mixed with warnings. First, the kind of learning we report here is at its beginning. Understanding more about doctoral students' learning prior to taking action to remedy their learning experiences is necessary. A great deal has been gleaned from the cases of Devon Brenner and Gloria Ladson-Billings; we urge that additional studies of this sort be carried out. Second, each school of education must design its own sites for learning about the learning of their own doctoral students and how best to bridge the various tensions described here. At the same time, there is much that professors of research in particular institutions can learn from professors of research in other sites. We urge a balance in the flow of knowledge and expertise between local, secluded efforts and efforts alive in other sites. Third, within schools of education, attempts to understand sensible reforms must occur at multiple levels—structurally in school, department, and program designs; operationally in the work of key governance structures; collegially among professors engaged in common programs or sharing in areas of specialized study; and also in the context of the adviser-student relationship, in the classroom, among students themselves, and among students, faculty members, and professionals with shared educational concerns. To focus reform and the design of reform in just one place, assuming that it will spread, whether through dictum or in other ways, is to risk its collapse. We believe that learning must begin in all these places at the same time.

Fourth, we recognize that despite the need to cast the net as widely as we have just suggested, doing so risks overloading what any school of education might do, leading it to a grinding halt. We suggest, therefore, that persons working at multiple levels and in multiple locations within schools of education be given choices of where and how to begin reform. Disparate efforts must be nurtured, studied, and followed with care, and persons working on related endeavors must be provided with means to learn together and from each other's successes and mistakes. We do not view a linear progression, whether top down or bottom up, as workable, preferring to rely on an organic vision that promotes natural growth.

Finally, although we emphasize the need to situate doctoral study carefully in students' lives, respecting their learning in multiple contexts, we suggest that the same respect and support be accorded professors. Their learning, and the support of their learning, amid such change and in new contexts is as much a priority for schools of education as is the learning of their doctoral students.

References

Atwell, N. *In the Middle: Writing, Reading, and Learning with Adolescents.* Portsmouth, N.H.: Boynton/Cook, 1987.

Ball, D. L. "With an Eye on the Mathematical Horizon: Dilemmas of Teaching Elementary School Mathematics." *Elementary School Journal*, 1993, *93*, 379–397.

Baumann, J. F. "Conflict or Compatibility in Classroom Inquiry? One Teacher's Struggle to Balance Teaching and Research." *Educational Researcher*, 1996, *25*(7), 29–36.

Brown, A. L. "Design Experiments: Theoretical and Methodological Challenges in Creating Complex Interventions in Classroom Settings." *Journal of the Learning Sciences*, 1992, *2*(2), 141–178.

Chubb, J., and Moe, T. *Politics, Markets, and America's Schools.* Washington, D.C.: Brookings Institution, 1990.

Cochran-Smith, M., and Lytle, S. *Inside/Outside: Teacher Research and Knowledge.* New York: Teachers College Press, 1993.

Collins, A., Hawkins, J., and Carver, S. "A Cognitive Apprenticeship for Disadvantaged Students." In B. Means, C. Chelemer, and M. Knapp (eds.), *Teaching Advanced Skills to At-Risk Students.* San Francisco: Jossey-Bass, 1991.

Collins, P. H. *Black Feminist Thought: Knowledge, Consciousness, and the Politics of Empowerment.* New York: Routledge, 1991.

Cooper, H. "Speaking Power to Truth: Reflections of an Educational Researcher After Four Years of School Board Service." *Educational Researcher,* 1996, *25*(1), 29–34.

Cronbach, L. J., and Suppes, P. (eds.). *Research for Tomorrow's Schools: Disciplined Inquiry for Education.* New York: Macmillan, 1969.

Geertz, C. *The Interpretation of Cultures.* New York: Basic Books, 1973.

Goswami, D., and Stillman, P. (eds.). *Reclaiming the Classroom: Teacher Research as an Agency for Change.* Upper Montclair, N.J.: Boynton/Cook, 1987.

Grossman, P. L., Wilson, S., and Shulman, L. S. "Teachers of Substance: Subject Matter Knowledge in Teaching." In M. Reynolds (ed.), *Knowledge Base of the Beginning Teacher.* Washington, D.C.: American Association of Colleges for Teacher Education, 1989.

Guba, E., and Elam, S. *The Training and Nurture of Educational Researchers.* Sixth annual Phi Delta Kappa Symposium on Educational Research. Bloomington, Ind.: Phi Delta Kappa, 1965.

Harnqvist, K. "Training of Research Workers in Education." In T. Husen and N. Postlethwaite (eds.), *The International Encyclopedia of Education.* (2nd ed.) New York: Pergamon Press, 1994.

Heath, S. B. *Ways with Words: Language, Life, and Work in Communities and Classrooms.* New York: Cambridge University Press, 1983.

Holmes Group. *Tomorrow's Schools.* East Lansing, Mich.: Holmes Group, 1990.

Holmes Group. *Tomorrow's Schools of Education.* East Lansing, Mich.: Holmes Group, 1995.

Howes, E. V. "Feminist Teacher Research and Students' Visions of Science: Listening as Research and as Pedagogy." Unpublished doctoral dissertation, Michigan State University, 1997.

Ingersoll, R. *Out-of-Field Teaching and Educational Equality.* Statistical Analysis Report. Washington, D.C.: National Center for Education Statistics, 1996.

Kerckhoff, A. C. *Diverging Pathways: Social Structure and Career Deflections.* New York: Cambridge University Press, 1993.

Kondo, D. *Crafting Selves: Power, Gender, and Discourses of Identity in a Japanese Workplace.* Chicago: University of Chicago Press, 1990.

Labaree, D. F., and Pallas, A. M. "Dire Straits: The Narrow Vision of the Holmes Group." *Educational Researcher,* 1996a, *25*(5), 25–28.

Labaree, D. F., and Pallas, A. M. "The Holmes Group's mystifying response." *Educational Researcher,* 1996b, *25*(5), 31–32.

Ladson-Billings, G. *The Dreamkeepers: Successful Teachers of African American Schoolchildren.* San Francisco: Jossey-Bass, 1994.

Ladson-Billings, G. "For Colored Girls Who Have Considered Suicide When the Academy Isn't Enough: Reflections of an African American Woman Scholar." In A. Neumann and P. L. Peterson (eds.), *Learning from Our Lives: Women, Research and Autobiography in Education.* New York: Teachers College Press, 1997.

Lagemann, E. C. *Contested Terrain: A History of Education Research in the United States, 1890–1990.* Chicago: Spencer Foundation, 1996.

Lareau, A. *Home Advantage: Social Class and Parental Intervention in Elementary Education.* Bristol, Pa.: Falmer Press, 1989.

Leinhardt, G., Zaslavsky, O., and Stein, M. K. "Functions, Graphs, and Graphing: Tasks, Learning, and Teaching." *Review of Educational Research,* 1990, *60,* 1–63.

Lensmire, T. J. *When Children Write: Critical Re-Visions of the Writing Workshop.* New York: Teachers College Press, 1994.

Meyer, J. W. "The Charter: Conditions of Diffuse Socialization Within Schools." In W. R. Scott (ed.), *Social Processes and Social Structure.* Austin, Tex.: Holt, Rinehart & Winston, 1970.

Meyer, J. W., Kamens, D., and Benavot, A. *School Knowledge for the Masses.* Bristol, Pa.: Falmer Press, 1993.

Moss, P., and others. "Inquiring About Inquiry: Reflections on an Introduction to the Philosophy of Social Science." Paper presented at the Annual Meeting of the American Educational Research Association, Chicago, 1997.

Neumann, A., and Pallas, A. "Moving Beyond the Middle: A Case Study of Transitions and Transformations in the Learning of Educational Research." Paper presented at the Annual Meeting of the American Educational Research Association, Chicago, 1997.

Neumann, A. "On the Making of Hard Times and Good Times: The Social Construction of Resource Stress." *Journal of Higher Education,* 1995a, *66,* 3–31.

Neumann, A. "Context, Cognition, and Culture: A Case Analysis of Collegiate Leadership and Cultural Change." *American Educational Research Journal,* 1995b, *32,* 251–279.

Neumann, A., and Peterson P. L. (eds.). *Learning from Our Lives: Women, Research, and Autobiography in Education.* New York: Teachers College Press, 1997.

Peterson, P. *School Politics Chicago Style.* Chicago: University of Chicago Press, 1976.

Peterson, P. L. "Why Do Educational Research? Rethinking Our Roles and Identities, Our Texts and Contexts." *Educational Researcher,* 1998, *27*(3): 4–10.

Peterson, P. L., and Knapp, N. F. "Inventing and Reinventing Ideas: Constructivist Teaching and Learning." In Gordon Cawelti (ed.), *The 1993 Yearbook of the Association for Supervision and Curriculum Development.* Washington, D.C.: Association for Supervision and Curriculum Development, 1993.

Peterson, P. L., Pallas, A. M., and Neumann, A. "Bridging Communities of Practice and Research: A Case Study of a Doctoral Student's Learning of Inquiry in Education". Paper presented at the Annual Meeting of the American Educational Research Association, New York, 1996.

Rosaen, C. "Collaboration in a Professional Culture: Renegotiating Barriers to Improve Practice." In Jere Brophy (ed.), *Advances in Research on Teaching* (Vol. 5). Greenwich, Conn.: JAI Press, 1995.

Rosenau, P. M. *Post Modernism and the Social Sciences: Insights, Inroads and Intrusions*. Princeton, N.J.: Princeton University Press, 1992.

Shulman, L. S. "Knowledge and Teaching: Foundations of a New Reform." *Harvard Educational Review*, 1987, *57*(1), 1–22.

Shulman, L. S. *To Know It Is to Psychologize It*. John Dewey Lecture presented at the Annual Meeting of the American Educational Research Association, San Francisco, 1995.

Shulman, L. S., and Quinlan, K. M. "The Comparative Psychology of School Subjects." In David C. Berliner and Robert C. Calfee (eds.), *Handbook of Educational Psychology*. New York: Simon & Schuster, 1996.

Sieber, S. D., and Lazarsfeld, P. F. *The Organization of Educational Research in the United States*. New York: Bureau of Applied Social Research, Columbia University, 1966.

Smith, D. E. *History of Mathematics, Vol. 2: Special Topics of Elementary Mathematics*. New York: Ginn Press, 1925.

Wilson, S. M. "Not Tension But Intention: A Response to Wong's Analysis of the Researcher/Teacher." *Educational Researcher*, 1995, *24*(8), 19–22.

Wong, E. D. "Challenges Confronting the Researcher/Teacher: Conflicts of Purpose and Conduct." *Educational Researcher*, 1995a, *24*(3), 22–28.

Wong, E. D. "Challenges Confronting the Researcher/Teacher: Rejoinder to Wilson." *Educational Researcher*, 1995b, *24*(8), 22–23.

Yerrick, R. (1994). "Science for All? An Insider's Account of Changing Classroom Discourse." Unpublished doctoral dissertation, Michigan State University, 1994.

The Changing
Infrastructure of Education Research

Allan Collins

T here has always been a great divide between education research and practice. Most practitioners regard education research as irrelevant to their day-to-day concerns, and so they pay little attention to what researchers recommend. This partly derives from the origins of education research in the field of psychology. The methods employed, based on laboratory studies, have led to a body of findings that has a problematic relation to questions of practice. Learning in the real world occurs in complex social situations, and laboratory methods of studying learnings so fundamentally alter the conditions of learning that it is not clear what to conclude from any such study.

Recently researchers have begun to study teaching and learning in the context of real-world learning environments. Their work is propelled by the desire to bridge the gap between research and practice and by the changing emphases in cognitive and sociocultural research (Greeno, Collins, and Resnick, 1996). These attempts to address the problems of practice are leading to changes in the infrastructure of education research. By infrastructure I mean the entire way research is carried out and communicated to the world.

Three examples of the changing infrastructure are embodied in the three chapters in this section: Chapter Fourteen by James G. Greeno and others represents what Ann Brown (1992) and Allan Collins (1992) refer to as a design-experiment methodology for developing and evaluating education innovations. Chapter Fifteen by Deborah Loewenberg Ball and Magdalene Lampert describes the development of representations of teaching and learning that can form the basis for a new kind of dialogue between researchers and practitioners. And Chapter Sixteen by Roy D. Pea describes the enrichment of communication among researchers and practitioners through new media. These chapters thus describe three different kinds of initiatives to change the infrastructure of education research.

DESIGN-EXPERIMENT METHODOLOGY

The evolving methodology of design experiments (Brown, 1992; Collins, 1992; Hawkins and Collins, forthcoming) began as a reaction to traditional psychological experimentation, which has dominated education research about teaching and learning. The methodology of psychological experimentation was based on notions of controlling variables in order to determine precisely what causes different effects. Researchers thus conducted experiments under laboratory conditions according to carefully defined procedures. Design experiments, in contrast, attempt to carry experimentation into real-life settings in order to find out what works in practice. This means giving up the notion of controlling variables and necessitates the development of a new methodology to carry out research.

One can illustrate the novelty of the design-experiment methodology most strikingly by comparing it to the experimental methodology used to study human learning in the psychological literature. Learning research started before the turn of the century with the German psychologist Hermann Ebbinghaus, who invented the nonsense syllable in order to study learning in its purest form. He identified many of the most important variables that affect learning, such as the similarity of stimuli to each other and the nature of the activity between learning and recall. This tradition of research on learning continues to this day and has evolved to address questions about how humans learn to solve problems and carry out complex tasks. It has produced many important findings about the conditions that affect both learning and transfer.

At least seven major differences can be identified between this kind of psychological methodology that has so dominated education research and the design-experiment methodology that is currently evolving:

1. Laboratory settings versus messy situations. Experiments conducted in laboratories avoid contaminating effects. Learners concentrate on the task without any distractions or interruptions. The materials to be learned are well defined and are presented in a standardized manner, rather than the manner a particular teacher may choose at any given moment. In fact, the presentation is usually one-directional, rather than relying on interactions between teachers and learners. In short, learning in a laboratory does not look anything like what goes on in a

typical classroom, workplace, or home, where most learning actually occurs. Design experiments are set in the messy situations that characterize real-life learning, in order to avoid the distortions of laboratory experiments.

2. A single dependent variable versus multiple dependent variables. Most psychological experiments have one dependent variable, such as the number of items recalled or the percentage correct on a test of some kind. Design experiments have many dependent variables that matter, although the experimenter may not pay attention to them all. They fall into three types: climate variables, such as engagement of the learners, cooperation among learners, and risk taking by learners; outcome variables, including the learning of knowledge, skills, strategies, and dispositions; and system variables, such as spread of use, sustainability, and ease of adoption. There are several characteristic ways of studying each of these types of variables: Climate variables can be studied by observation, interviews, and surveys; outcome variables can be studied by giving pre- and posttests or evaluating products and performances; and system variables can be studied by follow-up observations, surveys, interviews, and longitudinal studies.

3. Controlling variables versus characterizing the situation. Psychological experiments use a methodology of controlling variables borrowed from early physics. The goal is to identify a few independent and dependent variables and hold all the other variables in the situation constant. So, for example, if the experimenter regards amount of learning as the dependent variable, the goal will be to hold motivation constant. But the goal of teachers in classrooms is to find ways to motivate students, so that they learn something. Thus, holding motivation constant fundamentally undermines the usefulness of the results. In design experiments, there is no attempt to hold variables constant; instead the goal is to identify all the variables, or characteristics of the situation, that affect any dependent variables of interest. Not only is the goal to characterize what affects any dependent variable, it is also to identify the nature and extent of the effect.

4. Fixed procedures versus flexible design revision. Psychological experiments follow a fixed procedure that is carefully documented, so that it can be replicated by other experimenters. Design experiments, in contrast, start with planned procedures and materials that are not completely defined and are revised depending on their success in practice. In design experiments, the experimenter should characterize what happens as completely as possible and document any changes made in the plans, together with the reasons for the changes. The goal is to start

with teaching methods that are most likely to succeed but to monitor how they are working and to modify them when appropriate. This progressive refinement is standard practice in the product design community, as can be seen in the many refinements that are made in products over time. Until recently, however, progressive refinement was not the approach taken with education innovations, because of the strictures for replicability on the experimental methods inherited from psychology.

5. Social isolation versus social interaction. In most psychological experiments, the subjects are learning in isolation. They have no interaction with other learners and usually not with a teacher or expert either; the material to be learned is simply presented by text or video. By contrast, design experiments are set in complex social situations, such as a classroom. In consequence, students are sharing ideas, distracting and making fun of each other, being interrupted in their work, trying to make life difficult for the teacher, and so on. Design experiments have to cope with the noisy data that arise from such situations.

6. Testing hypotheses versus developing a profile. In psychological experiments, the experimenter has one or more hypotheses that are tested by systematically varying the conditions of learning. In design experiments the goal is to see what conditions lead to different effects. Design experiments ideally are much more like what *Consumer Reports* does when it evaluates the quality of different automobiles. The goal is to look at many different aspects of the design and develop a qualitative and quantitative profile that characterizes the design in practice. A large number of contextual variables determine the success of an innovation—for example: settings, such as homes versus schools and urban versus suburban schools; the nature of the learners, such as their age, background, turnover rate, and attendance rate; required support, including teacher support for students, technical support, administrative support, and parent support; professional development for teachers, administrators, technical people, and parents; financial support, including equipment costs, service costs, professional development costs, and replacement costs; and implementation path, describing how the innovation is introduced, the time devoted to it, and the duration of its usefulness. It is best if evaluation is done with respect to a number of dimensions in a comparative fashion, as when *Consumer Reports* evaluates different products.

7. Experimenter versus coparticipant design and analysis. In psychological experiments the experimenter makes all decisions about the design and analysis of the data, in order to maintain control of what happens and how it is analyzed. In design experiments there is an effort to

involve different participants in the design in order to bring their different expertise into producing and analyzing the design. Thus, teachers, curriculum designers, technology experts, cognitive psychologists, and anthropologists may all be involved in developing the design and evaluating its effects. Design experiments require many resources to stage, and hence it makes sense to bring to bear wide expertise in their design and evaluation.

Greeno and others describe in Chapter Fourteen how they developed and implemented a new curriculum for middle school mathematics, where students are faced with applied problems such as designing an energy-efficient building for the Antarctic. A number of aspects of their implementation reflect a design-experiment methodology: the work is set in middle school classrooms in a number of different schools; it is being evaluated on multiple dimensions; there is no control of important variables; the design is evolving by progressive refinement; the students and teachers are interacting in a variety of ways; the evaluation attempts to characterize richly what happens; and the design process involves people with different perspectives, including researchers, curriculum designers, and teachers.

The evolving design-experiment methodology is a radical change in the way education ideas are evaluated. It seeks to bridge the large gap that has existed in the past between research and practice. Such a radical change in methodology calls for equally radical changes in the way results are represented and communicated.

REPRESENTATIONS OF TEACHING AND LEARNING

With the development of video records, it has become possible to document teaching and learning in a much richer way than previously. Before the use of video, all analysis of teaching and learning was based on observation, field notes, behavioral checklists, and memory—methods with strong limitations. They all are biased by the point of view of the observer, and they do not provide a record of most of what happens in teaching and learning. Video, despite its limitations, provides a rich record that different observers can analyze. They can replay sections over and over to resolve issues and questions, and they can debate what really happened, what the students learned, what the teacher should have done, and the like. In this way it is possible to begin to develop a much deeper understanding of practice, which may lead to new ways of talking about practice and to appreciation of the subtleties of teaching and learning.

There are two ways that I see video records functioning to bridge the gap between research and practice. The first is to provide exemplars of teaching and learning. Teachers and researchers can come together to discuss and analyze what is happening in different settings. They can begin to develop a common language and common concerns for thinking about practice. In college courses, prospective teachers can use the archive to investigate questions they have about teaching practice. Teachers in the field can come together around such records to think about their practice. In fact, they can record their own teaching practice (Frederiksen, 1992) and use the archive as a basis for comparison. The power of this approach derives from seeing different teaching techniques and comparing them to one's own. This is called perceptual leaning in the psychological literature (Bransford, Franks, Vye, and Sherwood, 1989), when one learns by systematically comparing better and worse exemplars.

The second way video records may link theory and practice is to provide archives for extended analysis. Because video records are constructed to yield a rich representation of what happened, they can also serve as a basis for extended research into teaching and learning that has not been possible in the past. Researchers who did not participate in the original research can study questions of their own choosing about what happened in a particular setting. They may address questions that the original researchers never thought to ask. The archive of children's discourse that was put together for the study of child language served just this purpose, enabling researchers to discuss and analyze the same data from many different perspectives (MacWhinney, 1995). Such an archive provides a rich data source to researchers who are just starting their careers or are located in places with few resources to carry out their own research. Ideally future projects designed to improve teaching and learning will be documented in this way, so that extensive analysis can be carried out on the projects by researchers other than the designers.

Chapter Fifteen by Ball and Lampert addresses the issue of how to represent teaching and learning in order to give researchers and practitioners ways to look in depth at what happens in classrooms and other learning environments. These researchers have collected extensive records of their own teaching practice, including video and audio records of an entire year's math classes, all the students' written work during the year, field notes from classroom observers, and their own lesson plans and written reflections. They have also collected analyses by mathematicians and prospective teachers on the lessons, which other analysts can inspect. This is a remarkably rich documentation of classroom practice, but it is not the only such archive that has been compiled in recent years. For example, James Stigler and James Hiebert (1997) have compiled an archive of mathematics teaching in three countries at the eighth grade, consisting of videos and other materials for a random sample of one hundred teachers in the United States and Germany and fifty teachers in Japan. Another large archive has been put together on teaching practice in the Netherlands (Dolk and others, 1997). Ideally such records will also be collected to document teaching and learning in other environments, such as workplaces, museums, and homes.

These archives have the potential to change dramatically the ways teaching and learning are studied.

As Ball and Lampert point out, rich records will enable the education community to begin to develop a new language for talking about teaching and learning. Educators may begin to make distinctions between different types of teacher questions, dilemmas, or learning opportunities. By labeling such distinctions, a new vocabulary will emerge for talking about teaching and learning. This process of reification serves two important purposes: it helps to make certain concepts more available to support in-depth analysis of teaching and learning, and it makes it possible to communicate more precisely to others. John Frederiksen (1992) points out how language enables one to see in a new light what is going on in a particular situation. To take an example from Ball and Lampert's chapter, a common dilemma for teachers is whether to pursue a particular student's idea or to follow their prior plan for the lesson. But we have no name for this dilemma, and so it is difficult to communicate it to others. Furthermore, people who have not identified the dilemma before may not notice it when they view a classroom where the teacher is faced with it. As discourse around rich records of teaching and learning becomes common, we may expect that the language for talking and thinking about practice will greatly expand.

NEW MEDIA FOR COMMUNICATION

Reports of research have historically been limited to books and journals. These media are restricted to presenting text, diagrams, and pictures, which do not capture the richness of what is going on in teaching and learning situations. For example, it is difficult to tell from most written descriptions of innovations in schools what really happened. And so it has been difficult for practitioners to use the knowledge transmitted in this form; when they try, they often fail because critical elements to success are left out of the reports. Dissemination of innovations requires much richer descriptions and much more interaction than current media provide.

New media are changing scientific communication and are likely to have broad implications for education research. As communication moves more and more into electronic media, it becomes possible to communicate in much richer formats. Instead of being limited to text, diagrams, and pictures, it is possible to communicate about an intervention in a variety of formats, such as video that shows adults and children engaged in a learning environment; computer programs that enable one to explore and trace through what learners were doing when they were working in a computer environment; and on-line forums where researchers, teachers, and learners can interact with others about what went on in a learning environment. The ability to provide these additional kinds of records greatly extends the possibilities for the education community as a whole to analyze and reflect on teaching and learning in different settings.

Another new possibility for communication involves forming virtual communities of teachers and researchers over the Internet. Virtual communities developed within the science community, when the Internet made it possible for researchers at different sites to work together (Finholt and Olson, 1997). They provide links to other researchers and to shared resources, such as instruments, data sets, and computer tools. This model can be extended into education by bringing together researchers and practitioners into virtual communities. This is already happening among different teacher groups, which exchange ideas about teaching and learning. For example, one group of writing teachers meets every Tuesday night on the Internet to discuss issues in the teaching of writing. There are many more such groups that communicate using asynchronous communications, such as listservs.

If teachers and researchers form into a single community, they can explore questions of mutual interest. This will enable researchers to look at on-line data from many different classrooms (Scardamalia and Bereiter, 1996) and to carry out comparative analyses of classrooms not possible using current methods. It will also enable teachers and other stakeholders to have input into the research questions that researchers address. In such a community, teachers can share ideas and methods with other teachers who are pursuing similar goals, and researchers can share analysis tools and data sets. Such virtual communities would have profound effects on the kinds of research done and act to bring researchers and teachers closer together.

The fundamental goals of scientific communication are replication and evaluation: enough detail needs to be supplied so that other researchers can replicate the results and reach their own conclusions as to what led to the result found. To convey sufficient detail about what happens is more difficult in a classroom or workplace than it is in a laboratory experiment. That is why these new media are critical to the communication of what happens in the typical classroom. From the papers written about most design experiments, it is very difficult to tell what actually happened in the settings described.

As new kinds of education experiments are conducted and new media develop, new standards for reporting on experiments will evolve. This is a common pattern in the sciences. In psychology, for example, there developed in the first part of the twentieth century a standard in experimental research of not asking subjects what they were thinking or doing in order to ensure objectivity. Cognitive psychology, which developed in the 1950s and 1960s, rejected this standard, however, because researchers were interested in characterizing how people think rather than how they behave. This shift in the goal of research enabled researchers to collect "think-aloud" protocol data about what subjects were doing as they solved problems and carried out tasks. This in turn led to the evolution of new standards for collecting and reporting such data. Similarly, as education experiments move out of the laboratory into the messy settings of classrooms, workplaces, homes, and museums, it will become necessary to develop new standards for reporting what happens. These standards may well involve video and other technologies, just as the National Board for Professional Teaching Standards has required two unedited videos of their classes to be provided by any teacher who wants board certification as a master teacher. In coming years the community of education researchers will need to think more broadly about how to represent and communicate what is happening in the interventions they undertake.

In Chapter Sixteen Pea describes how these new media are being deployed currently in education and how they are being developed to exploit new possibilities. He discusses the rise of electronic journals and the formats for presenting information that these new media permit. He also describes the new on-line forums that have been developed for educational practitioners and the kinds of capabilities they offer. Education researchers are only in the initial stages of taking advantage of these developments.

CONCLUSION

The nature of education research is in a state of flux. We researchers are carrying out experiments in classrooms and workplaces rather than in laboratories. We are developing new ways to represent teaching and learning. We are increasingly using new technologies to communicate research to the education community. All these changes are interrelated. Design experiments demand rich representations to characterize what happens, and rich representations require new media to reach a large audience. The education community has not yet arrived at standards that reflect these changes and cannot do so until the changes stabilize. These ongoing changes in education research may serve to reduce the gap between research and practice that has been so destructive for the research enterprise in the past.

References

Bransford, J. D., Franks, J. J., Vye, N. J., and Sherwood, R. D. "New Approaches to Instruction: Because Wisdom Can't Be Told." In S. Vosniadou and A. Ortony (eds.), *Similarity and Analogical Reasoning* (pp. 470–497). New York: Cambridge University Press, 1989.

Brown, A. L. "Design Experiments: Theoretical and Methodological Challenges in Creating Complex Interventions." *Journal of the Learning Sciences*, 1992, *2(2)*, 141–178.

Collins, A. "Toward a Design Science of Education." In E. Scanlon and T. O'Shea (eds.), *New Directions in Educational Technology.* New York: Springer-Verlag, 1992.

Dolk, M., and others. A Multimedia Interactive Learning Environment for (Future) Primary School Teachers with Content for Primary Mathematics Teachers Education Programs. Utrecht: Nederlandse Vereniging tot Ontwikkeling van het Reken/Wiskindeonderwija, 1997.

Finholt, T., and Olson, G. "From Laboratories to Collaboratories: A New Organizational Form for Scientific Collaboratories." *Psychological Science,* 1997, *8,* 28–36.

Frederiksen, J. R. "Learning to See: Scoring Video Portfolios or 'Beyond the Hunter-Gatherer' in Performance Assessment." Paper presented at the Annual Meeting of the American Educational Research Association, San Francisco, 1992.

Greeno, J. G., Collins, A., and Resnick, L. B. "Cognition and Learning." In D. C. Berliner and R. C. Colfee (eds.), *Handbook of Educational Psychology* (pp. 15–16). New York: Macmillan, 1996.

Hawkins, J., and Collins, A. (eds.). *Design Experiments: Using Technology to Restructure Schools.* New York: Cambridge University Press, forthcoming.

MacWhinney, B. *The Child's Project: Tools for Analyzing Talk.* (2nd ed.) Hillsdale, N.J.: Erlbaum, 1995.

Scardamalia, M., and Bereiter, C. "Engaging Students in a Knowledge Society." *Educational Leadership,* 1996, *54*(3), 6–10.

Stigler, J. W., and Hiebert, J. "Understanding and Improving Classroom Mathematics Instruction: An Overview of the TIMMS Video Study." *Phi Delta Kappan,* 1997, *79*(1), 14–21.

CHAPTER FOURTEEN

Research, Reform, and Aims in Education

Modes of Action in Search of Each Other

James G. Greeno
Ray McDermott
Karen A. Cole
Randi A. Engle
Shelley Goldman
Jennifer Knudsen
Beatrice Lauman
Charlotte Linde

As education researchers we want and expect the field to provide a better understanding of the activities and practices of education and to contribute to the improvement of those activities and practices. Many ways of organizing education research and practice put distance and barriers between these goals, often by emphasizing the inclusion of education research in the basic research of academic disciplines. Although some aspects of distance and barriers can be beneficial, this chapter examines a way to organize activities of education research and practice so that they interact more directly.

As citizens we want and expect students to acquire a knowledge and appreciation of fundamental academic disciplines and to master the personal and institutional affairs of their current and future lives. Many ways of organizing

The Middle-School Mathematics Applications Project (MMAP) for curriculum development and research was supported by the National Science Foundation with grants MDR–9154119 and ESI–9452771. Our reflective analyses of the collaborative processes of design, development, and research in MMAP were supported by the National Science Foundation with grant ESI–9450522. We thank Rogers Hall for carrying out the transfer task for an early version of the Antarctica curriculum, Judit Moschkovich for her recollections about her role as assessment coordinator, 1994–1996, and Seth Chaiklin and Mariane Hedegaard for reading an early draft of this chapter. In his comments, Mike Atkin rightly pointed out that the tie between our theoretical frame (pragmatism and situative approaches to cognition) and our results may be happenstance. Other theoretical languages, for example, the language of action research (Atkin, 1992) or activity theory (Cole, 1996), may serve just as well. The framework we used worked for us, and we can recommend it without dismissing other theoretical languages.

school and nonschool activities put distance and barriers between these goals. Although some aspects of distance and barriers can be beneficial, this chapter examines a way to organize and use the activities of school mathematics learning so that they interact more directly.

The opportunity to confront the traditional barriers to cooperation across various interest groups concerned with schooling and education research developed as part of our research and development work on the Middle-School Mathematics Applications Project (MMAP). Since 1991 a group of researchers, curriculum developers, teachers, and occasional practicing mathematicians and scientists have been building, at the Institute for Research on Learning at Stanford University, applications-based design materials for children to learn mathematics in a hands-on fashion. Our goal has been to engage all children, including those currently underserved by the school system, in finding solutions to simulated real-world problems, in the process involving them in conversations and calculations leading to a mastery of proportional reasoning and function and other topics crucial to middle school mathematics. Each revision in the design has gone through multiple iterations, from idea to plan to mockup to classroom use to the analysis of classroom practices, and then back again through the same cycle before starting again. Teachers, researchers, and curriculum developers, both simultaneously and in sequence, have all touched most steps in each production cycle. Input and cooperation from many angles of vision have been so essential to each design that we have begun to think more carefully about how education research has become fractured and how it might be put back together.

Our argument, and the project in which we have developed it, draws much from a view of knowing and learning expressed by American pragmatists, especially John Dewey and George Herbert Mead. The domains of knowing, learning, and doing are often considered to be different, even immiscible. We argue —and support our argument with examples—that the boundaries separating these domains need not be as firm as they tend to be in American education and education research. That is, the aims and conduct of education and education research can be formulated and carried out to achieve more coordinated and integrated knowing and learning in action by students, educators, and researchers.

Our project, and the argument we have developed in it, complicates the relations of knowing and learning in disciplines with knowing and learning in practices where disciplinary knowledge is the resource. We do *not* argue that discipline-based knowledge for its own sake is unimportant. On the contrary, the development of concepts, perspectives, and methods for understanding fundamental principles in the inquiries of academic disciplines is a crucial part of the intellectual process. What we argue for is a different relation of that work to education. Regarding education research and practice, we complicate the relation between what is often cast as fundamental research or applied research and the conduct and reform of practice. Regarding the aims and conduct of education, we complicate the relation between what is often cast as knowing and learning abstractly in a discipline and knowing and learning grounded in and directed toward the experience and practical activities of students' present and future lives.

We have a conclusion: given an interactive formulation of the relations between theory and practice, it is possible for researchers, teachers, and curriculum developers to work together for extended periods of time in the development of environments in which children can learn. Something like this is said at the beginning of every research proposal. Why should we be surprised? We said it, for example, in our MMAP proposal (Goldman, Greeno, McDermott, and Pake, 1991), where we called for putting researchers and computer scientists in classrooms, for having teachers, mathematicians, and physical scientists build curricula together, and for having all of them in touch with the children who were being asked to learn. The surprise, in our case, is that it worked, and it is partly the job of this chapter to describe how that happened.

Somehow, in the United States, we have evolved education institutions that have obscured the relation between what has to be learned by children and what they need to know as adults (Varenne and McDermott, 1998). In contrast we must now struggle to build institutions where different kinds of knowledge —teacher knowledge, researcher knowledge, children's knowledge—are reintroduced and reunited in a vision of what adult citizens need to know and, accordingly, what children must learn in school. Our excitement rests in our gradually emergent understanding that the pragmatic and situative models of knowing and learning understood as practices—models that guided our development of curriculum materials and classroom practice—are also a good way to guide the interaction among the various interests that drive teachers, curriculum developers, and researchers. As researchers trying to organize a reform, we must be clear not only about the aims of education for children but about our own aims as well. We need to create a new kind of research community that reorganizes our engagements, knowledge practices, and educational products. Anything less is likely to leave established hierarchies in place, with researchers locked out of practice and practitioners locked out of research. Anything less, in leaving bad enough alone, stands to make things worse.

Almost a century ago, Mead argued that in a democracy, there should be little place for an expert to stand alone. Every attempt to direct conduct by a fixed idea of the future must be not only a failure but pernicious (1899, p. 371; see also Feffer, 1993, for the historical context). For Mead, as for his colleague Dewey (1927, 1938), expert knowledge is better seen as a working hypothesis that must enter a community of practice and jostle apparent knowledge until it takes root in a reorganization of what people can do with each other. "Reflective consciousness," warned Mead (1899), "does not then carry us on to the world that is to be, but puts our own thought and endeavor into the very process of evolution" (p. 371). Mead's position has strong implications for a conception of knowledge as it is gathered by researchers, used by practitioners and reformers, and learned by citizens seemingly not in the know. Because children are the most obvious case of people in need of received knowledge, viewing knowledge as a working hypothesis has vast implications for education.

In the century since the pragmatists started to build a democratic conception of knowledge as patterned activity in the world, the United States has moved as a culture into a deepening sense of theoretical knowledge as hierarchically arranged and separate from the activities of practitioners who would apply it in mundane settings. The division between theory and practice frames the terms in which the aims of education are formulated and achieved, as well as the ways in which knowledge about education is thought to be produced and used. Within this view, those interested in education and education reform face the problems of where to get knowledge, how to use it, and what its ends are. In the United States, there is the further problem that answers to these questions have been formatted and institutionalized: we operate as if we know that knowledge is in the academic disciplines. Within this formulation, to ask what students should learn is to ask what parts of the knowledge residing in the disciplines should be transmitted to students. It is authenticated by experts' telling educators what is valid for them to transmit. Similarly, to seek reform is to ask how knowledge in the disciplines of education research (psychology, sociology, and others) can be distributed by experts' telling practitioners what to do. Success is measured by tests that report how many specific bits of disciplinary knowledge students can demonstrate proficiently, whether measured by enhanced performance over set performance standards, over their peers, or over the collective performance of other nations.

Mead's formulation has more to recommend it than has much current practice. To the extent that received wisdom as to what knowledge is, how it is used, and how children learn it is part of the system that has manufactured so much failure in our schools, efforts at reform must do more than get new kinds of knowledge, apply it differently, and reconceive its assessment in the schools; such efforts must compete with received wisdom for epistemological authenticity and institutional license.

The authentication of knowledge entirely in academic disciplines conflicts with an important constraint on aims in education, stated by Dewey (1916) as follows:

> An aim must be capable of translation into a method of cooperating with the activities of those undergoing instruction. It must suggest the kind of environ-

ment needed to liberate and organize *their* capacities. . . . The vice of externally imposed ends has deep roots. Teachers receive them from superior authorities; these authorities accept them from what is current in the community. The teachers impose them upon children. As a first consequence, the intelligence of the teacher is not free; it is confined to receiving the aims laid down from above. Too rarely is the individual teacher so free from the dictation of authoritative supervisor, textbook on methods, prescribed course of study, etc., that he can let his mind come to close quarters with the pupil's mind and the subject matter. This distrust of the teacher's experience is then reflected in lack of confidence in the responses of pupils. The latter receive their aims through a double or treble external imposition, and are constantly confused by the conflict between the aims which are natural to their own experience at the time and those in which they are taught to acquiesce. Until the democratic criterion of the intrinsic significance of every growing experience is recognized, we shall be intellectually confused by the demand for adaptation to external aims [pp. 108–109].

Licensing knowledge for practice by standards unconnected with that practice conflicts with treating expert knowledge as working hypotheses. Nearly a half century after Mead's declaration that democratic knowledge must always be understood as a working hypothesis, Dewey (1939) noted his disappointment with the fate of working hypotheses if they are reentered not into a perfect democracy where they could be judged for the good of all, but into an America filled with competitive divisions and prejudices that hierarchically turn the losses of one side of the community into the gains of the other:

The problem of creation of genuine democracy cannot be successfully dealt with in theory or in practice save as we create intellectual and moral integration out of present disordered conditions. Splits, divisions between attitudes emotionally and congenially attuned to the past and habits that are forced into existence because of the necessity of dealing with present conditions are a chief cause of continued profession of devotion to democracy by those who do not think nor act day by day in accord with the moral demands of the profession [1939].

In such a world, research is difficult, and reform is even more difficult.

This chapter offers a report of progress in how we think about the knowledge we seek in our research and invite children to engage with in school. The key idea in both cases involves removing boundaries between knowledge in the disciplines and the domains of practical activity, while reforming the process of knowledge acquisition in middle school mathematics classrooms and in education research. We noted that the knowledge problem, as it is usually understood, is to figure out what knowledge is, how to use it, and how others can learn it, the order being from epistemological, through practical, to pedagogical. Our project took a different approach: we experimented with combining our ideas about social environments for learning, pedagogy, and mathematical practices in an agenda of both

research and practice. To change the mathematics learning of traditionally alien-
ated students, we had to reorganize their sense of how school mathematics is
accomplished and how and under what conditions they should act mathematically. We set out to work across the usual boundaries separating school curricula, mathematical knowledge, and real-world relevance. We did not have this
all figured out in advance, and we had to force ourselves to consider new ideas
of what constituted mathematics and mathematics knowledge—how it could
engage both teachers and students and how we (researchers, curriculum developers, teachers, and students) might recognize it if, in practice, it took different
communicative forms from the ones normally seen in classrooms.

With time, we have had results. We have seen mathematics classrooms function as a nexus of resources and challenges for encouraging growth in students'
knowing, understanding, and other activities. We can describe teacher and student knowledge interacting reflexively with researcher knowledge, thereby
working across the usual boundaries of education research, classroom and disciplinary practice, teaching, and assessment. We restructured these relations by
designing computational resources and curricula in a collaborative team of
teachers, author-designers, and researchers. Our task as researchers has shifted
to the documentation of border crossing in these classrooms as we have sought
new theoretical understandings, on the one hand, of the relations among disciplinary content, teaching, and learning and the production of classroom change,
on the other. The excitement is in seeing the two hands working together.

Our view stands in contrast to traditional ones, by which the teacher is a primary resource, responsible for organizing and monitoring students' activities.
In the standard view, the conceptual frames and materials provided for the
teacher and students—from textbooks to computer programs—are produced in
a two-stage process and delivered to classrooms. In the first stage, the community of disciplinary professionals produces the concepts, principles, and methods that are the certified contents of the curriculum. In the second stage, groups
of authors and designers produce the texts and other materials for classrooms,
either with a disciplinary professional included in the group or with such a person's consultation. Although the authors of curriculum materials often have
considerable teaching experience, the teachers who use the materials are generally considered as implementers and end users rather than as contributors to
design and content.

The guiding principle of our research and development project was to focus
on *participation structures* in which people from disparate communities could
construct practices productive for classroom learning and contribute to several
communities beyond the scope of our project. We focus on participation structures to alert readers to classroom work groups as the ultimate site for laying
out our mix of theory and practice. (The term has a more technical history in
the work of Phillips, 1972, and Erickson and Mohatt, 1982; it is directly related

to work on "involvement structures" [Goffman, 1971] and "attentional structures" [Chance, 1966] and less directly related to work on "behavioral settings" [Barker and Schoggan, 1973].) The classroom activities of our curriculum were designed to offer students connections between their experience with mathematics outside school, their experience with mathematics in school, and their projection into a life with mathematics beyond schooling. We were vigilant in maintaining authenticity in the mathematical content and practices invited by the curriculum, understanding that we owed students a legitimate introduction to the discipline. Teachers participated with us in curriculum development and research and with mathematics-using professionals in engineering, architecture, science, and other communities, in the hope that they could bring first-person experience to the students. The designer-authors were integrally involved in the research program and, with researchers, participated in the observational study of uses of their products in classrooms. The researchers participated in the design of materials, in working with the materials in middle school classrooms, and in discussions and analyses of learning and teaching practices.

Our description proceeds in an order that resembles how the work unfolded. We begin with the MMAP story and its consequences for how knowledge is approached in theory and practice. We explain the goals of MMAP and how we developed computer resources and curricula with the purpose of giving children reasons for learning mathematics and the material means for enhancing their efforts. Then we offer two case studies that illustrate our growing sense of how a learning community with shared, multiple commitments evolves knowledge and engages practical activities that, in turn, shape innovation. The overall story told through the case studies is that constant effort to keep researchers, teachers, and curriculum developers interacting and sharing their visions, concerns, and practices can strengthen what is ultimately made available to children in classrooms and offers all involved an alternative view of what counts as knowledge. The first case study concerns the problem of adequate assessment of students' mathematical knowledge, and our discussion covers two areas of concern: our gradual realization of the extent of work directly required on the problem of assessment and our efforts to design assessment systems that could meet the competing demands of teachers, curriculum developers, and researchers as they reported results to their professional communities. The second case study tells the same overall story, although it focuses on content issues in mathematics education. It describes the concern of researchers and teachers for a definition of "function" in middle school mathematics and reports how the research and development community acted on the concern.

Next, we offer a brief account of our work on issues of teaching practice that challenged the normal sense of what counts as mathematical knowledge in the classrooms, what counts as expert research knowledge once it is carried into classrooms, and what counts as contributions to research findings that can be carried back to the disciplines. We also report our growing sense of the gains to be made from cooperation among teachers, curriculum developers, and researchers.

THE MMAP CURRICULUM

MMAP makes a contribution to the goal of democratic learning that Dewey expressed as the pursuit of an educational aim translated "into a method of cooperating with the activities of those undergoing instruction" in "the kind of environment needed to liberate and to organize *their* capabilities" (1916, p. 108). The MMAP curriculum presents mathematics as a resource for activities not represented primarily by mathematics. Instead, the main activities are design projects—of floor plans for buildings, models for population growth and decline, codes, or geographical maps—all in the service of mathematical representation.

This approach to curriculum differs dramatically from the standard progression through mathematical topics, but its feasibility is supported by large bodies of research on everyday mathematics (Lave, 1988; Lave and Wenger, 1991; Nunes, Schliemann, and Carraher, 1993; Saxe, 1990) and on children's intuitive understanding of concepts of number and quantity (Carpenter, Fennema, and Romberg, 1993; Greeno, 1992; Harel and Confrey, 1994). The results of this research demonstrate that children are capable of significant mathematical understanding and reasoning when they are supported in activities that provide meaningful organization for the kinds of questions, problems, and representations that help mathematics make sense (Greeno and Goldman, 1998; Lampert, 1990).

As a MMAP curriculum is presented to children, first come problems in the world that require designs for their solutions—for example, a floor plan for a house that can be heated for ten years without exceeding certain cost limitations. Next come activities organized to achieve more specific solutions—for example, cutting outside wall space or increasing insulation to balance construction and heating costs. There is an obvious need for mathematics in these tasks. Sure enough, once the children have invested time and personal identity in modeling their house on the computer, they are excited about heating it efficiently. They willingly engage in mathematics work. They rarely ask why they have to learn mathematics, for the reasons are apparent in their design work. Everyone participates and hopefully prospers. Mathematics is accomplished. The children learn (and not just those who knew how to do the math before they started); teachers have a more informed group of students to teach; curriculum developers get new ideas from watching teacher and students in action; researchers get to restock conceptual tool kits as they see new kinds of results; and reformers can be reminded again of the power of the children who are usually left out of school mathematics.

Having gathered the best ideas and the right people, what was the possibility we could put our minds together to create materials that could help children learn mathematics, in a limited school-like fashion and, more important, in ways befitting citizens using mathematics to solve problems? Even if we assume that all parties to curriculum research projects are well intentioned, it was easy to imagine why they usually would not cooperate with each other extensively. "No time" is the most frequent and the most polite refrain. Nor is it ever difficult to elicit researcher accounts of what the teachers do not understand or teacher accounts of the airhead impracticality of researchers and their obtuse theorizing. Such tensions go deep in the education world, and they can kill discussion and cooperation before significant inputs can be given by the parties to any given project.

There may be a few reasons that MMAP was not plagued by such divisions. First, we were the beneficiaries of generous funding from the National Science Foundation (NSF), and we could pay teachers to participate. Second, many of our researchers had been teachers, and some of our teachers became researchers and curriculum developers. Third, we were integrating computers into the math curriculum, and the lure of technology allowed both a focus and a rallying point across groups. Fourth, and to us most important, the researchers and curriculum developers on our project generally believed that the teachers and children, in some significant sense, knew more about the circumstances of school than did the researchers and developers.

In planning the curriculum during the first summer of the project (1992), we met with about seven teachers for a five-week workshop (the project grew to over thirty teachers over the six years, and hundreds of teachers not associated with the project have used our early software efforts). When we began, we had curriculum principles, a prototype of a computerized design environment, and a few ideas about how to structure classroom activities. The teachers responded to these preliminary plans vigorously and in detail and collaborated with us in developing each new draft ad seriatim. As we proceeded, the teachers provided the decisive evaluations of what was and what was not working, basing their judgments on what was engaging and productive for their students. If something did not work in one iteration, then we had to change it for the next iteration, rather than assuming it was the fault of weak teaching or weak learning. We never allowed ourselves the luxury of a complaint about how our "clients" were not capable of doing what we had planned.

The realities under which we modified the curriculum were always in the classroom, always in the outcome as lived by teachers and students. Often we had to give up pieces of our distant vision in order to tune into classroom life. In our work with teachers about how they must pay attention to and learn from their students, we tried to create a community in which everyone could find the good sense of everyone else. As long as we stayed open to the teachers, we could together build materials that could stay open to the children; and if we did this together as part of a community, we might be able to make connections between the learning of children and the roles they might take on in their adult lives. Surprisingly, if we did all this, we could also make new connections between the knowledge the researchers gathered and the communities their ideas might serve.

In order to develop a new kind of math curriculum that would make a difference for underserved students, we were guided by the maxim that students would learn best from the same kinds of conditions we would build up for our own learning. If an approach were to meet our standards, it would not be enough to develop new classroom materials; rather, the materials would have to work in classrooms to invite children into conversations and inquiries about things they found relevant. We needed to stretch our researcher perspectives to work on curriculum, teaching, learning, assessment, and technology that would engage students' participation.

The challenge of MMAP was to embed democracy in a curriculum medium. Our commitments were these:

- To bring to the curriculum design process a collaborative community that included education researchers, teachers and teacher educators, curriculum developers, math-using professionals, and students

- To define and test the feasibility of an applications-based approach to learning math in middle schools by creating a series of units and assessments that responded to national standards

- To integrate technologies into the mathematics classroom

- To conduct research to improve on our materials design, generate new understandings of mathematics teaching and learning, and help reform math classrooms

MMAP is now a comprehensive middle school curriculum comprising three approaches to mathematics work: applications, extensions, and investigations. The nine applications projects plunge students into extended role play, in which they work for "design companies," creating codes, floor plans, and maps or biological models. Mathematical concepts and skills are integrated and developed along the way. The design contexts provide intuitively grounded reasons and resources for developing the mathematics. As a result, students who have previously been disengaged from mathematics can find new reasons to participate and find their common sense validated and applied to mathematics. Extensions, such as "Problems with Proportions" and "Counting in the Wild," build directly on the mathematical insights and skills students have developed within the major design units, introducing them to the standard mathematical notations associated with concepts, such as proportion, and helping them develop specific skills such as manipulating algebraic expressions or establishing a proof in geometry. Investigations, such as "Geometry in Quilting" and "Prove It!" introduce other mathematical concepts within more fanciful contexts or from a pure mathematics point of view. In these units, students learn, for example, geometric vocabulary in the context of quilting or methods of proof while exploring relationships between even and odd integers.

MMAP integrates computer software with all applications projects. To date we have developed four modeling and simulation environments supporting nine units of study. Each unit is designed to last for six weeks of classroom time, although there is considerable flexibility in how they can be used and how long they might last. Paper materials and technology are bundled together with guides for teachers to sequence lessons and activities. We offer three illustrative examples of the nine project-based units.

The Antarctica project places students in the role of architectural designers commissioned to create an economical and effective (well-heated) research station for scientists in Antarctica. Students use MMAP-designed ArchiTech software to create floor plans of their designs, investigate the relation of their design to varying environmental conditions, and generate and analyze data about building and heating costs. The central mathematical topics are scale, proportion, and functions. Students grapple with ratios as connectors between the real world and the ArchiTech screen. They come to understand subtle features of scaled representations, such as constancy, over the entire drawing, and they experience firsthand what it means to change an independent variable (insulation R-value), while holding others constant (outside and inside temperature), in order to investigate effects on dependent variables (the cost of heating). They carefully interpret graphs and charts of functional relations to make the best design to withstand Antarctic winters.

The Wolves and Caribou project requires students to explore dynamic relations among wildlife populations in Alaska. Students explore the question of whether and how to control wolf populations to increase caribou populations and then propose a policy to the state government. Students use HabiTech software to model population growth over time as it is affected by birth, death, and immigration and emigration rates. Middle school math topics of functions, rates, and use of variables are central to this unit aimed at seventh and eighth graders. Assessing and using "messy" data and discovering the limitations of models are other important insights made possible by this unit. Students must "crunch" a number of given rates into the one they need to determine birth and death rates for wolf and caribou populations. They enter this rate (in the form of a decimal or percentage) into a function box for birth rate or death rate and then set how often the rate will be applied (for example, monthly, seasonally). HabiTech shows students what happens to population growth as a result of these functions. As students try to emulate five-year population trends, they develop qualitative notions of how differences in rate affect populations. They carry out repeated experiments with various rates over a short period of time and get access to generated data in graph or chart form. Based on their mathematical model and comparisons with historical data, students then design a policy regarding wolves and caribou that the Alaskan government can put into action.

In Codes Inc.: Privacy, students are cryptologists who create privacy codes to a client's specification. Each client presents a different set of constraints, such as word length or use of numbers or letters in the encoded text. Students have two on-line coding tools available in the Coding Toolbox: a Function Tool and a Matrix Tool. These tools allow students to develop ideas and language around functions as well as number theory concepts to make and break codes. The view of functions is a set-theoretic one in which students learn about properties such as one-to-one correspondence, terms such as *domain* and *range*, and methods of determining formulas such as finite differences.

MMAP applications, together with extensions and investigations, form a balanced and comprehensive mathematical diet for middle schoolers. All National Council of Teachers of Mathematics (NCTM, 1989) Standards are addressed, and students have opportunities to develop important skills and concepts in each unit of study. MMAP abandons the traditional sequential approach to skill development and combines multiple mathematics topics in each single unit. The mathematical content of MMAP focuses heavily on two central areas of middle school mathematics: proportional reasoning and algebra/function. Middle school is the time for important transitions within each of these areas. Consequently math topics are revisited over a series of MMAP units in a variety of real-world and mathematical contexts. Although much of the context for learning is experiential, extensions make explicit implicit understandings developed within the applications projects and thereby allow students access to established mathematical tools and notations.

CASE STUDIES IN THEORY AND PRACTICE

We present two case studies that display the interaction of theory and practice in MMAP. One began as a teacher-initiated effort to deal with problems of assessment. The other began as a researcher-initiated inquiry into children's understanding of functions. In both cases, we offer an account of the practical problem (in the first case, a crisis) that brought our attention to an issue in the classroom and school, the curriculum rebuilding that attended to the problem, and the theoretical headaches that resulted from and guided work with the problems. For both cases, we can follow the problem management until it generated products: pedagogical practices for the teachers, software and text-based materials for the curriculum builders, and research reports for the theoretically minded. What happened between crisis and product is what we hope to reveal in our brief descriptions. In both cases, the description depends on an account of a rope built out of three fibers—teachers, curriculum builders, and researchers—for the purposes of accomplishing a long-term pedagogical goal.

The Assessment Case Study

From the onset of the project, like everyone else working on mathematics reform (Lesh and Lamon, 1992), everyone in our project was interested in alternative forms of assessment. The project was built around the creation of contexts in which children could participate in mathematics as it functioned in the real world, and we knew that traditional tests of skills out of context, as on standardized tests, would be systematically even more unfair to MMAP children than to the rest of the country's schoolchildren. Even in our proposal, we recognized the need for embedded assessments that would not only capture what the children had learned but ideally enhance what they were learning at any moment. That having been said, we did not know just what embedded assessments would look like in our classrooms, what teachers, students, and parents would want, or what would be most effective.

The First Stage: Identifying Our Problem. We started with two forms of embedded assessment that proved inadequate by everyone's standards. First, we had teachers keeping track of "math opportunities," those delicate moments in the children's interaction with MMAP materials when teachers would decide the time was right to introduce new mathematical concepts, activities, or skills to help the students with next steps in the project. Math opportunities would require students to ask questions or state observations when they were stuck; they would require teachers to track the students' mathematical engagements, activities, and conversations. We had hoped a record of the mathematical opportunities that children encountered in the course of working on a project would give us good, context-sensitive accounts of the children's learning; we also thought it would better enable teachers to offer a hand-tailored math program with systematic feedback to students as they were doing their work.

In our second form of embedded assessment, we asked the children to do presentations of their final designs to the whole class. In working with ArchiTech, for example, we asked them to present to the class the general features of the living space they designed on the computer and then to enter their design into a competition for its merit relative to the cost of building, cost of heating, efficiency of space, and the other parameters.

Two problems emerged across the first year. It seemed that not enough math opportunities were engaged by the children, or, if they were, they were not readily noticed as math moments by teachers or students. Most class time was videotaped, and it fell to the researchers to search for the math in the children's activities. In interviews the children told us they loved their new math class because it was fun to use the computers and great to pick up real-life architectural skills. When asked if they were learning any math, they looked blankly at us: "No math, but we're learning about the real world." Back with the videotapes, we saw students wrestling with scale and proportion and sometimes analyzing the complex relationships among variables in their designs, such as the costs of heating and the insulation values. But the students could not identify the math, and the teachers were uncertain about what math was actually accomplished in the groups. By the time the researchers found and described the math being worked on by the students, it was, relative to classroom realities, irrelevant. The question was: Is math really being accomplished if no one in the classroom can see it?

We had a crisis on all levels. The curriculum was not providing enough resources for locating math opportunities in student work. It needed boosting. The teachers had strong intuitions that kids were making important progress with mathematics, but the *en passant* approach to math opportunities was not productive for either teacher or student accountability. More opportunities were passed over than taken up, and too few memories of math moments appeared stored away for future use.

The embedded assessment situation further deteriorated when the final presentations offered little opportunity for students to demonstrate the complexity of their mathematics accomplishments. A presentation is a particular kind of social ritual (the same can be said of tests), and one's performance often bears little relation to what was worked on, learned for the moment, or really learned across time. Hours of argument, discussion, and experiments with variables in the designs came down to a sentence-long, matter-of-fact report about the final design product. On videotape, we saw children working hard during group time, yet in presentations they were reporting they "did nothing." When students were encouraged, as part of their presentations, to explain the mathematics they worked on, they almost all presented lists of rates and costs of specific design variables. They tended to have extremely limited ideas about what constituted mathematics. The research staff was part of the audience for the presentations and asked students questions. The students' answers made it clear that they were capable of talking in quite detailed ways about the math they had accomplished and how they had accomplished it. We knew the final presentations were an inadequate gloss on what the students knew.

With the teachers leading the way, we turned our attention to strengthening the unit activities with assessment opportunities. The teachers lamented that although they would sometimes have remarkably complex math conversations with children, they were hard pressed in meetings with parents to say what the children had learned. Imagine, for example, the children we interviewed telling their parents math class was great, because it was fun and helped to deliver life skills even if they did not do much math. We—researchers, teachers, developers, and children—were all potentially in trouble with parents and school administrators. We were all potentially in trouble with the communities we needed to speak to in our own work world—researchers to their respective fields and funders, teachers, principals, parents, and the curriculum developers to their peers, potential publishers, and potential users.

The Second Stage: Creating an Embedded Set of Assessments. The three groups—researchers, teachers, and curriculum developers—merged their interests and started to work on more specific unit activities and assessment tools that would improve the curriculum. Two sets of concerns emerged: first, the need for specific curriculum materials revealing students' everyday progress, and second, a worry that the high-stakes standardized test scores so integral to school life would be adversely affected by time spent in MMAP activities.

Developing materials and techniques to solve the assessment problem became a central project focus. The researchers began conversations with other assessment researchers and math projects. We tried to find out what progress others had made toward creating assessments that were full-bodied exhibitions of students' understanding as well as potential learning experiences in themselves, and not a waste of everyone's time. In weekly meetings, the group began to coordinate a set of activities, some based on techniques already in use and some newly created to address the unique applications-based experiences.

First, the assessment group worked out a variety of activities that would guide students to notice, name, and develop the math they encountered in their project work. The students were asked to write about their work in a math journal in which their daily writing focused just on math activities. Math reflections came at strategic points in the projects and invited in-depth accounts of how mathematics was used to improve some aspect of student designs. Math maps required students to produce pictorial accounts showing the unit as a journey through math topics. These documents, we thought, could be used as resources during conversations between students and teachers to bring mathematics front and center. They were meant to provide more opportunities for students to make mathematics connections orally, visually, and in writing.

Second, the assessment groups were interested in designing short tasks that would neatly but comprehensively capture the math power that students had developed during units. They designed a near-transfer task for one of the units and piloted it in field tests. The students were given a design for a dormitory for a warm climate, including the cost to heat it for ten years. The assessment task asked them to move the building to a cold area and to heat it for ten years without changing the costs; walls had to be moved, windows removed, insulation installed (one group wanted to buy all inhabitants sweaters, a change our software cannot accommodate). Many children found this task to be a good opportunity to articulate their learning.

Third, because we had noticed that teachers working with MMAP spent much of their time "grazing," that is, walking around during project work, finding out what students were learning, and orienting them toward the math in their work, we designed record-keeping devices that teachers could carry and use to make note of specific math concepts, skills, and strategies they saw during classroom lessons. We also added peer assessments for students to check on developments in the projects.

And fourth, members of the assessment group tried to catalogue the set of background concerns that guided teachers' day-to-day decisions (Knudsen, 1994; also discussed by Greeno and MMAP, 1997). Three major ongoing concerns were woven into the design of the assessment materials. First, there was a concern for getting the math in—making sure students spent their time productively learning math. Second, there was a concern for getting the math out—making sure math was extracted from projects in a way that satisfied accountability to the outside world. Third, there was a concern for equity—making sure all students had access to experiences that would help them both learn math and show their progress.

With these four interventions we hoped to produce a variety of assessment media that would give students with different strengths ways to display mathematical progress. The activities were designed to make conjectures, products, and explanations the focus of collective negotiation and provide opportunities for individual and group assessment. Our field tests confirmed that the assessment materials helped students to see their own mathematical growth and helped teachers judge student progress more fully. For each type of assessment activity, students produced examples of highly analytic and reflective mathematical thinking. We also found great variability in the quality of mathematical reflection in student assessment products. One student's journal entry might record a group's detailed analytic exploration and resulting new understanding, while another student's journal entry consisted of two sentences listing the day's classroom activities. Our videotapes and field notes showed that the quality of student assessment documents did not necessarily correspond to the quality of the work the documents were meant to record. Rich work sometimes resulted in fairly impoverished journal entries or presentations. Finally, we noted that any new assessment activity requires students to become familiar with new formats and standards, a significant effort when condensed into a single six-week unit. Students also needed to develop, as a regular practice, writing skills in the content areas if journals were to be successful assessment tools.

The Third Stage: Developing Assessments as Systematic Activities. Guided by such findings, new assessment materials were reviewed during teacher workdays, revised, and incorporated into all the curriculum units. Teachers began to use the techniques, researchers began to watch teachers use them, and developers continued to rewrite those that seemed to cause misunderstanding. During teacher work days, teachers shared student work that emerged from the MMAP menu of alternative assessment techniques, and they talked about what they got from the work and how they could evaluate it. There was no last word on alternative assessments. Some knowledge was held by the teachers, and some was emerging as working hypotheses for the researchers. Mainly the group was figuring out what it was doing as it went. Whenever assessment was the focus, teachers identified what they wanted students to learn, what they needed to do with assessments, and the information that would help them most.

The process of talking together about assessment was both productive and inescapable. A few people began to develop a video-based assessment casebook that would serve as a discussion catalyst for any group of teachers who wanted to talk about assessment. The raw material for the video cases came from research tapes, in which the researchers had captured teachers and students conversing mathematically. Piloting these cases at teacher work days convinced everyone that talking about assessment was worth continuing (IRL, 1998).

The Fourth Stage: Institutionalizing a Process Within the Community. The Assessment Club began as one teacher and one researcher who planned together and piloted the use of a MMAP assessment system. Others followed suit and began to focus on assessment during the 1996 MMAP summer institute. Soon most MMAP teachers were participating, and teachers from other reform projects started to join. The Assessment Club became part of every project work day.

The Assessment Club was built around the collaborative development of teachers' assessment systems. Given one teacher's success in integrating a few assessment techniques to form a coherent system, others were eager to try similar systems, and everyone worked together to plan systems that would be practical and useful in each club member's classroom. The focus of assessment research shifted to finding out how different techniques could be used together to help students proactively get more out of the curriculum.

To understand how the Assessment Club helped teachers improve their capacity to use performance-based assessments, consider the following events:

- A teacher shared journal entries in which her students wrote about fractions. Club members discussed what the writing revealed about each student's understanding of fractions and how to help students write entries that are more mathematical. The discussion helped teachers design better prompts for assessing through written assignments.

- An Institute for Research on Learning research scientist shared videos of peer reviews that took place in one club member's classroom. Noting some unnecessary student harshness toward the work of peers, teachers and IRL staff together developed an improved way to structure peer reviews. The new organization was then successfully piloted in another member's classroom and resulted in focused, businesslike peer reviews.

316 ISSUES IN EDUCATION RESEARCH

- The group created a project to find ways to have in-depth mathematical discussions with their students as a standard daily practice. Several teachers went back to their classrooms to have mathematical discussion conferences with small groups of students while the class worked on other activities. They came to the next Assessment Club meeting reporting that the conferences were both exhilarating and exhausting. The Assessment Club continued to work on ways to make the conferences more practical and useful.

- Applause all around, because a teacher who was afraid to use journals as an assessment had not only made it through a whole year of journals but decided to conduct professional development activities on student journals for other teachers in her school.

These stories illustrate a balance the Assessment Club managed to strike between structure and flexibility. The group met monthly and had an agreed-on set of working concerns, but goals, experiments, and materials all evolved out of the conversations and classroom experiences of teachers and researchers.

The story of the assessment struggle in MMAP is a demonstration of the problems and epistemological concerns we set out in the introduction to this chapter. There is certainly, in the world, received knowledge about assessment, even about nontraditional assessment. The researchers could have decided to conduct "Assessment Class" instead of Assessment Club and attempted to transfer this knowledge to teachers. Instead we all got smarter about assessment in much the same way we expect our middle school students to get smarter about mathematics. We got smarter the old-fashioned way, by working together.

The assessment group, however, had a problem. In search of a solution, we began by treating our own and others' experiences as working hypotheses. As we adapted and piloted assessments in teachers' classrooms, we changed our views about what assessments could and should do. We were always more interested in the "accessment" issues hidden in all school assessments. We had new working hypotheses about how to help students learn mathematics in ways that can be demonstrated to significant others—from parents, through institutional measuring systems, on out to research colleagues. The Assessment Club tried out hypotheses, and there was no end in sight. If our middle school students get to do the same with mathematics researchers with their reports, the circle of problem solving and progress may continue.

The Functions Case Study

With the MMAP curriculum, students participate by collaboratively evolving an understanding of the problem, knowing how to use the technology, and working toward solutions emergent in their activity. Development of a genre of activity organized in this way creates a basic dilemma. Teachers and curriculum developers are accountable for students' progress in learning in the subject matter discipline of mathematics, but their activities do not fit the patterns of standard mathematics classroom practices. As a result, an analysis of ways the activities of our curriculum achieve recognizability for learning mathematical concepts and principles is a consistent and significant task of our empirical and theoretical research. We—researchers, developers, and teachers—need constantly to characterize the contents of students' activities in relation to established mathematical concepts and principles.

As our second case study, we describe work on the concept of function as it emerged as part of the general issue of presenting mathematical content clearly and productively. From the beginning of the project, we discussed the concept of function, along with measurement and scaling, ratio and proportion, and percentage. Function is the central concept in high school algebra, and although it is not usually emphasized in middle school, some mathematics educators have been advocating the teaching of concepts of function earlier (Kaput, 1994). Research on children's implicit understanding of functions (Greeno, 1992; Piaget, Grize, Szeminska, and Bang, 1977) has shown that we could expect students to reason successfully about functional relations, and our observations of students' work confirmed this. At the same time, research in mathematics education (Leinhardt, Zaslovsky, and Stein, 1990; Romberg, Fennema, and Carpenter, 1993) has identified the concept of function as a difficult topic for both teaching and student understanding.

Although we had a strong intuitive sense that students were learning to reason about functions, our intuition, like the students' intuition, was quite inarticulate. This was unsatisfactory for teachers, developers, and researchers, for reasons distinct but interrelated. Teachers need to communicate with students, parents, other teachers, and administrators about the mathematical content that students are learning. Developers need to be able to say what mathematical concepts and principles are in their curricula. And researchers need to relate observed learning to the theories of reasoning and problem solving discussed in the literature on cognition and instruction.

In our summer workshops, we proposed topics for working groups. If there was sufficient interest by teachers in working on a topic, a group was formed. The topic of function was proposed and adopted during the workshop held in the summer of 1995. The group met for three weeks, with approximately three one- to two-hour meetings per week. Seven participants attended regularly and four occasionally. Of the eleven participants, four were teachers, two were MMAP staff who had been teachers in the recent past, and the rest were MMAP researchers and curriculum developers. One MMAP staff member had a specific assignment to develop materials for one or more extension units on the topic of functions.

The group had a two-part agenda: to discuss what was important for middle school students to know about functions and to develop materials for extensions on functions. The functions group did not have a sharp and pressing focus like the assessment group. The teachers had not thought much about the topic and were surprisingly vague about even a basic definition of mathematical function. Curriculum developers were surprised by the lack of strong definition and were concerned that it might be difficult to create materials to remedy the situation. The researchers had to worry if the literature they had been reading and writing was connected to any classroom realities.

In group discussion, teachers talked about their experiences working with students on understanding functions and described lessons they had presented with some success. The teachers were especially interested in developing activities that could be used as homework, and they were willing to consider the concept of function as recognizable to students and parents. Group activities also included reading and discussing published research articles on children's understanding of functions. Researchers gradually recognized that the conversation could develop theoretical distinctions considered in the research literature. One distinction involves two ways in which functions can be understood, as either processes or actions. The focus of these discussions evolved over time and centered on ways to help students use representations of functions in the forms of tables, graphs, and equations.

Work on the function concept illustrates a pattern in our project of inviting joint work on design followed by separate work on development, teaching, and research. The functions group came up with four goals for new MMAP materials on functions:

- To help students develop their work with functions as objects as well as processes

- To use multiple representations of functions to build students' facility with tables, graphs, algebraic symbols, and verbal descriptions of functions

- To develop students' awareness of functions in the real world, looking for and investigating the nature of changing and related quantities in the world

- To build on students' implicit reasoning about functions in the existing MMAP design units, tying it to standard representations and various mathematical viewpoints of functions

The functions group was not driven by pressures from the wider community, and the teachers were under no pressure to show how much their students learned about functions. Still, over the course of sporadic contacts, results began to appear. By the end of the summer workshop of 1996, much to the surprise of the participants, teachers had developed a new classroom focus, curriculum developers had new materials to seed and feed the teachers' focus, and researchers were writing a report on a new role of mathematical functions in the emergence of students' math skills.

The functions group had to work much less strenuously to cross the theory and practice divide than the assessment group, for the latter had to confront more deeply and aggressively a conception of knowledge as decontextualized skill. The functions group could develop in a more haphazard fashion. When the functions conversations began, one teacher was using Wolves and Caribou with her summer school class in the morning and attending the functions group in the afternoon. She brought back to her class expanded definitions of functions and activities to use with Wolves and Caribou to highlight the function concept. Because the MMAP extensions on function were not created yet, she relied on activities from the NCTM Standards addendum on functions (Phillips, 1991) and other resources that group members uncovered and analyzed. By 1996 the teachers had produced and distributed to the summer workshop a set of notes on functions, addressing definitions, what is important for middle schoolers to know, summaries of the research studied in the group, and prototypes of function activities based on MMAP units. They created a functions pamphlet for teachers that MMAP staff members used as a prototype for teacher-to-teacher communications on central math topics in middle school.

The work on functions developed across the entire MMAP community. The curriculum team created a series of extensions and investigations that deal specifically with functions and are meant to be used before or after larger design-based MMAP units. "Patterns and Functions" helps students move from visual representations of number patterns to tables and then to equations that describe the same pattern. "Direct and Inverse Variation" helps students work with functions as objects as they classify functions into these two families and identify the resulting properties. "Connecting to Algebra" helps students develop and solidify their use of algebraic symbolism for functions. "Functions in the Real World" looks at covariation in the world, helping students develop verbal, tabular, and graphic representations of functions not easily described by a simple algebraic formula. In "Functions from Various Views," students make explicit the different implicit views of functions they get within the Codes Inc. and Wolves and Caribou MMAP units.

We describe the investigation "Functions from Various Views" functions in which population sizes change from year to year. Children can define many kinds of functions, but the software and curriculum encourage two: one in which a quantity such as number of births per year is a constant and another in which the quantity is a constant proportion of the current value of another quantity, such as the population size. These two ways of specifying function result in linear or exponential functions of growth or decline. In the investigation, students examine and reflect on these two kinds of function, considering their general properties. In Codes Inc., students construct and analyze functions that map the numbers 1 through 26 (corresponding to the letters of the alphabet) to another set of numbers, and this mapping is used to construct a sequence of numbers that encodes any message. In the investigation, students consider families of these encoding functions. The activities include graphs of linear functions with different slopes and intercepts and quadratic functions with different parameters. The activities use standard mathematical terms for functions, including the concepts of domain and range. Finally, the linear and exponential functions from Wolves and Caribou are reconsidered, noting that the domain and range of these functions are time and population size and that the variable of time was not explicit in the equations that the students specified (that is, constant or linear difference equations). Students are guided to specify how the different equations correspond to the year-to-year changes in the functions of population versus time and to construct a graph of the increments versus time to reach further understanding of the components of the functions.

Using both discussions of the summer working group and records of students working with the Wolves and Caribou curriculum as data, research activity has been undertaken on the topic of functions. From an analysis of the videotapes, researchers were able to identify how students reasoned about functions. The data analyzed came from students' constructing models of wolf and caribou population sizes. Their understanding of functions was largely ordinal, involving sound expectations of the effects of increasing or decreasing the parameters of difference equations on rates of growth or decline of populations. It will be important to conduct further research in which we examine students' coming to understand the more explicit numerical properties and terminology of functions that are developed in extensions and investigations.

ISSUES OF TEACHING PRACTICE

The case studies in the previous section are examples of collaborative efforts to construct and modify working hypotheses for the dual purpose of developing different kinds of mathematics and mathematics learning, and of advancing scientific knowledge about the mathematics and mathematics learning we were developing. In this section, we report attempts to understand the participation structures we created. Our basis for this sketch is a set of conversations—a handful in the form of structured interviews with participating teachers and staff members. It includes our own reflective impressions, of course.

From the perspectives of MMAP teachers, the project offered them time to work with other teachers, researchers, and developers without the usual feeling of being told what to do, as if their knowledge did not count. We offer their opinions not as a confirmation that we did things right with them. As we elicited their opinions, there was no analytic reason for taking their statements to be wholly impartial. Rather, we present their voices as examples of how members of one mathematics learning and teaching community sing the community song that enables all those involved to work together. Our report is not disinterested. The evaluations we present were developed as part of the project we are offering as a case study. The conversations we had with MMAP staff and teachers were conversations among colleagues participating in the project and with a mutual interest in expressing positive feelings about the success of our joint endeavor. The merits of the opinions are less in the fact that we all provided positive evaluative remarks than in the substance of the remarks regarding the specific goals and the character of the interactions described.

To understand the interactions we had as researchers, developers, and teachers, it is useful to consider the curriculum materials we produced as boundary objects (Star and Griesemer, 1989), which are materials that function in more than one of the communities of an organization. Boundary objects can support the coordination of activities, to the extent there are significant commonalities in how the materials are interpreted and used.

Researchers with Curriculum Developers

The usual boundary between development and research was blurred in our activities. Most participants in MMAP arrived with nominal roles oriented primarily toward research or toward development, and many retained a specialization. Others have taken on multiple roles, and various roles have been adopted by people with different expertise. Crossover and overlap among roles and people has had important implications for shaping both reform and research efforts within MMAP. The organization of MMAP reflects the belief that many kinds of expertise can be useful in even fairly well-defined tasks. Participants become experts by activities in the MMAP community over time. Having a big-picture understanding allows individuals to contribute to a variety of tasks, and contributing to a variety of tasks improves big-picture understanding. Roles and tasks are constantly changing.

The curriculum materials served as boundary objects to support mutual participation between researchers and developers in three settings. First, in extensive discussions about features of the materials, researchers tended to focus on ways the materials might support the learning activities the project was committed to fostering, and developers tended to focus on issues of what features were feasible to create for practical use in classrooms. In these discussions, the participants all shared responsibility for the materials being designed. The materials themselves served as the boundary objects that researchers and developers jointly constructed. The second setting for joint participation had researchers and developers observing classroom uses of the software materials. Members of the team who were authors of materials participated in the field tests, along with researchers, by operating cameras and writing field notes; everyone shared responsibility for obtaining high-quality data from the classrooms. Third, developers and researchers participated in the interactional analysis of videotapes for understanding the classroom teaching and learning that our materials supported. The primary goal of this analytic work was a description of the learning activities of students with their teachers. Researchers would eventually use these descriptions primarily in empirical and theoretical reports, and developers would use them primarily in the design of future materials, but there was a strong sense of the interdependence of these two functions, especially since many of us had some responsibility for both.

Development of the Wolves and Caribou Unit. Wolves and Caribou, one of six units developed in MMAP during its first three years, involved many MMAP staff members and teachers at one point or another, and it serves as a good example of the way roles, tasks, and people were interwoven during the creation of a unit and the research emerging from it.

Wolves and Caribou invited work in six areas: curriculum development, software development, mathematical development, teaching and testing, publishing, and research. Almost everyone worked on multiple areas. Nine staff members and teachers were substantially involved in the Wolves and Caribou activity during its main development. Responsibilities were unevenly distributed, of course, but almost everyone was involved in most of the six areas of work. This reflects an approach to the work of designing, developing, evaluating, and analyzing the materials. There was recognition, for example, that those who were designing software would benefit from being up to date on the changing nature of the curriculum, which in turn was related to the information being obtained in research efforts, and that crosstalk would be more effective if people were engaged in all activities with a share in responsibility for their success.

Despite the complications of shifting roles among the individuals involved, project members generally appreciated the opportunity to work on the research, development, and reform agendas concurrently. We present statements made by three project members regarding what they found to be both satisfying and difficult about the shared roles and multiple agendas inherent in the project:

> For me, working on research and reform at the same time improves both activities, especially because I'm working with other people who also care about and engage in both activities. I can take what we learn in analysis of classroom activities and apply that immediately to curriculum or software design, and I can look at a classroom event and formulate research questions that I know will be useful in that context. The fact that everyone around is involved in similar activities makes it easy to do research that is well grounded in school problems, since everyone else has classroom experiences to share and everyone's research results keep popping up in classroom observations. And knowing about everyone's research problems makes it easy to keep pushing the limits of the curriculum: How can we improve it so that kids have more challenge, more enriching experiences, more contact with each other's ideas?

> I like having the reform be the goal of the research. I think that makes the research much more interesting. It also can be frustrating, because what I learned in classes about experimental paradigms isn't very useful in classroom,

reform-oriented research. But it is exciting to learn new ways of doing research that can inform the questions that come out of the classroom.

The basic message is that it's worth having the conflict. If I was only doing one —research or reform—I'd be frustrated because the problem really isn't separable. In the world people use paper curriculum and think about teaching and learning at the same time, so why shouldn't my job be that? It's like what I say about curriculum, that we're not creating a curriculum, we're creating supports for curriculum, since curriculum is what kids and teachers do in the classroom. The paper and software we write just support the curriculum that happens in classrooms. So if I care about making good paper and software, I have to go see how they're used, since that's what I say they're for.

There are inherent difficulties in working in many roles at once. For example, when helping a teacher plan, a staff member found herself trying to fill three roles in a single meeting: helping the teacher plan, improving the curriculum by making it more responsive to the teacher's needs, and using the conversation to understand more about teaching in ways that would inform research. She wanted to fill all the roles, but in practice each branch of the conversation could go in only one direction. In a single moment a staff member could work only with the curriculum, on the curriculum, or with the teacher's articulation of the curriculum; having chosen a path, it was difficult to retrace and begin another.

For many project members, time management became difficult as the number of roles increased. Relatively frequent deadlines in curriculum development, software design, and teacher support pushed research concerns aside more often than project members wished. A familiar frustration was coming to an exciting point in an analysis only to have to drop that project for two weeks to get ready for a classroom field test. Similarly, curriculum development responsibilities were pushed aside as a conference deadline approached. Although MMAP staff members experienced management difficulties, the problem was more acute for teachers. As if the demands of full-time teaching were not enough, many teachers served on a variety of math reform committees and projects. Some had mentor teacher responsibilities at their schools. Many found one staff day per month to be all they could commit to the MMAP project during the school year.

Despite the practical difficulties, there was a sense among those of us on the project that improving mathematics education is not a process that can be neatly separated into tasks and areas of responsibility. We sensed a growing realization of this problem in our annual meetings with other NSF-funded mathematics curriculum projects. As one member of another project commented, "I've also seen our colleagues in NSF-funded projects gradually take on more and more of the pieces. When we had the symposium on research on curriculum, a whole bunch of people said they were doing research, and they wouldn't have said that at the beginning. Year one they said, 'It's not my job to worry about how teachers are using the stuff.' Year two they said, 'How are we going to deal with teachers, assessment?' and year three they were talking about how they were dealing with it. The problem really isn't factorable, so it's better to start out with thinking that you're going to do it all."

Teachers with Curriculum Developers

MMAP's cyclic design process afforded at least three opportunities for teachers to participate in the design of curriculum. First, teachers were members of the work groups that conceptualized and wrote initial drafts of MMAP units. Second, teachers were invited to review draft materials for coherence, readability, utility, and mathematical sense. Third, teachers piloted the materials in their classrooms, and the pilots fed directly into the developmental process. The teachers interacted with developers and researchers in discussions of the materials that were helpful or problematic in achieving teaching goals. In all of these interactions, the curriculum materials were essential boundary objects between teachers and developers, who shared an orientation of valuing the materials primarily for their functionality in supporting students' learning.

The process of designing and developing materials overlaps with the process of teachers' trying them out, sometimes to the point of being indistinguishable. Draft materials are incomplete versions of units, and therefore much of what happens has to be initiated by the teacher, either on the spot or through activities planned the night before. These spontaneously created activities replace or at least supplement old draft materials. Because the design projects are created with the idea that mathematical content and teaching opportunities will emerge from the design process, no one really knows what students will uncover until the unit is used. Draft materials are only our best guess, and the materials designed in response to what students do are closer to meeting our original aims than the drafts could be. In one case, a teacher and MMAP staff created almost all of the Wolves and Caribou mathematics activities on an as-needed basis during the teacher's pilot. The teacher commented:

> Last year I did the first pilot of Wolves and Caribou. For me, that was exciting— to be in on the first time that it was gone through. To go through it. To start in on something when we didn't know where it was going to go, exactly. Learning as we were doing it. Teachers, researchers, and kids. Seeing what opportunities became available, what topics came out of it, and what seemed to be important. I welcomed the open-endedness of it. I just decided, I am going to do this, give it as much time as it needs. I think that we have developed a very fine curriculum, or it is developing by just jumping in and doing it.

The Wolves and Caribou pilot and development went on simultaneously, blurring the lines between piloting and developing. Other pilot tests have been less immediately tied to development, but all pilots resulted in changes in the materials based on what students did with them and teachers said about them.

Teachers pointed to two dimensions of their involvement in development. First, the teachers shared an interest in developing a version of mathematics embedded in activities. They did not want to neglect mathematics as such, but a commitment of the project was to present mathematics that makes apparent its usefulness. As one teacher put it: "I was in search of more interesting and challenging problem-solving materials that would really stimulate and cause students to think. MMAP was kind of like finding an oasis in a somewhat barren land. MMAP was not computational based, as the textbook basically is. It was more problem solving based, through applications. Its computation is embedded within the context of the problem whereby it makes sense."

Another teacher appreciated MMAP's use of computational technology: "MMAP involved the use of technology, which was one of the reasons I got into teaching, given my computer science background. Most of MMAP's work, the way I see it, is based on doing math through technology application. We know that kids are interested in working on computers."

The participating teachers did not necessarily see how the program of teaching mathematics through applications would work out, but they were interested in exploring the possibility. Said one, "So this is applications, but how real is it? But maybe that's okay—you still gain some mathematical sense. That is one question I had: What do we mean by 'applications'? Is it something going on in the real world, something scientists are using, or is it something we made up?"

The general idea of presenting mathematics as a resource was sufficiently broad to allow for considerable variation among different teachers' values and teaching styles. The materials were designed deliberately to encourage teachers to teach in various ways, and we have observed a significant variety of ways of teaching with the materials. This contrasts with some curricula developed in the reform movement that attempt to articulate a single, clear vision of what it means to teach. The relative lack of teaching protocols has its drawbacks, of course, but on the whole we believe that leaving room for variation is beneficial. It surely has provided a source of rich interactions between participating teachers and developers in exploring alternative techniques for using the materials. Room for variation has enabled the project to be more engaging to teachers than might be the case with a tightly specified approach.

Second, and perhaps more rewarding for us, were the teachers' testimonials about being full participants in the design of materials. In true collaboration, people feel listened to and recognized. As one teacher put it, "The biggest thing that was different between MMAP and any of the previous relationships we had was that MMAP's assumption was that the teacher was coming in on an equal footing as an authority and that what we were saying about how it actually works was valuable rather than our needing to be convinced of something needing to exist." Another commented, "I like the immediate feedback. I've been to conferences over the years where they ask the teachers' opinion and that's the end of it. We go through Wolves and Caribou, and next time we're here the changes have been incorporated into the thing. You get immediate gratification; you feel like you're doing something."

Teachers with Researchers

Movement across the boundary between teaching and research was less direct than across the boundaries involving development. Traditionally researchers have a responsibility for constructing reports that communicate with their colleagues in research communities. These reports are boundary objects for members of different communities of researchers, but in practice they are not especially effective for communicating with teachers. Teachers' activities included analytic work that contributed to their practices, such as reflections on their teaching and experimental trials of teaching methods. Teachers also generated questions that became incorporated in the research agendas. We also tried to have teachers participate directly in research-oriented analyses of videotape materials. This was not usually successful for the teachers, but it was a rich source of materials for our research endeavors.

Reflection on Teaching Practices. Opportunity for reflection on teaching, especially with others, is rare in many teachers' professional lives. Assuming teachers would be the ones to figure out what was important about teaching MMAP units, we inserted time for this in project work days and summer institutes. The teachers' reflections have been important for both individual teachers and MMAP's research on teaching.

Generating Research Questions. Teachers have influenced the research questions MMAP has pursued, and some MMAP teachers have formulated research questions as part of their talk about teaching. For example, teachers worried about the effects of computers on equitable classroom participation, and some devised policies for computer mouse use, assuming, quite naturally, that controlling the mouse indicated active participation. This led us to analyze tapes of students' working together at the computer, comparing the time spent holding the mouse with the numbers of design bids included in the children's final project. There was no correlation between these two counts (Cole, 1995). This result led MMAP teachers and staff to look at other ways to address the complex issue of gender equity.

Participation in Analysis of Classroom Data. Analysis of videotape is a central MMAP research activity. The video and ethnographic records obtained in the pilot tests are the primary research data. Teachers have often been asked to join this activity, and this has been valuable for some teachers, as the following testimonials show:

We were involved in commenting on what we saw, did we see math, in what to anyone else would look like a lot of down time—they're not concentrating. When we see the tape, looking at the kids, there's this natural flow that just has to come out. When you look at these tapes, you get to see the whole picture. Sometimes I look at the classroom and see only chaos, but when I look at the tapes, I saw a lot of talk about math, even though they did waste some time. I used to worry that some of the talking was unnecessary, but when I look at the tape, I see it is necessary; it's all part of getting that whole picture together. Each person is trying to understand the math for themselves, and they have to do it their own way. The conversation is necessary.

Finding visible examples of students' constructing their own knowledge is no easy task, especially if a teacher has thirty students in a class. Taking time out to view tapes of their students has helped some teachers see mathematical activity hidden "in real time." MMAP classrooms, along with other reform classrooms, look and feel different from traditional classrooms; there is more movement and noise, and a sense of "what's really going on" can seem elusive. Even the most dedicated reform teacher can use reassurance that the students really are learning mathematics amid the hubbub.

On the other hand, we have recorded comments that watching tape has not been useful. One teacher said that researchers and teachers have different needs:

There are places that we'll have to continue to work apart because our needs are disparate between people who are focused on research and people who are interested in actually getting in and making it work. For example, a researcher will evaluate a piece of tape and take a two-minute segment, and you will play it and play it and play it and ten-second things and go into minutiae, and you want to raise your hand as a classroom teacher and say, "Wait, these are middle school kids. They did not think before they spoke." The level of evaluation is far superior to their level of evaluation before they said what you're looking at. I know you need something to evaluate, but you need to keep in mind the reality of a middle schooler. It's just a disparate need. You need to have physical proof. Because what we work for is so much more fluid, it's like making us hold still. We're an asset to you as well as the other way around.

If tape viewing has been useful to some but not all, the comments of all teachers have been useful in the research process. For example, the explanation quoted above uses a sense of desperation to explain why a teacher is impatient with tape analysis and attributes that same sense of emergency to middle school children. This certainly points to how the MMAP curriculum must work to imitate the fast pace of attention and evaluation that marks real classrooms.

Videotape records of classroom activity are an example of a boundary object difficult to use to coordinate activities of researchers and teachers, because the members of the two communities are strongly inclined toward different interpretative frameworks for these objects. Researchers tend to interpret the tapes as data for developing and evaluating general hypotheses about learning and teaching and take a third-person stance toward the participants in the interactions they are observing. Teachers tend to interpret the meanings of the tapes much more as first-person experiences, as displays of either their own activity or the activity in which they could have participated.

A teacher who commented that tape viewing had been useful to her also asked for more direct feedback from the researchers' analyses of the videotapes: "They took videotape in both our classrooms, so they've studied it. I don't know what they've studied. I've just seen that one thing of one child. I just know that they look at it, and pull it apart and understand how the kids process stuff like that. I kind of wish that if someone is learning something that they would synthesize a few key ideas and share them with us." The comment points to a difficulty: for this teacher, research should result in synthesizable key ideas that can be immediately useful. The products of MMAP research so far are different. They are meant to help key ideas to emerge, but slowly. MMAP teachers are involved in this process, but the results can seem unrelated to neatly packaged quick results.

Observing Materials Design as Research. Joint participation in another research activity was less ambiguously successful. Developing teacher support materials to accompany MMAP units has been part of our research program. We began with this question: What can we do, with relatively cheap and accessible resources, to help teachers who want to use MMAP materials but who have not been part of our small core group? This was a practical question, because we have been faced with teachers throughout California using MMAP units. It was also a research question: Could we extend the community at a distance, through paper, video, and software? What are the important ideas about teaching and math that emerge as we create the products?

One result of our research-in-action was the *Teachers' Guide for the Antarctica Project,* which contains a paper document, a videotape, and a Hypercard stack. The paper document includes lists and stories, the two forms of communication the working groups thought speak best to teachers. The stories report classroom experiences, especially dilemmas resolved; the list sets out hints on logistics, questions to ask to promote math conversation, and activities for substitute teachers. The video shows actual classroom scenes with voice-overs from MMAP teachers addressing what we guessed would be the primary concerns of other teachers. The Hypercard stack provides access to all the student handouts, organized under various views of the project as a whole.

It is unusual to view such work as research, but it provided an important source of information for our research agenda. In developing material for other teachers, participating teachers articulated judgments about how to use software and curriculum materials productively, including evaluations of the resources. These judgments give us valuable information about their teaching practices as well as about the functionality of the materials. The materials developed for other teachers provided boundary objects for shared activity between teachers and researchers more effectively than did the videotape records of the teachers' classrooms. Researchers and teachers understood the materials as representing teachers' judgments and strategies and their function as presenting those judgments and strategies for outsiders.

We have to remind ourselves that activities such as designing the project's teachers' guide are partly research activities. Most MMAP activities are part of, or at least closely related to, research. At the very least, all our activities can provide data available for analysis. The *Teachers' Guide,* both product and process, provided data for an analysis (Knudsen, 1994) of MMAP teachers as "reform" teachers creating new ways of teaching mathematics. A stronger claim is that as teachers become involved in the research process, research products change. The *Teachers' Guide* is an example of a research product designed for the teaching rather than the research community. It meets teacher needs, within teacher time frames, with practical and challenging activities and suggestions. These research products should be judged by the standard of usefulness for practice, as well as by the theoretical and empirical validity of their assumptions and assertions. The guide addresses research questions with an exemplar that is open to inspection by others who can evaluate its usefulness.

A Teacher's Own Research Project. At least one MMAP teacher has carried out his own classroom research project. Following a summer workshop discussion of student journals, a MMAP teacher began using journals in his classroom as a way to find out more about what students were learning. His view of this activity in relation to research came up in an interview:

TEACHER: I do feel that I am researching journals, though. But that's for me; that's not for you guys. It's not a MMAP thing. It's a great idea that [a workshop visitor] brought in. So I guess that I'm doing my own personal research, seeing if I like it.

INTERVIEWER: So how do you see those as the same or different, besides the labels?

TEACHER: How does my research with journals, which is using the term lamely, differ from MMAP research?

INTERVIEWER: I don't think it is using the term lamely.

TEACHER: I do, because, well, how do they compare? Well, they can dovetail and intertwine because journals can certainly be used in a MMAP project.

INTERVIEWER: But maybe as far as methods.

ANOTHER TEACHER: I see it as trying out something new in the classroom.

TEACHER: Yeah, it's a lot of trial and error, guess and check. When we are doing lesson and activities for Wolves and Caribou over the summer, we are making these lessons, but we don't know if kids are going to like them, if they are going to work, what's going to happen, but you do them, you make them, and then you go out and give them to the poor teacher, make her do these things with kids, and then say, "Aha! We need to refine our guess!" So MMAP is using guess-and-check methods kind of thing, and that's exactly what I do with journals, is making it up as I go.

INTERVIEWER: Shorter feedback loop.

TEACHER: A much shorter feedback loop. I have a meeting with myself daily, hourly. So I guess they are similar that way.

Interviewer: Any big differences that you see?

TEACHER: I have a great interest in my journals because it's something I thought up. It's something I wanted to do, I wanted to learn about. I have a great interest in journals; I have an interest in MMAP. I guess that's a big difference. I have ownership. That's what it is.

What Counts as Research—According to Whom? Although we see research everywhere, our interviews with teachers revealed a different understanding. Most MMAP teachers claimed little involvement in MMAP research processes or products. Still, MMAP staff members view teachers' contributions to research as essential and significant. We are not sure of the implications of this difference. On the one hand, we are satisfied that teachers and researchers work together in MMAP both to create products and research their use. The mutual respect and sincere collaboration MMAP teachers report is practically and personally satisfying. On the other hand, if we really are making a new community of people worry about education reform together, it seems important to develop shared views of what we are doing.

Another concern, regarding the standing of teachers in the process, was expressed by a teacher: "For the reform to make some sense, we have to have more working with teachers and researchers, not two separate camps. Like that charter school in [a nearby city]; they had a teacher, two parents, and then they needed an expert in education. What about the teacher? Isn't she an expert in education? I feel like there's too much of that in the public—that if you're the teacher, you're not an expert in education. And if we're to be effective teachers, we have to become experts." This teacher saw the need for recognizing teachers' expertise. One way for teachers to claim expert status among the general public may be to be seen as researchers. MMAP teachers engaged in research activities could have currency in the public arena.

We have reached three conclusions:

1. It is good for both research and development that MMAP teachers are involved in all aspects of MMAP work.

2. It is not sufficient if teachers' contributions to research are recognized only by MMAP staff.

3. Teachers' research activity, if recognized, could support a more appropriate status in the public arena.

These conclusions are analogous to our concerns about students who are studying mathematics in MMAP classrooms. First, we are delighted with evidence of students doing mathematics while engaged in MMAP units. That they themselves did not recognize this as mathematics receded as we took pleasure in analyzing their activity as "proportional reasoning" or "using algebraic structure to solve a problem." Our own recognition of the mathematical content in students' design activities was an important first step. But if mathematics is social practice and students did not call what they are doing mathematics, then we had not completed the job of helping more students to be successful at mathematics. This problem clarified our next place to stand. It can be personally empowering and publicly effective to label as "mathematics" something that one does well and enjoys. The success of our research and development work depended on refocusing students to recognize their MMAP activities as mathematical and to use both that mathematical power and the recognition it may confer outside the classroom to build new contexts in which to use their mathematics. At the same time, we had to work toward a public and mutually shared view of research that helps teachers use research in their own practice and in support of their standing in the public arena.

CONCLUSIONS

Conceptions of knowledge, images of how knowledge is to be used, and the actual conditions under which knowledge might be useful, in varying combinations of fit and misfit, can differ radically from society to society, institution to institution (art versus science versus religion versus engineering versus bricolage), and setting to setting within the same institution. In this chapter, we have dealt primarily with knowledge as it is conceived, imagined, and used in school and school-related settings, first for children learning mathematics in classrooms and, second, for teachers, researchers, and developers working together on a reform curriculum. We have noted that these settings usually have a similarly static view of knowledge—how it is formed within disciplines and how it is passed on to teachers and in turn given to children.

We have contrasted the contemporary knowledge situation in schools with a more productive criterion as to what counts as knowledge in a formulation from Dewey (1916), to the effect that knowledge "must be capable of translation into a method of cooperating with the activities of those undergoing instruction. It must suggest the kind of environment needed to liberate and organize their capacities" (p. 108). This impulse has guided the work of the Middle-School Mathematics Through Applications Project. When applied in classrooms, the impulse has us building application materials for children learning mathematics; when applied in curriculum development situations, it has us building the applications with the scientists who model them and the teachers who use them; and when applied in educational research, it has us searching for ways to articulate findings consistent with patterns in the activities of all involved.

At its best, MMAP has taught us, at least partially, what is required if knowledge is to be redefined in terms of experience and practice in both classroom and research settings. What is required is an understanding of how knowledge is to be used in activities immediately at hand. Both teachers and children have had their fill of being told what the research shows, when in fact most of our research shows little of what is needed to be either taught or learned in classrooms. As we opened the chapter with a quotation from Mead about knowledge as hypothesis, we can close with Mead's complaint about mathematics education almost ninety years ago. He was discussing the "lack of interest we find in the problems which disgrace our arithmetics." He continued:

> They are supposed matters of converse, but their content is so bare, their abstractions so raggedly covered with the form of questions about such marketing and shopping and building as never were on sea or land, that one sees that the social form of instruction is a form only for the writer of arithmetic. When we further consider how utterly inadequate the teaching force of our public schools is to transform this matter into concrete experience of the children or even into their own experience, the hopelessness of the situation is overwhelming [1910, p. 691].

It would be better, said Mead, said Dewey, and says MMAP, to redefine knowledge in terms of what people have to know to proceed in the world, in terms of the activities of students undergoing instruction, in terms of the activities of teachers giving instruction. Mead continued with a description of what a good textbook might try to accomplish:

> It is not only that the material shows real respect for the intelligence of the student, but it is so organized that the development of the subject-matter is in reality the action and the reaction of one mind upon another mind [p. 692].

This is too much to ask of most texts, but it is not too much to ask of people in interaction with each other that they should have knowledge-producing actions and reactions, one on the other. MMAP has been our effort to build a setting, some of it predesigned on computer software and in curriculum units, and much of it invited in the form of teacher practice, in which the actions and reactions of minds on one another lead to growth in mathematics learning.

What is true for teachers and children learning mathematics was no less true for MMAP teachers, author-designers, and researchers building curriculum together. The excitement of the project is that it has given focus and encouragement for all three groups to use their minds together in the context of trying materials with real children in real classrooms. Barriers of hierarchy and misunderstanding gave way to the task at hand, and knowledge became less something one group owned while the other groups waited and more a set of working hypotheses all three groups were using in varying and mutually dependent ways. One result to date is an interesting set of materials that we hope will allow thousands of other teachers and children, researchers, and curriculum developers to enter the same conversations. A second result, more monumental and more tenuous, is a redefinition of knowledge as a set of working hypotheses that would be tested against their consequences for the body politic. There is no inherent reason for research to be pitted against reform, or theory against practice (Bernstein, 1971; Lobkowicz, 1967; Manicas, 1987). One pleasure of participation in MMAP so far is the weakening of these boundaries. There are many ways of knowing required in most human endeavor, and no one, and no one group, has an exclusive view of the whole operation. If we have a solid working hypothesis about how children can best learn in school and best assume places of citizenship after school, all kinds of knowledge should be allowed, indeed required. Students, teachers, administrators, parents, researchers, curriculum developers—all should be invited, indeed required, to contribute in ways helpful to the others. By their collective behavior, they can, in the words of Mead cited at the beginning of the chapter, "put their own thought and endeavor into the very process of evolution."

References

Atkin, J. M. "Teaching as Research." *Teaching and Teacher Education,* 1992, *8,* 381–390.

Barker, R., and Schoggan, P. *Qualities of Community Life.* San Francisco: Jossey-Bass, 1973.

Bernstein, R. *Praxis and Action.* Philadelphia: University of Pennsylvania Press, 1971.

Carpenter, T. P., Fennema, E., and Romberg, T. A. (eds.). *Rational Numbers: An Integration of Research.* Hillsdale, N.J.: Erlbaum, 1993.

Chance, M. R. A. "Attention Structure as the Basis of Primate Rank Preferences." *Man,* 1966, *2,* 503–518.

Cole, K. "The Mouse Trap: Alternatives for Judging and Encouraging Equity in Computer-Based Work." Paper presented at the Annual Meeting of the American Educational Research Association, New Orleans, April 1996.

Cole, K. Equity Issues in Computer-Based Collaboration: Looking beyond Surface Indicators. In J. Schnase and E. L. Cunnius (eds.). *Proceedings of the First International Conference on Computer-Support for Collaborative Learning.* Mahwah, N.J.: Laurence Erlbaum, 67–74.

Cole, M. *Cultural Psychology.* Cambridge, Mass.: Harvard University Press, 1966.

Dewey, J. *Democracy and Education.* New York: Macmillan, 1916.

Dewey, J. *The Public and Its Problems.* New York: Henry Holt, 1927.

Dewey, J. *Logic: A Theory of Inquiry.* New York: Henry Holt, 1938.

Dewey, J. *Freedom and Culture.* New York: Putnam, 1939.

Erickson, F., and Mohatt, G. "Cultural Organization of Participation Structures in Two Classrooms of Indian Students." In G. Spindler (ed.), *Doing the Ethnography of Schooling* (pp. 132–194). Austin, Tex.: Holt, Rinehart & Winston, 1982.

Feffer, A. *The Chicago Pragmatists and American Progressivism.* Chicago: University of Chicago Press, 1993.

Goffman, E. *Relations in Public.* New York: HarperCollins, 1971.

Goldman, S. V., Greeno, J. G., McDermott, R. P., and Pake, G. "The Middle-School Mathematics Applications Project." Proposal to the National Science Foundation. Palo Alto, Calif.: Institute for Research on Learning, 1991.

Greeno, J. G. "Mathematical and Scientific Thinking in Classrooms and Other Situations." In D. F. Halpern (ed.), *Enhancing Thinking Skills in the Sciences and Mathematics* (pp. 39–62). Hillsdale, N.J.: Erlbaum, 1992.

Greeno, J. G., and Goldman, S. "Thinking Practices: Images of Thinking and Learning in Education." In J. G. Greeno and S. V. Goldman (eds.), *Thinking Practices in Mathematics and Science Education.* Hillsdale, N.J.: Erlbaum, 1998.

Greeno, J. G., and the Middle-School Mathematics Applications Project. "Theories and Practices of Thinking and Learning to Think." *American Journal of Education,* 1997, *106*, 85–126.

Harel, G., and Confrey, J. (eds.). *The Development of Multiplicative Reasoning in the Learning of Mathematics.* Albany: State University of New York Press, 1994.

Institute for Research on Learning. *A Video Exploration of Classroom Assessment.* Macintosh and Windows 95 CD-ROM, 1998.

Kaput, J. "Democratizing Access to Calculus:. New Routes to Old Roots." In A. H. Schoenfeld (ed.), *Mathematical Thinking and Problem Solving* (pp. 77–156). Hillsdale, N.J.: Erlbaum, 1994.

Knudsen, J. "Aspects of Teaching in an Alternative Environment: The Case of Teachers Using and Developing MMAP Materials." Paper presented to the Annual Meetings of the American Educational Research Association, New Orleans, April 1994.

Lampert, M. (1990). "Connecting Inventions with Conventions." In S. P. Steffer and T. Wood (eds.), *Transforming Children's Mathematics Educational International Perspectives* (pp. 253–265). Hillsdale, N.J.: Erlbaum, 1990.

Lave, J. *Cognition in Practice.* New York: Cambridge University Press, 1988.

Lave, J., and Wenger, E. *Situated Learning: Legitimate Peripheral Participation.* New York: Cambridge University Press, 1991.

Leinhardt, G., Zaslovsky, O., and Stein, M. K. "Functions, Graphs, and Graphing: Tasks, Learning, and Teaching." *Review of Educational Research,* 1990, *60,* 1–64.

Lesh, R., and Lamon, S. J. (eds.). *Assessment of Authentic Performance in School Mathematics.* Washington, D.C.: American Association for the Advancement of Science, 1992.

Lobkowicz, N. *Theory and Practice: History of a Concept from Aristotle to Marx.* South Bend, Ind.: University of Notre Dame Press, 1967.

Manicas, P. T. *History and Philosophy of the Social Sciences.* Cambridge, Mass.: Basil Blackwell, 1987.

Mead, G. H. "The Working Hypothesis in Social Reform." *American Journal of Sociology,* 1899, *5,* 369–371.

Mead, G. H. "The Psychology of Social Consciousness Implied in Instruction." *Science,* 1910, *31,* 688–693.

National Council of Teachers of Mathematics. *Curriculum and Evaluation Standards for School Mathematics.* Reston, Va.: National Council of Teachers of Mathematics, 1989.

Nunes, T., Schliemann, A. D., and Carraher, D. W. *Street Mathematics and School Mathematics.* New York: Cambridge University Press, 1993.

Philips, S. *Participation Structures in Warm Springs Indian Classrooms.* New York: Teachers College Press, 1972.

Phillips, E., with Gardella, T., Kelly, C., and Stewart, J. *Patterns and Functions.* Reston, Va.: National Council of Teachers of Mathematics, 1991.

Piaget, J., Grize, J., Szeminska, A., and Bang, V. *The Psychology and Epistemology of Functions.* Trans. F. X. Castellanos and V. D. Anderson. Dordrecht: D. Reidel, 1977. (Originally published in French in 1968.)

Romberg, T. A., Fennema, E., and Carpenter, T. P. (eds.). *Integrating Research on the Graphical Representation of Functions.* Hillsdale, N.J.: Erlbaum, 1993.

Saxe, G. *Culture and Cognitive Development: Studies in Mathematical Understanding.* Hillsdale, N.J.: Erlbaum, 1990.

Star, S. L., and Griesemer, J. R. "Institutional Ecology, 'Translations,' and Boundary Objects: Amateurs and Professionals in Berkeley's Museum of Vertebrate Zoology, 1907–1939." *Social Studies of Science,* 1989, *19,* 387–420.

Varenne, H., and McDermott, R. *Successful Failure: The School America Builds.* Boulder, Colo.: Westview Press, 1998.

CHAPTER FIFTEEN

New Media Communications Forums for Improving Education Research and Practice

Roy D. Pea

W hat have been the early experiences in education and other disciplines with new computer-mediated technologies for the construction, submission, review, and publication of scholarly works? What new forms of scholarly communication are appearing that may contribute to knowledge about education in the future? How might the new communications technologies be shaped in ways that will improve what many see as the inexcusably weak links now present between education research and educational practice?

Scholarly publication in education today is predominantly print based. Yet the emerging interactive forms of publication, made possible by the explosive commercialization and democratization of access to the Internet and the World Wide Web, have tremendous potential for changing fundamentally how education research is conceived, conducted, authored, and critically responded to by its audiences. The new media forums could, moreover, serve to improve the understanding and practice of education, particularly in conjunction with design experiments in education settings, in which innovative practices are designed, implemented, assessed, and continuously adapted in dynamic partnership

I acknowledge National Science Foundation grant CDA–9720384 for supporting the Center for Innovative Learning Technologies, a context in which these concepts of new communications media for improving education research are being explored.

between social scientists and educators. The incorporation of primary audio-video data of classroom cases, interviews, and other educational artifacts in works published on-line could help to bridge the jargon gap between researchers and practitioners, linking them in a unified knowledge network. It even seems possible that as access to the Internet becomes more widespread, the fingertip availability of new media communications platforms such as the World Wide Web could advance a much-needed integration of the perspectives of education researchers, practitioners, and other education stakeholders in research inquiries.

The Internet and the Web are increasingly viewed as tools for capturing and composing digital multimedia documents, electronic publishing, collaborative reporting, and multiuser virtual environments, including virtual worlds. This chapter examines the use of these tools in a decontextualized manner, by situating them in specific pioneering efforts to transform scholarly communication in other disciplines and showing how the new media may fundamentally change every phase in the life cycle of education research. Those practicing disciplines such as physics, molecular biology, computer science, mathematics, and the humanities are further along than those in the field of education in thinking through the implications of these emerging genres, and their experiences and consequences for education research are explored here. The chapter provides a selective review of leading-edge developments in electronic journals, multimedia case presentations, moderated on-line conferences, and other more dynamic publication forums that engage significant audience participation. It concludes with a set of high-priority directions for developing new communications media to support education research, additionally addressing the requirements for creating a two-way, "live," and ever-evolving communications infrastructure for educational improvement.

Because the prospect of a rapidly changing role for the educator in the education research enterprise is a central focus of this chapter and because what I think about most is education research concerning cognition and instruction, teaching and instructional discourse, curriculum, and technology, much of my discussion and speculation concern these subareas. Specialists in history, sociology, or administrative studies will undoubtedly have different perspectives.

THE CURRENT STATE OF
SCHOLARLY PUBLICATION IN EDUCATION

Education research in its various facets is an extraordinarily broad-ranging enterprise. The comprehensive Scholarly Societies Project of the University of Waterloo, which analyzes the history of scholarly publication, makes the case that most journals—the predominant means for publishing and communicating research findings—have developed from the activities of scholarly societies. As of October 1998 the project has documented eighty-six societies devoted to the study of aspects of education (see http://www.lib.uwaterloo.ca/society/education_soc.html), ranging from subject matter teaching, as in physics, mathematics, and foreign languages, to the different levels of education, to curriculum and technology. For K–12 education and teacher education, an informative annotated list of 426 current education journals has been developed and is maintained by the staffs of the University of Wisconsin–Madison Instructional Materials Center and the Kansas State University Libraries (http:/wwwsoemadison.wisc.edu/IMC/journals/anno_AB.html).

What observations can one make about the production, publication, and consumption of scholarly research in education today? First, virtually all of education research is published exclusively in linear print media, and little use is made of more dynamic media such as animations, videos, or sound in communicating the processes and results of research. This is true even though a great deal of the primary data that are collected in education studies includes observations of classroom interactions and interviews with students, teachers, and other participants in education (Berliner and Calfee, 1996). In addition there has been little effort within the education research community to capitalize on the advantages of live links to other documents offered by current hypertext and hypermedia systems made broadly accessible through Web standards. The peer-reviewed electronic journal *Education Policy Analysis Archives,* edited by Eugene V. Glass, is one of the few scholarly electronic publishing efforts in the field of education (http://olam.ed.asu.epaa/). Twenty other electronic journals dealing with education are listed in the Education Electronic Library (http://wwwlib.waterloo.ca/discipline/education/journals.html), but with the exception of the 1996-initiated and award-winning *Journal of Interactive Media in Education* (*JIME*), they are on-line text-based journals. (The pioneering case of *JIME* is discussed later in this chapter.)

Second, the time lag between the write-up of education research results and journal publication is lengthy, often a year or more. After submission of the article, the peer review and author revision phase often takes six to eighteen months to complete. Although the period from acceptance to publication can be as short as about a year in journals like the *Educational Researcher,* the usual time cycle is another twelve to eighteen months (Denning and Rous, 1995). With electronic publishing, on the other hand, near-instantaneous sharing of research results is possible (although Internet-based communication is posing its own set of challenges to the economics of scholarly publishing, copyright protection, access, and the function of peer review).

Third, educators, the front-line agents for educational change, rarely read education research articles. A common lament among education researchers is that research knowledge of "what works" is not put into practice as broadly as "it should be" by educators (Kaestle, 1993). Complementary complaints among educational practitioners are that the information they want or need is hard to find, they have no time to read education research reports, and even if they did, such articles tend to be jargon filled, speaking to them in terms or in discourse frameworks that they cannot readily understand or put into practice (Kennedy, 1983).

Fourth, few educational practitioners produce reflective documents, in any media, about their teaching experiences that could help shape education research topics and strategies for improved learning. Absent experience with a readership for their works, it is a major challenge for teachers to learn how to write for others about what they are learning from their practices so that others may benefit. Yet the wisdom and learning that are embodied in classroom processes, orchestrated by teachers through their conceptual lenses, has extraordinary potential for producing actionable knowledge in education research. A strategy developed over the past several decades has been for scholars in education to work collaboratively with teachers to support their authorship of such reflective stories (Ruopp, Gal, Drayton, and Pfister, 1993).

These four features of education research could all change significantly as a function of the integration of new communications media in forums concerning research inquiry and educational practice and learning. The recent proliferation of experimentation in and commercialization of Web-based electronic publishing could reduce the time lag for education research publication, as it is doing in other fields. But even more to the point, widespread media-rich documentation of life in the classroom, and its interpretations by teachers as well as researchers, could altogether transform the properties of scholarly publication, the accessibility of research to educators, and the production of reflective documents by practitioners. Before considering these possibilities, it is worthwhile to highlight some distinctive aspects of education research inquiry.

THE NATURE AND PURPOSES
OF INQUIRY IN EDUCATION RESEARCH

As one of the primary generative functions of a society, well articulated by John Dewey and by developmentalists such as Erik Erikson, education is an exceptionally vital enterprise. Education fundamentally involves values and norms; it seeks through its activities to guide human development in the directions valued by the communities that educational enterprises serve (see also Moll and Diaz, 1987). The normative goals of education—what a society seeks to achieve through its activities—essentially involves renewal. In this sense, education is at once conservative—looking to the past and learning from it—and "subversive" and futuristic, second-guessing the needs of the possible worlds ahead and readying learners to adapt to them creatively and successfully over a lifetime of major changes in society, culture, and environment. Education research has the dual purpose of improving our understanding of the functioning of different levels of activity in education systems (such as conceptual change in physics for learners in a specific instructional environment or teacher development in the context of a reform-oriented school) and guiding improvements in practices (for example, in learning environment design or in administrative supports that facilitate effective reforms). Research in education thus has special properties as a field of inquiry and reporting; it is a fundamentally different kind of enterprise from research in physics or molecular biology.

There have been cycles of optimism and pessimism since the early twentieth century about the prospects for improving education practice through research, and recent years have seen a renewed call for researchers to show the practical value of their studies as well as to develop more collaborative methods involving scientists and educators (Huberman, 1989; McLaughlin, 1987). In response, there has been a growing use of design experiments to try innovations in the classroom and to assess new learning environments (Brown, 1992; Collins, 1992; Gomez, Fishman, and Pea, 1998; Hawkins and Collins, forthcoming; Salomon, 1995). But there are major issues of how to scale up such design experiments beyond a handful of schools.

Putting new curricula into daily practice is a hard task, and many curriculum researchers and reformers have seen the hoped-for reforms targeted by their innovations become "lethal mutations" when inappropriately interpreted in the classroom. Educators, in turn, have been frustrated with whole-cloth admonitions to transform their daily teaching practices with the latest research innovations. Although design experiments offer a promising approach to resolving these difficulties, their crucial feature—the collaborative engagement of researchers and educators in finding a common ground for advancing best educational practices around a reform agenda and set of reform strategies—presupposes an intimacy of communicative exchange that has escaped realization in the large. Why is this the case?

All curricula, and in particular new reform curricula, undergo significant adaptation during implementation in the classroom (Berman and McLaughlin, 1978). Curricula do not serve simply as scripts for transforming practice. Educators continue the design process for curricula in how they tailor learning activities, goals, and affiliated assessments in order to meet local circumstances. Such tailoring is challenging.

In addition, teachers work in a system, so that the tailoring process, although mainly centered in the classroom, is not limited to teachers using the curricula but expands to other members of the school community, including teacher colleagues, administrators, parents, and students. Curricular implementation thus offers up occasions, if the right kinds of support are provided, for educators to reflect on practice, consider new ideas, construct new understandings about practice, and reconstruct practice (Cohen and Ball, 1990).

The implications of this line of argument are significant for reflecting on design requirements for new communication forums for education research and practice. Educators and others involved in the enterprise could be better supported in the activities of tailoring new curricula to local contexts. Opportunities for this, and for sharing the successes and failures in the processes involved, should be explicitly built into new communication forums for education in the decade ahead. Media-rich annotations of curricula and other resources by education stakeholders, particularly teachers, could advance a form of "living curriculum," in which one's own experiences, and the plans and learnings of others, are shared and adapted within a broad-based, knowledge-building community. As yet we know little about how to do this.

One vehicle for beginning such experimentation would be an ever-evolving interlinked database, served by an open network, in which teachers could reflect on their tailoring experiences by posting on the Internet cases, from which others might learn. Like the personalized Web pages of educational resources that teachers have collected and shared with other educators, access to easy-to-use case development tools around curricular and other classroom practices could open up major venues for interteacher learning networks.

REPRESENTATIONAL MEDIA AND EDUCATION INQUIRY

Here I roughly delineate different phases in the life cycle of education research. These phases are useful in showing how representational media, and the properties of communication systems in which they are used, may lead to changes in the production and use of education research knowledge. In turn, I consider how traditional practices of conceiving, conducting, analyzing, authoring, and responding to and using education research may become transformed by these new media (and in some cases *should* become transformed because of the special normative properties of the field). Of course, in actual practice, these phases of the life cycle of education research are not strictly linear but are often iterative and embedded in structure.

I take for granted that different forms of representation may highlight or obscure aspects of the world they aim to represent (Mills and Pea, 1989). This position continues a line of argument well articulated by Kant and philosophers of the human sciences such as Giambattista Vico in the early 18th century, Johann Herder in the mid–18th century, and Wilhelm Dilthey's 19th-century writings on the history of culture, but most identified with the philosopher Nelson Goodman in writings such as *Ways of Worldmaking*. I apply this notion to the representations that we scholars of education use in our research publications (also see writings in the sociology of science by Latour and Woolgar, 1986; Lynch and Woolgar, 1990). The questions that arise, and the strategies that are used to pursue inquiry, often vary considerably across representational systems. For example, with respect to representing a physical system comprising an optical bench with a light source and a lens, very different properties are useful in different representations about, for instance, a photograph, a ray-tracing diagram embodying laws of geometrical optics, an algebraic equation for the depicted physical system, a written description of the scene, or an interactive simulation model of the optical bench physical system (Pea, 1992). Similarly, in presenting qualitative case studies of teaching and learning, there are distinctive strengths and weaknesses in the use of stories, time-coded observations of different categories of behavior, and edited videoclips of actual classroom interactions, depending on the aims of the inquiry. Questions about which representational forms to choose for depicting the results of scholarly investigations in education are not only about what it means to use the different forms, say video, in research to display data; they are "at a more fundamental level about what it means to do research," as Elliot Eisner rightly points out (1997, p. 5).

It is important to recognize that the alternative forms of data representation that have accompanied the proliferation of qualitative studies and their affiliated methods (from ethnography to discourse analysis) in education research over the past two decades are as much political as scientific contributions to the understanding of education. The same is likely to be true of representational revolutions in new communication forums for education research.

Conceiving Education Research with New Media

Education research is conceived and planned today largely by researchers outside the day-to-day concerns of educators. In its questions, methodologies, and reporting styles, such research tends to be driven by the professional standards of scholarly inquiry of the societies and journals of its constituent fields. The role of new media has been minimal thus far in transforming these traditional practices, although Nicholas Burbules and Chip Bruce (1995) illustrate, in their *Education Researcher* article "This Is Not a Paper," how the growing use of e-mail, listservs, bulletin boards, and newsgroups has started to transform the boundaries between correspondence and scholarly publication, personal and professional interchange, works in progress, and final publications and to challenge many fundamental assumptions about the production and ownership of intellectual works now largely resident in peer-reviewed print publications.

A listserv, a common Internet discourse medium, is simply an e-mail distribution list. For making announcements to sizable groups, or organizing discussion around a topic for a community of interest, it is a particularly valuable tool (for AERA's divisional listservs, see http://aera.net).

Yet in comparison with many scientific fields, education researchers engage in a small amount of electronic conferencing, and few experiments are under way to redefine the genre of scholarly communication. As of October 30, 1998, the *Directory of Scholarly and Professional E-Conferences* lists 265 different ongoing electronic conferences concerned with different facets of education research (http://wwwn2h2.com/kovaks/), and many of these are affiliated with divisions of the American Education Research Association (AERA). The AERA listserv moderated by Gene Glass (bitlistserv.aera) is listed as having fifty-three hundred readers, averaging twenty-seven messages contributed per day. Compare this to the much larger and far more active listservs devoted to topics as esoteric as vampires and furry-animal erotica.

This minimalist role of new media in the conceptualization of education research could change quickly if the gateways of communication *from* teachers in classrooms *to* the traditionally university-based education research community were opened up. As educators have begun to explore the internetworked world of information from their classrooms, the flow of learning could move from the classroom to the researcher, reversing the more traditional one-way transmission flow from theory and research into practice (Suppes, 1978).

Although unlikely to be sufficient in themselves, several preliminary conditions are necessary for such changes to occur. The first is broad-scale networking of classrooms, so that teachers have regular access to the Internet, preferably from home and school. The second is the existence of virtual "social places"—electronic hallways and other "places" in which discourse about practices among teachers (and perhaps for a research-interested community) could be conducted and well supported with communications tools, shared work spaces, and other resources. The third is simple-to-use tools for educators to author "cases" and publish them on the Internet. Cases, commonly employed in other fields such as business, law, and medicine, could provide a new kind of communication vehicle for teachers to share their experiences with colleagues and learn from one another through cumulative, reflective discourse about them.

Broad-Scale Networking of Classrooms. How realistic is it to expect that all classrooms in the United States will have access to the Internet and to Web sites for learning and teaching, and will thereby become richer resources for inquiries in the education research community? Until the past several years, the trend had been for schools to be internetworked, if at all, primarily for administrative purposes (Newman, Bernstein, and Reese, 1992). This is perhaps not all that surprising, since teachers are among the few professionals in our society who do not have a telephone for their work space, and an Internet connection to computers located in a classroom requires either a telephone (for dial-up modem access) or a faster connection, typically provided by an Internet service provider.

But rapid developments are occurring in internetworking classrooms and schools. As one example, during the first NetDay in 1996, over 250,000 volunteers helped wire 50,000 classrooms across the United States. Studies by the National Center for Education Statistics, U.S. Department of Education (NCES 1997, 1998), and the CEO Forum on Education and Technology (1997) provide complementary findings of an explosive growth in school and classroom Internet connectivity in the past two years, and school plans illustrate the same general fast growth trend. The proportion of schools that are able to access the Internet increased from 35 percent in 1994 to 78 percent in fall 1997, according to the National Center for Educational Statistics (NCES, 1998). A 1998 *Education Week* survey (Oct. 1) of all 96,000 public schools, conducted from February 1998 to June 1998, indicated that 85 percent have Internet access (compared to 76 percent for cable TV), but only 30 percent of schools (although 49 percent of districts) have a wide area network connection rather than modem dial-up (*EW*, Nov. 10, 1997). The proportion of actual classrooms from which teachers and learners can access the Internet is far smaller but also rapidly growing. The 1998 NCES survey showed only 9 percent of classrooms connected to the Internet in 1995, 14 percent in 1996, but a surge to 44 percent of classrooms in early 1998. Nationwide, the number of students per multimedia computer (including a sound card and CD-ROM drive) is still very spare, at thirteen to one (*EW*, Oct. 1, 1998). For comparative purposes, it is worth mentioning that a survey by the National Council for Accreditation of Teacher Education (1997) of 744 schools of education in May 1996 showed only 45 percent of faculty members using interactive instructional tools in their teaching and only 42 percent of education schools having at least one classroom wired for the Internet (Zehr, 1997). The current definition of a high-tech school—Internet access, local area network within the school, and better-than-average access for students to multimedia computers—is met by only 18 percent of schools nationwide, according to *Education Week* (Nov. 10, 1997).

Also, since 1997, IBM has been sponsoring the largest K–12 Internet project of our times. As part of the American School Directory (ASD) project, which is a collaboration of IBM K–12 Education, Apple Computer, Vanderbilt University, and Computers for Education, IBM is providing a free Internet Web site to all 106,000 K–2 schools and free e-mail accounts to every teacher and student in the United States. The objective of this project, announced in December 1996, is to provide an American School Directory (http://wwwasd.com/) so that teachers may access new resources for curriculum development, parents and other community members may connect to information on activities in their schools, and students may use free e-mail and other Internet resources for learning.

In another large program, Pacific Bell is spending $100 million between 1994 and 2000 for Education First, providing free ISDN (Integrated Systems Digital Network) lines to schools (much faster than today's dial-up modems) in California and on-site teacher technology training, Web site development, and related support.

In short, although networking all the classrooms in the United States and establishing Internet service does not by itself make for network-ready teachers, keen and able to put the Web's diverse resources to work for teaching and learning, as an essential condition of a new model for forging communication linkages between educational professionals and education researchers, it is well on its way to becoming widespread, and, I would expect eventually, universal.

Virtual Social Places for Teacher Networking. Current estimates are that only one in five teachers uses a computer regularly for teaching (CEO Forum, 1997; NCES, 1997). Could the appropriation curve be accelerated if teacher professional development organizations and teachers were to use the technology itself to learn more about how to integrate computing into their work practices?

Since 1996 SRI International's Center for Technology in Learning has been engaged in partnership with K–12 teacher professional development (TPD) organizations devoted to science education reform. Together they are developing, operating, and studying an easy-to-learn, on-line teacher professional development service called TAPPED IN (http://wwwtappedin.sri.com) (Schlager, Schank, and Godard, 1997). Using federal and private foundation grants to build this virtual learning community, the affiliated organizations—including the Lawrence Hall of Science in Berkeley, the Science Education Academy of the Bay Area, the Life Lab Science Curriculum Program, the California Science Project, and the Bay Area School Reform Collaborative—help underwrite the expenses of teacher participation and SRI's development of some of the TAPPED IN functions and services to meet their specific needs.

TAPPED IN integrates the best of current Internet communications tools, such as e-mail, listservs, Web pages, and newsgroups, into a Web-based graphical, multiuser virtual environment that simulates and extends face-to-face, real-time collaborative learning and mentoring situations. Geographically distributed teachers can meet and learn from one another by diverse levels of interactivity in the simulated graphical environment of a "conference center building" (a virtual place). Participants select an office in the extensible floor plans of TAPPED IN and bring in various informational resources for joint review or mentoring with colleagues and others (such as text and graphic "overheads," class notes or plans, articles, and pointers to Web pages). Whiteboards in meeting spaces may be written on, erased, and saved as meeting archives, along with textual discourse that participants contribute to a meeting. If TAPPED IN participants are using Web browsers supporting Java Telnet, they can collaboratively browse

Web pages together. Those who are sharing views on the same Web page can tour other sites together and make written commentaries as they go, which may be archived in TAPPED IN as a record of their meeting's activities.

TAPPED IN provides the technical infrastructure to support the TPD agendas and activities of each individual organization with which a teacher may be involved (such as workshops). Individual teachers may also "wander the halls" of the TAPPED IN virtual spaces, encountering other teachers, teacher professional developers, or researchers with whom they may share their experiences. They can thus use the collective TPD resources of the diverse set of participants TPD organizations beyond those of their "home" TPD provider.

Users of TAPPED IN can evolve the facilities and resources in this on-line center to suit their needs. They may link images (including three-dimensional objects using Virtual Reality Modeling Language) (http://wwwvrmlsite.com/), text, or Web pages via Internet links to virtual objects in the virtual space of the TAPPED IN on-line conference center. For example, the Lawrence Hall of Science maintains a number of virtual "rooms" around a reception area in TAPPED IN. One of these is the GEMS Room (Great Explorations in Math and Science). GEMS is a leading worldwide resource for supporting activity-based science and mathematics learning. It provides guidelines for how teachers without formal background in math and science can nonetheless use recommended everyday materials and foster student-guided discovery inquiry-based learning.

Although there are other network-supported teacher professional development forums, the TAPPED IN project illustrates the potential of new kinds of virtual places for filling crucial needs in the teachers' lifelong learning process. Schlager, Schank, and Godard's ongoing research examines the forms and experiences of teacher participation and learning that are found in a communication-rich, multiuser virtual environment of this kind.

More general developments of relevance for education and learning are occurring with "virtual world" technologies. It has been argued that the future of the Internet is a "social place," not a "digital library" (Curtis, Sonin, and Zaritsky, 1995). Patterns of usage for the Internet and systems such as America and CompuServe indicate that hundreds of millions of user hours are being spent on-line in chat rooms and other social places, in which users may connect through their computers to have textual conversations in real time. Inspired by these results, a number of Silicon Valley companies are seeking to provide the infrastructure to take the social desires of Internet users to the next level. These innovators have created tools for building and interacting in a variety of virtual worlds. Users can select or design "avatars"—graphical representations of "self" in cyberspace—and the objects and places in their interactive environments. They may then interact with others who happen to be connected to particular virtual world services (for example, The Palace, Worlds Away). Over two million downloads of The Palace virtual world software have been used to create and populate over a thousand virtual worlds, including some devoted to education and learning. Unlike present-day MUD (Multi-User Dungeons) and MOO (MUD, Object-Oriented), future virtual world users will be able to form large virtual communities and grow vast interconnected neighborhoods of their own design, which can scale nearly infinitely because of their distributed network architectural design.

In a specific education application of these ideas, Robert Kozma and Ruth Lang at SRI International are building "virtual places for collaborative science simulations." They are using undergraduate chemistry learning and precollege science teacher professional development as their domains and asking what specialized virtual places, resources, and capabilities are needed to support the social role and cognitive strategies involved in science learning. Based on their initial work, they are integrating client-server, multiuser virtual environment (MUVE) technologies like TAPPED IN (see Schlager et al., 1997) to provide diverse types of virtual places such as project rooms, lab benches, auditoriums, and digital libraries, with peer-to-peer synchronous multimedia collaboration technology. Such peer-to-peer collaboration will provide audio channels and simultaneous control and viewing of software applications such as simulations and tools for creating and manipulating other media used in learning and teaching (dynamic graphs, animations, equations, data tables).

Case Authoring Tools for Teachers to Share Their Experiences. In design experiments and other participatory design methods, the knowledge that teachers acquire, and their perspectives on such issues as what it takes to tailor an innovative project-based earth sciences curriculum to their inner-city social context and learning community, is not easily shared. Yet such sharing is likely an important factor in whether innovations in educational practice will scale up. The education research community is far too small to be directly involved in supporting such reflective processes among the roughly three million K–12 U.S. teachers. Are there ways that researchers could extend their reach through the use of new kinds of communications tools?

One need is for teachers to express more promptly their new learnings from the experience of tailoring innovations in context. Case tools can do this. Several prototypes already exist, including JavaCap and other case library tools from Georgia Institute of Technology's Edutech Institute (Kolodner and others, 1997; Shabo, Nagel, Guzdial, and Kolodner, 1997, pp. 241–249). Support to teachers who are learning to use reflective multimedia documents is provided in the work of Ricki Goldman-Segall (1990, 1998). Her *Learning Constellations* software provides multimedia ethnographic materials about grade 4–5 learners and their computer-rich classroom learning situations, so that different audiences can build connections among, and offer reflective commentaries about, these resources. For the purpose of communicating practices with preservice teachers about how to implement reform-oriented elementary mathematics teaching, Deborah Ball and Magdalene Lampert at the University of Michigan have also used hypermedia systems to create layers of interpretive annotations of videos of classroom teaching (see their chapter in this volume).

By means of case-based tools, teachers would be able to represent an experienced situation. Indexes would provide access to the cases by a user community seeking to learn from them (Ferguson, Bareiss, Birnbaum, and Osgood, 1992; Kolodner and others, 1997). Key research issues in using cases for supporting teachers' learning are how to select cases, how to identify which aspects of cases are crucial to facilitate learning, and what indexes will enable teachers to find the best cases for meeting the demands of a new problem they are facing. A common case architecture (Kolodner, 1993) is useful in this regard:

- The problem or situation the case is about
- The alternative means for addressing the issues in the problem or situation
- The results from carrying out the means used for addressing the issue
- An explanation for why the outcome occurred, whether expected or not (lessons learned)

Then, as Kolodner and others (1997) state, "While solving a problem or reasoning, a reasoner navigates to appropriate cases in the case library by using its indexed links. A case, told as a story about what happened in some situation, may suggest a way to solve a new problem, an issue that needs to be addressed, or a problem that might be expected to arise if some type of solution is put in place" (p. 151).

The importance of cases and stories to make education research more relevant to teachers' practices has also been highlighted (Carter, 1993; Connelly and Clandinin, 1990). Perhaps education research could become more relevant if researchers viewed the classroom as teachers view it, in their own terms (Kennedy, 1997). For example, one might imagine an extensive case library where teachers, working in diverse school settings with learners of different grade levels or abilities, would provide cases concerning how they went about appropriating a new technology or curricular innovation, such as the Internet project–based learning resources and teaching pedagogy in the atmospheric and earth sciences provided by the CoVis Project (Pea and others, 1997). Authored by teachers (perhaps with initial support from education researchers), the cases would summarize important aspects of their experience that they believe other teachers would find useful in the process of adapting these innovations to their own classrooms. Indexed at a useful level of detail, such a case library would help teachers who are new to those innovations more effectively manage their appropriation of these innovations. Cases from the field could perhaps serve as effective substitutes for, or complements to, the more traditional teacher professional development workshops at which such innovations are introduced, after which teachers are sent on their way to implement them locally. What specific form these tools would need to take, and in tandem with what types of personal and professional support for their use among the teaching community, are issues that must be resolved.

A working example from preservice teacher professional development suggests the utility of multimedia cases, even if they are not authored by teachers per se. Developed at the University of Michigan (Krajcik and others, in press), CaPPs (Casebook about Project Practices) provides a CD-ROM–based multimedia library of video clips and affiliated commentary that teachers can use for addressing their questions about project-based science (PBS). CaPPs is structured according to an exploration of teachers' questions concerning five key features of PBS: the use of driving questions, artifacts, collaboration, investigations, and technology. The concept is that new teachers can acquire a practical view of how PBS looks in real classrooms—and what its challenges and key properties are—by viewing video clips of experienced PBS teachers. These clips have annotations from researchers, other teachers, and the video-recorded teachers' reflections.

In summary, with the fulfillment of certain requisite conditions that are coming to fruition in new tools and practices in education research, new computing and communications tools may lead to sizable changes in how education research is conceived—changes that could provide a more substantial voice for practitioners than they now enjoy and changes in other phases of education research, particularly audience involvement in making formal research knowledge into actionable knowledge.

Conducting Education Research with New Media Tools

What implications do new communications media have for data representation issues (Eisner, 1997) in education research? (Fetterman, 1998, provides for a basic introductory article on kinds of computer and Internet resources for education research and instruction.) Although there is quite a lot of practical knowledge required to master the art of capturing good audio-video records in the noisy environments of classrooms (Roschelle and Zaritsky, 1995; Curtis, Sonin, and Zaritsky, 1997), the benefits of having accessible replayable records for research and instructional purposes (as for teacher professional development) have been long recognized. With the drop in costs for professional-quality recording and editing devices, inexpensive and easy-to-use computer video- and sound-editing tools, and the increased accessibility of digital cameras and video cameras that allow video and sound files to be imported directly into computer-based documents (http://wwwncsa.uiuc.edu/Cyberia/DVE/FusionDVE/html/future_developments.html),many researchers have begun to use new media in their education research.

A particular advantage of the new digital videorecorders is no loss of quality across generations of video editing. An area of emerging interest for researchers is computer-enhanced logging, coding, and retrieval of these audio-video records (for general issues, see Roschelle, Pea, and Trigg, 1990; SIGCHI, 1989; MacKay, 1995, pp. 138–145). Scanners also make it possible to assemble in one integrated medium a digital portfolio of students' work that may include paper lesson assignments, essays, videoclips of presentations and discussions, and other learning and teaching artifacts.

Analyzing Education Research Data with New Media

Once the researcher collects education research data, data interpretation and data analysis ensue. It is uncommon for the traditional subjects of such research—students, teachers, administrators, or others—to participate in the analysis of education research data. But the social science research community has begun to appreciate the value of having diverse perspectives on the patterns of data seen from learning and teaching settings (Brettell, 1993; Jordan and Henderson, 1993).

Some work involves teachers in watching videotapes of their own instruction or that of their peers and relies importantly on the perspectives that the participants in educational practice have on the meaning and coherence of their teaching activities. It is not too hard to imagine such involvement on a much larger scale (Sheingold and Frederiksen, 1995). What if participants in education research studies were provided with opportunities for making sense of the data that researchers have collected? What if they were allowed a voice in authoring the meaning of what transpires from a first-person rather than third-person perspective? This scenario does not eliminate the voice of the education researcher, but it opens up new lines of understanding for a broader audience. It is likely that a teacher-practitioner may find the categories of experience represented in other teachers' rendering of the meaning of their own practice more accessible than the theoretical categories common in the interpretive frames of the education researcher.

Authoring Education Research with New Media

Authoring education research articles for publication in a linear print medium today has much in common with authoring publications in earlier centuries. Paper (or more recently computer files) provides the inscriptional medium, and through a series of drafts, reviews (informal by colleagues and formal once submitted), and revisions, a final version is produced that is then archived in a paper journal or book. Publication of the research write-up may be individual or collaborative.

How is the nature of the work practices involved in this authoring process changing with the integration of communications technologies to serve old functions and with the invention of new forms that take advantages of the new properties of these media? I briefly describe a few of the ways, including changes in collaborative authoring, changes in media used to represent information in publications, and changes in the interrelationships of publications and their accessibility in an on-line medium (see also Burbules, 1998).

Collaborative Authoring. Consider the authoring involved in the composition of a report of education research. Collaborative research among education researchers is common, even across disparate empirical boundaries (for example, cognitive science, curriculum development, and teacher learning). As many scholars have pointed out, the networked communications recently made possible by the Internet over the past several decades have already provided new supports for such collaborative research and authoring in many scientific disciplines (Kiesler and Sproull, 1991), including education research to a small extent (Burbules and Bruce, 1995). As Peter Denning and Bernard Rous (1995) noted for computer science publications, "Authors are increasingly viewing their works as 'living on the Web.' . . . They see networks as new opportunities for collaborative authoring and for dynamic documents that incorporate other documents by link rather than by direct copying." More generally, the importance of distributed collaborative networks of researchers—dubbed "collaboratories" (NRC, 1993; Wulf, 1989)—has been heralded as the new organizational form for scientific research (Finholt and Olson, 1997; Johnston and Sachs, 1997).

At the most basic level, an author working in a location different from a coauthor's can work sequentially on a report on education research and, via electronic networks, nearly instantly send along the draft document for new work to be carried out by the collaborator. While undeniably important, this baton passing is a primitive form of networked collaborative authoring. Programs such as Microsoft Word now have group-writing revision facilities that provide support for many authors to propose revisions to a single document, which can then all be considered and accepted, rejected, or modified in a write-through pass by a lead writer. Also, screen-sharing programs such as Farallon's Timbuktu and shared whiteboards over the Internet such as those provided by TeamWave (http://wwwteamwave.com) make it possible for several researchers to work together at a distance on a text, using a parallel telephone channel or Internet telephone connection to mediate who has cursor control as a document is collaboratively elaborated in real time.

Multimedia Documents. Over the past several years, developments in software paradigms, such as Apple Computer's Quicktime for storing and replaying audio, video and animations in digital form, and object-oriented programming and component software, have made it possible to integrate graphical, video, and audio data files in text documents. Initially possible on stand-alone computers, these functionalities are now available over the World Wide Web, so that multimedia Web pages can be posted on one's Web site as documents that can be interacted with by users throughout the world across heterogeneous computer platforms (MacIntosh, PC, UNIX, NT). A great deal of experimentation in diverse fields of scholarship and teaching is evident as university faculty members, other researchers, and practitioners in the worlds of business and the arts explore the new genre for communicating the production of knowledge or works in their respective fields.

These developments are foundational. As Jay Bolter (1991) argued in his analysis of the history of writing, *Writing Space*, the representational media available for expressing, manipulating, and sharing the results of our thinking have had over the millennia a pivotal influence on what kinds of content were expressed, on who was able to benefit from these writings, and in how representational competencies were acquired (see also Lanham, 1993; Birkerts, 1994; Peek and Newby, 1996; Snyder, 1997). What might be possible and desirable in education research with multimedia documents?

Mitchell Nathan and others (1994) carried out some experimentation with the prospect of interactive multimedia journal (IMMJ) articles in education research. They argue for the utility of multimedia representations in capturing key aspects of educational contexts and of learning–teaching interactions (CTGV, 1994), as well as highlighting some risks and obstacles to using rich media for communicating the results of scholarly research in education. They do not include in their discussion hyperlinking resources within an interactive multimedia journal article, as is practiced in other fields, but restrict their consideration to a linear article model of a scientific report.

Among the IMMJ capabilities that Nathan and others (1994) consider to be important for communicating education research are the depiction of dynamic and interactive instructional materials and how they are used in instructional settings as well as concrete examples of how their use is received by learners. Summing up these properties, they argue that IMMJ articles can lead to more accurate mental models of instructional interventions among readers of these documents, provide valuable instantiations of abstract technical language used by education researchers (because actual classroom practices are depicted), and support more inclusive communication of research results to diverse audiences, including teachers, parents, school administrators, and community members.

Nathan and others (1994) also highlight some important limitations of IMMJ articles as they imagine them. One of these is the selective nature of video-recording in classrooms, which, although also present in other data collection activities, has the added burden of the video medium. Unlike textual descriptions, even when edited, such video data tend to convey a strong sense for the viewer of direct experience with the primary phenomena that are documented. A second issue is the integrity of video data that are being reported, where the concern is time sequence or time compression alterations distorting "the way it was." Another limitation they point to is the ethical dilemma posed when the visual identity, even without the name or location, of the participants in the research is revealed. Although this may not be problematic when the demonstrated effects of research interventions are profoundly beneficial, it could be damaging for the individuals involved when poor teaching practices or learners' faulty patterns of reasoning (important in the text-based educational research literature) are exposed. On this latter issue, they argue that only "very brief images that capture the global nature of the classroom intervention are generally safe to show because they do not center on any one person, do not reveal any particular behaviors that can be considered negatively, and still provide the reader of an IMMJ with a good feel for the execution of an instructional intervention" (p. 271). They recommend that individual teacher or student video depictions not be used until standards are agreed on for ensuring anonymity of video-based data.

The *Journal of Interactive Media in Education* (*JIME*), launched in September 1996 (http://www-jimeopen.ac.uk/jime/index.html), is the first electronic journal in education experimenting with issues of interactive media within its publications, for it fully integrates *JIME* articles with a structured (frame-based) Web discussion space to foster new models of scholarly practice (Sumner and Shum, 1996). For this purpose, *JIME* has adapted the National Center for Supercomputing Applications' HyperNews system so that reviewers may publish commentaries on articles under review linked to specific sections, figures and demonstrations, other reviewers' comments, and other resources considered relevant to the article by the commentator. An article is submitted, and reviewers and authors debate the submission, then open up the process to peer review. An edited version of this discussion is archived with the final publication, and subscribed authors and other interested parties receive e-mail announcing new postings about the article.

The editorial statement for *JIME* argues that a design field like interactive educational media must be able to present and critique its designs for scholarly progress to be appropriately conducted. To this end, *JIME* also allows authors to include interactive media demonstrations of instructional systems and users' uses of them in articles (in Macromedia Shockwave format). Thus far, they have not included the ethically challenging media of human-centered videos of instructional interactions.

Audience Involvement in Education Research with New Media

An important outcome of new media for authoring education research reports involves another major change: that the traditional audiences of a researcher's text can become much more interactively involved in the creation of the document and even in what counts as a document.

Unlike the cases I will consider of e-publishing in physics and in the cognitive sciences, the field of education research has the distinctive problem of needing to relate much more intimately to the phenomena of study—the participants in teaching and learning. Teachers, educational leaders, educational policymakers, and even parents are not only prospective audiences for education research but potential contributors to it. Education studies for a century have sought to illuminate and improve the scientific understanding of education, learning, and teaching. These other education stakeholders have a special insight into the day-to-day sites in which the theoretical knowledge and findings of educational inquiry could be applied; they also have the potential ability to tap new problems and solutions for long-standing concerns that should be shared with the education research community.

One of the most pronounced differences that has begun to emerge between print media and new interactive media is the relationship between author and reader. The boundaries between author and reader are familiar in the print medium. A work is authored, submitted to a publisher, and reviewed, revised for publication, and printed in quantities expected to be sufficient for projected sales. The reader buys and reads the work. Little communication transpires between reader and author.

In the emerging genre of new media on the Web, these relationships are much more intimate and are coming to change authors' and audiences' behaviors and expectations. Authors often now serve as hosts of America Online real-time chats with hundreds of participants concerning their print media or on-line works. Commentaries on an author's works are hyperlinked to drafts or archival versions of their publications on-line, and an author may be notified by e-mail when new commentaries appear.

Consider one preeminent example in some detail. The preprint phase in the history of scientific manuscripts is well known for its importance in the sociology of science. Traditionally a small number of close affiliates of a scientist or scientific team—an "invisible college"—are sent early draft versions of a scientific paper for remarks before the paper is formally submitted for publication. The preprints of papers actually submitted but not yet accepted for publication present another stage in the evolution of a scientific publication. Finally, there is the penultimate stage, when a scientific paper has been accepted by a journal, and the scientist or scientific team elects to send around the accepted manuscript to their scientific colleagues before it appears in print.

The preprint phase of this process is under radical transformation with the advent of the World Wide Web, most evidently in physics but also in many other fields. Widespread reliance on the uses of electronic preprints by scientists is commonplace in some fields of the hard sciences (http://xxxlanl.gov/)

and computer science (Association of Computing Machinery with its 80,000 members). Consider the famous case of the "e-print archives" at Los Alamos.

In August 1991, an electronic database of physics prepublications was initiated for a small community of under two hundred people, designated "hep-th" (for High Energy Physics, Theory). Within months, this Los Alamos physics e-print archive had expanded to over a thousand users, and by August 1994 it was used regularly by over thirty-six hundred (Ginsparg, 1994) of the world's estimated forty-five thousand physicists. The technical infrastructure for this system is automated, including the process of submitting preprints, and indexing their titles, authors, and abstracts. The archive may be accessed from the Web, FTP, or by e-mail. A crucial aspect of the e-print database is that it serves the needs of researchers who are presenting formal materials that they would ordinarily publish by conventional means in journals; the documents are not like usenet newsgroups or bulletin board systems. One of the most interesting results of this effort has been that in some subfields of physics, these on-line electronic archives rapidly became the primary means for researchers to communicate ongoing research, supplanting print journals (Ginsparg, 1994). As of October 1998, the http server statistics for the e-print archives indicate that roughly 500,000 connections are made to the server each week (http://xxxlanl.gov/cgi-bin/show_weekly_graph), with more than 2,200 new submissions during July 1997 alone (http://xxxlanl.gov/cgi-bin/show_monthly_submissions).

What are some of the other properties of e-Print archives that have become useful to its affiliated research communities? Besides the two-way submission and downloading of communications, authors can establish, and readers can follow, hyperlinked references within papers and use a password scheme that enables the author to transfer paper ownership to a journal or other party and to provide addenda. The history of revisions of a paper is also often saved in the archives for scholarly review.

Paul Ginsparg (1996) specifically notes that these archives do not constitute an electronic journal:

> The majority of authors continue to submit in parallel with conventional journal submission to take advantage of immediate distribution (and de facto precedence claim), and subsequent revisions frequently benefit as much or more from direct reader feedback as from the conventional referee process. Some authors feel more comfortable submitting only after a conventional refereeing process, with an attached "to appear in" comment, still taking advantage of both the advance distribution and archival availability. Certain journals have begun to accept the archive identifier as the electronic submission itself, and conduct their editor/referee interactions as well by means of the version retrieved from the archive. *Astrophysical Journal Letters* (published by the American Astronomical Society) actively encourages authors of accepted letters to place the "preprint" of the final accepted version in the astro-ph archive. The identifying

number is then used to add a link directly to the astro-ph from a Web page with a list of letters that have been accepted but not yet published. *Physical Review D* has similarly begun to add such link information to its own Web pages, and in addition uploads directly to the archive information concerning papers "to appear," and later their published status—the information is then available whenever users search the archive listings or browse abstracts. Better coordination with the existing archives could provide similar immediate benefits to readers of other APS journals.

Knowledge Networking:
Electronic Journals and On-line Forums

Much of the preceding section on new communication forums for different phases of the education research process is speculative in nature. Yet as the Los Alamos physics e-Print archives illustrate, disciplines besides education are further along in thinking through the consequences of new media for their genre of scholarly communication. What are the specific forms of new scholarly communication that are appearing, such as electronic journals, multimedia case presentations, moderated on-line conferences, and audience commentaries on materials made available in Web sites? What have been the early experiences in the disciplines, including education, with new media forums for the construction, submission, review, and publication of scholarly works?

Elsevier Science's debut of its electronic journal *New Astronomy* includes an illustration of a theoretical model that is a video simulation of binary pulsars, with two stars rotating around each other, evolving as one sucks up matter from the other, then explodes in a supernova. Springer-Verlag's *Journal of Molecular Modeling* is fully electronic, includes dynamic three-dimensional illustrations, and is on the Web. The next section includes a selective review of the leading-edge developments in electronic journals and other more dynamic publication forums that engage significant audience participation.

Three different forms of electronic journals have been distinguished: on-line, CD-ROM, and networked (Woodward and McKnight, 1995). Many of the features commonly recommended as beneficial to researchers, such as hyperlinked referencing to other papers, are not as well achieved in CD-ROM–only solutions to providing electronic journals.

Science, technology, and medicine (STM) are vibrant disciplines for the proliferation of peer-reviewed on-line journals (e-journals), with many hundreds of examples in place. Hitchcock and others (1998) estimate 3,000–5,000 peer-reviewed e-journals in all fields are available worldwide. Steve Hitchcock found three primary sources for STM electronic journals: commercial publishers, non-profit learned societies, and research institutions such as universities (Hitchcock, Carr, and Hall, 1996; also Mogge, 1996). Paper journals for STM disciplines are among the most expensive published, and document users would benefit considerably from electronic document access (Duranceau, 1995). Roughly half of those specialized, technical journals with typically high development costs (often involving expensive graphics) appeared in 1995, and, of the one hundred or so, close to half required paid subscription to view. Interestingly, nearly all from the university-based on-line journal developers were provided freely to readers (Hitchcock, Carr, and Hall, 1996). This situation may be contrasted with results from a recent study of 125 electronic journals by Harter and Kim (1996), which found that roughly 90 percent of the electronic versions of the journals reviewed—primarily in the social sciences, professions, and humanities, but also in some of the sciences—were available at no cost. Almost all peer-reviewed on-line journals are currently free, with publishers covering costs primarily from paper journal subscriptions or incremental revenues from site licenses paid by institutions from which users log in (Taubes, 1996).

Why have on-line journals exploded onto the scientific scene? As many authors have indicated, there are novel features of electronic publishing that provide a significant value added to the linear print medium—for example:

- Rapid access to disciplinary preprints
- Capacity to publish vast amounts of materials quickly and cheaply
- Searchability
- Hyperlinking to other papers and databases (primarily) and, in principle but rarely in practice, diverse dynamic media (such as animated graphics, video, audio, and interactive programs or simulations)
- Annotation capabilities so that readers may communicate with authors and one another
- Notification services, so that interested readers can be automatically notified by e-mail, discussion lists, or newsgroups when articles appear on-line in which they might have an interest

Perhaps one of the most intriguing findings from the first several years of experience with electronic journals is evidence pointing to the need for reinventing the user experience with the journal article, given the properties of this new publishing medium. In biology, scientists have recognized how electronic databases of three-dimensional graphical molecular structure representations could be made accessible through electronic publishing. And, as Gary Taubes (1996) noted, electronic journals in the sciences are already beginning to offer different forms of reader activity, author preparation requirements, and database interconnections:

Already a mouse click can take a subscriber from one article to related articles in the same journal, other journals, and resources such as databases of DNA sequences, protein structures, or galaxy images. By offering authors' raw data or the software used in the analysis, some of the journals will allow readers to double-check an author's work. . . . And any genes in JBC articles are linked to [GenBank] [GenBank http://wwwncbi.nlm.nih.gov/Web/Genbank/nar.edit.html], a service provided by the NIH's [National Institutes of Health] National Center for Biotechnical Information. Click on the gene, and you can go directly to the DNA sequence, if it exists. From GenBank [GenBank DNA Sequence Database], the NLM's [National Library of Medicine] own database structure allows users to jump in turn to other publications relevant to that sequence.

The Worm Community System (WCS) is an asynchronous collaboration system for the community of molecular biologists studying the nematode worm *Caenorhabditis elegans,* a model organism used for genetic sequencing in the Human Genome Initiative (HGI). The HGI aims to list in open databases the map and location of the full human genome and of other model organisms and to build up links to knowledge and scientific literature over the course of its scientific discoveries. The informatics needs of the HGI called for developments in advanced computing for distributed collaboration (Courteau, 1991; Frenkel, 1991; Pool, 1993) and could serve as an example to inspire the education research community. WCS was developed as a community system in molecular biology, an experiment of the National Science Foundation's National Collaboratory Project, and is often cited as the national model for future science information systems.

The aim of WCS (Schatz, 1991–1992; 1993; Schatz and others, 1996) is to support researchers within this biological research community in finding available knowledge, adding their own knowledge for others' use, and forming research knowledge interrelationships by connecting as well as annotating research entries (hyperlinking). In his design rationale for WCS, Bruce Schatz (1993) argued for the needs among community members for knowledge networks to span formal archival publications and informal "transient folklore."

WCS includes archival data (gene descriptions), physical maps, DNA sequences, cell lists and lineages, formal and informal literature, and analysis software programs. Given the rapidity of knowledge development in this area, and the fact that the diverse user communities for such knowledge (such as biologists specializing in other organisms or subfields of molecular biology) often do not share technical vocabulary (Furnas and others, 1987), WCS developed an algorithmic approach to the automatic generation of a domain-specific thesaurus by analyzing stored documents using externally acquired controlled term (keyword) lists, automatic indexing techniques, and statistics-based cluster analysis algorithms (Chen and Lynch, 1992). The WCS thesaurus that came out of this work captured domain-specific concepts and defines relevance interrelationship values between them, and allowed automatic updating. Then users of a simple browser to access WCS could use their own vocabularies and the semantics-rich thesaurus for finding related concepts.

Such experimentation with knowledge networks is not limited to the sciences but includes the humanities. Since 1985 the Perseus Project (Crane, 1996) has constructed a digital library for studying the ancient world of Archaic and Classical Greece with scholarly resources such as hundreds of Greek texts and translations; philological tools; extensive art catalogues of thousands of vases, sculptures, and other antiquities; and archaeological maps of hundreds of buildings and sites—in addition to color satellite map images annotated with ancient place names. *Thesaurus Florentinus* provides a large digital library of images of restoration under way at the Santa Maria del Fiore in Florence that can be used in different scholarship activities (Friedlander, 1996).

Nonetheless, experience to date (Hitchcock, Carr, and Hall, 1996) suggests that on-line journals have not mushroomed in fields such as computer science that lack a strong preprint culture (unlike physics or mathematics) and do not have important needs for wide distribution of results because others' work depends on them (as in physics).

The behavioral and brain sciences provide an example of advanced experimentation in on-line forums for scholarly communication using these new media. The prominent example of high interactivity between authors and readers is provided in the peer commentary, or "scholarly skywriting," advocated by Steven Harnad (Harnad, 1990, 1991), editor of *The Behavioral and Brain Sciences (BBS)* (see also Mason, 1992; Strangelove and Kovaks, 1992). In 1978, modeled after *Current Anthropology, BBS* began pioneering the publishing genre of "open peer commentary," in which fifteen to twenty-five scholars across specialties and around the world write critical reactions to target articles that are also rigorously peer reviewed, followed by an integrative response from the target article's author(s). Even in its early years, the citation impact of *BBS* was one of the highest in its fields (Drake, 1986).

Harnad now also edits the on-line American Psychological Association–sponsored journal *Psycoloquy* (http://wwwprinceton.edu/~harnad/psyc.html). *Psycoloquy* publishes articles and peer commentary in all areas of psychology, cognitive science, neuroscience, behavioral biology, artificial intelligence, robotics-vision, linguistics, and philosophy. With a combined listserv and usenet subscribership of more than forty thousand, it is a broad-based experiment in publishing refereed brief reports (around forty-five hundred words) of new concepts and results, for which the author wants rapid peer feedback, and of refereed peer feedback on these reports—thus the phrase "scholarly skywriting." Harnad has been a prolific contributor toward conceptualizing the revolutionary potential of the Internet (and more recently the Web) for electronic scholarly publishing (Harnad, 1990, 1991, 1995a, 1995b, 1997). Besides the advantages of more efficient and equitable peer review, Harnad (1995a) argues that the Web's true value for scholarly communications lies in the form of interactive publications that provide open peer commentaries on published and ongoing work.

Harnad's writings on scholarly electronic publishing have evoked considerable animosity in the publishing world and widely favorable reception among many academics (see Okerson and O'Donnell, 1995, for e-mail logs of the debates published as a book). Harnad (1991) argues for making electronic scholarly publications freely available over the Web for "esoteric" fields in the sciences, without "reader-end tolls" since their authors want readers and do not expect payment. But there is a large potential audience for actionable knowledge resulting from education research—millions of teachers and hundreds of millions of parents and community members. Is his argument inappropriately generalized to education research, not such an esoteric field because of its audience size? I do not believe so. Like information about health care and nutrition, information about learning and education is such a fundamental public good that universal access to it should be a priority of the e-publishing world.

Harnad demonstrates that free access is now possible with electronic networks, but until recently the economics of paper publishing have required scholars to make the Faustian bargain with publishers that a price tag will stand between them and their intended audience. Harnad's (1995b) "subversive proposal," issued in the summer of 1994 on the discussion list VPIEJ-L (Virginia Polytechnic Institute, Electronic Journals), is that publishers will not make this transformation themselves, so authors should make all their research papers available as unrefereed preprints over FTP servers (and now the Web) before publishing. His argument continues that when the paper then is accepted for publication in print, the author can replace his or her preprint on the server with the final refereed publication, no one will buy the journal, and publishers will transform their practices so that they charge authors for preparation and distribution but no longer charge readers for access. What scholars really need, he says, "is electronic journals that provide 1) rapid, expert peer-review (for quality control), 2) rapid copy-editing, proofing and publication of accepted articles (for dissemination), 3) rapid, interactive peer commentary (for attribution and desired feedback), and 4) a permanent, universally accessible, searchable and retrievable electronic archive (for access and academic credit)."

Another experiment with on-line forums in electronic journals is the new Elsevier molecular biology journal designed by Nigel Fletcher-Jones, *Gene-COMBIS*, a part of the preeminent journal *Gene* (see Taubes, 1996). In this case, besides hot links to other databases with pharmacological and biomedical information and abstracts and databases of nucleotide and protein sequences, discussion forums are provided that Fletcher-Jones describes as "virtual coffee breaks" akin to the hallway information exchanges at scientific conferences. E-mail from article readers is sent to the editors, who edit the best letters, which are attached on-line to the articles they are about.

While reasonably new in implementation, the widespread provision of Web document annotation tools is being explored in the research programs of several of the National Science Foundation's Digital Library research centers, including the developments represented in Stanford University's ComMentor (Röscheisen, Mogensen, and Winograd, 1995) and the University of California, Berkeley's multivalent annotation model for digital documents (Phelps and Wilensky, 1997). The model in each case, envisioned half a century ago in the seminal writings of President Roosevelt's science adviser Vannevar Bush (1945), is one in which an ever-expanding web of primary documents and annotations serves to grow an interpretive network of knowledge creation, use, and reflection. At Stanford Research Institute (now SRI International), Douglas Engelbart first implemented Bush's visions of hypertext journals (1975, 1984a, 1984b), and Theodore Nelson (1995, p. 32), the other hypertext pioneer who sought to instantiate Bush's vision, called this property of hyperlinked on-line journals and communication forums (only now widely possible with the Web) "transclusion"—"reuse with original context available, through embedded shared instancing." Since these efforts are only now becoming available, there has not been enough time to do the needed experimentation to find out what form electronic journals should take in different scholarly disciplines. But education research seems a prime candidate for such experimentation, given the special nature of inquiry in the field, which calls for better communication forums between researchers and practitioners than has been permitted by the traditional linear print publishing model.

OPPORTUNITIES AND CHALLENGES

What directions should new communications media take to support the specific needs of education research? And what are some of the critical obstacles to developing a two-way, live, and ever-evolving communications infrastructure for the improvement of education? Two general directions seem to me to provide the greatest breakthrough potential. The first is to pursue the goal of establishing mutually influential two-way communication of insights about learning and teaching—between education scholars as traditionally defined and educational practitioners. The second direction conceives of the Web not as a vast digital library but as a *social place*—one in which fluid social encounters occur routinely among participants in the diverse communities that can contribute to conversations about improving the education enterprise.

On the first direction, the field of education research will need to learn, through invention, field trials, and reflective analyses of experience, what genres of new media reporting work for the research community and for educational practitioners. To find the right form to the genres of reporting and community annotation, and to provide a more open-boundaried dialogue toward the achievement of actionable knowledge, much experimentation is needed in e-journals and other forums for research communication. As in physics and the brain and behavioral sciences, education researchers will need to take the lead in reinventing the work practices affiliated with their production of knowledge. A crucial part of the work ahead is to foster teacher involvement in these dialogues. It is frequently observed that teachers in the United States spend a greater proportion of their time in teaching than do teachers of other nations (Adelman, 1998; OECD, 1995; see also OTA, 1995), and so any proposals to involve them more integrally in reflective authoring and sharing of their learning about innovations in their classrooms confront the key obstacle of available time. Given the competing demands on their time, teachers need simple case-authoring tools for use in sharing their problems and learning experiences and in tailoring educational curricula and other innovations with one another.

As in the Worm Community System for knowledge networking among molecular biologists and other interested groups, advanced work on indexing, retrieval mechanisms, and meta-data for these cases will also be a priority. Meta-data are simply data about data. In the case of instruction, EduCom has organized a large consortium of organizations, including IBM, the U.S. Department of Defense, and others, to define the kinds of data about instructional management systems that could be used for indexing and retrieving educational materials over the Web. Such meta-data for instructional resources would define their own content domain, their indexing to standards, their age appropriateness, their media types, and so on.

Another challenge on the way to case development and sharing involves tackling successfully the complexities of establishing guidelines for ethical practice in media-rich representations of classroom practice, learning, and teaching events. In the use of primary, media-rich records of educational activities, no simple answers will be forthcoming. The contextualized information that makes a learning situation accessible to an observer of these records also identifies the look, if not the name and location, of the individuals involved. Aspects of the ethics of cyberspace research using on-line textual exchanges have recently been debated in a special number of *Information Society* (Kling, 1996; Thomas, 1996).

As for the second direction—making the Web a social place—I earlier discussed examples of multiuser virtual environments and "virtual worlds" technologies for learning and training. These technologies make it possible to establish neighborhoods, campuses, buildings, and other graphically depicted places to which people may come to meet and conduct various activities. Windows onto these worlds from computer screens may be opened up. Such windows enable geographically remote participants to return to persistent meeting places with persistent objects (such as document files, research lab equipment, portfolios of student work). In these virtual places, they can have real-time communication with others using media including voice, text, graphic, and shared action on simulations or with other applications. The potential benefits of such developments are wide-ranging, for these environments are readily extensible by users themselves and can be used to form virtual communities of learning around common interests.

As new media communication forums begin to open up the dialogue among the very diverse stakeholders in the education enterprise, issues of the need for universal accessibility to the Web's resources for improving education inevitably and justly arise. There are well-documented differences in computer availability at home and across schools as a function of income and funding levels (*EW*, Nov. 10, 1997). It is certainly a problem of social injustice if perhaps only one-quarter of the parents of school-aged children now are able to engage with knowledge networking about improving education from home over computer channels. Trends toward wiring all classrooms and toward including Internet-linked computers in public libraries and community centers will provide several ways of addressing such inequities. Furthermore, the advent in the past year of television set-top devices such as WebTV that sell for two hundred to three hundred dollars and require a monthly subscription fee of twenty dollars enables consumers to browse the Web over their television without owning a computer.

These trends toward universal access must continue. Many of the virtual world technologies presuppose a desktop computing environment today. But rapid developments in computer component miniaturization, wireless networking, handheld computing, and low-orbiting satellites capable of transmitting streaming audio-video communications suggest that we can anticipate virtual places for anytime and anywhere access to support learning communities within the next two decades. There are many economic and policy issues on the way to providing ubiquitous, fingertip access of new media communication platforms such as the Web, but the social costs of ignoring the need for universal access would be unacceptable.

References

Adelman, N. *Trying to Beat the Clock: Uses of Teacher Professional Development Time in Three Countries.* Washington, D.C.: U.S. Government Printing Office, 1998.

Berliner, D. C., and Calfee, R. C. (eds.). *Handbook of Educational Psychology.* New York: Macmillan, 1996.

Berman, P., and McLaughlin, M. W. *Federal Programs Supporting Educational Change: Vol. 5: Executive Summary.* Santa Monica, Calif.: RAND Corporation, 1975.

Berman, P., and McLaughlin, M. W. *Federal Programs Supporting Educational Change: Implementing and Sustaining Innovation.* Santa Monica, Calif.: RAND Corporation, 1978.

Birkerts, S. *The Gutenberg Elegies: The Fate of Proofreading in an Electronic Age.* New York: Fawcett, 1994.

Bolter, J. *Writing Space: The Computer, Hypertext, and the History of Writing.* Hillsdale, N.J.: Erlbaum, 1991.

Brettell, C. B. (ed.). *When They Read What You Write: The Politics of Ethnography.* New York: Bergin & Garvey, 1993.

Brown, A. "Design Experiments: Theoretical and Methodological Challenges in Creating Complex Interventions in Classroom Settings." *Journal of the Learning Sciences,* 1992, *2*(2), 141–178.

Burbules, N. C. "Essay Review: Digital Texts and the Future of Scholarly Writing and Publication." *Journal of Curriculum Studies,* 1998, *30*(1), 105–124.

Burbules, N. C., and Bruce, B. C. "This Is Not a Paper." *Educational Researcher,* 1995, *24*(8), 12–18.

Burbules, N. C., and Callister, T. A., Jr. "Knowledge at the Crossroads: Alternative Futures of Hypertext Environments for Learning." *Educational Theory,* 1996, *46*(1), 23–50.

Bush, V. "As We May Think." *Atlantic Monthly,* July 1945.

[http://www.isg.sfu.ca/~duchier/misc/vbush/vbush-all.shtml]

Carter, K. "The Place of Story in the Study of Teaching and Teacher Education." *Educational Researcher,* 1993, *22*(1), 5–12, 18.

Cognition and Technology Group at Vanderbilt. "From Visual Word Problem Solving to Learning Communities: Changing Conceptions of Cognitive Research." In K. McGilly (ed.), *Classroom Lessons: Integrating Cognitive Theory and Classroom Practice* (pp. 157–200). Cambridge, Mass.: MIT Press, 1994.

CEO Forum on Education and Technology. "The School Technology and Readiness Report: From Pillars to Progress." [www.ceoforum.org]. 1997.

Chen, H., and Lynch, K. J. "Automatic Construction of Networks of Concepts Characterizing Document Databases." *IEEE Transactions on Systems, Man and Cybernetics,* 1992, *22*(5), 885–902.

Cohen, D. K., and Ball, D. L. "Relations Between Policy and Practice: A Commentary." *Educational Evaluation and Policy Analysts,* 1990, *12* (13), 249–256.

Collins, A. "Toward a Design Science of Education." In E. Scanlon and T. O'Shea (eds.), *Proceedings of the NATO Advanced Research Workshop on New Directions in Advanced Educational Technology* (pp. 15–22). New York: Springer-Verlag, 1992.

Connelly, F. M., and Clandinin, D. J. "Stories of Experience and Narrative Inquiry." *Educational Researcher,* 1990, *19*(5), 2–4.

Courteau, J. (1991). "Genome Databases." *Science,* 1991, *254,* 201–207.

Crane, G. "Building a Digital Library: The Perseus Project as a Case Study in the Humanities." In E. A. Fox and G. Marchionini (eds.), *Digital Libraries 1996, Proceedings of the 1st ACM International Conference on Digital Libraries* (pp. 3–10). New York: Association for Computing Machinery, 1996. [http://www.perseus.tufts.edu].

Curtis, D., Sonin, J., and Zaritsky, S. "Digital Video in Education: A Joint Project of NCSA and NCREL." [http://www.ncsa.uiuc.edu/Cyberia/DVE/FusionDVE/html/dve_front_door.html]. 1997.

Curtis, P., and the Jupiter Team. "Not a Highway but a Place: Social Activity on the Net." [http://www.uni-koeln.de/themen/cmc/text/juptno1.txt]. 1995.

Denning, P. J., and Rous, B. "The ACM Electronic Publishing Plan." *Communications of the ACM*, Apr. 1995. [Also see http://info.acm.org/pubs/epub_plan.html.]

Drake, R. A. "Citations to Articles and Commentaries: A Reassessment." *American Psychologist*, 1986, *41*, 324–325.

Duranceau, E. F. (ed.). "The Economics of Electronic Publishing." *Serials Review*, 1995, *21*(1), 77–90.

Editorial Projects in Education. "Technology Counts '97: Schools and Reform in the Information Age." *Education Week*, Nov. 10, 1997 (special issue).

Editorial Projects in Education. "Technology Counts '98: Putting Technology to the Test." *Education Week*, Oct. 1, 1998 (special issue).

Eisner, E. W. (1997). "The Promise and Perils of Alternative Forms of Data Representation." *Educational Researcher*, 1997, *26*(6), 4–10.

Engelbart, D. C. "NLS Teleconferencing Features: The Journal and Shared-Screen Telephoning." *IEEE Catalog No. 75CH0988-6C*. 9tr (pp. 173–176). 1975.

Engelbart, D. C. "Collaboration Support Provisions in AUGMENT." *Proceedings of the 1984 AFIPS Office Automation Conference* (pp. 173–176). Los Angeles, Feb. 20–22, 1984a.

Engelbart, D. C. "Authorship Provisions in AUGMENT." *Proceedings of the 1984 COMPCON Conference* (pp. 465–472). San Francisco, Feb. 27–Mar. 1, 1984b.

Ferguson, W., Bareiss, R., Birnbaum, L., and Osgood, R. "ASK Systems: An Approach to the Realization of Story-Based Teachers." *Journal of the Learning Sciences*, 1992, *2*, 95–134.

Fetterman, D. M. "Webs of Meaning: Computer and Internet Resources for Educational Research and Instruction." *Educational Researcher*, 1998, *27*(3), 22–30.

Finholt, T., and Olson, G. "From Laboratories to Collaboratories: A New Organizational Form for Scientific Collaboratories." *Psychological Science*, 1997, *8*, 28–36.

Frederiksen, J., Sipusic, M., Gamoran, M., and Wolfe, E. *Video Portfolio Assessment.* Emeryville, Calif.: Educational Testing Service, 1992.

Frenkel, K. A. "The Human Genome Project and Informatics." *Communications of the ACM*, 1991, *34*(11), 41–51.

Friedlander, A. "Net Gains for Digital Researchers." *D-Lib* (issue 5). [http://www.ariadne.ac.uk/issue5/digital-researchers/]. 1996.

Furnas, G. W., Landauer, T. K., Gomez, L. M., and Dumais, S. T. "The Vocabulary Problem in Human-System Communication." *Communications of the ACM*, 1987, *30*(11), 964–971.

GenBank DNA Sequence Database. (n.d.). National Center for Biotechnical Information. [http://www.ncbi.nlm.nih.gov/Web/Genbank/nar.edit.html].

Ginsparg, P. "After-Dinner Remarks." APS meeting at LANL (Los Alamos National Laboratory). [http://xxx.lanl.gov/blurb/pg14Oct94.html]. Oct. 1994.

Ginsparg, P. "Los Alamos XXX APS ONLINE." APS News: APS Online (insert), p. 8. [http://xxx.lanl.gov/blurb/sep96news.html]. Nov. 1996.

Goldman-Segall, R. "Learning Constellations: A Multimedia Research Environment for Exploring Children's Theory-Making." In I. Harel (ed.), *Constructionist Learning* (pp. 295–318). Cambridge, Mass.: MIT Media Laboratory, 1990.

Goldman-Segall, R. *Points of Viewing Children's Thinking: A Digital Ethnographer's Journey.* Hillsdale, N.J.: Erlbaum, 1998.

Gomez, L., Fishman, B., and Pea, R. D. "The CoVis Project: Building a Large-Scale Science Education Testbed." *Interactive Learning Environments*, 1998, 6(1–2), 59–92. (Special issue on telecommunications in education.)

Goodman, N. *Ways of Worldmaking; Based on the Inaugural Series of Immanuel Kant Lectures at Stanford University, 1976.* Hackett Publishing, 1978.

Harnad, S. "Scholarly Skywriting and the Prepublication Continuum of Scientific Inquiry." *Psychological Science*, 1990, *1*, 42–43. [ftp://princeton.edu/pub/harnad/Harnad/harnad90.skywriting].

Harnad, S. "Post-Gutenberg Galaxy: The Fourth Revolution in the Means of Production of Knowledge." *Public-Access Computer Systems Review*, 1991, 2(1), 39–53.

Harnad, S. "Implementing Peer Review on the Net: Scientific Quality Control in Scholarly Electronic Journals." In R. Peek and G. Newby (eds.), *Electronic Publishing Confronts Academia: The Agenda for the Year 2000*. Cambridge, Mass.: MIT Press, 1995a.

Harnad, S. "Universal FTP Archives for Esoteric Science and Scholarship: A Subversive Proposal." In A. Okerson and J. O'Donnell (eds.), *Scholarly Journals at the Crossroads: A Subversive Proposal for Electronic Publishing.* Washington, D.C.: Association of Research Libraries, 1995b. [http://cogsci.soton.ac.uk/~harnad/subvert.html].

Harnad, S. "The Paper House of Cards (and Why It's Taking So Long to Collapse)." *Ariadne*, 1997, no. 8. [http://wwwariadne.ac.uk/issue8/harnad].

Harter, S. P., and Kim, H. J. "Electronic Journals and Scholarly Communication: A Citation and Reference Study." In *Proceedings of the Midyear Meeting of the American Society for Information Science*. San Diego, Calif., May, 1996 (pp. 299–315). [http://php.indiana.edu/~harter/harter-asis96midyear.html].

Hawkins, J., and Collins, A. (eds.). *Design Experiments: Integrating Technologies into Schools*. New York: Cambridge University Press, forthcoming.

Hitchcock, S., Carr, L., and Hall, W. "A Survey of STM Online Journals 1990–95: The Calm Before the Storm." [http://journals.ecs.soton.ac.uk/survey/survey.html]. 1996.

Hitchcock, S., Carr, L., Hall, W., Harris, S., Probets, S., Evans, D., and Brailsford, D. "Linking Electronic Journals: Lessons from the Open Journal Project." *D-Lib Magazine*, ISSN 1082-9873; December, 1998. [http://www.dlib.org/dlib/december98/12hitchcock.html].

Huberman, M. "Predicting Conceptual Effects in Research Utilization: Looking with Both Eyes." *Knowledge in Society: The International Journal of Knowledge Transfer*, 1989, 2(3), 6–24.

Johnston, W. E., and Sachs, S. "Distributed Environments (DCEE): Program Overview and Final Report" (draft, version 3). [http://www-itg.lbl.gov/DCEEpage/DCEE_Overview.html]. 1997.

Jordan, B., and Henderson, A. "Interaction Analysis: Foundations and Practice." *Journal of Learning Sciences*, 1993, 2.

Kaestle, C. "The Awful Reputation of Educational Research." *Educational Researcher*, 1993, *22*(1), 23–31.

Kennedy, M. M. "Working Knowledge." *Knowledge: Creation, Diffusion, Utilization*, 1983, *5*, 193–211.

Kennedy, M. M. "The Connection Between Research and Practice." *Educational Researcher*, 1997, *26*(7), 4–12.

Kiesler, S., and Sproull, L. *Connections: New Ways of Working in the Networked Organization*. Cambridge, Mass.: MIT Press, 1991.

Kling, R. (ed.). "The Ethics of Research in Cyberspace." *Information Society*, 1996, *12* (special issue 2).

Kolodner, J. *Case-Based Reasoning*. San Mateo, Calif.: Morgan Kaufmann, 1993.

Kolodner, J., and others. "Roles of a Case Library as a Collaborative Tool for Fostering Argumentation." In R. Hall, N. Miyake, and N. Enyedy (eds), *Proceedings of 1997 Computer Support for Collaborative Learning (CSCL97)* (pp. 150–156). Hillsdale, N.J.: Erlbaum, 1997.

Koselka, R. "Computers/Communications: The Hobby That Is Changing the Business World." *Forbes Magazine*, Oct. 6, 1997.

Kouzes, R. T., Meyers, J. D., and Wulf, W. A. "Collaboratories—Doing Science on the Internet." *IEEE Computer*, 1996, *29*(8), 40–46.

Krajcik, J., and others. "The Casebook of Project Practices—An Example of an Interactive Multimedia System for Professional Development." *Journal of Computers in Mathematics and Science Teaching*, 1996, *15*(1/2), 119–135.

Lanham, R. A. *The Electronic Word: Democracy, Technology, and the Arts*. Chicago: University of Chicago Press, 1993.

Latour, B., and Woolgar, S. *Laboratory Life: The Construction of Scientific Facts*. Princeton, N.J.: Princeton University Press, 1986.

Lynch, M., and Woolgar, S. (eds.). *Representation in Scientific Practice*. Cambridge, Mass.: MIT Press, 1990.

McLaughlin, M. "Lessons from Experience." *Educational Researcher*, 1987, *9*(2), 171–178.

MacKay, W. E. "Ethics, Lies, and Videotape." In *CHI'95 proceedings: Human Factors in Computing System* (pp. 138–145). New York: Association for Computing Machinery, 1995.

Mason, R. D. (ed.). *Computer Conferencing: The Last Word*. Vancouver, B.C.: Beach Holme, 1992.

Mills, M. I., and Pea, R. D. "Mind and Media in Dialog: Issues in Multimedia Composition." In K. Hooper and S. Ambron (eds.), *Full-Spectrum Learning*. Cupertino, Calif.: Apple Computer, 1989.

Mogge, D. (ed.). *Directory of Electronic Journals, Newsletters and Academic Discussion Lists* (pp. 7–32). (6th ed.) Washington, D.C.: Association of Research Libraries, 1996. [http://journals.ecs.soton.ac.uk/survey/survey.html].

Moll, L., and Diaz, S. "Change as the Goal of Educational Research." *Anthropology and Education Quarterly*, 1987, *18*(4), 300–311.

Nathan, M. J., and others. "Promises, Pitfalls, and Recommendations: Multimedia Journal Articles." *Educational Media International*, 1994, *31*, 265–273.

National Center for Education Statistics (NCES). *Advanced Telecommunications in U.S. Public Elementary and Secondary Schools, Fall 1996.* Washington, D.C.: U.S. Department of Education, National Center for Education Statistics, 1997. [www.nces.ed.gov/NCES/pubs].

National Center for Education Statistics (NCES). *Advanced Telecommunications in U.S. Public Elementary and Secondary Schools, Fall 1997.* Washington, D.C.: U.S. Department of Education, 1998. [www.nces.ed.gov/pubsearch/index.html].

National Council for Accreditation of Teacher Education (NCATE). "Technology and the New Professional Teacher: Preparing for the 21st Century Classroom." [ww.ncate.org/specfoc]. 1997.

National Research Council. *National Collaboratories: Applying Information Technology for Scientific Research.* Washington, D.C.: National Academy Press, 1993.

Nelson, T. "The Heart of Connection: Hypermedia Unified by Transclusion." *Communications of the ACM*, 1995, *38*(8), 32.

Newman, D., Bernstein, S., and Reese, P. A. *Local Infrastructures for School Networks: Current Models and Prospects.* BBN Report No. 7726. Cambridge, Mass.: BBN, 1992.

Office of Technology Assessment. *Teachers and Technology: Making the Connection.* Washington, D.C.: U.S. Government Printing Office, 1995. [www.wws.princeton.edu/~ota].

Okerson, A., and O'Donnell, J. (eds.). *Scholarly Journals at the Crossroads: A Subversive Proposal for Electronic Publishing.* Washington, D.C.: Association of Research Libraries, 1995.

Organization for Economic Cooperation and Development. *Education at a Glance: OECD Indicators.* Centre for Educational Research and Innovation. Paris, France: Organization for Economic Cooperation and Development, 1995.

Pea, R. D. "Distributed Intelligence and the Growth of Virtual Learning Communities over the Global Internet." Keynote address for symposium, Distributed Intelligence and Learners' Community: A New Direction for Computer Usage in Education. CIEC Annual Conference, Doushisha University Tanabe Campus, Kyoto, Japan, Aug. 4, 1997.

Pea, R. D. "Augmenting the Discourse of Learning with Computer-Based Learning Environments." In E. de Corte, M. Linn, and L. Verschaffel (eds.), *Computer-Based Learning Environments and Problem-Solving.* NATO Series, subseries F: Computer and System Sciences (pp. 313–343). New York: Springer-Verlag, 1992.

Pea, R. D., and others. "Science Education as a Driver of Cyberspace Technology Development." In K. C. Cohen (ed.), *Internet Links for Science Education* (pp. 189–220). New York: Plenum Press, 1997.

Peek, R. P., and Newby, G. B. (eds.). *Scholarly Publishing: The Electronic Frontier.* Cambridge, Mass.: MIT Press, 1996.

Peters, M., and Lankshear, C. (1996). "Critical Literacy and Digital Texts." *Educational Theory*, 1996, *46*(1), 51–70.

Phelps, T. A., and Wilensky, R. "Multivalent Annotations." In *Proceedings of the First European Conference on Research and Advanced Technology for Digital Libraries*, Pisa, Italy, Sept. 1–2, 1997.

Pool, R. "Beyond Database and E-Mail." *Science*, Aug. 13, 1993, pp. 841–843.

Röscheisen, M., Mogensen, C., and Winograd, T. *Shared Web Annotations as a Platform for Third-Party Value-Added Information Providers: Architecture, Protocols, and Usage Examples.* Technical Report STAN-CS-TR–97–1582, Stanford Integrated Digital Library Project, Computer Science Department, Stanford University, Nov. 1994 (updated Apr. 1995). [http://www-diglib.stanford.edu/diglib/pub/reports/commentator.html].

Roschelle, J., Pea, R. D., and Trigg, R. *VideoNoter: A Tool for Exploratory Video Analysis: Institute for Research on Learning*, Technical Report No. 17. Palo Alto, Calif.: Institute for Research on Learning, 1990.

Roschelle, J., and Zaritsky, R. "Video in Educational Research: A Starter Kit for Investigators of Learning." [http://www.covis.edu/ndec/ProjectPages/Raul_Video/VideoEdResearch.html]. 1995.

Ruopp, R., Gal, S., Drayton, B., and Pfister, M. *LabNet: Toward a Community of Practice.* Hillsdale, N.J.: Erlbaum, 1993.

Salomon, G. "Studying Novel Learning Environments as Patterns of Change." In S. Vosniadou and others (eds.), *International Perspectives on the Design of Technology-Supported Learning Environments* (pp. 363–378). Hillsdale, N.J.: Erlbaum, 1995.

Schatz, B. "Building an Electronic Community System." *Journal of Management Information Systems*, Winter 1991, *8*(3), 87–107.

Schatz, B. *National Collaboratories: Applying Information Technology for Scientific Research.* National Research Council. Washington, D.C.: National Academy Press, 1993.

Schatz, B. R., and others. "Federating Diverse Collections of Scientific Literature." *IEEE Computer*, 1996, *29*(5), 28–36.

Schlager, M. S., Schank, P. K., and Godard, R. "TAPPED IN: A New On-Line Teacher Community Concept for the Next Generation of Internet Technology." In *Proceedings of CSCL '97, The Second International Conference on Computer Support for Collaborative Learning*, Toronto, Canada, Dec. 1997.

Shabo, A., Nagel, K., Guzdial, M., and Kolodner, J. "JavaCAP: A Collaborative Case Authoring Program on the WWW." In R. Hall, N. Miyake, and N. Enyedy (eds.), *Proceedings of 1997 Computer Support for Collaborative Learning (CSCL97)*. Hillsdale, N.J.: Erlbaum, 1997.

Sheingold, K., and Frederiksen, J. *Linking Assessment with Reform: Technologies That Support Conversations About Student Work.* Center for Performance Assessment. Princeton, N.J.: Educational Testing Service, 1995.

SIGCHI. Special Issue on Video Use in Social Science Research. *Proceedings of ACM/SIGCHI Workshop on Video as a Research and Design Tool,* April. Cambridge, Mass.: MIT Press, 1989.

Snyder, I. *Hypertext: The Electronic Labyrinth.* New York: New York University Press, 1997.

Strangelove, M., and Kovacs, D. *Directory of Electronic Journals, Newsletters, and Academic Discussion Lists.* (2nd ed.) Washington, D.C.: Association of Research Libraries, Office of Scientific and Academic Publishing, 1992. [ftp://princeton.edu/pub/harnad/ Harnad/harnad91.postgutenberg].

Sumner, T., and Shum, S. B. "Open Peer Review and Argumentation: Loosening the Paper Chains on Journals." *Ariadne* [magazine of the UK Electronic Libraries Programme], Sept. 1996, *5*, 1 [http://www.ukoln.ac.uk/ariadne/issue5/jime/].

Suppes, P. (ed.). *Impact of Research on Education: Some Case Studies.* Englewood Cliffs, N.J.: Prentice-Hall, 1978.

Taubes, G. "Special News Report: Science Journals Go Wired." *Science,* Feb. 9, 1996, p. 764. [Also available in *Science Magazine On-Line* at http://science-mag.aaas.org/ science/scripts/display/full/271/5250/764.]

Thomas, J. "Introduction: A Debate About the Ethics of Fair Practices for Collecting Social Science Data in Cyberspace." *Information Society,* 1996, *12*(2), 107–117.

Woodward, H., and McKnight, C. "Electronic Journals: Issues of Access and Bibliographical Control." *Serials Review,* Summer 1995, pp. 71–78.

Wulf, W. A. "A National Collaboratory—A White Paper." In *Towards a National Collaboratory.* Unpublished report of a workshop held at Rockefeller University, Mar. 1989, pp. 17–18.

Zehr, M. A. "Teaching the Teachers." *Education Week,* Nov. 10, 1997, pp. 24–28.

CHAPTER SIXTEEN

Multiples of Evidence, Time, and Perspective

Revising the Study of Teaching and Learning

Deborah Loewenberg Ball
Magdalene Lampert

The activity of investigation is at the heart of many contemporary ideas about teaching and learning in classrooms. Whether students are studying temperature or democracy or poetry or probability, they are to learn from investigating phenomena and ideas. They are to learn from working on problems, talking with others about potential solutions, building on their own ways of thinking about concepts, and engaging with big disciplinary ideas. In mathematics lessons, for example, students are encouraged to investigate situations in which probabilistic events occur, construct ways of representing mathematical patterns, and debate the applicability of classic strategies for finding needed information. With literature, they are to consider texts closely, investigating and constructing alternative interpretations. Rather than simply assimilating conclusions, they are to engage in fundamental materials and ideas.

Two assumptions underlie this focus on investigation. One is that what there is to learn is more than conclusions—that the processes of knowing and figuring out are essential elements of knowledge of any field, in interplay with its core knowledge. Our thinking about this is related to the current literature on learning mathematics, or any other intellectual work, as being inducted into the culture of a "thinking practice." (See Lampert, 1998; O'Connor, 1998; Rogers Hall, Edward Silver, and other work by Magdalene Lampert.) Framing questions, deciding how to pursue them, being able to develop and evaluate reasonable interpretations and solutions—all of these both depend on and also generate knowledge. A second assumption is that investigation is itself a productive mode of learning. Investigation as we imagine it is supported by both constructivist and situated theories of learning (Cobb, 1994; see additional references).

We have been exploring how these ideas about learning could apply even to the study of teaching itself. (We use the word *study* here to encompass both inquiry of a scholarly nature and inquiry conducted for the purpose of learning to do or change teaching.) For the past two decades both of us have been teaching elementary school mathematics. Ball has been an elementary school teacher, teaching all subjects. Lampert taught mathematics first at the high school and then at the elementary level (Lampert and Ball, 1998). We have been teachers deliberately seeking to develop our practice—to improve the ways in which we engage our students in mathematics. As we each gradually became involved in broader conversations about the development of practice, in communities of researchers, teachers, and policymakers, we brought to them our experience as teachers. We considered our work "experimental"—that is, we were taking a stance of deliberate inquiry around our practice (Dewey, 1933). We were not teaching for the purpose of testing a curriculum or testing instructional strategies that might be shown to work and then widely disseminated. With the publication of the NCTM (National Council of Teachers of Mathematics) Standards in curriculum and evaluation (NCTM, 1989, 1991), our teaching was frequently cited as demonstrating the NCTM vision for mathematics teaching. We argued, however, that our practice was not best understood as modeling the Standards. Although we had been trying to develop the kinds of teaching and learning that many scholars wanted to know about but had trouble envisioning in real school classrooms, we were not aiming to apply theory to practice, working out the finer details so that others could adopt what we were doing.

Instead, we argued that we were investigating, as teachers, what is entailed in *trying* to teach mathematics for understanding. We sought to engage our young pupils in serious mathematical inquiry, and we tried to create classrooms in which children's ideas were used and respected by the teacher and by their classmates. Because we were teaching in a public school, we were also responsible to meet district curriculum objectives and for our pupils' preparedness for standardized tests. As we encountered challenges and dilemmas (Lampert, 1985), we tried to identify and understand better what shapes them and how we might manage them. For example, we often found ourselves struggling with how much to follow students' novel ideas and how much to steer the class's work back to the main path of currently accepted mathematics and the established school curriculum (Ball, 1993). We worked hard on issues of representation: in the choices of tasks and tools, how different contexts, materials, and questions shape the mathematics that students explore, and what they might learn about mathematics (McDiarmid, Ball, and Anderson, 1989; Wilson, Shulman, and Richert, 1987).

Amid many kinds of discussion about teaching and learning, we realized how often such conversations never developed past exchanges of judgment and opinion. We noticed also how frequently people sought to reduce the complexity of teaching. Faced with problems, teachers and professional development leaders alike promoted solutions. Students are having trouble learning to subtract? Use manipulatives. Motivation difficult? Teach through games. Children having trouble retaining what they are learning? Increase practice. Grappling with teaching ourselves, we eschewed these flat remedies. We realized that the inherent complexity of practice was a central premise for us. We assumed that the main work of teaching was in the "swamp" of the messy challenges of helping all students learn, where the work was multidimensional. Our daily work was embedded in difficult problems of practice, and what helped was better and better understandings of its complexity, not efforts to eradicate that complexity.

Despite repeated reference to our teaching as exemplary of the NCTM Standards, we began to think about how to use our teaching instead to produce *examples* of practice that could be studied by ourselves and others. We would be in the following sense "exemplary": our work would offer examples of certain ideas about and aspirations for teaching. Given our premise about the complexity of teaching and learning, we sought a complex knowledge of teaching that expanded what any one of us could see or hear. We assumed that increased and more finely tuned ability to examine and interpret teaching and learning would improve practice. We wanted more, not fewer, questions with which to listen to our students. We wanted more, not fewer, perspectives from which to consider what to do next. Rather than quieting the pedagogical discord, we sought perversely to increase its cacophony. With multiple voices shaping what we could see, hear, and imagine, we would be better prepared to face the complexities of practice. It seemed reasonable that one way to develop these multiple voices was to engage many different kinds of people in the investigation of a common context of practice (see Wertsch, 1991, on voices; also Heaton and Lampert, 1992).

We realized that if we could represent practice, then the possibilities for investigating and communicating about teaching and learning—by different communities—would be enhanced. Although others wanted to highlight our practice, what we needed to draw on was our knowledge of *investigating practice*, not our own evolving knowledge of practice itself.

We understood this as a problem of representation and communication. How could the many complex layers of practice be represented? And how could practice be engaged and discussed by a wider range of people concerned with teaching and learning? By making it possible for others to gain access to our classrooms, we envisioned that we could develop a common experience of classroom events to ground a more analytic discourse of practice. We imagined the possibilities that could ensue if more people were looking at the same classroom, bringing to bear different questions, experiences, and perspectives on the description, analysis, and appraisal of teaching and learning, and if, as part of that, the discourse of and about practice was shaped to center more on inquiry and analysis than on answers and evaluation.

The point was not to study Magdalene Lampert and Deborah Ball, or to study *our* teaching per se. Instead our vision was of using our classrooms as examples of a serious effort to teach elementary school mathematics for understanding and as a site for developing new ways to investigate teaching and learning. Viewed this way, what we envisioned can be seen as a special case of the genre of qualitative case studies. Like other case study research, this kind of work interweaves the empirical with the conceptual. Such case-based inquiry strives to illuminate broader issues, probe theoretical problems, and develop arguments and frameworks. A burden of proof rests with the investigator that something worthwhile can be learned from the close probing of a single instance. This raises the crucial question of what any "single instance" is an instance *of* (see Wilson and Gudmondsdottir, 1987; also Erlwanger, 1975). In our case, we sought to represent the teaching and learning in our classrooms as instances of elementary mathematics teaching and learning that aims at understanding.

We pondered what it would mean to make it possible for more people to have access to our classrooms as sites for investigating practice. What kinds of records would be needed to represent and communicate the complexity of these practices of teaching and learning? Whereas most researchers sample student and teacher work, discourse, and interaction, we engaged in a project to document classroom teaching and learning both extensively and intensively across an entire school year. During 1989–1990 we collected information about mathematics teaching and learning in our two classrooms. We collected video and audio records of small and large group work, copies of children's drawing and writing, quizzes, report cards, and our plans and notes. Over the past eight years we have been exploring the kinds of inquiry that access to this massive collection encourages and makes possible. Our inquiry into inquiry draws on our own efforts to study teaching and learning, as well as our observations of others' work with these materials (Schwab, 1961). To make still more fertile the terrain of inquiry, we have also been collecting and cataloguing annotations on the documents in the collection, building tools to analyze the records and annotations, and designing computer environments in which access to both records and analyses can be made available to both scholars and practitioners.

In this chapter we examine opportunities and problems in this approach to educational scholarship in which multimedia primary records of teaching and learning are made available to others. First we look more closely at what it might mean to investigate practice from multiple perspectives. Next we discuss what is entailed in collecting information to represent and communicate the complexities of teaching and learning. Third, we speculate about the role of new technologies in the development of a discourse grounded in instances of practice. What can we say about a technology that is fragile, rapidly developing, and expensive as a necessary tool for doing this kind of work? Finally, we conclude with a discussion of issues raised by our investigations of the investigation of teaching and learning.

INVESTIGATING TEACHING AND LEARNING

One thing we have learned is that discussions about practice are often more fruitful when they are situated in reference to a common context. A conversation about the teacher's role in class discussions, for example, can proceed with more depth when it is grounded in a common and concretely available instance of class discussion. Without a common context, it is possible for people to talk about teaching and learning without knowing whether they are agreeing or disagreeing about the meaning of terms, principles, and ideas. They can advocate for "hands-on" learning, "class discussion," or "problem-based" instruction, and not realize how differently they conceive these. Hence, to ground *this* discussion, focused on the investigation of practice, we begin with an illustration from a by-now widely familiar lesson in Ball's third-grade class. Our intention is to situate our consideration in and around a particular instance of practice, and to use it as ground for an examination of the investigation of teaching and learning. First we briefly recount the lesson (see also Chapter Twelve for a discussion of "Sean numbers"). Then we examine observations and questions that ensue.

The Lesson

In the middle of January, when the third-grade class was studying even and odd numbers, Sean[1] raised his hand and said:

> I was just thinking about 6, that it's a . . . I'm just thinking. I'm just thinking it
> can be an odd number, too, 'cause there could be 2, 4, 6, and two, three 2s,
> that'd make 6. . . . And two 3s, that it could be an odd *and* an even number.
> *Both! Three* things to make it and there could be *two* things to make it [Class
> data, Jan. 19, 1990].

Listening to this, Ball understood that in a certain sense, Sean was wrong. Six is not "an even number and an odd number." Even and odd numbers are mutually exclusive categories. But she guessed that he was connecting this to something that another child had just said—that some even numbers are "made of two even numbers" (8 is "made of 4 + 4," for example). And she thought

[1]All names used here are pseudonyms.

that Sean and his classmates could straighten this out with reference to the working definitions they had developed.

When she asked others what they thought of his claim, several other students tried to show him he was wrong. Cassandra used the number line to show him the consequences of thinking of 6 as odd. Pointing alternately to the numbers beginning with 0, she labeled them, "Even, odd, even, odd, even, odd, even . . . " and explained that calling 6 odd would make 0 odd as well, which did not make sense. But Sean only reasserted his point that 6 could be both even *and* it could be odd.

Hearing this exchange made Ball think that what she needed to do was to clarify the class's working definitions of even and odd numbers, which the class then took a few moments to do. Ball thought this cleared things up.

Still Sean persisted with his idea. The class was becoming more agitated. "Prove it to us! Prove it to us that 6 can be odd!" demanded Tembe. Sean willingly walked up to the board and calmly drew six circles and divided them into three groups of two (see Figure 16.1).

Suddenly Mei seemed to see what Sean was saying: "I think what he is saying is that, it's almost, see, I think what he is saying is that you have three groups of two. And 3 is a *odd* number so 6 can be an odd number *and* a even number."

Sean agreed with her, nodding.

Mei, however, having clarified what Sean was saying, said she disagreed with that. She went up to the board, announcing emphatically, "It's not *according* to how many *groups* it is."

She stood at the board, thinking. Then, suddenly sure of herself, she drew ten circles on the board (see Figure 16.2.).

"Let's see. If you call 6 an odd number, why don't you call 10, uh, like . . . uh, an odd number and an even number, or why don't you call *other* numbers an odd number and an even number?"

Figure 16.1. Sean's representation of the number 6.

Figure 16.2. Mei's representation of the number 10.

Mei seemed to think that this would convince Sean to give up his idea. Instead he looked at it and said, "I didn't think of it that way. Thank you for bringing it up, *so*—I say it's—10 can be an odd and an even . . . "

Other children grew more excited, and hands waved in the air. Mei, with rising conviction, exclaimed, "But what about *other* numbers?! Like, if you keep on going on like that and you say that *other* numbers are odd and even, maybe we'll end it up with *all* numbers are odd and even. Then it won't make *sense* that all numbers should be odd and even, because if all numbers were odd and even, we wouldn't be even having this *discussion!*"

What Do People See in Practice?

This episode from Ball's class has been examined by many different people (among them Rodney McNair, Penelope Peterson, Ralph Putnam, and Lee Shulman). Groups of policymakers, for example, have viewed the segment on videotape and have discussed how this classroom differs from the mathematics classes that they remember. They have investigated what students might be learning from their participation in this discussion and have considered their views of what is important to learn. Some have become deeply focused on issues of classroom culture. "How did the class develop into a place where children are able to show respect for one another's ideas?" Others have wondered what is going on with students who are not speaking, assuming that those who are not speaking are also not engaged.

Experienced teachers have watched the tape and examined the teacher's journal and the students' written work. They have investigated questions such as, "What did the students seem to know about even numbers and odd numbers?" "What is going on with the students who are not speaking?" "Is this worth spending time on?" They have discussed issues of being patient with children, of waiting, and wondered about when and how teachers should intervene. "Does Ball ever finally tell the students that 6 is not both even and odd?" "What do the students take away from this? Do some become more confused about even and odd numbers?" "Where does Sean get this idea in the first place?"

Whereas experienced teachers often focus on the students and the pedagogical decisions, preservice teachers' questions are often more immediate. "Does Ball do this every day? How does she cover the curriculum if she does this?" They worry about Sean's feeling embarrassed and about Mei's "showing him up." They see Sean as confused and want to locate where Ball "clears things up" and how she does this. They notice the classroom culture, although they rarely call it this, and they ask: "How did Mei and Sean come to treat each other like this?" "Is Sean getting backed into a corner by his peers?" "Is Mei trying to put Sean and his idea down?"

Mathematicians have viewed the episode with an eye toward the mathematics underlying the exchanges. At a recent conference, over one hundred mathematicians viewed the full lesson segment and investigated Sean's understandings.

They viewed the tape, examined the lesson transcript, and discussed their interpretations of the child's thinking. Asserting with great certainty what Sean knew or was doing, they were soon stunned to discover how differently they saw Sean. Heretofore content to assume that professional mathematical training could provide the intellectual tools to "hear" students, they confronted the interpretive nature of the work of understanding children's mathematics. And they contemplated the ambiguities and uncertainties inherent in this process. Whereas one mathematician was sure that Sean and the class were encountering modular arithmetic, specifically numbers congruent to 2 mod 4, another asserted equally definitively that Sean was operating on the desire to make the odd numbers closed under addition—that is, that an odd plus an odd ought also to be odd. Still another believed Sean was quite clearly confused as a result of the imprecise definitional language that the teacher had given the class. The "working definition" seen in the lesson is: *Even numbers are numbers that you can split evenly in half without having to use halves.* This definition was not necessarily given by the teacher, but the mathematician assumed that.

Education researchers also have viewed this episode. Their observations and questions, too, are shaped by their concerns and perspectives. On one occasion we showed this episode at a meeting focused on the study of classroom communication. A group of prominent researchers who study classroom teaching and learning watched the seven-minute film clip and began discussing the interactions among the children and between Ball and the children. One researcher asserted that Ball had a clear agenda and was doing all the talking, thus restricting children's opportunities to articulate their ideas. Another emphatically disagreed, arguing that Ball had all but abdicated her role in orchestrating or steering the discussion. The children, according to the researcher, were being allowed to meander, with little pedagogical guidance. Still another saw the lesson primarily in terms of patterns in who was talking, types of turns, and what this might reveal about status within the class. Another examined patterns of interaction by gender. Whereas the mathematicians attended closely to the content of the lesson, the educational researchers attended to interaction, classroom norms, and students.

STUDYING TEACHING AND
LEARNING FROM MULTIPLE PERSPECTIVES

Across settings, communities, and individuals we have seen how differently people see and interpret the video segment and the accompanying texts: children's work and the teacher's journal. Just as we expected, they bring their own training and perspectives to bear. Sociologists often notice patterns of interaction by groups. Psychologists comment on the children's development. Parents notice the children's interest level. Further, because classrooms are multidimensional, people do not confine themselves to those issues central to their own areas of experience. They are drawn, quite naturally and individually, into the complex tangle of practice. For example, mathematicians do not comment only about the mathematical issues, but also make claims about what children are learning, or they comment on the pedagogy. Policymakers become engaged in the mathematics of the children's talk. Psychologists examine the classroom culture. People do not see or hear the same things. What they see or hear is interpreted through the filters of their own knowledge and experience, both professional and informal (see Ball, forthcoming; Kelly and Lesh, forthcoming; and Lampert, 1998).

On one hand, then, we see the amazing array of perspectives that can be fruitfully brought to bear on practice from the outside. But what of the perspectives available from the inside? What we see and ask in examining the materials from our classrooms is from a viewpoint of insiders to the setting and the practice. We identify and ask about things that outsiders may not see. Having listened to dozens, even hundreds, of eight-year-olds, and knowing these particular eight-year-olds, means that we conjecture meanings in their talk that others may not. Deliberating on alternatives, we are aware of decisions we face that are invisible to observers. We can feel rhythms of timing that shape the motion of class. We are aware of the many cues we read off students' faces, words, and posture-composing our impressions of student engagement, boredom, understanding, confusion (Ball, forthcoming).

We return to the episode with Sean and the number 6. At the time, Ball remembers feeling conflicted and having many questions. She was pleased to see him so engaged, because he was not always so. But what was he really saying? Was he serious about thinking that 6 could be odd? Where were the other children on this? Was this discussion confusing them? Ball could see some possibilities around Sean's "discovery," but, she wondered, Is this worth spending more time on right now? The children had been engrossed in exploring conjectures about even and odd numbers, such as "even plus even equals even" and "odd plus even equals odd." They were working in small groups, seeking to figure out if these conjectures would be true for all even or odd numbers. This work, on the brink of early experience with formal proof, was exciting to the children, and to Ball as well. Was it worthwhile to divert this work to attend to Sean's idea about 6? Ball noted with pleasure how Mei and Sean were treating each other—with respect and seriousness, it seemed to her. Still, she wondered how Sean was feeling. Ball wondered whether and how best to exploit Sean's idea while also making sure the children got clearer about the definitions for even and odd numbers. Continuing the discussion for a while, a pattern was identified for other numbers like Sean's 6: 10, 14, 18, 22, 26, and so on. (Each of these numbers, like 6, has an odd number of factors of two.) They even discovered that 2 fit the pattern, for it has *one* group of two, and 1 is an odd number. Ball felt torn: she could see that the children had wended their way into some interesting mathematical territory. But she also could see the third-grade curricular schedule before her eyes, and she continued to question what this exploration, however mathematically intriguing, was doing for all the students.

Just as disciplinary perspectives—mathematical, sociological, philosophical, and so on—can illuminate aspects of practice not otherwise focal, perspectives drawn from inside the practice of teaching also expand our collective understandings not only of the practice but also *of what there is to investigate about practice*. Lampert's work on dilemma management, for example (Lampert, 1985), emerged from her own experience of facing mutually incompatible goals and concerns as a fifth-grade teacher and yet having to maintain attention to them in her moves and decisions. Facing the multiple aims and considerations was not a matter of choice, she argued. Her analyses and those of others who drew on her conceptualization of "dilemmas of teaching" have since opened a perspective on the challenges of practice that broke with the ways in which others had written about dilemmas in teaching (see, for example, Berlak and Berlak, 1981). Heaton's (1994) work on the experience of an accomplished teacher who seeks to learn to teach for understanding by teaching fourth-grade mathematics illuminates the confusions and insecurities that a teacher in such a position might face—confusions and insecurities that would be difficult for an outsider to recognize. Ball's examination of the episode with Sean highlights the endemic tension in honoring both students and subject matter (Ball, 1993).

These and many other questions like them, articulated from inside practice, are both multidisciplinary and extradisciplinary in nature. Their pursuit entails empirical, conceptual, and philosophical considerations. Many of these questions, central as they are, are also fundamentally unknowable. There is no single or conclusive answer to whether pursuing Sean's idea is mathematically worthwhile, or to what the other children are getting from this discussion. The complexity of practice makes it a terrain of uncertainty rather than conclusiveness. Infrequently are the central questions matters for which definite answers can be found: despite the fact that "What is Sean thinking?" is a question at the heart of practice, it is not one that can be definitively answered. Yet investigation and careful analysis can finely map an issue in such a way that it can be seen and considered from more perspectives. Although this does not lead to answers, it does lead to improved understanding of the multiple constituents and interactions within any particular slice of teaching and learning.

CREATING A REPRESENTATION OF TEACHING AND LEARNING

Because we were convinced that a kind of investigation of practice was needed that was at once built from the inside and developed with multiple perspectives from the outside, we set out to represent the terrain of practice. Despite our conviction, we had many questions: Are there ways to record and represent practice that would enable us to interrogate its complexities more effectively? Can tools be designed that would support multilayered investigations of practice, not just by us but by others? What might such materials and tools make possible? What problems and issues might emerge?

We chose to document closely a year of teaching and learning in our own classrooms because we were willing to be recorded day after day, to have our students' work scrutinized, and to keep careful records of our own plans and reflections. Committed to the idea that teaching practice could not be captured in a few model lessons, we were willing to have documentation occur no matter what was happening in the room. We wanted to learn about what it might take to crisscross the terrain of practice, to learn about teaching from the inside of the practice itself. A problem we faced was how to represent the teaching and learning in our classrooms in ways that would make it possible to investigate practice.

Teaching and learning are seamless activities that occur in the streams of human experience and interaction. One does not start teaching when the morning bell rings or stop learning when it is time for recess. The events we would call "teaching" and "learning" do not have neat boundaries around them. Although they are interactive, they do not occur only when teacher and students are face to face. Any particular event is connected in multiple and complex ways to the events that preceded it. From the inside, it seemed to us that the problem of capturing a year-long record of everything we did as mathematics teachers and everything our students did as mathematics learners was similar to the problem faced by the mapmakers in Borges's imaginary kingdom, who thought the best map should represent exactly in one-to-one scale everything in the kingdom. Even if it were possible to run several video cameras from the start of the 1989 school year to its end, we reasoned, we would have an inadequate record, because the stream of events so recorded could be understood only in the context of past experience, suggesting the even more absurd idea that if we really wanted to document teaching and learning, we should have been videotaping everything in the lives of the players since their births. We would have to choose to collect a limited set of records. That was clear. But how would we choose? We could have decided on a "story line" at the outset like "the development of students' capacities to represent their ideas in multiple formats" or "the establishment of a classroom culture that supports mathematical discourse" or "the teacher's and students' roles in determining lesson content" and collected the records we would need to tell that story. But many such "stories" could be told about any class over a one-year period, and we wanted to make a collection that would make it possible to assemble numerous stories after the fact. With this goal in mind, we made our decisions about the structure of the collection as a whole and about what should be collected on any given day and periodically throughout the year. We were guided throughout by the idea of producing multiple representations of the phenomena under study. We began in September 1989 with the idea that we would record an entire year's worth of teaching and learning. (This work was funded by the National Science Foundation under grants TPE 89–54724.)

The idea that what we were producing would be a representation of practice meant that we wanted to collect multiple records of what was happening. (We recognize that all records are in some sense interpretations and that records and interpretations exist along a continuum of documentation of experience. Hence, no data are "raw"—that is, complete and unbiased.) To make records, we wanted to add to our capacities to perceive and remember what was happening and produce multiple images of events for others to look at and listen to. Such a multiplicity of images would enable post hoc triangulation and description.

Ordinary Artifacts of the Practices of Teaching and Learning

In this category are the records that we would routinely keep for the purposes of planning and reflecting on our teaching and student assessment: daily teaching journals and student class work, tests, and homework, as well as reports to students and their parents on students' work. These artifacts serve as both records of what occurred and as representations of what one *does* in the course of doing the kind of teaching and learning we wanted to study.

As teachers we had been keeping journals as a matter of course for more than ten years. Except for the rule that we would write something every day, entries in these journals were not standardized. We generally wrote for an hour for each hour of teaching time and variously included notes on lesson preparation and evaluation, including long- and short-term plans, observations on individual students, design of mathematical problems for each class session, and comments on general pedagogical problems. We did not alter this practice during 1989–1990, nor did we make any changes to the form of our journal entries. Because teacher thinking is a central component of teaching practice, we reasoned that those who wanted to study teaching and learning in our classrooms would need access to these notes in order to get some insight into our insights, perspectives, reactions, plans.

As we wrote in our journals across the year, in bound notebooks, with pens, our writing and drawing was transferred to electronic text and graphics so that it would be possible to do word searches on the text to find information about particular students, issues, and problems.

We had also developed as a regular part of our practice routines for students to record their work on mathematics in and out of the classroom in a bound notebook. At the fifth-grade level, students wrote down the "problem of the day," recorded their experiments with aspects of the problem, stated their conjecture about a solution, and composed a reasoned argument for why their solution "made sense." In the third grade students also copied the day's problem and worked on it, first individually and often with a partner as well. During the class discussion of the problem, they continued to write and record ideas and representations. Students in both classes used their notebooks to illustrate ideas they were trying to explain to other students. In addition to being a running record of what students did during the mathematics class besides think and talk, the notebooks document something about the content of the lessons for each student. Because of the way lessons were structured, students differed in their experiences of and interpretations of the curriculum, so it would not have been enough simply to record each day's assignment. For any particular day, we wanted a record of what mathematics students were working on. The notebook as a whole could offer perspectives on each student's experience on a given day and over time.

These notebooks were collected and reviewed regularly by each teacher. Lampert wrote comments on the students' work for them to read and respond to; Ball took notes in her teaching journal and also spoke with the children individually about what she saw in their notebooks. We collected and catalogued homework assignments in order to demonstrate the nature and role of homework in relation to classwork and show the teacher's decisions about what students can profitably do at home. We continued this practice during 1989–1990. The student notebooks were collected weekly and photocopied. Once the notebooks were photocopied, page numbers were added to each page, and they were filed by date and student. We also photographed the notebooks on occasion to record the sense of the whole.

In addition to the daily notebooks, we collected all homework, quizzes, and reports to parents in order to have a complete record of all existing written information about students' work and learning.

Records Collected: Videotapes and Audiotapes, Transcripts, Observers' Notes as Records of Lessons

Beyond the collection of materials generated in the course of routine practice in our classrooms, we also collected records that would make more available the multiple events and levels of experience. We used videotape and audiotape to record lessons and other conversations with the children outside of class. Structured field notes on every lesson were also written during class by observers. (We are indebted to Fred Erickson and Jan Wilson, 1982, esp. pp. 39–47, for guidelines for collecting multimedia records in classrooms derived from the standards set in ethnographic.)

We collected extensive video and audio documentation of both classes. Although the people who did the taping did not have professional videography skills, they brought school-sensitive tact, knowledge, and insight to the task that technical assistants might have lacked.

We began taping each day as students came in the door for recess and continued taping for a few minutes after each lesson was over to get a more complete class period. We wanted to portray the fact that teaching and learning go on outside the conventional lesson boundaries imposed by bells or the teacher's announcements. Students often do or say things as they come in the room or as they are packing up their books that are highly connected to what goes on during a lesson. In both classrooms, the formal lesson period had roughly three parts: a short beginning segment in which the teacher communicated the "problem of the day," about a half-hour during which students worked in groups of four to six on the problem, and another half-hour of teacher-led discussion of some aspect of the mathematics in the problem.

Considering possible types of shooting and editing, we chose neither conventional documentary procedures in which we would collect shots varying greatly in scope and piece them together in an order different from the original sequence in which they were shot, nor the opposite extreme of "locking on" the camera to one perspective and letting it run for the duration of the lesson. Instead, we filmed long takes, with the camera zooming in and out and the camera person moving around focusing on salient details. This allowed us to acquire a continuous record of events while at the same time doing some situated interpretation (see Feld and Williams, 1975, for an argument supporting this approach).

During all of the time we taped, there were many different kinds of activities going on simultaneously. When watching earlier tapes we had made, viewers often asked, "What is the teacher doing when . . . ?" or "What is the rest of the class doing while . . . ?" Although we could not realistically capture everything viewers might want to see, we decided to have two cameras running simultaneously during all times—one that would follow the teacher and one that would roam off the tripod during small group activity. Although keeping the camera on a tripod was less distracting for students, we knew we wanted close-ups of student work while it was in production, as well as documentation of students' talk and body language as they tried to communicate their mathematical ideas to their peers.

We decided each day which children to focus the cameras on to vary who was being recorded and take advantage of the variety of activity available to record. Much of the time, the cameras captured several small groups seriatim as they worked on the problem.

We audiotaped all lessons in order to generate a complete record of whole group interchanges. We also decided to audiotape conversations in small groups in order to expand the regions of the classroom that were recorded. The daily audiotapes also made it easier to produce "first-pass" transcripts of each lesson. These transcripts were then corrected, and the detail added "enhanced" by a member of the research team who could recognize individual students' speech patterns since they had made extensive observations in the classroom. We anticipated that transcripts would be invaluable to users unfamiliar with the classroom and its discourse, even if the sound on the videotapes was of good technical quality.

We decided to supplement the audio and video records of the classes by having observers write summaries of each lesson describing mathematical content, pedagogical representations, problems that arise from the perspective of the students, activities of five focal students in each class, incidents of potential interest to teacher educators and teacher preparation students, and comments on the overall agenda. These standardized semianalytic field notes would provide a complex index of lessons that would make possible searches of various kinds. We rotated the preparation of notes among observers with mathematical background, teaching experience, and teacher education experience to vary the perspective of the notes and avoid a singular focus.

ACCESSING, LINKING, AND ANNOTATING THE RECORDS: USING NEW TECHNOLOGIES TO CREATE A MULTILAYERED DISCOURSE OF PRACTICE

In 1989 we made a request to Apple Computer for some equipment to start experimenting with building tools that would give us and other investigators access to all of these records and the capacity to record and browse multiple interpretations of teaching and learning events. We argued:

> Given access to a rich collection of documents in multiple media, users should
> be able to form their own hypotheses about teaching and learning and to test
> those hypotheses against a wealth of data from the two classrooms. . . . In the
> hands of a user who seeks to learn about teaching, the system would enable and
> encourage exploration and investigation. . . . In the system we propose to
> design, users will have the capacity to do research on their own questions about
> how teaching and learning proceed in classrooms where a different kind of
> mathematics is being taught. They will have access to tools which enable them
> to move through material (audio, video, written transcripts, voice/written anno-
> tated notes by the instructor or other students), to construct their own interpre-
> tations [Lampert and Ball, 1998].

The technical capacities of hypermedia were just beginning to be realized in 1989 with the commercially available but simplified software produced by Apple called Hypercard and in more sophisticated environments like that created in Brown University's Intermedia. The tools for investigation produced by Intermedia were impressive: in biology, history, and English literature, faculty members and students were able to browse many kinds of documents in a nonlinear

fashion, creating their own links among ideas and evidence and making annotations on varieties of text and graphics. But Intermedia depended on a whole
laboratory full of developer–programmers and hardware designers—as well as
very expensive UNIX computers for each student workstation (Yankelovitch,
Han, Meyrowitz, and Drucker, 1988). And although Intermedia made it possible to link and annotate text and graphics, it did not include video or audio as
sources of information. At the same time that Intermedia was presenting a
hypertext "proof of concept," Apple was beginning to market Hypercard and
had even produced a booklet for university instructors on how to design and
market multimedia course materials and some demonstration videos of projects
under development (Apple, 1988). The company suggested that not only text
and graphics but video and audio could be linked and annotated. We saw in
hypermedia the technical capacity to make records of teaching available to multiple investigators. We imagined that with Hypercard, we could build interactive multimedia tools that would run on personal computers (see Ambron and
Hooper, 1988, for several case studies of development projects in the education
sector).

At the MIT Media Lab in the 1980s, researchers were beginning to explore the
use of video in documenting multiple perspectives on classroom teaching and
learning and experimenting with Hypercard as a program for editing, linking,
and annotating that record (Goldman-Segall, 1990; Harel, 1990). These
researchers argued that hypermedia could provide multiple perspectives on classroom activity, since records of the learner's work, the teacher's work, the results
of that work, and interpretations of it could all be linked and made available to
anyone who was interested in seeing what went on. They deliberately rejected
the "documentary" genre of videography as representative of a single (the editor's) point of view on classrooms and chose instead to build systems that would
enable users to make their own "documentaries," to be able to view the documentaries of others, and to have the flexibility to remake the story over and over.

Coincidentally, while we were engaged in the study of education practices
and thinking about hypermedia as a tool for communication about those practices, a team of researchers at the University of Illinois, led by Rand Spiro, was
studying medical practice with similar problems in mind. They wanted to be
able to represent diagnostic practice in order to communicate better with medical students about how doctors used knowledge. They went beyond the classical case-based instruction then popular in medical schools, claiming that
real-world cases had a multifaceted complexity and thus needed to be represented in lots of different ways to bring out those multiple facets. They criticized written cases for being unilateral and for representing their author's
perspective. The metaphor that Spiro and his colleagues used for their hypermedia development work was drawn from Wittgenstein's ideas about knowledge as a terrain to be explored by multiple journeys through it, none of which

would entirely capture the terrain in its entirety. This metaphor seemed power-ful to us, given what we wanted to represent about teaching. When Wittgen-stein set out to summarize his thoughts about the nature of knowledge into a coherent whole "with a natural order and without breaks," he instead produced *Philosophical Investigations* (1963), a series of remarks representing different journeys across the intellectual terrain that relates meaning, understanding, logic, consciousness, and other things. He says of this work in the Introduction:

> After several unsuccessful attempts to weld my results together into such a whole, I realized I should never succeed. . . . My thoughts were soon crippled if I tried to force them on in any single direction against their natural inclination.—And this was, of course, connected to the very nature of the investigation. For this compels us to travel over a wide field of thought crisscross in every direction.—The philo-sophical remarks in this book are, as it were, a number of sketches of landscapes which were made in the course of these long and involved journeyings [Wittgen-stein, 1963/1968].

Wittgenstein's frustrations felt familiar. His notion of knowledge as a terrain has persisted in our thinking about teaching and learning as a domain of study.

Although we did not have access to tools that would make it possible for us to collect records of teaching and learning in digital form, we did want to col-lect them in a form that could later be digitized and stored in a computer. We gambled on the fact that the tools for digitizing would become cheaper and more widely available in the near term, making the idea of computer storage and soft-ware-driven access realistic. We used hi−8 video cameras, audio recorders, and still photographs. We used black pens on white paper for all material that was to be photocopied and later scanned. Software for making these records digital was in its infancy, and we tried a variety of graphics and word processing programs simultaneously, producing filing cabinets full of tapes and paper versions of tran-scripts, students' work, observers' notes, and teachers' notes.

We had set out on our quest to collect a rich set of records of practice. What we wound up with was a multifaceted archive produced using various computer applications that had very quickly outdistanced HyperCard's capacity for filing and linking. Database software that would make a system of even simple cross-referencing available was growing and changing quickly, but at the time we needed it, none was available for use on standard personal computer hardware that could cope with the many different kinds of information we were collect-ing. None could make links between, for example, the seating chart for a given day and the work of the students sitting in a particular group. Only recently have databases been able to deal in any way with more complicated data such as complex text, and multimedia and most databases provide only the limited ability of storing all such complex data as an indistinct unit that can be saved and retrieved, but not searched or manipulated.

The archive of classroom records we collected is very complex in terms of its structure and the way that one piece relates to others. It encompasses a large number of different types of objects. Database programs typically track a limited number of things (like an inventory system, where there are many different objects that are tracked, but technically each object is treated as the same) and treat complex objects as uniform and undifferentiated. Storing, accessing, and manipulating data of the type we have collected by several simultaneous users is still on the leading edge of computer science research. Making a user interface that clearly communicates what is there and how to get to it complicates the problem even further. (See Moody, 1996, for the story of the software development team that worked on a children's multimedia encyclopedia for a year.)

INVESTIGATIONS IN PRACTICE

We grappled with what was involved in representing teaching and learning with more complexity. We worked to create an accessible and flexibly manipulable terrain of representation that could be crisscrossed by investigators seeking to learn about teaching and learning. Throughout, we have been actively engaged in experimenting with what happens when such materials, even in less than full format and without the most sophisticated tools, are engaged and explored by others. Our core aim is to examine what happens and what might be learned when investigators seek to learn about practice through close examination of artifacts of teaching and learning. In the last section of this chapter, we return to the episode about Sean and the number 6 and discuss what we have been learning from our forays.

What Stands Out About Others' Inquiry into Practice?

What stands out about what is entailed in understanding teaching and learning from the many times we have shown materials from this class to individuals and groups? What we have usually made available for these investigations includes a videotape of twenty-one minutes of class—although we usually show only approximately eight minutes—copies of children's writing from their notebooks from that day, and the teacher's journal entries for that day and several days thereafter.

Number and Scope of Questions. One thing that has repeatedly struck us is the range and variety of questions that are provoked from one segment of a classroom lesson. Additionally striking is the many domains from which these questions emerge and in which their pursuit heads. Some questions bore down into the data at hand. Who is talking, and what kinds of turns do they take? What is Ball saying, and what do her moves seem to do? Other questions require more interpretation: What is the mathematical essence of what Sean is saying? Is he confused or onto something mathematically profound? These questions seek to understand and explain the episode itself.

Other questions extend beyond the boundaries of the seven minutes of tape. Asking what students take from this episode and whether they become confused as a result is a question that requires examining evidence beyond that lesson. Asking how the classroom culture developed by January to make this episode possible requires looking at data from the beginning of the school year. It also requires examining what are consistent features of this classroom's culture. These questions examine this classroom more broadly. Both these and the previous questions are about the particulars of this episode and this classroom. Making the connection from particulars to more general questions or issues of teaching and learning is far from automatic.

Still other questions jump off the episode, and even off the data, into a host of crucial normative issues. Is Sean's idea worth discussing, or should the teacher simply tell him and his classmates that even and odd numbers are mutually exclusive sets and review the definitions of each? Should the teacher let a couple of children talk in front of the class, or should she put them in small groups so that everyone gets a chance to talk? These questions, and others like them, raise issues of value and norms, prompted by but not confined to the particular episode.

The Relations of Observations and the Observer. Noting the range of questions that emerge repeatedly reminds us of the deeply theoretical nature of observation. What people see and inquire about is shaped by what they know, believe, and assume (see Latour and Woolgar, 1979, on how scientists use theory in their observations). Events, relations, ideas, and patterns are not "in the data," to be apprehended by viewers. Quite obvious is the fact that an experienced elementary teacher will see things on the tape that will be invisible to a policymaker—the structures of the pedagogical moves, for instance. A mathematician will see things not likely to be noticed by an educational researcher, and vice versa. Take as an example an excerpt from the commentary produced by the mathematician Hyman Bass (1997):

> Ball and the other children have implicitly taken as understood that a number cannot be both even and odd. While Sean consistently (with one small exception) speaks of 6 being even *and* odd, letting these qualities comfortably coexist in his mind, Ball often paraphrases Sean as proposing that 6 is even *or* odd, suggesting that it is ambiguously one or the other, rather than both at the same time, as Sean wishes to allow. Ball's use of "or" conveys a source of the conflict that we witness, and which Sean's "and" did not intend. Ball at one moment thinks that Sean, in saying that 6 is odd, is saying therefore that 6 is *not* even, and [concludes that] Sean must be confused about the definition of even numbers.

Taking note of the difference in meaning between "6 could be both even and odd" and "6 could be even or it could be odd" is a subtle but critical observation, linked to significant differences in the mathematical conjecture. In his written commentary on this lesson, Bass frequently notes mathematical moves and uses of language that highlight for him, as a mathematician, what is going on mathematically among the children and their teacher. For example, he points out that Sean's idea is confined to the number 6. It is only when Mei offers 10, presumably as a challenge to the implication of Sean's idea, that his idea begins to be generalized, setting the stage for the students' later discovery that 14, 18, and 22 are all also examples of his idea. Bass's comments often point to issues of knowledge invisible to others whose experience and training point them to other salient elements of the lesson which are, in turn, obscure to Bass and his colleagues.

The Inherent Incompleteness of Any Representation of Practice. A third, and related, issue is what constitutes the "data" for investigating teaching and learning. No data comprise all there is to "see" or to inquire about (see Erickson and Wilson, 1982). Despite the vastness of our database and despite our attention to collecting extensive daily video and written information about these classes across an entire school year, the information is nonetheless necessarily incomplete. The camera takes aim and makes choices the investigator may rue. What is the small group sitting at the front right of the class doing at the beginning of the small group work time? This question is out of bounds unless that region of the classroom was in the camera's eye at that moment. The children's written work is a cognitive archaeology that defies the desire to examine the layers and their temporal development. Did Ofala make that picture of even numbers before or after Nathan said his idea? When did Riba cross out her written definition? Was Daniel looking at Harooun's notebook, or vice versa, or did they work together, recording as they went? Answers to these critical questions of practice are impossible from the temporally compressed records we have collected. What was the teacher's intention in asking a particular question, and how did the students interpret it? Our claim here is not that any other practice is somehow more possible to document completely. Instead we seek to highlight the crucial elements of incompleteness in records of teaching and learning.

The Relations of Question and Terrain for Inquiry. A fourth issue we have grappled with is what constitutes an appropriate or adequate terrain for a question—for example, the question of what the children take from the discussion of Sean's idea that 6 is both even and odd. One place to look for an answer is in their notebooks, to see what they wrote at the end of this lesson. Another is their subsequent quiz on even and odd numbers. But another is how they use and interact in class discussions in the future. Yet another is their reference to and use of even and odd numbers in subsequent class work.

Each path offers the possibility of a different insight into the question of what children are taking from the lesson. No one is any more complete than another, nor do they sum to the truth. Still, the possibility of looking from multiple perspectives offers a kind of insight less likely to be attained in other ways (see Schwab, 1961, on polyfocal conspectus).

Considering where to look to investigate issues of teaching and learning is a matter almost without bound. Like the rational number line, the information at a given moment in time is infinitely dense. And like the number line, the places to look extend infinitely in either direction—the past, present, and future.

The Interdisciplinary Nature and Scope of Useful Materials for Inquiry into Practice. Beyond the records of classroom interactions, teacher notes, and children's written work, other resources play a role in examining teaching and learning. For example, determining whether Sean's notion about 6 is worth spending time on is not merely a matter for idiosyncratic contemplation. More than a matter of personal opinion, this question might be informed by access to third-grade curriculum guidelines: What is expected that children should learn at this level? But it might also be informed by reference to a longer view of curricular expectations: What are students to learn over time in school mathematics, and how does an unexpected student idea such as Sean's fit on this longer trajectory of mathematics learning? Still, decisions about worth are more than matters of mapping against the extant mathematics curriculum. They may be referenced to disciplinary knowledge apart from its current school translation.

Because teaching and learning are webs of theory and practice, their investigation is inherently multidisciplinary. For example, embedded in the episode with Sean are philosophical issues to be examined about the aims of education and about alternative perspectives on the nature of knowledge: What are the issues about what is worth knowing? Is it about even and odd numbers? About the construction of knowledge in mathematics? How do ideas about democratic participation, and about the moral aspects of teaching, illuminate the episode?

And there are issues about mathematics. Is Sean misunderstanding, or is he doing something fundamentally mathematical in identifying a new class of objects? What should a mathematical definition do? How do alternative mathematical definitions of even numbers offered by the students map against one another? How are the teacher's and different students' moves in the conversation seen from a mathematical perspective?

Perspectives derived from psychology, sociology, and political science all can highlight elements of the episode otherwise left unexamined. The list extends indefinitely. And such disciplinary perspectives interact in practice. Empirical questions about what the children learn, for example, entail psychological theory, philosophical considerations of what counts as knowledge, and mathematical perspectives on what to pay attention to in the students' talk and

writing. Investigating teaching and learning in ways that afford deeper understandings of practice depends on tools built from fields far from the buzzing life
of third-grade mathematics.

But the materials useful in shaping and conducting inquiry into practice are
broader yet than the disciplines. We still have a lot to learn about the range of
ideas and materials that offer perspectives on practice.

The Underdeveloped Nature of Discourse About Practice. The multidisciplinary nature of practice and its investigation raises important questions about
the discourse of knowing teaching. First, different groups of people know and
seek to make claims about teaching. They come from different communities
with different norms for what counts as knowing and for expressing and giving
evidence for knowledge claims. The culture of professional mathematics, for
instance, socializes mathematicians toward a more certain view of knowledge
than is customary among social scientists. The mathematicians who have investigated our materials have consistently made much more definitive assertions
and reached final conclusions. When knowing is seen as more interpretive,
knowledge claims are made more tentatively. Sean is seen as *possibly* confused
or *possibly* seeing the pattern of 2 mod 4; evidence can be marshaled for both
interpretations. Less easily claimed would be the assertion that Sean does not
understand what an even number is at all. In contrast to mathematicians, we
may ask, How do teachers or policymakers treat knowledge claims about teaching and learning? How various are their views within these communities? What
are the pressures in practice that might lead to greater certainty or tentativeness
in knowing? The point is that across communities, different patterns exist for
knowing and communicating about knowing (how consistent these are, how
much is formed through professional socialization and enculturation into ways
of knowing, and how much is personal and idiosyncratic—questions about
which we yet know too little).

Related to this is a lack of standards for what counts as evidence, or adequate
evidence, for making claims about teaching and learning. Investigators of this
material differ widely in what they seem to count as adequate warrants for an
assertion. One person will say, "Only a small number of children are following
this discussion," and refer to how children appear on the videotape—that is,
many are looking down or writing in their notebooks. Another will examine the
children's notebooks and see many of them filled with the very material that is
being discussed by Mei and Sean at the board and use this to claim that these
children are engaged in the discussion and are learning. Someone else will argue
that whether children are writing in their notebooks or not does not adequately
answer the question of what it means to be "engaged" in a discussion when
you are not one of the principal speakers. Knowing whether children are
"engaged" in a classroom lesson, and what would count as adequate basis for
knowing, is in fact a question of compelling importance to teachers and

researchers alike. Hence, issues about standards of evidence are critical across communities of those who seek to learn about practice.

A third element that complicates discourse about teaching is the sparseness and unevenness of language for describing teaching. Describing the nature of the teacher's moves in the course of the class, for example, is complicated by the few terms we have for discriminating and labeling different kinds of questions or responses. A question like, "Are you saying all numbers are odd and even?" is very different from the question, "Sean is saying that some numbers, like 6, could be both even and odd. What do other people think about this?" And both of these are different from, "Who can think of a number to test Ofala's conjecture about odd numbers?" or "Who can tell Sean why 6 is not odd?"

Asking, "Are you saying all numbers are odd and even?" can be seen as a mathematical move, seeking to engage the children in the mathematically important question of the scope of the discovery one has made. It is a question that presses on the central mathematical aim of generalization. Pressing children to generalize is not necessarily germane to discussions of poetry or historical events. It is an example of a pedagogical move deeply rooted in the specific subject matter. In contrast, asking, "Sean is saying that some numbers, like 6, could be both even and odd. What do other people think about this?" is a generic pedagogical move useful across subjects. A teacher might ask this when she is unsure whether other students are following a classmate's claim or in order to invite more students into the conversation. It underscores and revoices a student's idea (see O'Connor, 1998), seeking to make it focal for more of the class. One might imagine such a question in any class. Asking, "Who can tell Sean why 6 is not odd?" is a common move made by teachers that at once signals to everyone that something is wrong and also demands that the other children search their knowledge. It is a different move from simply explaining to Sean that 6 is not odd and reminding him of why. But as a question, it is also different from the two previous ones.

The purpose of this slightly extended foray into the territory of teachers' questions in the course of conducting content-based class discussions is to illustrate the vast uncharted terrain of practice. We lack maps, location, and names for many parts of the terrain. This observation highlights the exciting expanse of investigation that lies ahead for those who seek to learn about teaching and learning and who do so in the context of much richer records of practice. The sparseness of maps and language, however, also highlights the complexities of exploration and communication that lie ahead.

Investigations in Practice: Multiples of Time, Evidence, and Perspective

Across our investigation of the study of practice, in our own work, and in the work of others who have investigated our materials, we have been struck with multiplicity along three dimensions. First is multiplicity of time. Two aspects stand out. Our practice-based decision to use the school year as the case means that investigators seeking to understand what the third graders took away from the discussion of "numbers that could be both even and odd" face complex judgments about when to look. Does one answer this question by what the students say, do, and write on this particular day during class? Through the ensuing days of work on even and odd numbers? Later in the year? Multiplicity of time is in part the opening up of teaching and learning, acknowledging and grappling with its unboundedness, both before and after any given episode. A second facet is the capacity within this kind of inquiry to examine and reexamine practice. That the materials capture and hold still the sweep of time passing in classrooms allows investigators to delve deeply into phenomena that in real time are much less apprehensible.

A second dimension of multiplicity is that of evidence. The variety of materials comprising this representation of practice means that investigators have access to a wide variety of information pertinent to any particular question. On one hand, this allows a richer exploration of a question. Seeking to learn what other children in the class were taking from the discussion of Sean's idea might involve examination of the written transcript, the children's written work, or the video. Each of these offers different information. On the other hand, these kinds of information do not necessarily converge. Quite often interpretations grounded in one piece of information seem to conflict with what is gleaned from another. Confronting and considering this multiplicity of evidence is both an affordance for the study of practice and a phenomenon of practice with which teachers—and others—must contend and not ignore.

A third dimension of multiplicity is the rich potential inherent in convening interpretations around a common context, and learning through and about the diverse perspectives that different investigators and communities of investigators bring to their inquiries. The webs of complex insight and interpretation produced by literally hundreds of diverse traversals of the episode about Sean offer remarkable insights and enhance subsequent investigations. Important work lies ahead in investigating what is seen within and across multiple perspectives and what is entailed in crossing the boundaries across such perspectives. How does experience with multiple interpretations of a common phenomenon shape investigators' intellectual dispositions and habits? How do we make sense of the multiple, and often conflicting, interpretations? What do we "know" from across these?

CONCLUSION

New ideas about the nature of practice and what it means to know it are combining with new technologies to make possible the accrual of a discourse about teaching that begins in the study of teaching and learning. Having access to shared records of practice, and to multiple interpretations of those records, can shape one's own internal discourse and the discourse within one's own community. It may also make possible a transcending of community boundaries and, hence, views of teaching and learning, what it means to know, and what is possible to know or appreciate about practice.

Fundamental questions concern what is entailed in "knowing" about teaching and learning and how what we are doing fits with other traditions of scholarly and practical inquiry about teaching. In a sense, we are pressing on some elements of qualitative research, blurring the boundaries of insider-outsider, and throwing questions of knowledge open to question. That more people can have access to the same data also means that data can lend themselves to more interpretations. How might we think about what would count as standards for good work of this kind, and how would such conversations proceed, across time, perspective, and the purposes of different communities? Who are the communities that might contribute to the development of a discourse about practice, and how might the availability of common materials of teaching and learning affect the traditional chasms among such communities? As in the investigation of practice, these questions central to the investigation of the study of practice are themselves multidisciplinary and will be honed and informed through perspectives on inquiry and knowledge in other domains.

Toward that end, we have strived in our work to bring multiple external voices to the study of teaching and learning. There is obvious value in illuminating different perspectives and questions about practice. New points of view highlight heretofore invisible elements of teaching and learning. But to what do these all sum? There is no algorithm for combining multiple perspectives to produce interpretations and understandings that are somehow "better" because of their variety. Multiplicity does not necessarily yield more refined views of practice.

Moreover, not only is there no formula for combining different points of view; we have also seen that perspectives from these different realms do not even "talk" to each other. It usually takes translations, and people who are border crossers, to lend authority and comprehensibility to these perspectives. We and others have worked as ambassadors or border crossers, visiting—and even inhabiting—these different worlds. We have spoken of practice with policymakers and researchers. We have engaged them in problems of practice. As teachers we have carried ideas from outside into the realm of practice.

What we are contending with is the challenge of developing practices of knowing and norms of discourse that can facilitate communication about teaching and learning within and across communities and that are centrally concerned with fashioning a distinctive vocabulary, syntax, and rhetoric of practice. A discourse and epistemology of practice will, in part, borrow profitably from the disciplines from which teaching and learning draw. In the academic world, we assume that these multiple perspectives, in conversation and in interaction with one another, could support the construction of better understandings of practice. In the world of practice, we assume that being able to access and support internal and joint arguments among the many voices that bear on practice could enhance teachers' capacities to see, hear, deliberate about, and know in practice.

Some elements of the discourse that we need for the investigation of practice, however, transcend particular disciplinary tools, language, structures, and syntax. The study of practice requires more than intercultural or interdisciplinary discourse. We ask, How might a "borderland" (Delgado-Gaitan, 1997; Anzaldua, 1987) be created in which a disciplined and multivocal discourse of practice might be developed? What would an epistemology of practice look like that could involve people from different worlds and perspectives but would also provide language for a focus on practice, grounded in its particular structures?

What would such an epistemology of practice entail? It would embody a respect for the complexity of practice. It would seek to illuminate, not solve, its intricacies. Knowledge in and of practice would be seen as inherently interpretative rather than certain and real. Norms would be created for distinguishing and mediating among various kinds of claims. Empirical questions ("Does the teacher always let students shape the agenda of class so strongly?") are different from normative ones ("How can seriously exploring a confused student's idea be justified?"). Some claims are logical or analytic ("The press to symbolic representation of mathematical relationships and ideas is in tension with situated theories of knowing and learning"), and others are matters of pedagogical appreciation or taste ("The teacher does not support the children's risk taking"). A discourse of practice needs discussable standards for validating different kinds of claims and for distinguishing better from less well-grounded assertions. Finally, and perhaps most complex, the study of practice requires methods for mediating across multiple claims. If "polyfocal conspectus" (Schwab, 1961) on teaching is to yield the richness of understanding it promises, then mechanisms are needed for reconciling or holding in interpretative complement different interpretations of teaching and learning.

We are left, as usual, with more questions. We need more systematic opportunities to examine the kinds of inquiry conducted across our forays with this material. We need to examine the relations between investigations conducted within the particular contexts of our classrooms and the construction of more general hypotheses, questions, and knowledge about teaching and learning. We are reminded of Mei, the young girl in Deborah's class, who presses Sean about his wonderment over the number 6. If these questions about what it would take to combine multiples of time, evidence, and perspective were less central to improving what we know about practice and how we know it, then "we wouldn't even be having this discussion."

References

Ambron, S., and Hooper, K. (eds.). *Interactive Multimedia: Visions of Multimedia for Developers, Educators, and Information Providers.* Redmond, Wash.: Microsoft Press, 1988.

Anzaldua, G. *Borderlands/La Frontera: The New Mestiza.* San Francisco: Spinsters/Aunt Lute, 1987.

Apple Computer. The Apple Guide to Courseware Authoring. Cupertino, Calif.: Apple Computer, 1988.

Ball, D. L. "With an Eye on the Mathematical Horizon: Dilemmas of Teaching Elementary School Mathematics." *Elementary School Journal,* 1993, *93*(4), 373–397.

Ball, D. L. "Working on the Inside: Using One's Own Practice as a Site for Studying Mathematics Teaching and Learning." In A. Kelly and R. Lesh (eds.), *Research Design in Mathematics and Science Education.* Norwell, Mass.: Kluwer, forthcoming.

Bass, H. "Commentary on Sean." Paper presented at National Science Foundation conference, Building on Our Strengths, Mar. 5, 1997.

Berlak, A., and Berlak, H. *Dilemmas of Schooling: Teaching and Social Change.* New York: Methuen, 1981.

Cobb, Paul. "Where Is the Mind? Constructivist and sociocultural perspectives on mathematical development." *Educational Researcher,* 1994, *23*(7), 13–20.

Dewey, J. "Empirical and Experimental Thinking." In *How We Think.* New York: Heath, 1933.

Erickson, J., and Wilson, S. *Sights and Sounds of Life in Schools: A Resource Guide to Film and Videotape for Research and Education.* Institute for Research on Teaching, College of Education, Michigan State University, Research Series No. 125. East Lansing: Michigan State University, 1982.

Erlwanger, S. "Benny's Conception of Rules and Answers in IPI Mathematics." *Journal of Children's Mathematical Behavior,* 1975, *1*(2), 7–25.

Feld, S., and Williams, C. "Toward Researchable Film Language." *Studies in the Anthropology of Visual Communication,* 1975, *2*(1), 25–32.

Goldman-Segall, R. "Learning Constellations: A Multimedia Research Environment for Exploring Children's Theory Making." In I. Harel (ed.), *Constructionist Learning* (pp. 295–318). Cambridge, Mass.: MIT Media Laboratory, 1990.

Harel, I. "The Silent Observer and Holistic Note-Taker: Using Video for Documenting a Research Project." In I. Harel (ed.), *Constructionist Learning* (pp. 327–344). Cambridge, Mass.: MIT Media Laboratory, 1990.

Heaton, R. "Creating and Studying a Practice of Teaching Elementary Mathematics for Understanding." Unpublished doctoral dissertation, Michigan State University, 1994.

Heaton R., and Lampert, M. "Learning to Hear Voices: Inventing a New Pedagogy of Teacher Education." In D. Cohen, M. McLaughlin, and J. Talbert (eds.), *Teaching for Understanding* (pp. 43–83). San Francisco: Jossey-Bass, 1992.

Kelly, A., and Lesh, R. (eds.). *Research Design in Mathematics and Science Education.* Norwell, Mass.: Kluwer, forthcoming.

Lampert, M. "How Do Teachers Manage to Teach? Perspectives on Problems in Practice." *Harvard Educational Review,* 1985, *55,* 178–194.

Lampert, M. "Studying Teaching as a Thinking Practice." In J. Greeno and S. G. Goldman (eds.), *Thinking Practice.* Hillsdale, N.J.: Erlbaum, 1998.

Lampert, M., and Ball, D. L. *Multimedia, Mathematics, and Teaching.* New York: Teachers College Press, 1998.

Latour, B., and Woolgar, S. *Laboratory Life: The Social Construction of Scientific Facts.* Thousand Oaks, Calif.: Sage, 1979.

McDiarmid, G. W., Ball, D. L., and Anderson, C. W. "Why Staying Ahead One Chapter Doesn't Really Work: Subject-Specific Pedagogy." In M. Reynolds (ed.), *The Knowledge Base for Beginning Teachers* (pp. 193–205). New York: Pergamon and the American Association of Colleges of Teacher Education, 1989.

Moody, F. *I Sing the Body Electronic: A Year with Microsoft on the Multimedia Frontier.* New York: Penguin Books, 1996.

National Council of Teachers of Mathematics (NCTM). *Curriculum and Evaluation Standards for School Mathematics.* Reston, Va.: National Council of Teachers of Mathematics, 1989.

National Council of Teachers of Mathematics (NCTM). *Professional Standards for Teaching Mathematics.* Reston, Va.: National Council of Teachers of Mathematics, 1991.

O'Connor, M. "Language Socialization in the Mathematics Classroom: Discourse Practices and Mathematical Thinking." In M. Lampert and M. Blunk (eds.), *Talking Mathematics in Schools: Studies of Teaching and Learning.* New York: Cambridge University Press, 1998.

Schwab, J. J. "Enquiry and the Reading Process." In I. Westbury and N. Wilkof (eds.), *Science, Curriculum, and Liberal Education: Selected Essays.* Chicago: University of Chicago Press, 1961.

Wertsch, J. *Voices of the Mind: A Sociocultural Approach to Mediated Action.* Cambridge, Mass.: Harvard University Press, 1991.

Wilson, S., and Gudmondsdottir, S. "What Is This a Case Of? Exploring Some Conceptual Issues in Case Study Research." *Education and Urban Society,* 1987, *20*(1), 42–54.

Wilson, S., Shulman, L. S., and Richert, A. "150 Ways of Knowing: Representations of Knowledge in Teaching." In J. Calderhead (ed.), *Exploring Teachers' Thinking* (pp. 104–124). Eastbourne, England: Cassell, 1987.

Wittgenstein, L. *Philosophical Investigations.* New York: Macmillan, 1968. (Originally published in 1963.)

Yankelovitch, N., Han, B. J., Meyrowitz, N. K., and Drucker, S. "Intermedia: The Concept and the Construction of a Seamless Information Environment." *IEEE Computer,* 1988, *21,* 81–96.

POSTSCRIPT

Some Reflections on Education Research

Jerome Bruner

Education research as an empirical enterprise should have been quite unproblematic. Its progress might well have been expected to parallel what happened in other forms of "engineering," where theoretical knowledge is applied to practical problems—like biology applied to medicine or physics to bridge building. But its history, since its beginnings in the latter part of the nineteenth century, has been anything but. It does not seem to have succeeded in the usual way of establishing practices that eventually came to be taken for granted, like vaccination or pasteurization. If education research has established any taken-for-granted practice, it is the measurement of individual differences, whether in mental accomplishment or mental ability. But even this achievement was limited. Although the *reliability* of mental measurement has not been seriously questioned, its *validity* has been: you can give the test again and get the same scores, or show that the odd and even items yield comparable scores, but what do the scores *mean*?

Reservations about validity are telling, for they amount to saying, perhaps unjustly, that education research has "succeeded" by generating methods that may be pragmatically useful but lack theoretical depth—low-grade engineering at best. This shallowness was exemplified, for example, by the early school survey movement (Casswell, 1929), whose essential program was to measure, say, the "efficiency" of schools in teaching such subjects as spelling by doing census-like inquiries into the spelling performance of schoolchildren, with little if any concern for the theoretical niceties involved, say, in language acquisition.

This has led critics to contend, perhaps unjustly, that education research has mainly been involved in redescribing culturally canonical common sense in more statistically reliable, pragmatically useful ways—"intelligence" as IQ, or musical aptitude as a score on the Seashore scale. The pragmatic utility of such procedures comes from their predicting fairly well how children will do in school or in their music classes, without shedding much light on the nature of intelligence or of musical talent as such.

Such seemingly rigorous redescriptions of canonical common sense, critics further claim, and again perhaps unjustly, often misinterpreted what they were intended to redescribe, with unfortunate results. Sometimes these misinterpretations are simply in the interest of seeming to be "scientific"—like arguing that test reliability is an "operational definition" of validity, as in the silly claim that "intelligence is what intelligence tests measure." But sometimes (if only inadvertently), such claims lead to grievous (if implicit) political and ideological consequences— as when the claim is made that IQ is "constant" over age and experience, a finding achieved by systematically eliminating test items from IQ tests that are known to change with "experience" and exposure to a culture's tool kit. In consequence, a short generation later, immigration quotas disfavoring Southern and Eastern European immigrants are justified by reference to their scoring norms on the Army's General Classification Test! (For a general account of the issues surrounding IQ, see Gould, 1981, and what is in effect a rejoinder to it, Herrnstein and Murray, 1994.)

It is not surprising, then, that test-based education research is condemned not only for its theoretical shallowness but for its political-ideological insensitivity. The charge has been that it is more often guided by short-term policy considerations (like classifying recruits in World War I) than by long-term aspirations to "improve the educational system" or "realize human potential."

So despite its modest achievements, the findings of education research have frequently fueled bitter controversies—ideological and political ones at that. One expects of such research that it might shed light not only on the nature of mind but on how to cultivate its powers and sensibilities. And the critic's claim is that education research became so enamored of its own self-made image as a "rigorous science" that it opted for a dispositional theory of mind that left little room for questions about how its powers and sensibilities are cultivated—as with its mantras about the so-called constancy and heritability of the IQ. In so doing, it left itself open to attacks on even its principal methodological premise. Is mental ability, whether specialized or general, really amenable to measurement by standardized tests employing uniform criteria? What of cultural diversity? Do abilities always express themselves in the same way? Do different cultural settings require the same kinds of sensibility? And besides, given that these questions are at all contestable, who finally sets the "official" uniformity standards for assessing mental abilities? While these are, as it were, all technical questions, they are ideological ones as well. And in the eyes of many critics, the education research community has been notoriously blind about the lethal mix with which it is dealing. Nor is there much sympathy for the usual sociology-of-science excuse that, after all, education research was only trying to find a place for itself above the salt at the scientific banquet table (Lagemann, 1997).

So its start and its first round have not been very auspicious—certainly unlike the opening histories of other engineering enterprises, like medicine or civil engineering.

WHAT IS DIFFERENT ABOUT EDUCATION RESEARCH?

I would like to stand back a little from all this early contentiousness and consider whether there are deeper and more endemic reasons that education research is not like those other forms of engineering that make progress by applying principles from the natural sciences to practical problems. It seems to me that there have been several obstacles to progress in education research that are inherent in the enterprise.

Perhaps the most important is that its objectives—the cultivation of mind, the betterment of life, or whatever else—are in principle culturally contestable issues that inevitably become ideological or political issues not readily resolved by scientific research alone. There is always disagreement about what "being educated" entails—what skills and sensibilities, what stock of knowledge and beliefs, what values constitute the educated person (Bruner, 1996).

A second inherent difficulty is that education research relies on general principles drawn from the human sciences. And these principles, it is said, are "not up to the job." They are "immature" (according to one view) or inherently different from the "prediction-and-control" pattern of the natural sciences (according to another).

And finally there is the troubling question raised by the topic of this book. What kind of research can be useful in setting education's aims or, more broadly, in guiding educational policy? Education is a public undertaking, and the policies that guide it, although ultimately aimed at individuals, are designed for institutions. Can education research properly address itself to these institutional questions, given its tradition of individualism as both a field of scholarship and a methodology?

I am concerned with all three of these broad problems. But I have intentionally avoided treating them separately, for they are highly interconnected.

COPING WITH THE DIFFERENCE

Consider first the charge that education research must rely on principles drawn from the human sciences that are not "up to the job" of engineering. The conventional way of characterizing this shortcoming is by invoking the immaturity of the human sciences. But to accept the charge of "immaturity" at face value may obscure an even more important matter—a difference in kind between the human and the natural sciences that makes education research an entirely different form of "engineering" from those based on the natural sciences.

Indeed, the human sciences seem to become even more different from the natural sciences as they mature—with more emphasis on understanding and less on explanation in Georg von Wright's (1971) sense. This same trend seems characteristic of education research as well. As it develops, the less it seems to resemble standard research in the interest of guarding public health or building better bridges, even granting that there are some surface similarities. One can argue, for example, that the discovery of the power of literacy is analogous to the discovery of radar or an anticholera vaccine (see Olson, 1996).

So what is the difference between, say, wiping out an epidemic or building a good bridge and deciding how best to educate a new generation?

The answer is surely plain. Deciding how to educate a new generation not only lacks the a priori singularity of purpose of, say, protecting their health; indeed, it even involves making decisions about what constitutes "good education." It is banal to say so, but death, even its prevention, is not a controversial issue: whether to end a cholera plague is not a contestable matter. It is self-evident. Death is inherently undesirable, and it is a secondary matter whether it is "understood" scientifically or, as in some indigenous societies, it is thought that witchcraft is part of its epidemiology (Evans-Pritchard, 1937). Disease and death, whatever else they may be, are facts of nature.

Education is of quite a different order. Its aims are culturally constituted—generated within a culture. "Educating" somebody is drastically different from keeping the person alive or preventing death. There was nothing "naturally" desirable, for example, about teaching young ladies in antebellum Virginia to speak and read French. It was simply taken as a sign of cultivation among Virginia's gentry. The only consequence for failing to become cultivated in this way might be exclusion from the higher reaches of plantation social life. So how did a mastery of French become a trope for "being cultivated" in that society?

Doubtless, all societies everywhere have some sort of criterion for distinguishing "cultivated" from "uncultivated" people, and one can even make up an evolutionary Just-So story about why that should be. But the particular criterion chosen to stand for being cultivated seems, if not arbitrary, then at least rooted in tradition rather than in nature. And who knows how French speaking gained its symbolic power! Was it the Enlightenment, the reflected charms of French court life, an instinctive alignment with England's classic antagonist—what?

Doubtless, too, all cultures recognize, promote, and even reward "cultivatedness," whatever form it may take. It stands for behaving in a fashion acceptable to those who matter in the broader sodality—one's reference group. Its "value" is symbolic, deriving not from laws of nature but from some cultural consensus, from some canonical pattern that emerged after long, often fitful maturing. In consequence, "cultivatedness" takes many forms in different cultures—modes of thought and expression, even ways of dress that are taken by other members of the culture as "signs" of somebody participating in the maintenance of the culture. In that sense, cultivatedness is a conservative virtue.

But to survive, a culture must also look to the future. (See, for example, Roy Pea's thoughtful chapter in this book.) For although we educate young people to honor the culture's traditions of sensibility or cultivatedness—its past—we also seek to equip them with "flexibility" and "resilience." We even rewrite the past and its canonicities with a view to relating it to our hopes or fears about the future—as in Anglo-American common law, where precedents are meant to guide rather than to determine judicial decisions. And so, for example, we tinker with history curricula to update our traditions better to fit them to the present—and presumably the future. Even the sciences and mathematics do not escape such tinkering. The "new" mathematics, for example, was dismissed as faddish when first proposed. The argument against it was that you could not balance your bank account in the "new math"—a bit like arguing that you cannot pave a road in plane geometry. The covert message was, of course, that education (including mathematics) should have a practical aim, a latter-day twist on the "cultivatedness" theme (or a counter-twist on it). So when the information revolution finally spewed computers into the consumer market, the "new" mathematics ceased being faddish and yesterday's "nerd" might now be a Bill Gates in the making. Characteristically, we are uneasy about balancing the past and the future, almost Hamlet-like—keen for "world history" curricula yet banning foreign books from the school library. Perhaps it is in the nature of culturally constituted aims, including educational aims, that this be so. Human cultures, in negotiating their normative standards, typically establish a dialectic between the canonically expectable and the imaginatively possible—the canonical embodied in such coercive institutions as the law, public education, and other "standard operating procedures"; the imaginatively possible in theater, literature, and "cultural criticism," as we have come to call it. (For a fuller discussion of this view of "cultural dialectic," see Amsterdam and Bruner, forthcoming; they exemplify this dialectic process by reference to common law practices.)

To revert to my earlier point about the difference between the constituted nature of educational goals in contrast to the stark nonnegotiability of medical goals, one other point needs to be made. There is a sense in which one's very position—one's social class and status—depends on how conventionally well educated one is. For "being educated" itself becomes a mark of social class and status, or being educated at certain prestigious institutions, whether The Ivy, Oxbridge, or *les grands écoles*. Access to education, then, provides entry into the power structure of a society and the criteria by which one gains access become ever more contentious—as if a multiplier had been inserted into the contestability equation.

Or, to put it in Pierre Bourdieu's (1977) terms, a society's ways of distributing status-endowing symbolic resources to its members is a major factor in determining one's "market" position within the society. It is this fact that makes education such an intensely political issue and that makes it so difficult to maintain a balance between the traditional and the innovative. Stakeholders in the status quo panic at the possibility of lost status; aspirants for new status become enlivened by a "revolution of rising expectations." And the "education wars" heat up into political battles. It is all too familiar.

Which brings us back to the political climate in which education research must operate. It is all well and good to determine, say, that one way of teaching reading is better than another—a finding surely worth its salt. But though a technical discovery, it leaves untouched such surrounding political issues as who shall be taught to read in what language in which school with teachers of what qualifications. These turn out to be cultural-political as well as cognitive-intellectual issues. Witness, for example, the recent battle over Black English.

But return now to the human sciences and the manner in which they differ from the natural sciences. In response to such issues as those we have been discussing, they have taken a much more interpretative stance. (For discussion of the nature and role of interpretation in the human sciences, see Bruner, 1991, 1996.) And although that stance is still an unsettled one, it already has led to important changes, not only within its constituent disciplines (like psychology, sociology, anthropology, even linguistics) where one finds a new emphasis on constructivism and pragmatism, but in educational research itself. There are now lively disciplines like educational anthropology, educational sociology, and even educational political science. Their objective is to examine more directly the cultural dialectic by which a society expresses its values through its educational practices. It takes for granted that educational aims are culturally constituted, rather than given or neutrally natural. These new developments (well represented in this book) do not by any means bar education research from using the scientific method or the reasoning of population statistics. They simply underline the importance of recognizing that education as such is guided by contestable cultural norms and that, for example, although there are biological constraints on educability, they do not speak for themselves. It may be a "scientific fact," for example, that the children of the better educated get the best education. But it is also a fact that it does not justify itself on the ground, for example, that these children are "naturally" brighter. Perhaps the culture's Golden Apple should go to those educational institutions that can do best for children whose parents never went to college. After all, we need to be sensitive to the dangers of creating an inherited meritocracy.

Education research, if it is to be effective in the broader society, must extend its concern, as it is now doing, beyond the classroom and beyond pedagogy narrowly defined. It needs also to participate in the task of discerning the consequences of such culturally constituted ends as a society prescribes for its education system.

Education research, under the circumstances, becomes a cultural science, however much it may rely on methods developed in the natural sciences.

RESEARCH FOR GOAL SETTING

I want to turn now to how (or whether) research may be used to help set our educational aims or goals. The first question is whether research ever determines the aims of any enterprise. Research traditionally is about how: how to achieve ends arrived at by conviction or faith. But that surely is not the whole story, for research can also establish an existence theorem—that is, it can establish what is possible. And, indeed, education research has been, and continues to be, involved in such research. Many of the chapters in this book report just such "existence theorem" research projects—all of which is not to say that just because some educational objective can, contrary to common belief, be achieved it is, *eo ipso*, desirable. But it may be. If a cooperative classroom regimen produces as good or better results than a competitive one, it is worth considering whether we should encourage, even institutionalize systems that foster cooperative learning (Brown and Campione, 1990; Bielaczyc and Collins, forthcoming).

Indeed, it is not just Q.E.D. existence theorem research that can have such a "renewing" effect on educational aims, but theoretical formulations as well, even when they are only en route to being established (or rejected). I offer as examples the idea of a "spiral curriculum" (Bruner, 1960) based on the notion that a conceptual structure is first grasped intuitively and then only later reformulated in more formal symbolic terms, or the idea that the important thing about a child's answer is not simply whether it is right or wrong but what question the answer is addressing.

But breakthrough theorems are rare, if precious. We also do research to determine whether, once established, our ends have been achieved and, if not, what prevented this. Why aren't first-year high school students mastering algebra, or third graders showing more respect for school property? Indeed, it is from such studies that we often learn what our aims really were. Aims are odd in that way. What makes them so is that "policy" is often an amalgam of what we want to achieve framed in terms of how we want to achieve them. Policy evolves over long periods of time, often given symbolic shape by watershed conflicts along the way, usually in the form of contested measures—some new statute or ordinance opposed, a bond issue that barely squeaked through, a lost school board election. In the process of this contesting, means become (or seem to become) ends. (It has always been my view, for example, that "foreign policy" gets made in cables sent out to American embassies abroad in response to particular problems. It is this truism that led eventually, some say, to creation of a Policy and Planning staff in the U.S. State Department, one of whose chief tasks is to monitor the policy that emerges from this dynamic process.) The grand aims of "policy" easily get lost or obscured by the means chosen to achieve them. Indeed, aims rarely are discussed save cloaked in the limiting rhetoric of local and concrete proposals like bond issues, teachers' pay, charter schools, and the like. Policies, in this sense, accrete rather messily, and they get "taken" over in all their messiness by advocates and activists. New Labour in Britain, for example, wants accountability through a national curriculum and national assessments (taking a leaf from their Conservative forebears), but it also wants teachers to show initiative in their teaching (Broadfoot, 1997) and to feel identified with New Labour! So it is not the least anomalous that they now feel the need for research to discover what this stance has done, what the costs are in educational practice for "capturing the political center." Nor is it surprising that, say, Project Head Start leaders feel the need for research to determine what their professed policies actually led to in practice, in how Head Start *really* operates locally (Lubeck, 1998). The looseness of Head Start's policy directive, ironically enough, is almost a contrast case to the National Curriculum/National Examination rigidity of British education, yet both of them end up in doubt about what praxis their respective policies led to.

We all know full well that the formulation of a policy, while it may signal an intent, can also set self-defeating traps. Richard Daugherty (1995) has recently related the history of the effort of the British Conservative government in 1988 to gain control over local educational authorities by introducing the National Curriculum and National Assessment. By 1994 the Ministry of Education had had to make so many compromises that it was itself confused about its policy. But what it had accomplished (research was to show) was that it had turned teachers and politicians into enemies— hardly intended! Reviewing Daugherty's masterful if rather depressing account, Patricia Broadfoot (1997, p. 404), a particularly shrewd and knowledgeable observer of the British scene, concludes that the thing that was missing in this period of policymaking was not so much substance but "mutual understanding, . . . mutual respect, and trust." As she puts it in effect, you cannot simply formulate a policy to control and monitor an education system by curriculum and assessment requirements, when that system had before been so "free" that its only "requirement" had been that there be a weekly hour of religious instruction, which itself was mandated to be nonpartisan. In fact (and not surprising), teachers and local authorities interpreted the Education Act of 1988 as a sign of distrust on the part of the Conservative government. The issue at hand was one of political-cultural trust with long roots into Britain's class-ridden history. Would purely *education* research have been sufficient in such a setting?

And so it is with education research bearing on education's aims and policy. It cannot be exclusively concerned with classrooms and pedagogy.

I want to offer an American version of what I have just recounted—the 1988 Charlottesville Declaration. The Governors famously proclaimed in Charlottesville that in order to keep America competitive in world markets, we must improve the quality of American education generally, but particularly (and this was taken as virtually self-evident) by improving the teaching of science, mathematics, and literacy. Teachers were not part of the decision process. But this time another kind of anomaly produced the trouble. For within a decade, research studies began showing that the Charlottesville "policy" was based on a misleading oversimplification of the relation between means and ends. Even taking it for granted that one of the aims of education is to maintain or improve one's share of world markets, doing so required far fewer technically trained people and far more middle managers than had been supposed (Carnevale and Rose, 1998). The aim of "science and mathematics for all" was plainly an incomplete and a shortsighted one. At just about the same time, incidentally, it was found that American high school students scored far down in the science-mathematics league standing as revealed by the respected TIMSS (Third International Mathematics and Science Study) testing program—and at a time when the United States was thriving on world markets.

Should these findings lead us to reconsider the "aims" of our education policy? Perhaps. They might even lead us to look at history a little differently. After all, Britain's world power (market share included) was achieved during a period in which an Oxbridge "first" in Classics put one at the head of the competitive pack. A narrower technical degree was hardly despised, but a large number of them was never thought of as crucial to Britain's success.

This is not to say that Charlottesville was "wrong"—only that it was unsubtle in its setting of educational aims. But note again that the matter arising from this is no longer strictly educational. The real question that remains is what it takes to run a highly technical, highly successful economy. And not surprising, that question is now being taken back to the drawing board, so to speak, in order to assess what one should expect from an educational system in support of a nation's struggle for world markets.

But that question immediately poses another one. Even if one were so utilitarian as to entertain the idea that a nation's educational aims should be dictated by struggle for world markets, does it suffice to emphasize technical skill alone, or even managerial skills for that matter? Can we maintain a democracy on such a narrow base? What of maintaining a sense of participation in the democratic process or, indeed, of cultivating a proper skepticism about the exclusive place of economic and corporate ends in designing educational policies? Is not the dignity and worth of the common man proclaimed in our democratic Constitution also a crucial end to be sought? After all, was not John Locke's radical doctrine of empiricism, emphasizing each man and woman's ability and right to decide things on their own, as much an educational as a political doctrine? In thinking about educational policy, we do well to remember that Locke's words were being heeded not only at Constitution Hall, where the framers were forging a new Constitution, but at Germantown Friends Academy, not far down the road, where the school's masters were framing a new curriculum for the children of the founder generation (Brinton, 1965). And as the times have changed, we have gone on reframing our curricula to meet the changing times in much the same spirit as our courts have gone on reframing their interpretations of our Constitution with that end in mind. Education—and education research—cannot be kept separate from the life of the culture at large.

FURTHER THOUGHTS

And that, in effect, leads me to the one broad conclusion that I must draw from these reflections: education research should never have been conceived as principally dedicated to evaluating the efficacy or impact of "present practices." The major research question that it faces is *not* simply how well our schools and systems of pedagogy teach spelling or mathematics or literacy. Rather, the master question from which the mission of education research is derived is: *What should be taught to whom, and with what pedagogical object in mind?* That master question is threefold: what, to whom, and how? Education research, under such a dispensation, becomes an adjunct of educational planning and design. It becomes design research in the sense that it explores possible ways in which educational objectives can be formulated and carried out in the light of cultural objectives and values in the broad. To put it in a metaphor, the Charlottesville Declaration should have followed a long period of education research into the possible roles of education in American life and in America's place in the world economy.

I commented that the trend in education research was precisely along the lines of the conclusion I have just stated—toward a broader, more general mission. But I want to be clear that I am not proposing a technocratic solution to the effect that education research should establish our education goals as well as help design the methods of achieving them. Rather, the proposal is that modern societies are sufficiently complex so that even the task of setting the goals of education requires careful research as to what may be needed in order to achieve such goals as may be set. Perhaps such prior research would save us from such simplicities as those contained in the Charlottesville Declaration—that to compete in a global economy, what you need is simply more and more training in science and math. Had there been further thought on the matter, perhaps the first conclusion might have been that we needed much better knowledge about the role of education and schooling in shaping the ways of the society. Schools and the education system, we finally realize, are as much a cultural problem as they are a solution to one. Perhaps the new age of education research should begin with a searching study of the costs and benefits of using schooling as our mode of (presumably) bringing the young into the culture.

References

Amsterdam, A. G., and Bruner, J. *Minding the Law*. Cambridge, Mass.: Harvard University Press, forthcoming.

Bielaczyc, K., and Collins, A. "Learning Communities in Classrooms: A Reconceptualization of Educational Practice." In C. M. Reigeluth (ed.), *Instructional Designs Theories and Models*. Vol. 2. Hillsdale, N.J.: Erlbaum, forthcoming.

Bourdieu, P. *Outline of a Theory of Practice*. New York: Cambridge University Press, 1977.

Brinton, C. *The Anatomy of Revolution*. (Rev. and exp. ed.) New York: Random House, 1965.

Broadfoot, P. "Assessment: The English Panacea." *Oxford Review of Education*, 1997, *23*(3), 401–405.

Brown, A., and Campione, J. C. "Communities of Learning and Thinking, or a Context by Any Other Name." In D. Kuhn (ed.), *Developmental Perspectives on Teaching and Learning Thinking Skills: Contributions in Human Development, 21* (pp. 108–126). Basel: Karger, 1990.

Bruner, J. *The Process of Education*. Cambridge, Mass.: Harvard University Press, 1960.

Bruner, J. *Acts of Meaning*. Cambridge, Mass.: Harvard University Press, 1991.

Bruner, J. *The Culture of Education*. Cambridge, Mass.: Harvard University Press, 1996.

Carnevale, A. P., and Rose, S. J. *Education for What? The New Office Economy*. Princeton, N.J.: Educational Testing Service, 1998.

Casswell, H. L. *City School Surveys: An Interpretation and Analysis*. New York: Bureau of Publications, Teachers College, Columbia University, 1929.

Daugherty, R. *National Curriculum Assessment: A Review of Policy*. Bristol, Pa.: Falmer Press, 1995.

Evans-Pritchard, E. E. *Witchcraft Among the Azande*. New York: Oxford University Press, 1937.

Gould, S. J. *The Mismeasure of Man*. New York: Norton, 1981.

Herrnstein, R. J., and Murray, C. *The Bell Curve: Intelligence and Class Structure in American Life*. New York: Free Press, 1994.

Lagemann, E. C. "Contested Terrain: A History of Education Research in the United States, 1890–1990." *Educational Researcher*, Dec. 1997, 5–17.

Lubeck, S. *Research on Head Start*. Report to a Spencer Foundation conference on Culture, Human Development, and Education. Cambridge, Mass.: Harvard Graduate School of Education, Oct. 1998.

Olson, D. *The World in Print*. New York: Cambridge University Press, 1996.

von Wright, G. H. *Explanation and Understanding*. Ithaca, N.Y.: Cornell University Press, 1971.

NAME INDEX

A

Addams, J., 53
Ahmed, A., 127
Alexander, C., 52
Appiah, K., 140
Apple, M., 130
Archer, M., 100
Asante, M., 140
Atkin, M., 299
Atkinson, P., 231
Atwell, N., 249

B

Bacon, F., 206
Bakhtin, M., 217
Ball, D. L., 6, 263–265,
    289–290, 294, 295, 348,
    371–398
Barnard, H., 44, 49
Barnes, C. A., 17–41
Bascia, N., 177
Bass, H., 389–390
Bennett, W., 171
Berliner, D., 26
Bestor, A., 21, 53
Bidwell, C. E., 85–104
Blau, P., 91
Bloch, M., 146–147, 148

Bolter, J., 352
Bourdieu, P., 116, 117,
    129–130, 131, 404
Bowles, S., 129, 131
Brenner, D., 247; experiences
    teaching writing, 248–249;
    impact of cross-disciplinary
    studies on, 274, 276; initial
    assumptions about
    research, 254; initial
    experiences in graduate
    school, 252; as member of
    professional and local
    communities, 252–254; as
    member of teaching and
    research communities, 254–
    256; as public intellectual,
    279–280; tension between
    research and practice, 267–
    269
Broadfoot, P., 406
Brophy, J., 26, 36
Brown, A., 5, 14, 183, 184,
    238, 289
Bruce, C., 342
Bruner, J., 121, 227, 228,
    399–409
Bryk, A., 28, 33

Burbules, N., 342
Burgess, E., 88
Bush, G., 77
Bush, V., 361

C

Carnoy, M., 132
Chaiklin, S., 299
Chittenden, T., 63
Chomsky, C., 208
Cisnerso, S., 211
Clark, A., 107
Clemens, E. S., 105–120
Clinton, W., 32
Cohen, D. K., 17–41
Cole, K., 299–335
Coleman, J., 22–25, 29–30,
    93, 94, 96
Collins, A., 289–298
Collins, H. M., 108
Collins, P. H., 140, 268, 275
Collins, R., 100
Comer, J. P., 33, 59
Conant, J. B., 21
Cooley, W., 26, 36
Corrigan, P., 134
Counts, G., 19–20, 22, 54
Crane, J., 4

411

SUBJECT INDEX

Globalization and education
(*continued*)
knowledge, 124–128; understanding student responses to schooling, 130–132. *See also* Cultural influences in research; Local cultures
Goals and standards, 12–15; misleading public with standardized testing, 71–73, 400–401; rethinking testing and student assessment, 80–81; setting for education research, 405–408; standardized testing, 65, 79–80; standards for education experiments, 296–297; for status attainment research, 90–91; undermining test goals with coaching, 69–70. *See also* Testing
Graduate studies in education research: allowing student-directed research, 190; avoiding compartmentalization, 175–178; core knowledge and necessary competencies, 170–171; critical thinking as part of, 185–188; current absence of core studies, 185; curricula changes and institutional reform, 204, 213–215; developing core studies, 166–170; directing graduate research projects, 193–194; effect on educational researchers, 252–261; epistemologies of students in, 258–261; examples of core knowledge and skills required, 171–175; framing workable problems, 184–185, 371; making claims for educational methods, 180–184; mastery of core knowledge in other fields, 167–169; mentoring and apprenticeships, 194–200; personal accounts of, 252–258; providing depth of content knowledge, 178–180. *See also* Cross-disciplinary studies; Scholarship

Graduation rates, 72–73
Great Society, 21, 24, 26, 54
Group inclusion and exclusion, 136–138

H
Historical instability of research community, 10–12
History of Mathematics (Smith), 264
Holmes Group, 266, 267
Horace's Compromise (Sizer), 77
House on Mango Street, The (Cisneros), 211

I
Identity, 135–143; debates over epistemological issues and curricular content, 138–139; group inclusion and exclusion, 136–138; identity formation for students, 139–143. *See also* Individualist turn; Status attainment research
In the Middle (Atwell), 249
Indexing research databases, 362
Indirect data, 63–64
Individualist turn: defined, 85–86; study of status attainment and, 90–94; trends supporting, 94–98
Individuality (Thorndike), 19
Inequality (Jenks), 24
Information Society, 362
Inquiry: decision-driven v. conclusion-driven, 43; in education, 43–44; foundation of educational, 60; in mathematics classes, 372; process-focused, 52–55; public pull for decision-driven, 44; purpose of in education research, 339–341; representational media and, 341–342; tension between basic and applied, 43–48. *See also* Investigation
Intellectual community. *See* Building research community
Intellectual segregation, 257

Interactive multimedia journal (IMMJ) articles, 352
Interdisciplinary materials, 391–392
Internet in education research, 295–297, 336–370; analyzing education research data with new media, 350; audience involvement in online education research, 363–366; authoring education research with new media, 350–353; current state of scholarly publications, 337–339; electronic journals and online forums, 356–361; influence on conception of education research, 342–343; nature and purposes of inquiry in education research, 339–341; networking classrooms, 343–345; newsgroups, 296; representational media and education inquiry, 341–342; research opportunities and challenges, 361–363; teacher networking online, 345–347; teachers' tools for designing research, 347–349; using video and sound files, 349–350; Web as social place, 361. *See also* Computer-based media
Interpretation of Culture, The (Geertz), 258
Introduction to the Science of Sociology (Park and Burgess), 88
Investigation: archiving and accessing research records on video and audio, 385–388; Ball's example used for teaching and learning, 375–378; choosing where to look for, 390–391; complexity of investigating teaching practices, 373–374; creating representation of teaching and learning, 380–382; finding what to investigate, 378–380; as incomplete representation